Rabbinic Authority

Volume 4

Rabbinic Authority

The Vision and the Reality

THE *HALAKHIC* FAMILY, THE CHILD'S WELFARE AND THE *AGUNAH*

Beit Din Decisions in English

Volume 4

RABBI A. YEHUDA (RONNIE) WARBURG

URIM PUBLICATIONS
Jerusalem • New York

Rabbinic Authority: The Vision and the Reality:
The Halakhic Family, the Child's Welfare and the Agunah –
Beit Din Decisions in English, Volume 4

by A. Yehuda (Ronnie) Warburg

Copyright © 2018 by A. Yehuda (Ronnie) Warburg

Editor and preparation of Index Sources: Rabbi Dov Karoll

Printed in the United States of America

First Edition

ISBN: 978-1-60280-306-0

Library of Congress Control Number: 2013492287

Urim Publications, P.O. Box 52287, Jerusalem 91521 Israel

www.UrimPublications.com

רב דוד באבד, פוסק מפורסם של המאה התשע עשרה מוסרה לנו מסורה שקיבל:

"מריש כל אמינא מה ששמעתי מפי הגאון רבי בעריש רפפורט . . . שהיה מקובל מפי רבו
הגאון נודע בשערים האבד"ק לובלין, בבוא לפניו איזה שאלה, מקודם הי' שוקל בשכלו על
אמיתת העניין לפי שכל האנושי האיך הוא, ואם נראה לו לפי שכל האנושי שהדבר אמת,
אז הוא מעיין עפ"י חוקי תוה"ק מה משפטו – וכן הוא אצלי, בבוא לפני שאלת עגונה
וכדומה, אם ברור הדבר בעיני לפי השכל ודעת בני אדם שהדבר אמת, אז אנכי מיגע א"ע
למצוא צד היתר עפ"י חוקי ומשפטי תוה"ק וכו'"   (שו"ת חבצלת השרון ב:כ"ח)

Rabbi Dovid Babad, a renowned 19th century authority communicates to us the following *mesorah* that he received:

"I heard from *ha-Gaon* Rav Barish Rappaport . . . that he had a
mesorah from his Rav, *ha-Gaon* Noda Bashearim, ha-Av Beit Din
of Lublin, that upon receiving a question to address, he would
first weigh in his mind the truthfulness of the matter according to
what human reason dictates and if in his estimation human reason the matter is true, then he will delve into *Halakhah* to arrive
at a decision."   (Teshuvot Havatzelet Ha-Sharon 2:28)

"כל רב בישראל רוצה בתקנת בנות ישראל ויודע גודל המצוה להתירה מעיגון והאיסור
הגדול לעגן כשהיה בידו לתקן ולא תיקן"(רב משה פיינשטיין, אגרות משה אה"ע א:קי"ז)

"Every *rav* in *Yisrael* wants to promote the welfare of the daughters of *Yisrael* and he is aware of the greatness of the *mitzvah* to
free her from *igun* and it is a major prohibition "to leave a wife in
chains" if one has the ability to address the situation and does not
resolve it."   (Rabbi Moshe Feinstein, Iggerot Moshe EH 1:117)

"וכל מי שמתיר עגונה אחת בזמן כאילו בנה אחת מחורבות ירושלים העליונה"
(הב"ח, שו"ת בית חדש החדשות סימן ס"ד)

"Freeing one *agunah* is like rebuilding one of the ruins of the
ruins of the heavenly Jerusalem"
          (Rabbi Yoel Sirkes, Teshuvot Bayit ha-Dash ha-Hadashot 64)

"הנני מסכים . . . להתיר האישה מכבלי העיגון . . . ויען שמבואר בתשובת ב"ח החדשות
. . . כי מי שמתיר עגונה אחת בזמן הזה כאלו בנה אחת מחורבות ירושלים העליונה
וכן נדחקתי לגמור התשובה ביום הצום על חרבן בית תפארתנו [תשעה באב]"
(הרב שלום שבדרון, שו"ת מהרש"ם א:פ"ד)

"I agree to free a woman from the chains of *igun* since it states in
Teshuvot ha-Bah "freeing one woman is like rebuilding the ruins
of the Heavenly Jerusalem" therefore I pushed myself to finish the
teshuvah (the ruling) on the fast day which commemorates the
destruction of our glorious temple [=*Tisha be-Av*]"
          (Rabbi Shalom Schwadron, Teshuvot Maharsham 1:84)

Contents

Foreword from Volume One

IN REFERRING TO THE HIGHEST LEVEL of truth finding in a judicial proceeding, our Sages use of the phrase, *"Ha-dan din emet la-amito."* What is being conveyed here is that knowledge of the law is not sufficient to render a verdict of truth. In order for the *dayan* to arrive at the correct verdict, the precise facts of the case must be discovered as well.

A beth din panel is not only thoroughly versed in the relevant halakhot, but is also well-equipped by virtue of educational background and professional work experience to grasp the reality on the ground. This entails a relentless commitment to relevant fact finding, taking nothing at face value, and understanding the implications of the facts for the commercial behavior of the parties.

A second characteristic of the halakhic-judicial process dealing with monetary matters consists of the documentation that must accompany the verdict that the panel hands over to the litigants at the conclusion of the proceedings. The claims of the plaintiff, as well as the respondent's rebuttals and counterclaims, are meticulously recorded. Next, a thorough discussion of the issues from a halakhic perspective is presented. Finally, the verdict is rendered, and this verdict is demonstrated to have flowed from the halakhic discussion.

R. Dr. A. Yehuda Warburg has assumed a vital role in implementing this vision of a "double level" of truth in the Beth Din of America and on other panels. In the present work, *Rabbinic Authority: The Vision and the Reality*, R. Warburg presents a number of his judicial rulings. What stands out in these decisions is the halakhic framework, legal perspective, and "reasoned opinions" R. Warburg sets up to support his decisions.

For a number of decades, I have been involved on an ad hoc basis as a *dayan*, including serving on judicial panels for the Beth Din of America.

In this capacity, I have often crossed paths with R. Warburg and served together with him on the same judicial panel. In each panel we served on together, R. Warburg's outstanding Torah scholarship was always in evidence, scholarship motivated by a perfectionist's drive to achieve new vistas in advancing the "double dimension" of truth that stands as the ideal for the halakhic-judicial process.

R. Dr. Aaron Levine, *z"l*
19 Adar 1, 5771
February 23, 2011

Preface

THE PRESENT VOLUME IS the fourth in a series of volumes intended as an introduction to a subject perhaps unfamiliar to many – rabbinic authority in our *halakhic* sources. The subtitle, "The Vision and the Reality," points to the themes being addressed in this work.

In addressing the "*halakhic* vision" of rabbinic authority,[1] we will offer a systematic inquiry of *Ein Tenai be-Nissu'in* which was published in Vilna in 1930. This work is a compilation of letters composed by rabbinical figures who opposed the introduction of *kiddushin al tenai* (loosely translated as conditional marriage) for a prospective Jewish couple who were embarking upon marriage which was suggested as a solution to deal with freeing wives who subsequently were unable to receive a *get* from their husbands. Our inquiry will address the *halakhic* and meta-*halakhic* factors involved in rejecting the proposed formula for a conditional marriage authored by French rabbis in the late nineteenth century. Furthermore, based upon our review, we will understand the significance of the title of this work and the line of argumentation found in these letters which subsequently propelled a rabbinic rejection of twentieth century solutions proffering other types of *kiddushin al tenai* which were proposed to deal with the *agunah* problem.

Since we are dealing with "the world of *issurim* (prohibitions)" due to the *halakhic* concern of *hezkat eishet ish* (the status of a married

---

1. As we know, *Halakhah* distinguishes between the theoretical law, which emerges from an abstract study of the sources of *Halakhah*, and the law that is applied in a particular factual context, i.e. *Halakhah lema'aseh*. See *Bava Batra* 130b and *Talmud Yerushalmi Beitzah* 2:1 (R. Yohanan's statements).

However, whereas "the vision" portion of the presentation deals with the decisions of *Halakhic* authorities as memorialized in *sifrei pesak* (restatements of *Halakhah*) and *sifrei teshuvot* (responsa), "the reality" portion of our presentation focuses upon the *halakhic*-judicial rulings of a *beit din*.

woman) as well as other factors, authorities were unwilling to release a wife without her receiving a *get* from her husband and therefore rejected these proposals for implementing conditional marriages. Nevertheless, when dealing with monetary matters, generally speaking, *Halakhah* allows individuals including prospective spouses to determine their own monetary relationships, provided that the arrangement complies with a proper form, i.e., *kinyan*, and is not violative of any prohibitions such as theft or the interdict against taking *ribbit* (*halakhic* interest).[2] Consequently, it is unsurprising that there is much discussion how to draft a proper prenuptial matrimonial property agreement. As such we focus our attention upon the proper formula to be employed when executing such an agreement and whether it can be executed prior to the engagement or prior to the marriage.

The ability of prospective spouses to contract is not limited to the drafting of a prenuptial marital property agreement. Should a prospective spouse renege on "a promise to marry," will he/she be able to sue in a *beit din* for reimbursement of wedding-related expenses due to a breach of an engagement? Are gifts that were given in the anticipation of the marriage recoverable? These questions are discussed in chapter three of our monograph.

The marital relationship itself may be said to be a contract, albeit a very special contract which establishes "a personal status" based upon the willing consent of the parties. Should a Jewish man and woman marry, *Halakhah* attaches certain consequences to that status. Among the monetary consequences to being married is a husband's obligation to provide support for his wife as well as his children. On one hand, spousal support and child support is examined in the Talmud. On the other hand, there is no Talmudic discussion whether a father is dutybound to pay for the medical expenses of his child. Despite the fact that this issue is only briefly analyzed among post-Talmudic decisors, in chapter four we were able to distill three different *halakhic* models for establishing a father's duty to provide for reimbursement of his child's expenses for medical assistance.

In chapters five and six, we deal respectively with how American law and *Halakhah* address the matter of meting out corporal punishment of children and the dynamics of the child custody decision making process as reflected in the decisions handed down by the Israeli rabbinical courts.

---

2. *Kiddushin* 19b; *SA, EH* 38:5; *SA, HM* 291:17; *Beit Yosef, Tur HM* 305:4; *SA, HM* 305:4; *Rema, SA HM* 344:1.

In chapter seven, in the wake of *get* recalcitrant husbands receiving a *halakhically* improper *heter nissuin*, permission to remarry without giving a *get* to their first wife, we present the underpinnings of the ruling of the late Rabbi Yosef Elyashiv z"l who permits the execution of a *get zikui* in the case of a husband who remarries another woman (without a proper *heter nissuin – halakhic* permission to remarry) without giving a *get* to his first wife.

The "reality" of rabbinic authority presented in this volume deals with one type of authority – the Jewish court, the *beit din*. The cases chosen for this volume entail excursions into the universe of *"bittul kiddushin,"* voiding a marriage which results in the wife being able to remarry without a *get*. According to *Halakhah*, dissolution of the matrimonial bond requires the voluntary agreement of both spouses and failure of one party to assent to to the divorce action precludes execution of the divorce. Under certain conditions should a husband be threatened to give a *get* and subsequently he consents to give it, according to most *Poskim* the resultant *get* is viewed as a *get me'useh* (a coerced *get*) and it is null and void and should she remarry any children sired from this relationship will be considered *mamzerim* (*halakhic* bastards).[3] In short, Jewish divorce must be consensual. In the event that a *get* is not forthcoming from a husband, we address whether there are grounds to void a marriage of a woman to an apostate, to a husband who is incapable of copulation, a husband who engages in spousal rape and a husband who fails to provide support for his wife. Furthermore, we address whether there is a basis to void a marriage of a husband who suffers from delusional jealousy disorder, a husband who is physically abusive and/or emotionally abusive to his wife and/or children and a stepfather who engages in pedophilia with his stepdaughters. Finally, if a husband prior to the marriage contracted HIV and he failed to disclose this matter to his wife until after their marriage, is the wife permitted to continue to live with him and simultaneously request that her marriage be voided due to his *mum gadol*, major defect(hereafter: *mum* or defect)? Or if a wife knew prior to her marriage that her husband suffers from severe depression, is there any *halakhic* credence to her claim that after being

---

3. However, according to the minority view of Rambam, the resulting *get* would be *pasul*, rabbinically invalid. As such, should she remarry under such circumstances any offspring sired from that relationship would be kosher. See *MT, Gerushin* 2:7, 10:2. For an unintentional misconstrued understanding of his view, see this writer's *Rabbinic Authority: The Vision and the Reality* (hereafter: Rabbinic Authority) vol. 1, 175, text accompanying n. 51.

married to him she suddenly discovers that she cannot tolerate the situation and wants to have her marriage voided? Finally, there may arise in a situation where it is our understanding and assessment that a wife would have never agreed to the marriage if she had been aware of the lot that would befall her, namely remaining an *agunah* forever. In such a situation, may the marriage be voided? In two cases we explain why a wife's allegation that her husband failed to disclose prior to the marriage that her husband suffered from severe depression and contracted HPV will not serve as justifications for voiding the marriage. In our analysis, under certain conditions we apply the avenues of *"kiddushei ta'ut"* and *"umdana"* in order to void a particular marriage.[4]

In chapter eight, we have included eight presentations, many of them inspired by reasoned opinions handed down as a *dayan* at the International Beit Din located in New York City. In each presentation, we offer a rendition of the facts of the case. Subsequently, there is a discussion of the *halakhic* issues emerging from the facts, followed by a decision rendered by the *beit din* panel. To preserve the confidentiality of the parties involved in these cases, all names have been changed, and some facts have been changed and/or deleted.[5] To expand the reader's horizons we have incorporated an introduction to chapter eight which elucidates the dynamics underlying the *halakhic* reasoning utilized in arriving at the various decisions presented there.[6]

As we elucidated elsewhere,[7] the majority of authorities argue that it is a *nohag*, a practice rather than a *halakhic* duty to enlist the support of an outside rabbinic authority (ies) prior to rendering a decision regarding marriage and divorce in general and voiding a marriage in particular. Recently, Rabbi Refael Shlomo Daichovsky, retired dayan from the Beit Din ha-Rabbani ha-Gadol in *Yerushalayim* published an essay wherein he contends that a credentialed *beit din* who has a track record of issuing *piskei din*, decisions is empowered to render a judgment without seeking outside rabbinic approval provided there has been a critical investigation

---

4. For a detailed analysis of these two techniques, see this writer's *Rabbinic Authority* vol. 3, 134–176. For other avenues which have been utilized to void a marriage, see *Rabbinic Authority*, vol. 3, 231–263.

5. Additionally, we have included another line of argumentation for voiding the marriage which did not appear in two of the original decisions examined in chapter 8. See infra chapter 8c, text accompanying note 61 and chapter 8f, text accompanying nn. 49–51.

6. See Introduction infra text accompanying notes 25–48.

7. See this writer's *Rabbinic Authority*, vol. 3, 256–262.

of the *halakhic* sources as well as a thorough scrutiny of the facts.[8] As he notes there is the Talmudic imperative that "a *dayan* must be guided by what his own eyes observe"[9] and consequently, even if a second opinion questions the merit of the *dayan's* argumentation since he has not participated in the actual rabbinical court proceeding he should rely upon the *dayan's* position.[10] Finally, contends Rabbi Daichovsky that the *psak din* is valid even if other rabbinic decisors dissent from its conclusion or if the ruling is in error.[11] As long as we are dealing with a credentialed *beit din* (even *hedyototh* – laymen) that errs, "*shelo ke'din*" (in R. Gartner's words), argues *Dayan* S. Tzvi Gartner though there is no *mitzvah* to accept the ruling from the perspective of the matter under deliberation by the *beit din*, nevertheless there is a *mitzvah*, a duty to adhere to the words of Torah scholars.[12]

---

8. "May a *dayan* retract his decision" (Hebrew) 37 *Tehumin* 343, 345 (5777).

9. *Bava Batra* 131a.

10. *Teshuvot Hut ha-Meshullash* 9. For other understandings of this principle see *Sanhedrin* 6b; *Nidah* 20b; *Rashbam, Bava Batra*, supra n. 6, s.v. *ve-al tigmeru*; *Hiddushei ha-Ran Bava Batra*, supra n. 7; *Yad Ramah, Bava Batra* 8:135; *Teshuva Rabbi Avraham ben ha-Rambam* 97.

11. See supra n. 8; *Teshuvot Lev Shomeia le-Shlomo*, 2: 37. For some of the authorities that Rabbi Daichovsky relies upon to reach his conclusions, see *Sefer ha-Hinnukh, mitzvah* 496; *Derashot ha-Ran, ha-Derush* 11; *Taz, Divrei Dovid al ha-Torah, Shofetim* 17:11; *Iggerot Moshe, Orah Hayyim*, Introduction.

In a matter of *horo'ah* (ritual law) such as marriage and divorce should the *beit din* err in *devar Mishneh* (a matter explicit in the *Mishneh* – loosely translated as black letter *Halakhah*) it is null and void or if the error is in a matter of *shikkul ha-da'at* (a matter of *halakhic* discretion) which is not linked to *sevara* (*halakhic* logic) the decision is null and void. See *Sanhedrin* 33a; *Hiddushei ha-Ritva, Avodah Zarah* 7a; *Shakh, SA YD* 242:58. It is only when a decision where the error is in *shikkul ha-da'at* which is linked to *sevara* that the decision is final. See *Torah Temimah, Devarim* 17:11.

Should the error be submitted for deliberation to the local Torah scholars and to the arbiter who rendered the decision and if the *dayan* continues to affirm his own ruling, one cannot force him to change his mind. Since he was authorized to render a ruling, in accordance with the aforementioned *Poskim* his ruling is final even though it is based upon an error. Clearly, other authorities are entitled to disagree with his position.

For definitional guidance regarding these two types of error in *devar Mishneh* and in *shikkul ha-da'at* see *Sanhedrin* 33a; *Beit ha-Behirah, Sanhedrin* 33a; *ha-Maor ha-Gadol*, on Alfasi to *Sanhedrin* 12a; *MT Sanhedrin* 6:1–2; *Piskei ha-Rosh Sanhedrin* 4:6.

12. *Kefiyah be-Get*, 20, 152. However, Rabbi Gartner seems to argue subsequently that should the *beit din* actually err there is no duty to comply with their words. See *Kefiyah be-Get*, 153. See also, File no. 306044470-21-4, Yerushalayim Regional Beit

To state Rabbi Daichovsky's posture differently, for those *Poskim* who refrain from seeking *halakhic* approval of their rulings prior to handing them down, implicit in their position is that a credentialed arbiter who is imbued with *yirat shamayim* (fear of heaven) is empowered to render a decision that may be at variance with a ruling handed down by any of his predecessors provided that the ruling is reflective of an analysis of applicable *halakhic* sources and based upon a scrutiny of all the facts. As such, it is readily understandable that the seeking of "an outside rabbinic opinion" by a credentialed *beit din* in order to endorse voiding a particular marriage is a *nohag* rather than a *halakhic* duty.[13]

Chapter three has originally appeared in The Jewish Law Annual, chapter four has originally appeared in Dine Israel, and chapters five and six have originally appeared respectively in Tradition and in Israel Law Review. All of these published essays appear here in an expanded and updated form.

As we have shown elsewhere,[14] there is an ongoing debate whether voiding a marriage is *halakhically* proper as a solution to "the plight of the *agunah*". Offering us an intriguing interpretation of the Talmudic *halakhic*-philosophical statement "*Elu ve-elu divrei Elokim hayyim*" (lit. these as well as these are the words of the living God), Rashi of eleventh century France teaches us,[15]

> When the two rabbis of the Talmud disagree with each other concerning the *Halakhah* . . . there is no untruth here. Each of them justifies his view. One gives a reason to permit, the other gives a reason to forbid . . . It is possible to state "both speak the words of the living God". At times, one reason is valid; at other times, another reason. For reasons change even in the wake of only slight changes in the situation.

Din, June 10, 2008.

13. *Piskei ha-Rosh, Sanhedrin* 4:6; *Teshuvot ha-Rosh* 55:9; *Derashot ha-Ran, ha-Derush* 7; *Rema, SA HM* 25:2; *Teshuvot Hut ha-Meshullash* 9; *Ha'amek Davar, Bereshit* 49:4, *Devarim* 1:3; *Ketzot ha-Hoshen*, introduction; *Arukh ha-Shulhan HM* 8:3, 25:2; *Introduction to Sefer Dor Re've'ei, Tractate Hullin*; Hazon Ish, *Kovetz Iggerot* 2:15; *Iggerot Moshe*, supra n.11, *Orah Hayyim* 4:11, 39, *Yoreh De'ah* 1:101,3:88,5:8, *Dibrot Moshe, Shabbat* 10:2. See further this writer's *Rabbinic Authority*, vol. 1, 44–64.

14. See this writer's *Rabbinic Authority*, vol. 3, 134–176.

15. *Ketuvot* 57a,s.v. *mai kamashma lon.*

In the wake of the increasing number of *agunot* both in our Orthodox Jewish and non-Orthodox Jewish communities, an *agunah's* unwillingness to be extorted by her husband in order to procure her *get*, the lingering fear of an *agunah* to decide "to leave the fold" due to her plight and the contemporary inability in the Diaspora to physically coerce a husband to give a *get* represent in Rashi's words "slight changes in the situation" which dictate the adoption of "the reason" which is permissive. As such, in circumstances where all attempts to procure a *get* for the wife fail, "the reason" that ought to be ruling the day is to void the marriage based upon techniques which have been expounded in *Halakhah* dating back to the early thirteenth century.

Hopefully our presentation will educate our community regarding the parameters and scope of rabbinic authority in general and "shatter the silence" surrounding how rabbinic authorities and *battei din* (rabbinic courts) have dealt with *bittul kiddushin* in particular. In the wake of *get* recalcitrance, for those *agunot* who avail themselves of the services of a *beit din* who is willing to critically investigate the possibility of voiding a marriage, it becomes a life-defining moment for them. They deserve no less. As the late Rabbi Avraham Shapiro, former Chief Rabbi of Israel states,[16]

> . . . . a *beit din* is obligated to pursue a (*halakhic* – AYW) solution in order that the wife does not remain an *agunah*.

A. Yehuda (Ronnie) Warburg
22 Kislev 5777
December 22, 2016

---

16. *Teshuvot Minhat Avraham* 4:6.

I Rabbinic Authority
The Vision

Chapter 1

An inquiry into the interaction of the *halakhic* and meta-*halakhic* argumentation of *Ein Tenai be-Nissu'in* (Vilna, 1930)

IN 1884, LEGISLATION WAS enacted in France which established that its judges would address a marital dispute and should the spouse's (or spouses') arguments be valid reasons for executing a divorce they would be authorized to dissolve the marriage even against the husband's will and the man and woman were free to remarry. In light of this new legislation of civil divorce and in the wake of instances where wives in the French community became *agunot* due to their inability to receive a *get* from their husbands, upon the counsel of Rabbi Eliyahu Hazan of Alexandria, Egypt,[1] in 1887 some members of the French rabbinate introduced the solution of a conditional marriage where the husband would state to his spouse:

> You are betrothed to me, should the civil judges divorce us and I will not give you a divorce in accordance to the religion of Moshe and Yisrael, this betrothal shall not be effective.[2]

In short, the execution of this *kiddushin al tenai*, conditional marriage,[3] obviates the need for a *get*.

---

1. *Teshuvot Talumot Lev* 3:49.
2. *Ein Tenai be'Nissu'in*, 5.
3. Formally speaking the condition is linked to the establishment of *kiddushin*, betrothal. However, today, as is the case for centuries the act of *nissu'in*, marriage transpires "on the heels of the act of *kiddushin*," therefore we are addressing simultaneously the issue whether we can condition the validity of the *nissu'in*. See *Teshuvot Terumat ha-Deshen* 223; *Teshuvot Hikrei Lev EH* 58 in the name of Rosh. Consequently, it is unsurprising that the collection of the letters which addresses the propriety of the French conditional *kiddushin* executed at the time of *kiddushin* is

Rabbi Michal Weil of France and formerly "Grand Rabbi" of Algiers suggested that wives would be considered *halakhically* divorced based upon a constellation of factors: namely the power of the rabbinate to annul the betrothal (*hafka'at kiddushin*), recognition of a civil divorce as well as reliance upon the opinions of Rabbi Akiva and Rabbi Shimon ben Gamliel which validated a Jewish divorce executed in non-Jewish courts.[4] Various renowned rabbis from different lands including Chief Rabbi Zadok Kahn of Paris, Rabbi Elhanan Spektor,[5] Rabbi Naftali Tzvi Berlin of Yeshivat Volozhin and Rabbi Meir Hildesheimer of Berlin, Germany, opposed the propriety of such a solution in writing.[6] Due to strong opposition to these solutions from various rabbinical authorities, in 1907 at the general meeting of some of the members of the French rabbinate, without mentioning the Jewish divorce in the *tenai*, another conditional marriage was proposed which states that at the time of the marriage the prospective husband says to his prospective wife that she is betrothed to him on the condition that should she remain an *agunah* due to him after the civil judges divorced them the betrothal is void.[7] Given Rabbi Weil's endorsement of marriage annulment, the approval of the French conditional marriage by Rabbi Eliyahu Hazan, the passage of the newly drafted version of the conditional marriage of 1907, a 1924 Constantinople Beit Din proposal of a conditional marriage and the appearance of Rabbi Yosef Shapotshnik's controversial writings in 1928 and 1929 which attempted to address the *igun* problem with the introduction of a new formula for conditional marriage and invoking the power of marriage annulment, one naturally would expect a rabbinic response. At the request of Rabbi Hayyim Grodzinsky, Rabbi Yehuda Lubetsky of Paris, France, accompanied by the assistance of Rabbi Moshe Weiskopf of Paris, France who collected over thirty letters from rabbinical authorities who rejected these solutions accompanied by the signatures of dozens of rabbis who opposed the *tenai* their response was published in 1930 in a book entitled *Ein Tenai be'Nissu'in*.

The purpose of the review of this book is to examine the *halakhic* and meta-*halakhic* reasoning memorialized in these letters regarding the

---

entitled *Ein Tenai be'Nissu'in*.

4. A. Freiman, *Seder Kiddushin ve-Nissu'in*, Jerusalem, 1964, 389, n. 1.

5. *Ein Tenai be'Nissu'in*, 4.

6. *Teshuvot Meishiv Davar* 3:49; A. Hildesheimer, "Objections to the Proposal of a Conditional Marriage," (Hebrew) 9 *Yeshurun* 712 (5761).

7. For various versions of the legislation which the rabbinic assembly considered, see *Ein Tenai be'Nissu'in*, 12.

merits of the French *tenai*[8] and subsequently to understand the import and significance of the chosen title of this compilation of letters, *Ein Tenai be'Nissu'in*.

Addressing the propriety of the French conditional marriage, Rabbi Yosef Glicksberg aptly observes:[9]

> This is a very sensitive topic since in addition to the clear *halakhic* problems that have a basis in the Talmud and early *Poskim* (authorities – AYW), we find here moral issues of strengthening the Jewish family . . . and therefore there are *teshuvot* and letters of scholars of the generations that have been collected into the book *Ein Tenai be-Nissu'in*.

In short, upon analyzing a *halakhic* issue, one must distinguish between the views which stake out a position based upon their understanding of the mishnaic and talmudic sources as interpreted by post-talmudic authorities as well as the invoking of public policy (or some have labeled a meta-*Halakhah* principle[10]) considerations of *Halakhah*. In other words, it may be that an arbiter sincerely accepts that a particular practice is permitted by the *Poskim* but nevertheless chooses to prohibit it due to the fact that it may create a *hillul ha-Shem*, a desecration of God's name, may lead people to engage in other prohibitions, imbibes the practices of non-Orthodox movement (or movements), may undermine a certain

---

8. In pursuance to *SA EH* 149:5, there are various requirements which must be complied with regarding a *tenai*. Some are mentioned in these letters and others are not. There is no attempt here to review the French condition in light of these requirements.

Here we are simply addressing the reasons for the rejection of the French condition as they emerge from the letters. Clearly, there are additional issues which ought to have been addressed by the proponents and opponents of this *tenai* and inadvertently omitted, but discussion of these matters in the text is beyond the scope of our presentation which is limited to the argumentation advanced in these letters. Some discussion of a portion of these outstanding issues has been relegated to the footnotes of this review.

9. "*Kiddushin al tenai*," (Hebrew) 12 *Torah She'ba'al Peh* 134 (5730).

10. The term meta-*Halakhah* is translated as "above the *Halakhah*." Seemingly it would mean that there are two dimensions, one dimension is *Halakhah* and the other is something beyond or outside of *Halakhah*. However, our understanding is that these meta-*halakhic* principles are an integral part of the *Halakhah* rather than emerging from the norms of another foreign legal system or non-*halakhic* framework of values. These principles reflect certain values which emerge from the norms of *Halakhah*. Changed circumstances will determine whether there is need to refrain from continuing to advance a certain public policy consideration(s).

revered *halakhic* institution or lead individuals to conclude that another practice which is prohibited ought to be permitted because it is similar to the sanctioned practice based upon *medameh milta le'milta*, analogical reasoning. Clearly, there is a need for an arbiter to distinguish between these two different dimensions when issuing a *halakhic* ruling lest he be in violation of *bal tosif*, adding to the Torah, lying, or misrepresentation of what constitutes *Halakhah* and what is *halakhic* public policy.[11] Invoking such meta-*halakhic* considerations within the context of a *psak*, ruling, in the arbiter's mind means that compliance with his judgment is obligatory rather than optional or supererogatory.

With that in mind, we will review the letters which have been memorialized in the book and discuss the lines of *halakhic* argumentation against the implementation of *kiddushin al tenai*[12] based upon a scrutiny of the sources and rulings of our *Poskim* as well as the objection of this tool as a vehicle to deal with *igun* based upon *halakhic* policy considerations. To fully understand the substance of the opposition to the French conditional marriage, we will present how earlier *Poskim* addressed in other contexts the various issues raised by this proposed solution.

1.

The threshold question is the propriety of such a *tenai*. In the Torah, we are taught that the husband writes a *get* and hands it to his wife.[13] That being said, since the *tenai* withholds a husband's right to refuse a *get*, is such a condition to be subsumed in the category of "stipulating against the Torah" and therefore will be null and void?

A *baraita*, a source from the time of *Tannaim*, cited in Talmud Bavli states the following:[14]

> [If a prospective husband states] I betroth you, on the condition that you have no claim against me for food, clothing or conjugal relations, she is betrothed and the condition is void, so states

---

11. A. Frimer and D. Frimer, "Women's Prayer Services – Theory & Practice Part 1," 32 *Tradition* 5, 39, 60–69, (1998).

12. The issue of marriage annulment which is readily distinguishable from the merits of a *tenai* is beyond the scope of our presentation. In short, acknowledging the propriety of a particular *tenai* does not hinge upon endorsing *hafka'at kiddushin* and therefore non-compliance with a bona fide *tenai* will result in voiding a marriage even if *hafka'at kiddushin* is proscribed. See *Mahberet Kiddushin al Tenai*, 57–58.

13. *Devarim* 24:1.

14. *Ketuvot* 56a; *Bava Metzia* 94a.

Rabbi Meir. Rabbi Yehudah states, private ordering (contracting out of a law found in the Torah) concerning monetary issues is valid.

For Rabbi Yehudah, the condition which seeks to release the prospective husband from his monetary obligations such as food and clothing is valid even though these duties are mandated by the Torah. On the other hand, seeking a release from a nonmonetary matter such as engaging in conjugal relations will not be recognized. Arguing with this position, Rabbi Meir contends that under all circumstances, even monetary matters, a prospective husband is proscribed from advancing such stipulations because in effect his request is either that the Torah obligation should be inapplicable to him[15] or that he is requesting that upon the establishment of the marriage his prospective wife waive her right to these matters.[16] Disagreeing with Rabbi Meir, for Rabbi Yehudah a wife can waive her right to monetary matters such as food and clothing but since abstaining from intimate relations entails "a *tza'ar ha'guf*," pain to the body, a wife cannot waive such a matter.[17] The common denominator between Rabbi Yehudah and Rabbi Meir is that private ordering via the execution of a *tenai* is proscribed in nonmonetary matters. Based upon the foregoing, the French proposal which is dealing with divorce which entails a matter of an *issur*, a prohibition (releasing a wife from a *hezkat eishet ish*, presumed status as a married woman), ought to proscribe any such private ordering in the form of *tenai* according to both Rabbi Yehudah and Rabbi Meir.

Moreover, the premise of the French *tenai* assumes that a wife will be free to remarry even if the husband is refusing to give a *get*. Such a premise is contrary to what is written in the Torah that a *halakhic* divorce is contingent upon a husband giving the *get* voluntarily rather than a ruling rendered by a civil court and therefore such a *tenai* which

---

15. *Hiddushei ha-Ramban Bava Batra* 126b; *Ketzot ha-Hoshen* 209:11.

16. *Hiddushei ha-Ritva Kiddushin* 19b; *Shitah Mekubezet Ketuvot* 56a in the name of Rashba.

17. *Rashi, Kiddushin* 19b, *Bava Metzia* 51a; *Tosafot Ketuvot* 56b; *Rashbam, Bava Batra* 126b; *Mishneh le-Melekh, Ishut* 6:10. Nonetheless, though Ritva views private ordering through the *halakhic* prism of *mehilah*, waiver, nonetheless, he contends that a wife can waive her right to conjugal relations. See *Hiddushei ha-Ritva Kiddushin*, supra n. 16, *Bava Metzia* 51a and *Bava Batra* 126b. His position has been subsequently endorsed by others. See *Mordekhai, Ketuvot* 213; *Teshuvot Maharik, shoresh* 10; *Beit Shmuel, SA EH* 69:5.

may result that a wife will be divorced against her husband's will ought to be invalid.[18]

Given that the Torah's directive of "if she doesn't find favor in his eyes ... and he will write for her a bill of divorcement and put it in her hand"[19] is undermined by the French *tenai* which empowers the civil court to issue a divorce even against a husband's will, therefore such a condition is invalid in the eyes of Rabbis Lubetsky, Weiskopf, Friedman, Grodzinsky, Rappaport, Tenenbaum (known as Lomza Rov), Danishevsky, and Meir Simcha ha-Kohen, known by the authorship of his *sefer* (book) as Ohr Sameah.[20]

Notwithstanding Rabbi Meir Posner who raises the possibility of prohibiting such a condition which results in a *halakhic* divorce without a *get* if a prospective husband conditions his marriage that he will divorce his prospective wife if he refuses to give a *get* at the time of the divorce,[21] Rabbi Weil contends that a review of the talmudic discussions and post-talmudic rulings clearly sets down when a husband is free to contract out of certain marital duties and when he is prohibited to seek release from certain obligations vis-à-vis his wife.[22] In effect, the husband is conditioning the marriage that his wife forgoes certain rights. A review of these rulings does not prohibit a prospective wife to marry her prospective husband on the condition that he will divorce her even if he refuses to do so at the time of the divorce. Consequently, Rabbi Weil argues, the proposed conditional divorce is in consonance with *Halakhah* and therefore ought to be valid.

In response to Rabbi Weil's contention, Rabbi Lubetsky claims that in fact such a condition is in variance to the Torah and therefore invalid. Though Rabbi Lubetsky refrains from explaining his posture, the rationale which is already enunciated in *Tannaitic* and *Amoraic* passages is that the conditional *kiddushin* entails a matter of *issur*, prohibition, freeing a wife from the status of *eishet ish*, a married woman and consequently one cannot formulate such a condition.[23] However, this rationale cannot serve as the sole justification for outlawing the use of a *tenai*. As we will see, even with regard to matters of *issur* such as divorce[24] or

---

18. *Devarim* 24:1–3; *Ketuvot* 83b–84a.

19. *Devarim* 24:1.

20. *Ein Tenai be'Nissu'in*, 7, 13, 16, 25, 32–33, 35, 36–77.

21. *Teshuvot Beit Meir* 38.

22. *Tur EH* 38:12–13; *SA EH* 38:5, *Tur HM* 67:12; *HM* 67:9; *Tur HM* 227:24–26; *SA HM* 227:21.

23. Supra n. 18.

24. See infra text accompanying n. 28.

halitzah, a conditional *kiddushin* will be allowed under certain circumstances. The focus of the objection to the proposed *tenai* lies elsewhere. A husband may request that a wife forego her rights prior to consummating the marriage, but he may not condition the establishment of the marriage on the condition that his wife has no such rights according to *Halakhah*.[25] As such, we may apparently understand the rejection of the French conditional *kiddushin* which assumes that the husband is bereft of the right to refuse to give a *get* that will not be recognized due to its denial of the Torah directive.[26]

However, despite the fact that Rabbi Posner's words are presented as a possibility rather than as a staked out position, Rabbi Lubetsky in very trenchant terms characterizes Rabbi Posner as "a well-respected latter day *Posek*" and "one cannot reject his reasoning like straw."[27] Nonetheless, as he notes, Rabbi Posner alludes to the dissenting opinion of Rashba who recognizes the right of a prospective wife to consummate a *kiddushin* on the condition that the couple will divorce willingly at a future time[28] which serves as the factor of Rabbi Posner's reluctance to advance his thoughts as a full-blown position. Nevertheless, Rabbi Lubetsky contends that Rashba's conditional *kiddushin* is factually distinguishable from the French conditional *get*. Whereas, in the Rashba's case the condition states that she will be his wife for a prescribed duration of time and at the end of the time he may divorce her or not,[29] in the French *tenai* there is no set time for the divorce and the divorce is dependent upon third parties or his wife rather than the husband. Since the execution of the *get* is predicated upon the fact that the husband authorizes the writing of the *get* and the French proposal assumes that the husband has not given such instructions (in fact, he refuses to give a *get*) therefore such a condition is contrary to the Torah.[30]

---

25. *Tosefta Kiddushin* 3:8.

26. See supra text accompanying n. 18. Consequently, it is unsurprising that in the 1907 proposal, the French rabbinate deleted any mention of the *get* as well as the husband's refusal to give one to his wife.

27. *Ein Tenai be'Nissu'in* 7.

28. *Hiddushei ha-Rashba Gittin* 84a; *Ein Tenai be'Nissu'in* 8.

29. The fact that he may subsequently change his mind later and decide not to divorce her will not impact on the propriety of the condition. See *Teshuvot ha-Rosh* 33:1; *Teshuvot Torat Emet* 64. Since there is no certainty at the time of executing the condition that he will become *get* recalcitrant, the condition is not contrary to the Torah.

30. However, there are others who reject the view of *Beit Meir*. See *Avnei Miluim, Ishut* 38; *Hazon Ish, EH Kiddushin* 56.

Summarizing the argumentation of Rabbi Eliezer Berkovits,[31] Rabbi Yehudah Abel aptly notes:[32]

> In the case of one who marries on the condition that he will divorce; the condition is not that he shall divorce *against his will*. No-one forces him to marry this woman and if he agrees to the condition (to divorce) because he wants the marriage, at least for a time, then he also *wants* to give the divorce because he wants the marriage. True, it may be that when it comes to giving the divorce he may have changed his mind and not want to give it but this is not at all clear *at the time of the making the condition*, and the Rosh has already ruled in section 33 of his *responsa* that so long *at the time of making the condition* it is not clear that the fulfillment thereof will be against the Torah such a condition is not "a condition against the Torah". . . .
>
> It is furthermore possible to say that even if we judge the situation from the point of view of that which obtains in the end, when he is not willing to divorce and only does so reluctantly, only to avoid the retroactive annulment of the marriage that also is considered "of his own free will."

To state it differently, if the prospective husband would have conditioned the marriage upon refraining from writing the bill of divorcement and/or give it to her that would be grounds to invalidate the *tenai* and the marriage would be viewed as an unconditional one, requiring a *get* should the couple divorce. However, the French *tenai* states at the time of the marriage the prospective husband says to his prospective wife that she is betrothed to him on the condition that should she subsequently become an *agunah* due to him and the civil judges divorced them the betrothal is void. Contrary to Rabbi Lubetsky's reasoning, here there is no attempt to uproot any Torah mandate[33] and consequently the *tenai* ought to be recognized.

Secondly, lest one contend that the *tenai* creates a situation of a *get me'useh*, a coerced *get*, by dint of the fact that he agreed that his wife may be divorced against his will; nothing could be further from the

---

31. E. Berkovits, *Tenai be'Kiddushin u-ve-get*, Jerusalem, 5727, 64–65.

32. *Confronting Igun*, London, 2011, 31–32.

33. As will demonstrate in our presentation the *halakhic* mandate that is being set aside is the involvement of the civil court in the *halakhic* divorce process. See infra, text accompanying notes 87–92.

truth. Firstly, nobody coerced the husband to set up this arrangement. It was his choice to propose the *tenai* and with the marital breakdown, he was not coerced to give a *get*. He could refuse and in light of the *tenai which he established at the time of the marriage* the marriage would be voided. Relying upon Tashbetz,[34] as *Dayan* Yosef Goldberg, *av beit din* of Yerushalayim Regional Beit Din and an international expert on *get* coercion, states:[35]

> Since our Sages have revealed to us that *get me'useh* entails taking away his ability to decide and he is unable to decide whether to become divorced or not under such circumstances it is invalid . . .

Here, the French *tenai* is premised upon the husband's ability to decide at the time of the execution of the condition regarding his divorce.

Whether one views the French conditional *kiddushin* as a bona fide condition or as "in variance to the Torah" ought to be resolved in favor of the former position since we are well aware that there are *Poskim* who validate a condition to the act of the *kiddushin* which precludes the possibility that should the husband die childless and he was survived by his brother, the brother is dutybound either to marry her (*yibum* – levirate marriage) or release her via the performance known as *halitzah*. By preempting this possibility, in effect the arrangement via the execution of the condition is seemingly contrary to the Torah[36] and yet there are authorities who validate it. Aware of the fact that some *Poskim* such as *Teshuvot Shevut Ya'akov* 1:127 and *Nahalat Shivah, Nusah Shtar Halitzah* 22 recognize the execution of a *kiddushin al tenai* regarding *yibum*, Rabbis Lubetsky and Weisskopf argue that the matter of *yibum* is a unique situation due to the fact that it is unclear whether in fact the *tenai* will materialize (namely the *yavam* will be an apostate or he will disappear) and even if it happens, the condition transpires after the husband's death.[37] Moreover, though some *Poskim* validate a conditional marriage for the purpose of avoiding the possibility of a *yibum* situation with a *yavam* who is a *mumar*, an apostate Jew, petitioners who wrote to Rabbis Ya'akov Reicher and Meir Posner note that even in the absence of the *tenai*, according to some authorities there is no obligation upon

---

34. *Teshuvot Tashbetz* 1:1.
35. Y. Goldberg, *Get Me'useh*, Jerusalem, 5763, 160.
36. *Devarim* 25:5–10.
37. *Ein Tenai be'Nissu'in*, 13.

the widow to marry her brother-in-law who is a *mumar*![38] Furthermore, Rabbis Hoffmann and Tenenbaum contend, without the execution of a *tenai* nobody will marry a man whose brother is a *mumar* and he will never be able to fulfill the *mitzvah* of procreation.[39] As such, we may refrain from addressing the propriety of the *tenai*. On the other hand, the circumstances addressed by the French *tenai* are markedly different from a *yibum* situation. Namely, divorce is more likely to happen with a couple than *yibum* and the voiding of the marriage would transpire during the husband's lifetime rather than after the husband's demise.

Furthermore, if one delves into the parameters for permitting *kiddushin al tenai* in relation to the matter of *yibum*, one will better understand the propriety of the French *tenai*. Already Talmud Yerushalmi rules that if a prospective husband conditions his marriage that "upon my demise, she will not be required to undergo *yibum* (levirate marriage)," such a stipulation is invalid.[40] As elucidated by Rabbi Shimon bar Tzemah Duran, better known by the acronym: Tashbetz, the Yerushalmi's conclusion is due to the fact that such a *tenai* is at variance to the Torah's explicit directive that upon the demise of a husband, his childless widow is obligated to engage in *yibum*.[41] Many Sephardic decisors including Rabbi Yosef Karo oppose such a *tenai*.[42]

Notwithstanding Rabbi Yisrael Isserelein's view,[43] Ashkenazic decisors concur with the *mesorah* found in Talmud Yerushalmi. Citing the Mahari Brin, Darkhei Moshe rules:[44]

"Even though one cannot stipulate that she is not required to undergo *yibum* because 'it is stipulating against the Torah,' however if he betroths her with a double condition if she falls in front of a *yavam*" such a condition is valid.

Subsequently, Rema in his glosses of *Shulhan Arukh* repeats his ruling by stating:[45]

---

38. *Teshuvot Shevut Ya'akov EH* 1:127; *Tzal'ot ha-Bayit*, 6. Obviously, since most *Poskim* validate a woman marrying a *mumar*, this solution falls by the wayside.

39. *Ein Tenai be'Nissu'in*, 13,32(= *Teshuvot Divrei Malkiel* 5:121).

40. *Talmud Yerushalmi, Bava Metzia* 7:10.

41. See supra n. 36; *Teshuvot Tashbetz* 2:17.

42. *Beit Yosef, Tur EH* 157; *Teshuvot Hayyim Sha'al* 2:38; *Teshuvot Beit David EH* 97; *Teshuvot Devar Moshe* 1, *EH* 26.

43. *Teshuvot Terumat ha-Deshen* 223. Alternatively, Mahari Brin, infra. text accompanying n. 44 embodies his *tenai* or changes the formulation of the *tenai*.

44. *Darkhei Moshe Tur EH* 157.

45. *Rema, SA EH* 157:4

> [If a man] betroths a woman and he has a brother who is a *mu-mar*, he may betroth and stipulate a double condition that if she falls to an apostate *mumar*, she will not be betrothed.

In other words, in pursuance to the condition of Mahari Brin and Rema, we are not dealing with a condition being stipulated against the Torah. The husband has no intent to consummate a *kiddushin* that will nullify the institution of *yibum*. Rather the condition is linked to a *fact pattern* (rather than a *Halakhah*) namely that should he die childless, she should not have to marry his brother who is a *mumar* and such *kiddushin* will retroactively be voided.[46] This distinction emerging from Rema's works is subsequently affirmed by others.[47]

Based upon the foregoing, the formulation of the French *tenai* is based upon a fact pattern rather than uprooting a *Halakhah* and consequently ought to be valid. In fact, in contradistinction to Rabbis Lubetsky, Weiskopf and others who claim that the French *tenai* was "contrary to the Torah," in his letter, Ohr Sameah aptly notes that the above-cited parameters needed are obtained in the stipulation of a *tenai* regarding *yibum* and abstains from even addressing the merits of the French *tenai* from this perspective.[48] The implication to be drawn from his silence is that the French *tenai* was properly drafted. In short, the permissibility of executing a *tenai* to address the issue of *yibum* to a man who is Torah-observant or a *yibum* to a man who is a *mumar* serves to corroborate that the condition is not contrary to the Torah and serves as proof that the French *tenai* is equally not in variance with the Torah.

2.

Assuming that the French *tenai* does not entail "a stipulation contrary to the Torah," if a *tenai* was executed during the *kiddushin* when the prospective husband gives a ring to his prospective wife in the presence of two eligible witnesses and the condition was not repeated at the time the couple engaged in *nissu'in*, marriage (which comprises *hupah*, the blessing recited under the canopy, *yihud*, seclusion and *bi'ah*, intercourse) the

---

46. See *Tosefta Kiddushin* 3:7–8; *Teshuvot Noda be-Yehudah,* Mahadura Kama *EH* 56.

47. *Teshuvot Rabbi Akiva Eiger* 1:93; *Teshuvot Me'il Tzedakah* 1 in the name of Rabbi Yona Lanad; *Teshuvot Shev Ya'akov EH* 2:39; *Noda be-Yehudah,* supra n. 46; *Arukh ha-Shulhan EH* 157:13. For a more nuanced distinction, see Y. Eibschutz, *Bnei Ahuvah, She'eilot u-Teshuvot,* 15–17.

48. *Ein Tenai be'Nissu'in,* 29.

emerging question is whether the *tenai* still has validity or do we argue that the fact that the husband failed to repeat it at the time of *nissu'in* means that he waived the *tenai* and she requires a *get*? Addressing the case of a prospective husband who executed a *tenai* that he was betrothing a woman on the condition that she is not subject to vows which proscribe her from engaging in certain practices (or has no *mumim*, defects[49]) and subsequently marrying him unconditionally without engaging in *bi'ah*, there is a controversy between Rav and Shmuel whether a *get* is required.[50]

For Shmuel, there is an implicit assumption that a prospective husband insists that the *tenai* of *kiddushin* extends itself to the marriage and consequently there is no need to repeat the *tenai* at that time even prior to having intercourse.[51] Consequently, in the event that unbeknownst to the husband his wife was subject to vows, the husband was engaging in *be'ilat zenut*, illicit intercourse. As such, in accordance to Shmuel, we don't recognize the *hazakah*, presumption that a person doesn't engage in *be'ilat zenut*.[52]

On the other hand, in pursuance to Rav, the *tenai* must be repeated at the time of *nissu'in*. Consequently, should a prospective husband execute a conditional *kiddushin* followed by an unconditional marriage, the wife is required to receive a *get* if the *tenai* has been unfulfilled. Elucidating upon Rav's view, Abaye teaches us that Rav recognizes the *hazakah*[53] and in effect with the act of *bi'ah* the original act of *kiddushin* becomes operative.[54] As such, in the wake of a conditional *kiddushin* followed by an unconditional marriage, the giving of a *get* is mandated if the *tenai* has not been fulfilled. In this fashion, one preempts the possibility that the relationship may be retroactively illicit should the *tenai* be unfulfilled and the marriage would be voided retroactively.[55] Alternatively, since the man is fearful that his *kiddushin* may be retroactively voided and his intercourse will be construed as an act in promiscuity, consequently an unconditional *nissu'in* implies in accordance to Rav that he was *moheil*, he waived the *tenai*.[56]

---

49. *Rashi, Ketuvot* 72b, s.v. *kinsah stam.*
50. *Ketuvot* 72b–73a.
51. *Hiddushei ha-Rashba, Ketuvot* 73b, s.v. *ha'he na'me.* See Shmuel's dictum in *Yevamot* 110a.
52. *Rashi, Ketuvot* 72b; *Hiddushei ha-Ritva, Ketuvot* 73a.
53. *Ketuvot* 72b.
54. *Beit Shmuel, SA EH* 38:59.
55. *Tosafot, Yevamot* 107a, s.v. *amar Rav Yehudah.*
56. *Ketuvot* 73a; *Yevamot* 110a.

Significantly, Abaye contends that the requirement of mentioning the condition again at the time of the *nissu'in* for Rav is predicated upon the fact that he betroths a woman with a *tenai* that she isn't subject to vows and then divorced her. He then decided to betroth her again and marry her without repeating the *tenai*. Subsequently, it was discovered that she has engaged in making vows. Under such circumstances, when a divorce transpires between the first *kiddushin al tenai* and the *nissu'in*, we assume that the husband's intent is to engage in an act of *kiddushin* rather than illicit intercourse and no *get* is required. Similarly, should a man betroth a woman conditionally and subsequently *nissu'in* is consummated under the *hupah*, Rav claims that there exists a requirement to repeat the *tenai* at the time of the *bi'ah*[57] lest the relationship be viewed as illicit and should the *tenai* not be recited again a *get* is required.

Given that we are dealing with a controversy between Rav and Shmuel, there is talmudic rule that in matters of *issura*, prohibitions, we follow the position of Rav.[58] Therefore, in pursuance to the Talmud's posture this reflects Rav's view,[59] and in accordance to Abaye's understanding of his position, most *Poskim* endorse his posture that a *get* is required should the *tenai* fail to be repeated at the time of the *nissu'in* which is consummated subsequent to the execution of the *kiddushin*.[60]

The proponents of the French *tenai* only require that the condition be recited at the time of *kiddushin*. Consequently, since normative *Halakhah* endorses Rav's view that the *tenai* must be repeated upon *bi'ah*, it is unsurprising that Rabbis Lubetsky, Hirsch, Danishevsky and Shapiro contend that the French *tenai* needs to be repeated at that time.[61] In fact, as we mentioned, Rabbi Hazan endorsed the French *tenai* but mandated that it be repeated again only at the time of *nissu'in* and *yihud*.[62]

However, even if the French rabbis who supported the *tenai* would

---

57. *Alfasi, Ketuvot* 73b; *Rashi, Ketuvot* 73b, s.v. *makholet be'ta'ut; Hiddushei ha-Ritva, Ketuvot* 73b, s.v. *ela amar Rava.*

58. *Nidah* 24b.

59. *Ketuvot* 74a.

60. *Hagahot Maimoniyot, Mishneh Torah* (hereafter: *MT) Ishut* 7:7; *Tur EH* 39; *Bah, Tur EH* 38:12; *Beit Yosef, Tur EH* 38:46; *SA EH* 38:35, 149:5; *Beit Shmuel SA EH* 38:59. Whether there is a *get* requirement on biblical or rabbinic grounds is subject to debate. See infra, n. 66.

There is Rabah's understanding of Rav which is recorded in *Ketuvot* 73b which would exempt the giving of a *get* in this situation but we do not rule in accordance to his interpretation of Rav's posture. See *Ran on Alfasi, Ketuvot* 34a; *Hiddushei ha-Ritva, Ketuvot* 74a, s.v. *u-le'inyan psak Halakhah.*

61. *Ein Tenai be'Nissu'in*, 8, 19–20, 34–36, 40.

62. *Talumot Lev*, supra n. 1

have mandated a repetition of the condition at the time of *kiddushin*, the opponents of the proposed solution to the *igun* problem lodged two additional reservations in their letters concerning the proposal. Firstly, given that the *tenai* ought to be repeated prior to the *bi'ah*,[63] Rabbis Lubetsky, Weiskopf, and Ohr Sameah argue that there is a requirement of the presence of two witnesses who will affirm that the *tenai* was repeated. Since such a procedural requirement will not transpire, there will be no demonstrable proof that the condition was in fact repeated.[64] However, in defense of the proponents of the French *tenai* there is Ra'ah's view which is supported by other renowned authorities that since people are aware that the couple is living together, they serve as *"anan sahadei"* (lit. we are the witnesses) to the act of *bi'ah*.[65] As such, it is sufficient that the *tenai* is repeated at the time of *bi'ah* and there is no need to have two witnesses present who attest to the act.

Secondly, if the husband proposes a conditional *kiddushin* and fails to mention the *tenai* at the time of the *nissu'in*, the wife requires a *get* even if the condition did not transpire. The assumption is that there is a presumption that the husband does not engage in promiscuity and he nullified the *tenai* at the time of *bi'ah*.[66] Should the husband repeat the

---

63. Since today, the *hupah* and *kiddushin* transpire at the same time under the *hupah*, there is no need to recite the *tenai* twice while the couple is under the *hupah*. However, it ought to be repeated equally at the later stage of *yihud* (see *Ein Tenai be'Nissu'in* in the name of Rabbi Danishevsky, 36). But the *Poskim* when addressing the *nissu'in* usually focus upon the final stage of *bi'ah* only which requires a repetition of the condition. For a list of authorities who mandate the repetition of the *tenai* at the time of *bi'ah*, see *Teshuvot Rav Pe'alim*, vol. 2 *EH* 6. Cf. Rabbi Yehezkel Landau and Rabbi Y. Eibschutz who mandate that the *tenai* be recited at the time of *kiddushin, nissu'in, yihud* and *bi'ah*. See *Noda be-Yehudah*, supra n. 46 and *Bnei Ahuvah, She'eilot u-Teshuvot*, page 17. Additionally, there is the opinion of Rabbi Akiva Eiger cited in *Pithei Teshuvah* that the husband would swear in the presence of his prospective wife at the time of the execution of the *tenai* prior to the *kiddushin* that he will never void the condition and that their intimate relations forever will be in accordance to the *tenai*. See *Pithei Teshuvah, SA EH* 157:9 in the name of *Teshuvot Rabbi Akiva Eiger* 1:93. See also, *Noda be-Yehudah, op. cit.; Teshuvot Shivat Tzion* 71; *Bnei Ahuvah*, op. cit. (who required that the wife would equally execute an oath); *Teshuvot Beit Shlomo* 147; *Talumot Lev*, supra n. 1 who concurs with Rabbi A. Eiger.

64. *Ein Tenai be'Nissu'in*, 9, 14, 29–30.

65. *Hiddushei ha-Ra'ah, Ketuvot* 73a; *Rema, SA EH* 149:1; *Bi'ur ha-Gra SA EH* 26:3; *Beit Shmuel SA EH* 26:1,31:22, 155:32; *Teshuvot Mishkenot Ya'akov EH* 109 in the name of many *Rishonim; Teshuvot Re'em* 1:96; *Gan ha-Melekh* 16; D. Friedman, *Yad Dovid, Ishut* 1, 3:81,4:275. See also, *Teshuvot Beit Av She'vei, Helek Ezrat Avraham, EH* 14(3); *Zekher Yitzhak* 17 in the name of Rambam; *Teshuvah Shelemah* 2:17.

66. *Tur EH* 38; *SA EH* 38:35, 149:5. A *get* is required on rabbinic grounds due to

tenai at the time of *nissu'in*, in accordance with the above view the *tenai* is valid and noncompliance with this condition results in voiding the marriage.[67] However, there is the view of Riaz that even if the *tenai* had been repeated again at the time of *bi'ah*, a *get* is required due to the fact that we presume that the love emerging from the final stage of *bi'ah* engenders a waiver of the condition![68] Based upon Riaz's approach, Rabbis Lubetsky, Weiskopf, Danishevsky and Shapiro reject the French *tenai* or for that matter any conditional *kiddushin/nissu'in* due to the fact that the act of *bi'ah* will summarily nullify any previous condition.[69] Aware that in matters of marriage and divorce (excluding *igun* matters), many authorities will factor into consider all opinions including a stringent minority view,[70] Rabbi Danishevsky exclaims:[71]

> Though there are authorities who disagree with this [view – AYW] and argue that if an explicit *tenai* was stipulated at *nissu'in* and *bi'ah* it would be valid, who is capable to tip the scale against Riaz and Shiltei ha-Gibborim who cited him?

Clearly the scale can be tipped in favor of the authoritative *Poskim* whom we cited who reject such a position![72] What is driving and compelling Rabbi Danishevsky as well as the others to adopt this singular view of Riaz and Shiltei ha-Gibborim may be found in their respective letters which raise the concern for *hezkat eishet ish*, the presumptive status of being a married woman as well as meta-*halakhic* considerations. Invoking Riaz and Shiltei ha-Gibborim's opinions serves to avoid breaching the walls of *davar she'be'ervah*, a matter of incest. In fact, Rabbi Yehiel Weinberg contends that the adoption of this minority opinion by Rabbis Lubetsky,

---

the existence of a factual doubt whether the husband waived the *tenai* even if the living together transpired shortly after the *kiddushin*! See *SA EH* 38:35; *Beit Shmuel SA EH* 38:59; *Helkat Mehokeik, SA* 38:48. See also, *Beit Yosef, Tur EH* 38:35. Cf. *Taz, SA EH* 38:18.

67. *Bi'ur ha-Gra SA EH* 157:13; *Teshuvot Maimoniyot, Nashim* 29; *Helkat Mehokeik, SA EH* 38:49 in the name of Hagahot Ashrei and Rosh; *Beit Shmuel SA EH* 38:59 in the name of *Tosafot* and Hagahot Ashrei.

68. *Shiltei ha-Gibborim* in the name of Riaz, *Ketuvot* 34a on Alfasi. See also, *Talmud Yerushalmi, Kiddushin* 2:4, *Korban Eidah*, ad. locum; *Beit ha-Behirah, Yevamot*, end of Perek 1.

69. *Ein Tenai be'Nissu'in*, 13, 35, 40.

70. *Tosafot Yevamot* 36b; *Teshuvot Kedushat Yom Tov* 9; *Simhat Yom Tov* 11; 75; *Teshuvot Maharival* 4:19.

71. *Ein Tenai be'Nissu'in*, 35.

72. See supra text accompanying notes 66–67.

Weiskopf, Danishevsky and Shapiro was for the purpose of rejecting any *igun* solution based upon employing the technique of conditional marriage.[73]

3.

Assuming that the French *tenai* does not entail "a stipulation contrary to the Torah" and it is initially explicitly stated at the time of *kiddushin* and subsequently repeated during the various stages of *nissu'in* (namely *hupah*, *yihud* and *bi'ah*), there is a question whether in fact the proposed *tenai* in actuality is really deemed *halakhically* a condition.

To respond to this argument, we need to understand the following: Encyclopedia Talmudit states:[74]

> Every condition that a person stipulates, that if the condition transpires the action will take effect and if the condition is unfulfilled the action will not take effect, and the condition involves a matter that he intends to fulfill and is able to fulfill it, the act occurs through the fulfillment of the condition, and this is not dependent upon the Halakhah of *bererah*, retroactive clarification.
>
> However, if he stipulates a condition that he is unable to fulfill, and during the time of the condition it is a doubt and the condition occurs by itself, this is dependent upon retroactive clarification.

To state it differently, the fulfillment of a condition is linked to an action whereas retroactive clarification involves the human will. For example, if a prospective husband states, "I will betroth this woman on the condition that I don't have to support her," given that the establishment of the *kiddushin* is linked to the man's compliance with an action, namely refraining from supporting her, the betrothal is *halakhically* valid should he refrain from maintaining her. On the other hand, if at the time of the *kiddushin* the prospective husband states to his prospective wife that she is betrothed to him on the condition that should she remain an *agunah* due to him and the civil judges divorced them the betrothal is void since the condition is linked to a future event, namely the court's

73. E. Berkovits, *Tenai be'Nissu'in ve-Get*, Jerusalem, 1966, Introduction by R. Weinberg.

74. *Encyclopedia Talmudit*, vol. 4, page 224.

rendering of a civil divorce. As such, based upon the *halakhot* of *bererah* as understood by Ramban,[75] we understand that retroactively the ties of the couple which were established were one of *pilagshut*, concubinage rather than marriage.[76]

Ascribing to Rambam that any relationship created outside of *kiddushin* is to be viewed as *pilagshut* and therefore prohibited,[77] Rabbi Dovid Tzvi Hoffmann entertains the possibility that since the majority of marriages will not result in civil divorce and even in the few cases that they do the husband will give a *get*, therefore marital dissolution resulting in *pilagshut* will rarely occur. Consequently, given that there exists a *safek*, a doubt regarding the future of the marriage, Rabbi Hoffmann claims that some may contend that we follow majority rule and construe the ties as marital rather than *pilagshut*. In effect, the French conditional *get* ought to be construed as a bona fide condition rather than be governed by the halakhot of *bererah* resulting in retroactive *pilagshut*.[78]

Implicit in this approach to validate the French conditional *kiddushin*, Rabbi Hoffmann argues, is that at the time of the *kiddushin* we are relying on the majority opinion that the marriage will be valid and will not result in *pilagshut*. However, Rabbi Hoffmann rejects this approach because the majority rule emerges in order to address a situation, *be-diavad*, *ex post facto* namely to address an emergency situation when the husband refuse to give a *get* and therefore cannot be invoked *le-khatehila*, *ex ante*. In short, the French conditional *kiddushin* may result in retroactive *pilagshut* and therefore cannot be executed.

However, the foregoing presumes that the French *tenai* is governed by the halakhot of *bererah*. Notwithstanding Ramban's distinction between *tenai* and *bererah*, following in the footsteps of Rambam, Ran, and others Shulhan Arukh contends that a condition that is linked to compliance with the human will is a bona fide *tenai* rather than subject to the *halakhot* of *bererah*.[79] As such, the condition is valid and will in effect avert the dissolution of the marriage resulting in retroactive concubinage.

---

75. *Hiddushei ha-Ramban, Gittin* 25b.

76. *Ein Tenai be'Nissu'in*, 18.

77. For some of the earlier authorities who endorse this understanding of Rambam, see *Teshuvot ha-Rivash* 395 (end); *Teshuvot ha-Rashba* 4:314; *Magid Mishneh, MT Ishut* 1:4. Cf. *Beit Shmuel SA EH* 26:2; *Bi'ur ha-Gra, SA EH* 26:8; *Teshuvot Maharashdam EH* 232; *Teshuvot ha-Radvaz* 4:225; *Sefer ha-Mikneh, Kiddushin, Kuntres Aharon* 26.

78. *Ein Tenai be'Nissu'in*, 17.

79. *MT Ishut* 7:1; *Hiddushei ha-Ran, Ketuvot* 25b; *SA EH* 38:8.

4.

In short, based upon the foregoing presentation there is a well-trodden *mesorah*, tradition to validate certain aspects the French *tenai*. Aware that there is an abiding *halakhic* concern of *hezkat eishet ish* lest one permit a wife to remarry without a *get* which may result in the *creation* of *mamzerut* (*halakhic* bastardy), nonetheless Rabbi Hazan communicates his endorsement of the *tenai* to the French rabbinate in order *to prevent mamzerut* by unintentionally allowing *agunot* to engage in promiscuity due to their inability to receive a *get*.[80]

On the other hand, our review has demonstrated that Rabbis such as Hayyim Soloveitchik and Dovid Friedman either explicitly or implicitly articulated their *halakhic* concern to preempt the emergence of the phenomenon of *mamzerut* should the *tenai* be validated.[81] As such, some authorities contend we can well understand why some *Poskim* validated a *tenai* regarding *yibum* due to the fact that there is no concern of *mamzerut* in future generations.[82] Absent a matter of *yibum*, when dealing with a divorcing Jewish couple we need to be concerned with proper marital dissolution lest the wife remarry and sire offspring which will be tainted by *mamzerut*. As such, the invoking of the *tenai* should be ineffective. Yet, in defense of the French *tenai*, one can claim that the validation of a conditional marriage has not only been applied to a *yibum* instance but equally to a deaf husband or a mentally dysfunctional one.[83] As such, the *tenai* ought to be effective in the conventional case of a divorcing couple. Again, though as we have shown that there are *seemingly* grounds to validate the *tenai*, due to the *halakhic* concern for *hezkat eishet ish* and meta-*halakhic* factors the opposition was unwilling to validate the *tenai*.

Furthermore, in response to Rabbi Weil's clarion call that we need to endorse the French proposal lest we cause "a *hillul ha-Shem*," a desecration of God's name, Rabbi Lubetsky retorts, do you think that "the Catholic religion adapts (its beliefs – AYW) to be in consonance with secular laws?" On the contrary, Rabbi Weil argues, the Catholic religion does not recognize the institution of civil divorce. As such we are performing a *Kiddush ha-Shem*, a sanctification of *Hashem's* name

---

80. *Talumot Lev*, supra n. 1.
81. *Ein Tenai be'Nissu'in*, Statement by Rabbi Hayyim Grodzinsky, 26, 28, 55.
82. *Ein Tenai be'Nissu'in*, 4, 15, 32.
83. *Nahalat Shivah, Shtar Halitzah* 22:8; *Shev Ya'akov*, supra n. 47.

if we retain our religious practices![84] Even assuming that there are grounds to validate the proposed conditional marriage, examining the *hillul ha-Shem* from a different angle, Rabbi Hoffmann contends that Reform rabbis will exclaim that the Orthodox rabbis have conceded that their laws are no good and the temper of the times cannot tolerate their observance. In effect, they will argue that for the Orthodox Jews the prevailing times are mightier than antiquated laws. Rather than create in his words "a *hillul ha-Shem*," Rabbi Hoffmann asserts that the proposed conditional *kiddushin al tenai* should be rejected.[85] Finally, obviating the need of requiring a *get*, for Rabbis Hoffmann, Breuer and Tovish, undermines the institution of marriage.[86] For these three meta-*halakhic* considerations as well as others, there was strong rabbinic opposition to the proposed *tenai* and therefore their *halakhic* argumentation served as a vehicle to object to the proposed condition.

5.

As we mentioned, based upon our examination *seemingly* there are *halakhic* grounds to validate the French *tenai*. However, as Rabbi Lubestsky notes, the *tenai* fails to address the rudimentary *halakhic* requirement that "the dissolving of the marital ties is incomplete, since the *dayanim* have to permit her to remarry . . ."[87]

In the event that that there is a dispute between a Jewish couple whether there is a basis to dissolve their matrimonial ties or if a husband refuses to give a *get* or the wife is recalcitrant concerning accepting the *get*, it is incumbent upon a *beit din* of three or a rabbi to determine whether there are grounds to compel [assuming one is legally permitted to utilize such means], obligate, or recommend the giving and the accepting of a *get*. Pursuant to normative *Halakhah*, once such a determination has been handed down then and only then may a civil court enforce the rabbinic decision.[88] Here, the French proposal of a conditional marriage

---

84. *Ein Tenai be'Nissu'in*, 6.

85. *Ein Tenai be'Nissu'in*, 18.

86. *Ein Tenai be'Nissu'in*, 17, 21, 26.

87. *Ein Tenai be'Nissu'in*, 6.

88. *SA EH* 134:7–9. Whether a non-Jewish court must state to the husband "do as the *beit din* mandated" or if it suffices for a civil court to state "give her a *get*" even though the *beit din* directed the civil court to coerce the giving of the *get* is a subject of debate between Rosh and Rama. See *Tur EH* 134. According to some authorities we accept Rosh's view that it suffices for the civil court to state "give a *get*". See *Tur*, op. cit.; *Beit Shmuel, SA EH* 134:15. For further discussion of this controversy, see

presupposes that a civil court rather than a *beit din* is empowered to arrive at the determination that there are grounds for the couple to divorce. Such an arrangement is in contravention of *Halakhah*.[89]

Moreover, the establishment of the act of marriage as well as the termination of the marital relationship through the execution of a *get* is grounded in the voluntary action of the couple rather than a judgment handed down by a rabbinical arbiter or *beit din*. As Torah states, "if she doesn't find favor in his eyes . . . and he will write for her a bill of divorcement and put it in her hand" and with the advent of Rabbi Gershom's legislation the writ of divorce must be accepted by her.[90] As such, the French proposal not only advances the unacceptable idea that a non-Jewish court is the arbiter of the grounds for the Jewish divorce but as renowned Rabbis Friedman, Grodzinsky, Y. Epstein, Meir ha-Kohen, Tenenbaum and others contend, the proposed arrangement implicitly denies that the execution of the *get* is solely in the hands of both parties.[91] In fact, in accordance with this proposal, the wife spearheads the marriage dissolution against her husband's wishes. In effect, as noted with chagrin by Rabbi Meir ha-Kohen,[92] the proposed *tenai* allows for the Jewish couple to be entitled to participate in *the halakhically prescribed arrangement of a non-Jewish marriage* where there is no mandate for a written divorce document and that either spouse may unilaterally decide to dissolve their matrimonial ties![93] The proposed *tenai* is the embodiment of nineteenth century French law whereby it is the state not the petitioning party (in this case the wife) in a divorce action who dissolves the marriage.

For the above reason alone, there is no basis for recognizing such a *kiddushin al tenai*. Whereas, concerning the other issues relating to the *tenai* there is a *mesorah* to validate it, however, absent a *beit din* directive to recommend or obligate a *get*, there are no grounds to recognize the proposed condition which empowers the sole involvement of the civil court in the *halakhic* divorce process.Consequently, it is unsurprising that approximately seventy five years later, following in the footsteps of

---

Kovetz Sha'arei Torah, vol. 3, kuntres 11, siman 63; vol. 4, kuntres 2, siman 9; vol. 4, simanim 34, 53.

89. *Iggerot Moshe EH* 3:44.

90. See supra n. 19.

91. See supra text accompanying n. 20. See also, *Ein Tenai be'Nissu'in*, 3, 17, 33, 38.

92. *Ein Tenai be'Nissu'in*, 29.

93. *Talmud Yerushalmi, Kiddushin* 1:1; *MT, Melakhim* 9:8.

the proponents of the Kushta *tenai*,[94] Rabbi Eliezer Berkovits' proposed *tenai* is predicated upon the involvement of the divorcing parties rather than the participation of a civil court.[95]

6.

The final issue is what was the thrust of the opposition to the French *tenai*? Were the *Poskim* opposed to the particular *tenai* due to certain *halakhic* shortcomings or was there a principled rejection of recognizing any *tenai* regarding *nissu'in*? Clearly, a cursory review of the applicable *halakhot* memorialized in certain views found in Ketuvot 73b, 74a, Yevamot 15a, and Bava Kama 110b validate the implementation of a *tenai* under certain prescribed conditions. [96]Hence, it is unsurprising that in a series of three letters written during the years 1912, 1928–1929, the renowned Rabbi Hayyim Ozer Grodzinsky explicitly states that his rejection of the French *tenai* is that there is no basis to introduce any *tenai* in the format of a *takanah*, rabbinic legislation concerning marriage.[97] To state it differently, *halakhically kiddushin al tenai* is a possibility, however, to suggest it as a global solution in the form of a *takanah* for marriage annulment is prohibited. In fact, Rabbi Hayyim Ozer Grodzinsky accompanied by Rabbi Friedman explicitly note that their opposition to the French *tenai* was due to the fact that the obligation of divorce was left in the hands of the civil court.[98] In other words, should the *tenai* have passed *halakhic* muster, in terms of a *tenai*, it would have been validated. However, even if the *tenai* would be recognized, due to the fact that the *tenai* was being presented as an avenue to annul a marriage (*hafka'at kiddushin*), it found disfavor in the mind of Rabbi Grodzinsky. Decades later, Rabbi Menahem Mendel Kasher equally understood that the rejection of the French *tenai* was grounded in the opposition of introducing the *tenai* as a vehicle to annul marriages.[99]

Nonetheless, in *Ein Tenai be'Nissu'in*, there is a letter authored by Rabbi Yehiel Michel Epstein, known for the authorship of his book Arukh ha-Shulhan, who states that the proposed condition runs afoul of

---

94. See *Mahberet Kiddushin al Tenai*.

95. *Tenai be'Nissu'in ve-Get,* supra n. 73, 57–58.

96. See also *Tosafot Ketuvot 73a,* s.v. lo ta'ma; *Beit ha-Behira Yevamot* 107a; *Hiddushei ha-Rashba, Yevamot* 107a; *Pnei Yehoshua Ketuvot* 73a.

97. *Ein Tenai be'Nissu'in,* R. Grodzinsky's public statement; 56, *Kovetz Iggerot Ahiezer,* Part 2, *Iggeret Rav,* 361–362.

98. *Ein Tenai be'Nissu'in,* 16, 56.

99. M. Kasher, *"Be-Inyan tenai be-nissu'in,"* (Hebrew) 12 *Noam* 338, 348 (5729).

the Talmudic directive *"ein tenai be'nissuin"*.[100] And in fact, the chosen title of the collection of letters which is under review here is *Ein Tenai be'Nissu'in*. Seemingly, endorsing this Talmudic mandate means that *Halakhah* rejects *kiddushin al tenai*. And Rabbi Grodzinsky agreed that *"ein tenai be'nissuin."*[101]

However, as we mentioned, the Shulhan Arukh recognizes the implementation of *kiddushin al tenai*. And in fact, discussion of this technique is strewn throughout the pages of other *sifrei psak* (loosely translated as codes) and *she'eilot u-teshuvot* (responsa). In fact, Rabbi Moshe Sofer, a leading *Posek* for early nineteenth century European Jewry introduced his own text for a *kiddushin al tenai!*[102] Moreover, explicitly or implicitly following in the footsteps of *Tosafot*,[103] some *Poskim* understand the aforementioned Talmudic mandate to mean that *bittul kiddushin*, voiding a marriage via the tool of conditional marriage is infrequently used rather than proffering a *halakhic* ruling prohibiting its use.[104] Other authorities understand the statement *"ein tenai be'nissuin"* as a *Halakhah* to be utilized in terms of resolving a particular issue rather than a Talmudic ruling that a conditional marriage is to be outlawed under all circumstances.[105] For example, addressing earlier attempts to permit a conditional marriage, Rabbi Yosef Henkin states:[106]

> *Ein tenai be'nissuin* is a clear *Halakhah* and finds support upon firm foundations that will not collapse . . . a condition is effective at the time of *kiddushin* and not at the time of marriage and only (valid – AYW) at the time of intercourse.

Yet, we need to understand why the title chosen for this collection of letters was *Ein Tenai be'Nissu'in*. Firstly, as noted by Rabbi Grodzinsky as well as Rabbi Menahem Kasher, given that authorities are not empowered today to annul a marriage in these circumstances, consequently the

---

100. *Ein Tenai be'Nissu'in*, 17.

101. *Teshuvot Ohr Sameah* 3:10.

102. *Teshuvot Hatam Sofer EH* 1:111.

103. *Tosafot, Yevamot* 107a, s.v. *Beit Shammai*

104. *Shivat Tzion*, supra n. 63; *Teshuvot Radakh* 9; *Avnei Miluim* 39:1; *Teshuvot Mishpetei Uziel* 2, *EH* 46(4).

105. *Ohr Zarua, Yibum and Halitza* 617; *Lehem Mishneh, MT, Gerushin* 10:6; *Beit Shmuel, SA EH* 157:6; *Teshuvot Hut ha-Meshullash*, 3:3; *Teshuvot Ahiezer* 1. *EH* 9(1); *Teshuvot Mishpetei Uziel* 2, *EH* 44(2).

106. Y. Henkin, "Regarding the matter of the Conservative reform of *kiddushin*" (Hebrew), 1 *Noam* 70, 73 (5718).

proposed conditional marriage which in part is based upon *hafka'at kiddushin* is ineffective. To state it differently, should the *tenai* fail to be fulfilled, seemingly the rabbis are empowered to annul the marriage. As such, the title was chosen to communicate to the community that annulment may not be invoked in the wake of *tenai* noncompliance.[107]

Secondly, as we noted in our introduction, one of the events which precipitated the publication of *Ein Tenai be'Nissu'in* in 1930 is the 1924 Constantinople Beit Din proposal of conditional marriage known as the "Kushta *tenai* ".[108] Approximately 20 years after the appearance of the French proposal, rabbis of Istanbul suggested a formula for a conditional marriage for the purpose of dealing with matters of *igun* in their community. A 58-page treatise entitled *Mahberet Kiddushin al Tenai* published at that time outlined the basis for their proposal. In the wake of instances of *agunot* and the concomitant fear of promiscuity, they proposed retroactive voiding of the marriage if the husband abandoned his wife for a lengthy period of time, or if he became mentally dysfunctional or contracted a contagious disease,[109] or if he refused to comply with a *beit din* judgment of divorce or if the wife wanted to have *halitzah* from a *yavam* who disappeared or a recalcitrant *yavam*.[110] Should any of these conditions materialize, the *tenai* executed between the couple authorized the *beit din* to annul the marriage and the annulment was based upon the agreement of the *benei ha'ir* (the representatives of the community) who had rabbinic authorization to be *mafkir* (expropriate) the ring of the *kiddushin* and thus dissolve the marriage.[111] Given that the husband would swear never to cancel the *tenai*, the condition was stated at the time of the *kiddushin* and *hupah* ceremony and did not need to be repeated at the time of *yihud* or *bi'ah*.

Whereas, as we have seen that absent the decision of some members of the French rabbinate to authorize the civil court to determine the merits of becoming divorced there was a well-trodden *mesorah* to validate other portions of the proposed *tenai*. As such, one may have

---

107. See *Mahberet Kiddushin al Tenai*, supra n. 12 where the authors of their proposed *tenai* recognize the *halakhic* integrity of the condition to effectuate the voiding of the marriage without employing *hafka'at kiddushin*.

108. Rabbi Grodzinsky, *Kovetz Iggerot Ahiezer*, supra n. 97.

109. If the husband either failed to disclose a psychological disorder or a disease that he contracted prior to the marriage or a mental disorder or disease which he contracted during the marriage which would be intolerable for marital living, these situations would serve as grounds for voiding the marriage.

110. *Mahberet al Kiddushin*, 6.

111. *Mahberet al Kiddushin*, 5.

expected that the Kushta *tenai* which empowered a *beit din* rather than a civil judicial forum to establish whether there are grounds for the divorce would have received maximal *halakhic* approval from rabbis who were uninvolved in the drafting of the *tenai* or minimally would have submitted constructive criticism to amend the *tenai* to pass *halakhic* muster. In fact, the rabbis who composed *Mahberet Kiddushin al Tenai* not only articulated many of the identical authoritative expositions that were advanced to defend the French *tenai* but offered numerous other lines of argumentation to buttress their position that the Kushta *tenai* was a valid technique to address the matter of *igun* in their community.

Though some authorities endorsed the Kushta *tenai*,[112] there were a few Ashkenazic and Sephardic authorities who opposed the Kushta *tenai* on substantive *halakhic* grounds as well as for pragmatic and meta-*halakhic* considerations. However, except for a portion of Rabbi Ya'akov Toledano's criticism which appeared during the same year of the appearance of *Ein Tenai be'Nissu'in*[113] the other reactions appeared *after* the 1930 publication of this collection of letters.[114]

Now we can better comprehend the selection of the title of this compilation – *Ein Tenai be'Nissu'in*. Despite the fact that our review of these letters indicates that the criticism which was elicited was a frontal attack upon the merits of the French *tenai* without offering constructive avenues to propose a *halakhically* bona fide condition, yet as we noted earlier for Rabbi Yehiel Weinberg the title which was chosen for this collection was chosen to communicate the impropriety of invoking *any kiddushin al tenai* to solve the *agunah* problem in the nineteenth century French community.[115] The appearance of the Kushta *tenai* was the wakeup call that there is an acute and dire need to understand that the meta-*halakhic* considerations of undermining the institution of marriage, *hillul ha-Shem*, and ideological assimilation as well as the *halakhic* concern for *hezkat eishet ish* are hanging in the balance again. Yes, there may be grounds *halakhically* to validate the Kushta proposal, a *tenai* which clearly resonated *halakhically* in contradistinction to the French *tenai*, but at the end of the day the message was clear: *"ein*

---

112. *Teshuvot Mishpetei Uziel* 2, *EH* 44.

113. Y. Toledano, *"Kiddushin al tenai ve-Hafka'at Kiddushin,"* (Hebrew) 6 *Otzar ha-Hayyim* 201 (1930).

114. Y. Toledano, *Teshuvot Yam ha-Gadol EH* 74 (1931); S. Hillman, *"Teshuvah be-Kiddushin al Tenai,"* (Hebrew) 1 *ha-Maor* 13 (1933), 2 *ha-Maor* 43 (1933), 3 *ha-Maor* 63 (1933), 4–5 *ha-Maor* 83 (1933), 1–3 *ha-Maor* 27 (1934); *Mishpetei Uziel*, supra n. 112.

115. *Tenai be'Nissu'in ve-Get*, supra n. 73.

tenai be-nissuin." For Rabbi Grodzinsky, the appearance of the Kushta *tenai* was a *kol korei*, a clarion call to instruct that the *musar haskel*, the *halakhic*-moral lesson derived from the proposed French *tenai* is that *hafka'at kiddushin* was neither an option in the past nor an option for the present and future.[116] In effect, even though the Kushta *tenai* may be proper in terms of the *halakhot* of *tenaim*, conditions; nonetheless, it was argued that we must reject its use since the proponents of the *tenai* secondarily legitimate its use based upon the technique of *hafka'at kiddushin*.[117] Consequently, the Kushta *tenai* ought to be banned. Others opposed the Kushta *tenai* on its own merits in light of its compliance with *hilkhot tenaim*.

On the other hand, the title of the compilation *Ein Tenai be'Nissu'in* was chosen for two reasons: Firstly, to voice an objection to recognizing the tool of *hafka'at kiddushin*. Secondly, even though the primary focus of the letters was to elicit criticism of the merits of the French *tenai*, nevertheless, due to the *halakhic* concern of the *hazakah* of *eishet ish* as well as certain meta-*halakhic* or public policy considerations, we must conclude that "*ein tenai be-nissuin*" even relates to other *tenaim* including the Kushta *tenai*. Notwithstanding the problematic nature of introducing the French civil court as an integral part of the *get* process, it is clear that the other arguments advanced against the French *tenai* would be equally applicable to many other *tenaim* proposed by others including the one suggested years later by the rabbis of Istanbul and Rabbi Eliezer Berkovits.[118] To state it differently, had the opposition focused solely on rejecting the French *tenai* due to the role played by the civil court, this line of argumentation would have sufficed to marginalize the proposed French *tenai*. The fact that they advanced additional arguments against the *tenai* proves that the *halakhic* concern of *eishet ish* and meta-*halakhic* factors were in play here which were introduced in order to convey the message "*ein tenai be'nissu'in*." Though their argumentation clearly is based upon a *mesorah*, as we have demonstrated there are equally other persuasive *mesorot* which may validate other *tenaim*. The fact that the opposition chose to invoke opposing traditions indicates that a *halakhic* concern for the *hazakah* of *eishet ish* and meta-*halakhic* factors were at work here. Even prior to the published rabbinic opposition to the Kushta *tenai*, the utilization of the *tenai* was summarily banned with the

---

116. See supra text accompanying n. 108.

117. See supra n. 107.

118. Cf. Rabbi Berkovits, supra n. 73, at 167 whose claim that the reasons for the *halakhic* opposition to the French *tenai* relates only to that proposal is incorrect.

publication of *Ein Tenai be'Nissu'in*.[119] Similarly, though Rabbi Henkin offered another solution which entailed in part the use of a conditional marriage,[120] due to the appearance of *Ein Tenai be'Nissu'in*, he understood the import of its publication and retracted his proposal.[121] Finally, prior to presenting his meta-*halakhic* and *halakhic* opposition to the *kiddushin al tenai* proposed by Rabbi Ben Tzion Uzziel, the initial argument advanced by Rabbi Shlomo Zevin is to state that even if his suggestion is different from the French *tenai*, the compilation of *Ein Tenai be'Nissu'in* precludes the introduction of a different *tenai*. Though Rabbi Uzziel's suggestion diverges from the French *tenai*, in Rabbi Shlomo Y. Zevin's words "it is of no importance" whether the proposal differs from the French *tenai* or not.[122]

In conclusion, since the appearance of *Ein Tenai be'Nissu'in*, there have been over ten different proposals for introducing conditional marriage as a solution for the matter of *igun*. Some of these solutions have been summarized in 2000 in a series of articles entitled *Ein Tenai be'Nissu'in*.[123] Notwithstanding the practical reasons for opposing the Kushta *tenai* and rejecting the Kushta endorsement of *hafka'at kiddushin*, during the 1930's after the appearance of *Ein Tenai be'Nissu'in* Rabbi Shmuel Hillman, Av Beit Din of London Beit Din and father-in-law of Rabbi Yitzhak Herzog invokes various arguments including the Talmudic statement "*ein tenai be-nissuin*" to delegitimize the integrity of the Kushta *tenai*.[124] Whether the rationale of "*ein tenai be-nissuin*" was articulated or not concerning these proposed *tenaim*, their fate was identical. The majority of these proposed solutions neither were implemented globally or even locally nor were the subject of systematic and extensive critical review. For example, in 1966, Rabbi Berkovits published a thorough analysis of *kiddushin al tenai* and explained in detail how his proposal differs from the French *tenai*. In particular, unlike the French *tenai* which empowered the civil courts to play a decisive role in the *get* process, in his solution he elucidates how the *beit din* assumes para-

---

119. See supra text accompanying n. 113.

120. *Perushei Ibra* 5:25.

121. See Henkin, supra n. 106; *le'Dor Aharon*, 110–111.

122. S. Zevin, "*Ein Tenai be-Nissu'in*," (Hebrew), 4–5 *ha-Maor* 87–88 (1933).

123. Z. Gartner and B. Karlinsky, "*Ein Tenai be-Nissu'in*," (Hebrew), 8 *Yeshurun* 678 (5761), 9 *Yeshurun* 669 (5761), 10 *Yeshurun* 711 (5762).

124. S. Hillman, "*Teshuvah be-Kiddushin al tenai*" (Hebrew), 1 *ha-Maor* 13 (1933), 2 *ha-Maor* 43 (1933), 3 *ha-Maor* 63 (1933), 4–5 *ha-Maor* 83 (1933), 1–3 *ha-Maor* 27 (1934); Z. Gartner and B. Karlinsky, "*Ein Tenai be-Nissu'in*," (Hebrew), 9 *Yeshurun* 678 (5761), 714–717.

mount importance.[125] Yet, here again, notwithstanding Rabbi Menahem Kasher's article published almost a half century ago and Rabbi Yehudah Abel's recent comments published in 2011 regarding Rabbi Berkovits' contribution,[126] since the appearance of Rabbi Berkovits' proposed solution in 1966, to the best of our knowledge there has been no systematic critical inquiry into the merits of his suggestion.

In short, the publication of *Ein Tenai be'Nissu'in* in 1930 and the appearance of the series of these articles in 2000 entitled *Ein Tenai be'Nissu'in* serve metaphorically as bookends for the issue of conditional marriage dating back to the French *tenai* of 1887.

In other words, *kiddushin al' tenai* in any shape or form may not be advanced as a solution to resolve the plight of the *agunah*. Nonetheless, relying upon the text of *kiddushin al tenai* proposed almost two centuries ago by Rabbi Moshe Sofer,known by the acronym Hatam Sofer[127] the late Rabbi Yehuda Amital, Rosh Yeshiva of Yeshivat Har Etzion in *Eretz Yisrael* employed the technique of *kiddushin al tenai* at least two times to address potential marital issues of three marrying couples.[128] Do we continue to follow the *halakhic* public policy which began with the publication of *Ein Tenai be'Nissu'in* in 1930 and rebuff any proposal of *kiddushin al tenai* despite a *mesorah* of rulings in *sifrei psak* and *teshuvot* which permit the deployment of *kiddushin al tenai* under certain conditions [129] or do we follow in the footsteps of Rabbi Sofer's solution, those who proposed the Kushta *tenai*, the proposed *tenai* suggested by Rabbi Berkovits and Rabbi Amital and attempt to address the *agunah* situation? Do we ascribe to Rabbi D. Hoffmann's view that any proposal for *kiddushin al tenai* ought to be respected only if it has been suggested by a renowned rabbinic authority that is erudite in this realm of *Halakhah*?[130] Do we subscribe to the opinion of Rabbi Kook that any

---

125. *Tenai be'Nissu'in u-ve-Get*, supra n. 73, 57–71, 165–172.

126. See M. Kasher, "In the matter of a condition in marriage," (Hebrew) 12 *No'am* 335(5729); *Confronting 'Iggun*, supra n. 32, 3–45.

127. See supra text accompanying n. 102.

128. Sarah and Dov Weinstein, "*Kiddushin al tenai* which was prepared by the late Rabbi Yehuda Amital," (Hebrew), 36 *Tehumin* 248 (5777).

129. *Teshuvot ha-Rif* 118; *Teshuvot ha-Rosh* 35:8; *Rema, SA EH* 157:4; *Bah, Tur EH* 157:4; *Taz SA EH* 157:1; *Tzal'ot ha-Bayit EH* 6; *Teshuvot Noda be-Yehudah*, Mahadura Kama *EH* 54; *Teshuvot Hayyim ve-Shalom*, vol. 2 *EH* 103; *Teshuvot Maharam Schick EH* 70; *Teshuvot Mahaneh Hayyim*, vol. 2, *EH* 21; *Teshuvot Rabbi Akiva Eiger*, Mahadura Kama 93; *Teshuvot Shevut Ya'akov* 1:127; *Teshuvot Hikrei Lev EH* 58; *Teshuvot Ma'aseh Avraham Ashkenazi EH* 7; *Teshuvot Sha'arei Rahamim*, vol 2 *EH* 6; *Teshuvot Me'il Tzedakah* 1–4; *Teshuvot Imrei Eish EH* 95.

130. *Teshuvot Melameid le'Ho'eil* 3:22.

proposed *kiddushin al tenai must* be approved by renowned and erudite rabbinical authorities? [131] Or do we continue "to bury our heads in
the sand" and proclaim *ein tenai be-nissuin* without initiating a critical
inquiry into the issue of *kiddushin al tenai* with the avowed purpose to
hopefully, *be'ezerat Hashem* receive *halakhic* acceptance of a proposed
kiddushin al tenai by renown authorities of the Torah observant Jewish
community?

---

131. *Teshuvot Ezrat Kohen* 42.

Chapter 2

The propriety of certain types of prenuptial property agreements

DESCRIBING THE THREE-FOLD *HALAKHIC* classification of the matrimonial property system, the late Ben-Zion Schereschewsky, a leading expert in *halakhic* marriage law and former Israeli Supreme Court Justice writes:[1]

> Dowry or *'nedunyah'* means all property of whatever kind brought by the wife to the husband upon their marriage . . . those assets of the wife which she of her own free will entrusts to her husband's responsibility. . . ."*Nikhsei tzon barzel*" (lit. "the property of iron sheep") is a term derived from the name of a transaction in which one party entrusts property on certain terms, the latter undertaking responsibility . . . for return of the capital value of the property as at the time of his receipt thereof . . . Upon dissolution of the marriage, this obligation of the husband is governed by the rule that any appreciation or depreciation in the property is his . . . *Melog* property is property of which the principal remains in the wife's ownership but the fruits thereof are taken by the husband, so that he has no responsibility . . . in respect of the principal, both its loss and gain being only hers, and upon dissolution of the marriage such property returns to the wife . . . This category embraces all the property of the wife

1. B.Z. Schereschewsky, "Dowry," in M. Elon (ed.), *The Principles of Jewish Law*, Jerusalem, 1975, 390–392. For a comparison of the *halakhic* property regime with the community and common-law matrimonial property systems, see N. Rakover, "Property relations between spouses," (Hebrew), 12 *Torah She'ba'al Peh* 115, Jerusalem, 1970; A. Rosen-Tzvi, *The Law of Matrimonial Property* (Hebrew), Jerusalem, 1982, 121–134; Z. Warhaftig, "Community property between husband and wife," (Hebrew), Proceedings of the Fourth World Conference for Jewish Studies, Jerusalem, 1965, 189–194.

falling outside the category of *nikhsei tzon barzel* – save for property of the kind described in the next section – whether brought by her at the time of entering the marriage, or acquired thereafter, e.g. by way of inheritance or gift . . . A third category is property of the wife concerning which the husband has no rights at all, neither as to the principal nor the fruits thereof. This includes property acquired by her after the marriage by way of gift, the donor having expressly stipulated that it be used for a specific purpose . . . or that it be used for any purpose of her choice without her husband having any authority . . . or property given to her as a gift by her husband.

Although marriage does not affect a husband's property, a wife's property is impacted by marriage. Though the title to the wife's property (movables and immovables) and *tzon barzel* property of immovables resides with her, the husband has exclusive rights to its management, income, and profits, to be used for "the comfort of the home."[2]

The question arises whether there can be a prenuptial agreement whereby the property arrangement may be modified. Assuming such a possibility exists, at what juncture in time may such an agreement be finalized?

Let's focus upon the wedding ceremony, the event that established the marriage between the couple. To understand the background and building blocks of this practice, we need to offer some *halakhic* background. Recognizing that marriage consists of two separate acts, called *kiddushin* (i.e. act of *halakhic* engagement without cohabitation) and *nissu'in* (marriage with cohabitation) respectively, Rabbi Norman Frimer and Rabbi Dov Frimer note:[3]

> In practical terms, *kiddushin* as the primary state of Jewish marriage can be . . . normatively constituted through the presence of five *halakhic* elements . . . At the helm stands *kavanah*: intention. But intention for what? Two divergent directions emerge . . . According to one authority, the intent of the couple must be for at least the most minimal and natural characteristics of the marital experience . . . That decision, however, must also include the stipulation that the wife shall be exclusively related

---

2. Schereschewsky, supra n. 1, at 147–153.

3. N. Frimer and D. Frimer, "Reform Marriages in Contemporary Halakhic Responsa," 21 *Tradition* 7, 9–11 (1984).

to her husband and prohibited to all others. From this intent of *leshem ishut* will then flow all other authority which will bestow legitimacy and direction upon the formal ceremony and simultaneously form the foundation of the *kiddushin*. The other view finds the natural standard utterly inadequate . . . What, then, shall be the normative canon for *kavanah*? It must be *le-kiddushei Torah* or *leshem kiddushin* . . . a conscious awareness that the ceremony must be *kedin*, in faithful fulfillment of the hallowed imperatives of Jewish law . . .

. . . the intention to marry must be visibly objectified, in order both to articulate as well as to inculcate the core ideas of that *kavanah*. Jewish tradition, therefore, devised two more patterns of action to achieve tangibility. One of them was the *amirah*, an official verbal declaration of marital *kavanah* to be made directly by the groom to his bride in a formal and public style . . . The other act . . . was the *netinah*, giving, initiated again by the groom and complemented by the parallel *kabbalah*, receipt, by the bride. These sequential acts of "give and take" involve an object . . . traditionally a ring . . .

But not only must these facets of *kavanah* be shared between bride and groom. Normally, the *halakha* also demands . . . *ratson* – a fourth element, involving the couple's voluntary assent to all parts of the *erusin* (i.e. *kiddushin* – AYW). . . .

Finally, a Jewish marriage must be witnessed by at least two qualified *edim*, whose responsibility is two-fold. When necessary, they . . . can help establish the facts and certify the . . . degree of compliance with the prerequisites of Jewish marriage law. Yet, even more critical is their role . . . who by their very presence and participation at the ceremony constitute the validity of the *ma'aseh kiddushin* (i.e. an act of *halakhic* engagement – AYW).

In short, the subjective marital intentions of the Jewish man and Jewish woman are translated into reality via verbal articulation; concretization of this intent must occur under the scrutiny of two eligible witnesses and in the presence of an officiating rabbi and public assemblage (minimally ten adult male Orthodox Jews) for the expressed purpose of establishing a consensual marital union. With the finalization of the act of *nissu'in*, the Jewish man becomes a husband and is obligated to engage in conjugal relations and perform certain monetary duties such as supporting and clothing his wife. Moreover, with the advent of *nissu'in*, the aforementioned marital property regime emerges as governing the property relations between the couple.

That being said, at what point can the property arrangement established by *Halakhah* be modified? Let's assume that there is a monetary agreement executed by a couple prior to their marriage whereby all the property owned by the woman, the man is *mo'hail*, waives entitlement to the profits of these assets labeled *nikhsei melog* as well as future entitlement to her *ma'aseh yadeha*" (literally her handiwork) which minimally refers to a wife's domestic chores[4] (hereafter: future rights)? If the agreement was executed prior to the act of the *kiddushin*, then the *mehilah* is ineffective due to the fact that the accrued profits of *melog* property and a wife's earned income represents a future right which will be exercised by the man upon *nissu'in*. To be capable of waiving such right, one must possess the right at the time of the *mehilah*. As such, one cannot waive future rights.[5] Prior to the *kiddushin*, no such entitlement exists for the prospective husband. Should the agreement be executed via a *kinyan* (symbolic act of undertaking an obligation), the *kinyan* would be ineffective because the future rights are a *davar she-lo ba la'olam* (something not yet in existence). Consequently, the execution of a *kinyan* under such conditions is a *kinyan devarim* (an undertaking of words).[6] Similarly, if the man *obligates himself* accompanied by a *kinyan* to waive his entitlement to these future rights, then the arrangement would be invalid.[7] Based upon the foregoing presentation,

---

4. *Shulhan Arukh* (hereafter: *SA*) *Even ha-Ezer* (hereafter: *EH*) 69:4. Whether he is equally entitled to receive her earned income should she be employed is subject to debate. See this writer's *Rabbinic Authority*, vol. 2, 221–222.

5. *Teshuvot ha-Rashba* 5:180; *Teshuvot ha-Ran* 23; *Rema, SA Hosen Mishpat* (hereafter: *HM*) 209:4; *Bi'ur ha-Gra, SA HM* 209:17; *Teshuvot Shoeil u-Meishiv*, Mahadura Kama 3:158; *Teshuvot Beit Yitzhak EH* 1:112. Cf. some *Poskim* who validate such a *mehilah*. See *Beit ha-Behirah, Ketuvot* 83a; *Teshuvot ha-Bah* 124; *Teshuvot Kedushat Yom Tov* 6 in the name of Rashbam.

6. *Teshuvot ha-Rashbash* 243; *Teshuvot Havot Yair* 163; *Pnei Yehoshua, Ketuvot* 83a.

7. On the other hand, if he obligates himself to sell something which is not yet in existence and it is finalized with a *kinyan* the duty is *hal* (loosely translated: resides) upon the person who is the obligor rather than upon an item. See *SA HM* 60:1. In fact, Rabbi Daichovsky claims that if the man obligates himself prior to *kiddushin* that he will not have rights in his wife's assets, the arrangement is valid based upon the *halakhah* of a hiring a worker. In other words, he agreed to her request and married her in exchange for allowing the rights to remain in his prospective wife's possession. See S. Daichovsky, "In the matter of a husband's rights in his wife's assets," (Hebrew), *Le-David ad Olam*, 107, 117.

unless one accepts the position, albeit a minority view, that in principle a man may be *mo'hail* his future rights prior to *kiddushin*, or due to it being a rabbinic right it is waivable,[8] such a prenuptial agreement would not be recognized.

The outstanding question regarding this arrangement is whether *mehilah* will be effective *after* the act of *kiddushin* prior to the act of *nissu'in*. As we know, a husband inherits the assets of his wife upon her demise.[9] Despite the fact that after *kiddushin*, a husband cannot inherit his prospective wife's assets should she die prior to their marriage, there is a relationship established (*"age'da bei ketzat"*) which emerges as a result of *kiddushin*[10] between the man and woman which suffices to remove the inheritance right from the category of a *davar she-lo ba la'olam*. As such, after *kiddushin* he is authorized to engage in *siluk* (*haf-ka'ah* – renouncing) of his right to his wife's inheritance.[11] Analogously, a *siluk* performed by the prospective husband after the *kiddushin* ("I have no claim whatsoever upon the fruits of your estate and your earned income when you will marry") would equally be effective.[12] As such, if a

---

8. See supra text accompanying n. 5.

9. *SA EH* 92:8; *Beit Shmuel, SA EH* 92:19; *Helkat Mehokeik, SA EH* 92:16.

10. The consequences of consummating the act of *kiddushin* is that the woman is betrothed to the man but *halakhically* they may neither engage in conjugal relations with each other nor have marital relations with a third party. See *SA EH* 55:1. Yet should they decide to refrain from consummating a marriage, a *get* is required. See *SA EH* 26:3. Yet, upon consummating *kiddushin*, there is "a link to the properties" which will remove a prospective husband's right to his wife's inheritance from being classified as a *davar she'lo ba le'olam*. See *Tur* and *Beit Yosef EH* 69; *Helkat Mehokeik, SA EH* 69:12. As such, *siluk* of this right couched in a *tenai* will be effective if executed after *kiddushin* and upon marriage he will be unable to benefit from her inheritance. See *SA EH* 69:6–7; *Rema, SA EH* 92:7–8; *Helkat Mehokeik, SA EH* 92:4; *Beit Shmuel, SA EH* 92: 6.

11. *Teshuvot ha-Rashba* 1:960, 2:132; *Teshuvot ha-Rivash* 404; *SA EH* 69:6–7, 92:1; *Rema SA EH* 92:7–8; *Taz SA EH* 92:8; *Helkat Mehokeik, SA EH* 69:12, 92:4–5; *Beit Shmuel, SA EH* 92:6; *Bi'ur ha-Gra SA EH* 92:11; *Avnei Miluim* 92:5.

Our conclusion assumes even if the husband's inheritance rights of his wife's assets are of a Biblical status. See *Hiddushei ha-Ramban, Bava Kama* 49a; *Piskei ha-Rosh, Bava Batra* 16 and *Teshuvot ha-Rosh* 55:1; *Magid Mishneh, MT Ishut* 23:1.

12. *Rivash*, supra n. 11; *Rashba*, supra n. 11; *Rabbeinu Yeruham, Sefer Meisharim*, 23:4; *Hiddushei ha-Ritva, Gittin* 77a, s.v. *amrei*; *Mishneh Torah* (hereafter: *MT*), *Ishut* 23:1; *Rema SA EH* 92:1 in the name of Ran, *Beit Shmuel*, supra n. 11; *Helkat Mehokeik*, supra n. 11, 69:12; *Sma SA HM* 209:21; *Shakh, HM* 66:134; *Teshuvot Shoeil u-Meishiv*, Mahadura Kama, 3:158, Mahadura Tlita'ah, 3:22; *Avnei Miluim*, supra n. 11; *Mishneh le-Melekh, Ishut* 15:1, 23:1; *Teshuvot Divrei Malkiel* 4:155; *Hazon Ish EH* 77:9–10; *Minhat Asher, Bava Batra* 36(1); File no. 836209/1,2, Beit Din ha-Rabbani ha-Gadol, July 6, 2016.

prospective husband is *mo'hail* (rescinds) his future rights after *kiddushin*, such an agreement ought to be effective. Implicit in this conclusion is that either *mehilah* and *siluk* are synonyms for waiving a right or that they are different institutions, however concerning their effectiveness in dealing with future rights they yield the same results.[13]

Nevertheless, despite the above grounds for validating, after *kiddushin*, a prenuptial agreement entailing *siluk* or *mehilah*, there are *Poskim* who validate an arrangement of the *siluk* of future interests even prior to *kiddushin*.[14] Implicit in this position is that *siluk* differs from *mehilah*. The *sevara* (line of reasoning) offered by Taz is the following: Should a person engage in *siluk* it means that he has no interest in being *zokheh* (receiving the privilege of benefiting) the right and therefore he is empowered to renounce the right before he receives it.[15] Therefore, we can understand those *Rishonim* who will validate a *siluk* arrangement even regarding a future right which is of a Biblical status.[16] However, there is the view of some authorities that one can waive such a right prior to *kiddushin* because it is a rabbinic privilege to receive the accrued profits of a wife's *melog* property.[17] The rationale is that since this right was

---

Even if the *siluk* agreement was performed prior to the *kiddushin* (or even after the *kiddushin*) by the execution of a *kinyan*, the agreement is invalid. Since the man is renouncing future rights rather than transferring them, there is no requirement of a *kinyan*. See *MT, Ishut* 23:1, *Magid Mishneh* and *Mishneh le-Melekh*, ad. locum. *SA EH* 92:1, 7; *Helkat Mehokeik, SA EH* 92:4; *Beit Shmuel SA EH* 92:6; *Avnei Miluim*, supra n. 11; *Teshuvot Havot Yair* 46. He must declare the arrangement in writing or in the presence of two witnesses.

13. Though *Ketuvot* 83a is dealing with a case of *siluk* from a wife's assets, numerous *Rishonim* utilize the word *mehilah* in their respective commentaries regarding *Ketuvot* 83a. See *Rashi, Ketuvot* 83a, s.v. s.v. *me'makom*; *Tosafot, Ketuvot* 83a, s.v. *ve'savar*; *Hiddushei ha-Ritva, Ketuvot* 83a, s.v. *Rav Ashi*. And some *Poskim* equate the two at least with regard to future rights. See *Sma*, supra n. 12; *Teshuvot Havot Yair* 47; *Netivot ha-Mishpat HM* 209:6; *Shoeil u-Meishiv*, supra n. 12.

14. *Mordekhai, Ketuvot* 212 in the name of Maharam; *Rema SA EH* 90:17, *HM* 209:8; *Bah*, supra n. 5; *Teshuvot Havot Yair* 50 in the name of Rabbi G. Ashkenazi. Given that prior to the *kiddushin* there is no *halakhic* bond between the couple (see supra n. 10), many authorities invalidate a *siluk* agreement prior to *kiddushin*, see supra n. 12.

15. *Taz, SA HM* 209:4; *Ketzot ha-Hoshen* 209:11; Y. of Lissa, *Beit Ya'akov EH* 69:6; *Mishneh le-Melekh, MT Ishut* 23:1. Cf. Rabbi Daichovsky who argues that Taz sanctions a *siluk* arrangement only after *kiddushin*. See Daichovsky, supra n. 7, at 112.

16. *Bnei Binyamin*, 182 in the name of Ramban, Ra'ah, Rashba and Ran; *Avnei Miluim* 92:4 in the name of Rashi; *Hiddushei ha-Rashba, Ketuvot* 83a; *Mishneh le-Melekh*, supra n. 15 in the name of Ran. Cf. *Tosafot Ketuvot* 83a, s.v. *ke'de'rav*.

17. *Rashi, Ketuvot* 83a, s.v. *me'makom ahair*; *Rashbam, Bava Batra* 49a, s.v. *be'odo*; *Tosafot Rid, Ketuvot* 83a; *Hiddushei ha-Ra'ah, Ketuvot* 66a; *Hiddushei*

established to financially benefit the domestic household,[18] should the prospective husband decide that there is no need for this benefit, he may renounce his right. On the other hand, if the privilege is grounded in Torah law, one cannot engage in *siluk* because the Torah is absolute and is not dependent upon his will that if he rejects it he will not benefit from it.[19] Similarly, given that a husband's entitlement to her domestic chores is a rabbinic privilege in exchange for supporting his wife in order to avoid animosity between the couple,[20] should he decide that to forego this benefit, he may renounce his right.

Furthermore, notwithstanding some authorities,[21] this *siluk* arrangement may take place after *shiddukhin* (engagement) prior to *kiddushin*. In certain circles, it is customary for the prospective couple to have prepared a *shtar tenaim*, a list of conditions upon the occasion of *shiddukhin* with certain various parental and spousal obligations and the anticipated month of the wedding (or the actual date). The *siluk* arrangement is validated by these *Poskim* either because a man may renounce a future right, "these are matters that can be acquired via the medium of speech"[22] or the stating of such an agreement accompanied by a penalty and a *herem* (a threat of excommunication) will be effective.[23]

Taz's *sevara* for validating the power of *siluk* may be translated into at least two indigenous *halakhic* categories. Firstly, as we know, a husband

---

ha-Rashba, *Ketuvot* 83a in the name of Tosafot; *Tosafot Gittin* 77a, s.v. *ve-khi'de'Rav Kahana*; *Tosafot, Bava Batra* 49a, s.v. *ve-khi'de'Rav Kahana*.

Addressing a case of *siluk*, renunciation of marital property, both *Pnei Yehoshua, Ketuvot* 83a and *Arukh ha-Shulhan HM* 241:6 argue that it is effective due to being a rabbinic privilege. Assuming that the term *siluk* is identical to the term *mehilah* or that the two institutions are readily distinguishable and one can derive *halakhot* of *mehilah* from the *halakhot* of *siluk*, one can arrive at the conclusion that *mehilah* will be validated concerning a rabbinic privilege. Therefore, such an agreement will be validated even if finalized prior to the marriage.

For the privilege viewed as a rabbinic one, see *Tosafot Bava Batra*, 136b, s.v. *Rabbi Yohanan*.

18. *SA EH* 85:17; *Helkat Mehokeik, SA EH* 85:41; *Beit Shmuel, SA EH* 85:38.
19. B. Lipkin, *Bnei Binyamin* 173, 178–179; *Minhat Asher, Bava Batra* 36.
20. *SA EH* 69:4.
21. *Sefer Beit ha-Behirah, Ketuvot* 83a; *Yeshuot Ya'akov* 92:2; *Sefer Nahalat Shivah* 20 (2).
22. *Ketuvot* 102a-b; *SA EH* 51:1.
23. *Hiddushei ha-Hatam Sofer, Ketuvot* 83; *Teshuvot Hatam Sofer EH* 2:166; *Teshuvot Oholei Ya'akov* 101; *Teshuvot Havot Yair* 50 in the name of Rabbi G. Ashkenazi. Rabbi Y. Bachrach argues that if the *siluk* is accompanied by a *kinyan*, it will be effective after *shiddukhin*. See *Teshuvot Havot Yair* 47.

is obligated to support his wife.[24] Addressing the situation of a wife who agrees that she will not be supported by her husband, Rabbi Ya'akov of Lisa concludes that this act of *siluk* from her right to *mezonot* (support) is to be construed like *shi'yur*, a reserve clause.[25] In effect, the wife is limiting her monetary entitlement emerging from her marriage (*shi'yur*) by engaging in renouncing her right to *mezonot* from her husband.

The reserve clause is being couched as a *tenai*. Usually, the *tenai* is a condition for the validity of a transaction between two parties and therefore the condition must be couched according to *mishpetei ha-tena'im*, the *halakhot* of conditions.[26] For example, if Reuven gives money to a poor man to purchase a shirt, he may not buy a coat because he disregards the owner's wishes.[27] Should the poor man disregard the person's instructions in effect he is viewed as a thief due to the fact that he disregarded the conditional clause in Reuven's request. Becoming a thief is contingent upon the fact that a *tenai kaful*, a double condition, has been drafted, i.e. "On the condition that the poor person purchases the shirt with the man's money, it belongs to him. If he purchases the coat with the man's money, he is a thief." The transaction will be valid if the *tenai* is fulfilled. However, if the *tenai* is not complied with, the transaction is deemed misappropriation. In other words, whether the act will occur is contingent upon the fulfillment of a *tenai*.

In contradistinction to utilizing a *tenai* to set the parameters of a transaction between parties, here when dealing with a *siluk* arrangement we are focusing upon utilizing a *tenai* regarding the rights between a prospective couple. Implicitly following Rambam and others,[28] in the words of *Dayan* Eliezer Goldschmidt, we have a *tenai* which conceptually is "*bil'vad*" (loosely translated: limiting).[29] We are dealing with limiting the monetary scope of the husband's rights in the wife's property during their marriage rather than whether a particular act of marriage will materialize or not. Whether the act will transpire is not dependent upon the fulfillment of the *tenai*. Rather we are focusing upon a *tenai be-derekh hagbalah*, a condition which is limiting, specifically of the benefits enjoyed by the husband in his wife's property. The marriage will

---

24. *SA EH* 70:3.

25. For the effectiveness of *shi'yur*, see *SA HM* 209:7–8, 212:3; *Rema SA HM* 212:3, 214:5.

26. *SA EH* 38:2, *HM* 241:12; *Rema, SA EH* 38:3

27. *Bava Metzia* 78a.

28. *MT Zekhiyah u-Matanah* 3:8.

29. *Piskei Din Rabbanayim* (hereafter: *PDR*) 1:289, 306–307. See also *PDR* 9:60, 62.

take place and it is not linked to the compliance with a *tenai*. The parameters of the couple's monetary relationship in the marriage, whether the
husband will benefit from certain rights, is dependent upon whether a
tenai was executed. Consequently, in our context though a *tenai* is being
employed to limit the husband's rights, given that it is a *tenai bil'vad*,
notwithstanding *Tosafot*, and others,[30] it need not comply with *mishpetei ha-tena'im*.[31]

In other words, in the case presented to him, where the wife is stating
in the form of a *tenai* that this privilege will not be given to her by dint
of marriage, Rabbi Ya'akov of Lisa argues that such an agreement is recognized.[32] Similarly, Rabbi Ya'akov of Lisa contends that by executing a
siluk arrangement concerning his future rights in the form of *tenai* the
prospective husband has the prerogative to forego future rights due to
the fact that the arrangement preempted the creation of this matrimonial privilege.[33]

This solution poses two difficulties. Firstly, one cannot employ a
reserve clause regarding a matter which is a *davar she-lo ba la'olam*.[34]
Secondly, given that we are dealing with a *davar she-lo ba la'olam*, therefore these future rights possess no height, width or depth and therefore
are to be classified as a *davar she'in bo mamash*.[35] While *hilkhot hiyuvim*,
the law of obligations, fully recognize the validity of a reserve clause, this
type of clause is invalid when the right which is withheld is intangible.

Notwithstanding the above, one can couch the reserve clause as a
tenai and it will be effective because a *tenai* is valid regarding a *davar
she-lo ba la'olam* as well as a *davar she'in bo mamash*.[36]

Alternatively, Rabbi Arye Leib Heller contends that the efficacy of a
siluk arrangement which states, "on the condition that I have no claim

---

30. *Tosafot Ketuvot* 56a, s.v. *harei*; *Teshuvot ha-Rosh* 81:1; *Teshuvot Imrei Mishpat* 11.

31. *Teshuvot ha-Rashba* 2:140; *Hiddushei ha-Ritva. Kiddushin* 23b, s.v. *ve'ha'na-
khon*; *Teshuvot Maharit* 1:45; *Mahaneh Ephraim, Zekhiyah u-Matanah* 10; *Bnei
Aharon, Hiddushei HM* 241; *Batei Kehunah, Beit Din* 1:6; *Tosafot Rabbi Akiva Eiger,
Pe'ah* 6:69; *Beit Ya'akov EH* 92:7. For the distinction between a *tenai* which must
comply with *halakhot* of conditions and one which is valid without fulfilling such
requirements, see *Hiddushei ha-Ritva, Kiddushin* 23b; *Teshuvot ha-Rashba* 2:140.

32. *Beit Ya'akov EH* 69:6, 92:7.

33. *Tosafot Ketuvot* 83a, s.v. *ke'derav*; *Beit Ya'akov*, supra n. 15.

34. *Tosafot Bava Batra* 148a; *Tur HM* 209; *SA HM* 209:7; *Arukh ha-Shulhan HM*
209:13.

35. Rabbi Hai Gaon, *Sefer ha-Mekah ve-ha-Memkar*, Sha'ar 2.

36. *Rema, SA HM* 209:8; *Arukh ha-Shulhan HM* 212:14; *Pithei Hoshen, Kinya-
nim* 20:19 (74–75).

(benefit – AYW) of the *Halakhah* of future rights in your property" is that it is drafted as a *tenai*. And even though this *tenai* is "contrary to what is written in the Torah" since *Halakhah* recognizes a husband's rights in his wife's property it is valid due to the fact that the agreement entails monetary matters, namely the future rights of a husband in his wife's properties. And monetary issues are subject to modification based upon the employment of a *tenai*.[37] This conclusion finds its precedent in Talmudic rulings found in Kiddushin 19b, Ketuvot 56a and Bava Metzia 94a. As Rabbi Heller notes, Rashba opines should a prospective husband state at the time of the *kiddushin* that the *kiddushin* is "on the condition that he does not need to provide to his wife support and clothing," the arrangement is valid due to the fact that he wants to be *mo'hail* his duties rather than renounce (*siluk*) his obligations.[38] Based upon his rationale the validity of a condition in monetary matters does not provide for uprooting *halakhot*. Otherwise, *siluk* would have been effective. Responding to this challenge, Rabbi Heller offers his solution which was earlier presented by Rabbi Shimon bar Tzemah Duran, better known by the acronym: Tashbetz, who notes the following:[39]

> We do not say a condition contrary to what is written in the Torah is null, unless he explicitly conditions that what is written in the Torah ought to be nullified. However, if he conditions *himself* that he will not fulfill what is written in the Torah, his condition is not void . . . since he is conditioning himself and waives the privilege that the Torah entitled him to have.

In short, implicitly endorsing *Taz's sevara* and following Tashbetz's reasoning, Rabbi Heller is validating a *siluk* arrangement for future interests even prior to the act of *kiddushin* by couching it in terms of employing a *tenai* which is in variance to what is written in the Torah.

Notwithstanding, Tashbetz's and Taz's understanding, Rabbi Heller's view finds precedent in the Talmud. As we know, the *Shemitah* (Sabbatical) year provides that creditors may not pursue debtors for outstanding loans. What if, at the time of the loan transaction, the parties draft an agreement in the form of a *tenai* that there will be no release from debt in the upcoming *Shemitah* year? The validity of the agreement

---

37. *Ketzot ha-Hoshen* 209:11.

38. *Shitah Mekubetzet, Ketuvot* 56a in the name of Rashba.

39. *Teshuvot Tashbetz* 1:94. See also, *Rashi Makot* 3b; *Hiddushei ha-Ritva, Makkot* 3b; *Teshuvot ha-Rosh* 77:4.

will be contingent upon the wording of the *tenai*. If the *tenai* is that "the *Shemitah* year does not cancel the debt," then the agreement will not be recognized because it is in variance with the Torah's directive that the debt is cancelled by the *Shemitah* year. On the other hand, if the *tenai* is drafted "that you do not cancel the debt due to me in the *Shemitah* year" – meaning that you do not take advantage of the *Shemitah* year – it becomes a *tenai* between the creditor and debtor and the debt remains "alive" despite the coming of the *Shemitah* year.[40] Similarly, if prior to the *kiddushin* the man states in the form of a *tenai* that he does not want to benefit from future rights in the marriage, the agreement is valid.

The common denominator between Rabbi Ya'akov of Lisa and Rabbi Heller's views is that despite the fact that the *siluk* agreement transpires prior to *kiddushin*, it will be effective due to couching the arrangement in a *tenai*.[41] Implicitly, they are subscribing to the view that the execution of a *tenai* will be valid even when dealing with a *davar she-lo ba la'olam*.[42]

Alternatively, a *siluk* arrangement may be executed employing the language of *hithayivut* (obligation) such as "I obligate myself via a *kinyan* to return all that I will be privileged to receive (*zekhiyah*) from her properties due to being married to her properties as well as its fruits."[43] Utilizing this terminology of *hithayivut* is effective even prior to *kiddushin*.[44]

Finally, notwithstanding some *Poskim*,[45] a *siluk* arrangement will be effective by employing *kinyan udita* by stating that "I admit that all the properties and their fruits that will fall into my possession due to my marriage with my wife belong to her."[46]

In contradistinction to *siluk*, as we have shown, *mehilah* deals with a situation where the man possesses an existing right[47] and consequently if the right is not yet in existence such as prior to *kiddushin*, it will not

---

40. *Makkot* 3b.

41. See also, *Mahaneh Ephraim*, supra n. 31; *Teshuvot Maharit* 1:45; *Teshuvot Divrei Malkiel* 4:155; Beit Din ha-Rabbani ha-Gadol, supra n. 12; Cf. *Mishneh le-Melekh, MT Ishut* 23:1 (end) who claims that *siluk* couched as *shi'yur* is effective without employing a *tenai*.

42. *Rema, SA HM* 209:8; *Mahaneh Ephraim, davar she'lo ba la'olam*, 5.

43. *Rema SA EH* 92:7.

44. *Pithei Teshuvah SA EH* 92 in the name of Noda be-Yehudah.

45. *Ketzot ha-Hoshen* 194:4; *Teshuvot Shai le-Mora* 42.

46. *Rema SA HM* 257:7 and *SA HM* 209:5,250:3; *Minhat Hinnukh, mitzvah* 336:5; *Ketzot ha-Hoshen* 194:3; *Netivot ha-Mishpat* 60:17.

47. *Rashba*, supra n. 5; *Ran*, supra n. 5. Cf. others who disagree and affirm a *mehilah* agreement. See supra n. 14.

be recognized.[48] However, the act of *kiddushin* generates *"age'da bei ketzat,"*[49] therefore executing a *mehilah* of future rights at this juncture has validity.[50] Yet, others reject the efficacy of such an agreement.[51] However, if the *mehilah* is executed in the format of a *tenai* it is valid.[52] For example, if at the time of *kiddushin*, the prospective husband agrees with his prospective spouse that she may marry him on the condition that he is absolved from feeding her and clothing her, the agreement is deemed valid.[53] Similarly, if he is *mo'hail* in the form of a *tenai* his future rights *vis-à-vis* his prospective wife's properties it is valid.

In short, given the fact that there exists a debate regarding the propriety of both a *mehilah* agreement as well as a *siluk* arrangement, it is recommended that a *tenai* be executed prior to the marriage that the marriage ought to be established whereby the husband will not be the beneficiary of the rights in his wife's properties. Alternatively, as suggested by others, prior to the *kiddushin*[54] or under the *hupah* between the *kiddushin* and the *nissu'in*,[55] an agreement should be drafted, signed by the parties accompanied with a *kinyan* which states that the husband will neither benefit from rights in his wife's property nor gain title to her earned income. Obviously, the scope of these prenuptial agreements may extend well beyond the future rights that we addressed to encompass other matters such as that neither party will have a right in each other's respective properties which exist at the time of marriage nor in properties that they may acquire in the future.[56] Lastly, a prenuptial agreement may address the possibility that should a divorce ensue that

---

48. *Rema SA HM* 209:4; *Mishneh le-Melekh*, supra n. 41.

49. See supra n. 10.

50. *Sma*, supra n. 12; *Shoeil u-Meishiv*, supra n. 12

51. *Taz*, supra n. 15; *Beit Yitzhak*, supra n. 5; *Teshuvot Pnei Moshe* 2:110.

52. *Tosafot Rabbi Elhanan, Ketuvot* 56a–b, s.v. *harei*; *Shitah Mekubezet, Ketuvot* 56a in the name of Rashba; *Mishneh le-Melekh, MT Ishut* 6:10.

53. *SA EH* 69:6.

54. In the form of a *hithayivut*, a duty, the prospective husband can obligate himself even regarding *davar she'lo ba la'olam*. See Daichovsky, supra n. 7, 117.

55. At the time of signing of the agreement under the *hupah* the husband will declare that the *hupah* will not serve as means to consummate the marriage until after the recitation of the blessings of the *nissu'in*. See *Pithei Teshuvah SA EH* 92:1 in the name of Yeshuot Ya'akov; *Teshuvot Imrei Mishpat* 11; Beit Din ha-Rabbani ha-Gadol, supra n. 12.

Alternatively, under the *hupah*, the arrangement ought to be executed via a *tenai*. See *Teshuvot Bikurei Goshen*, vol. 1, 14:4–5.

56. For a sample agreement, see T. Ben Ya'akov, *Mishpatekha le-Ya'akov* 2, 572–580.

the issue of the division of marital assets ought to be resolved by a *beit din* in accordance with *Halakhah*.[57]

---

57. For a debate regarding the propriety of recognizing secular law as an avenue to resolve marital financial matters, see A. Sherman and S. Daichovsky, "The Law of Marital Partnership: The Law of the Land," (Hebrew) 18 *Tehumin* 18, 32, (5759), "The Law of Marital Partnership – Non-Recognition in Jewish Law," (Hebrew) 19 *Tehumin* 205, 216 (5759); U. Lavi, "Division of Marital Property in accordance to the law of monetary relations after accepting a *kinyan*,"(Hebrew) *Kenas ha-Dayanim*, 71–94 (5761). See also, this writer's, "Varying approaches toward the division of matrimonial property upon divorce," (Hebrew), 71–72 *ha-Darom* 129 (5761) and this writer's *Rabbinic Authority,The Vision and the Reality*, vol. 1, 189–193, 195–199 (2013).

Clearly, the Israeli *battei din* under the Chief Rabbinate will resolve end of marriage issues such as division of marital assets in accordance with secular law. One of the reasons is that civil law determines the expectations of the parties, i.e. *umdana*. See *Hazon Ish, Sanhedrin*, Likkutim 16:1; *Teshuvot Minhat Yitzhak* 2:86; *PDR* 16:312; *Iggerot Moshe HM* 1:72; *Teshuvot Havalim ba-Nei'imim* 5:34; *Teshuvot Ateret Shlomo* 1, page 360. Others have relied upon *minhag ha-medinah* (the national practice) in order to validate a recognition of civil law. See File no. 80581-21-1, Tiberias Regional Beit Din, June 24, 2009; File no. 798217/2, Beit Din ha-Rabbani ha-Gadol, August 1, 2011; File no. 873705/1, Beit Din ha-Rabbani ha-Gadol, November 7, 2012. Unwilling to rely upon *umdana* or *minhag ha-medinah* many *battei din* mandate that the parties execute a *kinyan*, a symbolic act of undertaking an obligation to have their monetary matters resolved in accordance with civil law. See File no. 593163/2, Tiberias Regional Beit Din, January 5, 2014; File no. 899102/4, Tiberias Regional Beit Din, June 7, 2017; File no. 1073595/4, Haifa Regional Beit Din, June 28, 2017.

Chapter 3

Breach of a promise to marry

THIS PRESENTATION EXPLORES HOW the *halakhot* of *hi-yuvim*, obligations, deal with the breach of promise to marry.[1] In the wake of a breach, what are the *halakhic* consequences? How do the rabbinical courts which are under the Chief Rabbinate of the State of Israel regulate what happens when there is a breach of *shiddukhin*, an engagement? Consider the following case: The plaintiff, relying upon the defendant's promise of marriage, advanced nonrefundable deposits for a reception hall, an orchestra, a photographer and a custom-made wedding gown. One month before the scheduled date of the wedding, the prospective groom, the defendant, informed the plaintiff that "all wedding plans were off" and would not be keeping his promise to marry her. Subsequently, she cancelled all the wedding plans and brought an action against her former fiancé in a *beit din* for imbursement of her wedding-related outlay of expenses which had been expended in the reliance upon the unfulfilled promise to marry. Given that "the promise to marry" has been *halakhically* characterized as an instance of "two who have undertaken an obligation,"[2] how do the *halakhot* of *hiyuvim* define this "obligation"? Does it really constitute a *hithayivut*, an obligation in the formal sense of the word? Is one obligated to marry one's prospective spouse? Can one recover damages for a breach of promise to marry? Are

---

1. For earlier treatments, see E. Shochetman, "More regarding damages arising from breach of promise to marry," (Hebrew) 9 *Mishpatim* 109 (1978); D. Frimer, "Returning engagement gifts upon breach of a promise to marry in light of the new civil legislation," 10 *Mishpatim* 329 (1980); P. Shifman, *Family Law in Israel* (Hebrew), Jerusalem, 1984, 121–145; E. Kanarfogel, "Rabbinic Conceptions of Marriage and Matchmaking in Christian Europe," ed. E. Baumgarten, et al. *Entangled Historians: Knowledge, Authority and Jewish Culture in the 13th Century*, Philadelphia 2017, 31–33.

2. *Teshuvot Rabbi Akiva Eiger, Mahadura Tinyana* 75. See also *Teshuvot Shivat Tzion* 88.

there grounds for reimbursement of wedding-related expenses due to a breach of an engagement? Are gifts that were given in the anticipation of the marriage recoverable?

Professor Ben Tzion Schereschewsky, an expert in *halakhic* family relations and a former Justice serving on the Israeli Supreme Court writes:[3]

> The party committing a breach of promise – that is, not marrying the other party – may be liable to compensate the other party for any actual damage sustained, such as the expenses of the preparations for the marriage, and may also be obliged to return the gifts he received on the occasion of the *shiddukhin*, whether from any party or from relatives and friends.

According to Professor Schereschewsky, a plaintiff may recover breach-of-promise damages that are tortuous (causing damage) such as unreimbursed expenditures made in preparation for the impending marriage. Since a plaintiff can also recover engagement gifts under *halakhot* of *hiyuvim*, Professor Schereschewsky maintains that both claims associated with the breach of promise, a claim associated with *nezikin*, torts, and the claim related to *hilkhot hiyuvim*[4] are recovered based upon an *umdana*, as assessment of intent that can be presumed to be correct.[5] In other words, would the prospective wife have incurred wedding expenses had she known her fiancé would break their engagement? Are the engagement gifts to be construed as conditional gifts? Is the condition in question the actual occurrence of the marriage and in the event the marriage fails to transpire the gifts are returnable? Or might it be that gifts are not recoverable when the donor changes his mind, as long as the recipient has taken steps to fulfill his or her part of the agreement? Employing Schereschewsky's analysis, invoking the technique of *umdana* in order to establish the basis for a tort claim and *hiyuvim* claim, translates in our situation into recovery of damages for unreimbursed expenditures and recovery of gifts by the aggrieved party.

But does the breach-of-promise claim resemble a tort or a *hiyuvim* claim? Is the employing of an *umdana* a suitable avenue for recovery of

---

3. B.Z. Schereschewsky, *Family Law in Israel*, (Hebrew), Jerusalem, 1993, 16.

4. Clearly, a tort claim is an illustration of a claim in *hiyuvim*. But for the sake of our presentation, we are referring here to a duty which emerges from a written agreement between the parties.

5. Ibid.

expenditures and return of gifts? Do Professor Schereschewsky's sources corroborate his conclusion?[6]

A related issue may shed light on the nature of the duty inherent in the act of *shiddukhin*. If, in a divorce agreement, a married couple takes upon the obligation (*mit'hayvim*) to dissolve their marriage, is such an agreement valid? The following reply was given by an Israeli Rabbinical Court:[7]

> It is clear that a divorce decree issued following a mutual agreement to be divorced, even though the parties undertook the obligation via *kinyan* (a symbolic act to undertake a duty – AYW), does not obligate them to become divorced . . . each party may withdraw from the agreement . . .

In other words, such an agreement is null and void. Numerous Israeli *battei din* (rabbinical courts) have adopted this position.[8]

It has been argued that the same conclusion should apply in a situation where two parties undertake an obligation to bind themselves in marriage. Both agreements have been characterized as *"kinyan devarim,"* a promise.[9]

Why doesn't *Halakhah* uphold such agreements whereby the parties obligate themselves to a marriage or a divorce? Though the *battei din* in question did not respond to this issue, the answer is nonetheless clear.[10] The Talmud states that the execution of a *kinyan* between two partners for the express purpose of dividing a plot of land equally between them is a *kinyan devarim* and therefore void.[11] As numerous authorities have explained, the effectiveness of utilizing a *kinyan* in this context is predicated upon the transfer of an object.[12] In rabbinic parlance, we speak of

---

6. Ibid., 16 n. 17.

7. *Piskei Din Rabbanayim* (hereafter: *PDR*) 8:175, 179.

8. *PDR* 1:257, 262; 2:289, 290; 3:322, 323; 8:3, 9, 175, 179; 10:121, 126; 11:89, 91.

9. *PDR* 4:374, 377; 8:175, 179. See further B. Lifshitz, *Promise: obligation and acquisition in Jewish Law* (Hebrew), Jerusalem, 1988, 110–12, 383.

10. Generally, the rulings of these *battei din* reflect normative *Halakhah*. See I. Warhaftig, *The undertaking in Jewish Law: Its validity, character and types*, (Hebrew), Jerusalem, 2001, 197–199, 471–472. For dissenting opinions, see *Teshuvot Kol Aryeh EH* 85; *Teshuvot Torat Hesed* 228; *Teshuvot Mateh Aharon* 8–9; *Teshuvot Nahal Yitzhak HM* 60:3. For a discussion of other dissenting views, see B. Lifshitz, *Employee and independent contractor: contractor – acquisition and obligation in contrast*, (Hebrew) Jerusalem, 1993, 118–133.

11. *Bava Batra* 3a.

12. See Warhaftig, supra n. 10, at 206–215.

a *davar she'yesh bo mamash* (something which is tangible) which when it exists imparts validity to a *kinyan*. In this context, tangibility is defined as something which has height, width and depth.[13] Ownership in something which is intangible (*davar she'ein bo mamash*) such as dividing up land and therefore the land cannot be transferred.[14] A *kinyan* can only in halakhic parlance be "*nitfas*"[15] (secured) or *hal* (executed)[16] with something which is tangible.

An obligation between two parties to behave in a certain manner in the future – for example to divide up land – is characterized by the Talmud as a *kinyan devarim* and is understood by the authorities as an example of the ineffectiveness of the execution of a *kinyan* in the absence of *davar she'yesh bo mamash*.[17] A promise to perform an action in the future ("we will divide up the land") cannot constitute a *kinyan* which is a symbolic act to undertake a *hithayivut*.[18] Such an undertaking does not transform a promise of a future action into a *davar she'yesh*

---

13. Rabbi Hai Gaon, *Sefer ha-Mekah ve-ha-Memkar, sha'ar* 2. See I. Brand, "Transactions in incorporeal estate: from philosophy to law," (Hebrew), 21 *Shenaton ha-Mishpat ha-Ivri* 71 (2000).

14. *Shulhan Arukh* (hereafter: *SA*) *Hoshen Mishpat* (hereafter: *HM*) 203:1, 212:1–2.

15. *Tur HM* 212:2; *SA HM* 212:1

16. *Perishah, Tur HM* 212:1; *Teshuvot Mateh Aharon* 1:9; *Torat Hesed*, supra n. 10.

17. *Sma, SA HM* 157:5; *Netivot ha-Mishpat HM* 157:4; *Arukh ha-Shulhan HM* 157:2.

18. *Rashi, Bava Batra* 3a, s.v. *kinyan devarim hu*; *Piskei ha-Rosh Bava Batra* 1:3.

Alternatively, the invalidity of a promise to perform an action in the future is due to the absence of *gemirat da'at* (firm intent and resolve to act) on the part of those involved. See *Torat Hesed*, supra n. 10; *Mateh Aharon*, supra n. 16. Adopting this view that a promise to marry falls under the category of acts predicated on *gemirat da'at*, see *Teshuvot Imrei Yosher* 1:203.

The ineffectiveness of a promise to perform a future action at a later date, as noted above, extends to a case where a prospective spouse commits to marry via execution of a *kinyan*. See *Teshuvot Maharbil* 1:59; *Teshuvot Lehem Rav* 147; *Arukh ha-Shulhan HM* 60:11. Cf. *Teshuvot Mateh Aharon* 1:7–9; *Knesset ha-Gedolah* gloss on *HM* 203.

However, despite the problem of *kinyan devarim*, some decisors argue that the violation of a penalty clause for a breach of an engagement is actionable in a *beit din* for a claim for emotional pain. See *Tosafot, Bava Metzia* 66a; *SA HM* 207:16; *Shakh SA HM* 207:24; *Sma, SA HM* 207:24. The Vilna Gaon agrees that such a claim be submitted to a *beit din* for this reason, provided that the local practice is to impose such a penalty. See *Bi'ur ha-Gra SA HM* 207:4. Rabbi Yosef Kolon contends that even in the absence of a penalty clause, the jilted party must be compensated for emotional stress. See *Teshuvot Maharik, shoresh* 29.

bo mamash. Applying the following line of reasoning to our situation, since the tangibility requirement is a condition for the effectiveness of performing a *kinyan,* and a promise to perform a future action is bereft of this integral component, an agreement to marry is invalid.

This explanation affords us to understand the *battei din's* view as to the ineffectiveness of the commitment undertaken by both parties to the *shiddukhin* and a married couple who decides to get divorced. In the scenario we are exploring here, where the parties exchanged a mutual promise to marry at a future date, such an agreement lacks validity.

In light of the ineffectiveness of the promise to marry, given the scenario that we have envisaged, grounds for reimbursement of wedding-related expenses? Though a promise to marry at a future date is invalid, if a document of *tenaim* (conditions for marriage)[19] is signed at the time of *shiddukhin* which specifies "an obligation to pay" (*hithay-ivut*) and a monetary penalty to be imposed on the party in default, the agreement is valid.[20] For as soon as the monetary obligation is created, the parties become debtors, in contrast to having merely exchanged mutual promises to carry out a future action.[21] Consequently, reliance on the penalty clause seems to be grounds for recovering expenses for a breach of a nuptial promise.[22] Nevertheless, the conventional explanation for the inclusion of this penalty clause is that it is intended to provide the aggrieved party compensation for *boshet,* the embarrassment and emotional anguish of a broken engagement rather than to provide a

---

19. In various communities, it is customary at the time of *shiddukhin* to sign a document called *tenaim,* enumerating various parental duties relating to the affianced couple, the anticipated date or month of the wedding and a provision for a monetary penalty to be paid should a party to the agreement default. On the different formulations of this document, see *Sefer Nahalat Shivah* 7–8; *Tikun Soferim* 11 and *Teshuvot Zera Avraham* (Yitzhaki) *HM* 11.

In the wake of *asmakhta*-related issues generated by the penalty clause, in certain communities the *tenaim* document did not provide a penalty clause for breaching the agreement. See S. Tavish, *Teshuvot Sheilat Shalom,* Mahadura Tinyana, 279.

20. For the effectiveness of a clause of *hithayivut,* see *Sma, SA HM* 245:2; *Teshuvot Hatam Sofer EH* 112, 135; *Teshuvot Beit Yitzhak,* 1:111. For different formulations of the provision, see *PDR* 4: 275, 278–279; 11:131, 140–145; 14:337, 339.

21. For an explanation of how a binding obligation is generated by a *tenaim* document, see *Sma, SA HM* 243:12. Cf. *Sefer Nahalat Shivah* 9:3. See also *Teshuvot Zera Emet Yoreh De'ah* (hereafter: *YD*) 236; *Sha'arei Yosher, Sha'ar* 5, perek 2.

On imposing an oath to impart validity to an agreement to marry at some future date, see *Teshuvot ha-Rashba* 3:213; 4:157; 7:502; *Teshuvot ha-Rivash* 191,208; *Teshuvot Zera Emet YD* 94; *Teshuvot Zikhron Yehonatan* 4.

22. *Teshuvot ha-Mabit* 2:98.

basis for recovery for expenses incurred in contemplation of marriage.[23] Therefore, even if the *tenaim* were written at the time of the engagement, this will not be a basis for resolving our issue of compensation for wedding-related expenses due to the breach of an engagement agreement.

Though the *halakhot* of *hiyuvim* seem to preclude recovery for financial loss relating to wedding-related expenditures, nevertheless adopting the approach of numerous *Poskim*,[24] many Israeli *battei din* view a breach of a promise as a *hezek* (an injury) which entitles the aggrieved party to damages.[25] This question whether there is responsibility for a *hezek* when an engagement is broken is a matter of controversy between Rambam and Ra'avad. As Rambam rules:[26]

> My teachers have ruled that it is the custom of the land that each man when he is betrothed (via the act of *kiddushin* – AYW) should arrange a feast for his friends or distribute money to the religious functionaries of the community, and if he follows the custom of all people and then she retracts, she must refund his expenses, because she has caused him to spend his money; and whoever causes another to lose money must pay for it.
>
> This applies only if he has witnesses to testify how much he spent. . . .

In his critical gloss, Ra'avad demurs and states:

> I do not concur with his teachers regarding this matter. That indirect causation is akin to seeds in the garden that did not grow; regarding which one pays only expenses. The principle of the matter is that monetary loss indirectly caused to him, the person is exempt from responsibility.

---

23. *Beit Shmuel, SA Even ha-Ezer* (hereafter: *EH*) 50:14; *Shakh, SA HM* 206:24; *Teshuvot Ridvaz* 1:129; *Teshuvot Hagam Shaul* 23; *Teshuvot Maharash* 4:78; *PDR* 3:57, 59–61. See also, Kanarfogel, supra n. 1, at 32.

Whether recovery for emotional harm in fact requires a binding agreement such as a *tenaim* document is a matter of debate. See supra n. 18; Shochetman, supra n. 1, at 117–121; Shifman, supra n. 1, at 142–144.

24. *Otzar ha-Poskim, EH* 50:3, sections 24–26. See also *Teshuvot Halikhot Yisrael* 25–26.

25. *PDR* 3:18, 31–32; 57, 63; *Piskei Din, Beit Din for Monetary Matters and Verification of Jewishness of the Chief Rabbinate* 3:205, 208–209.

26. *Mishneh Torah* (hereafter: *MT*), *Zekhiyah and Matanah* 6:24.

In other words, whereas according to Rambam a breach of a promise to marry is actionable, pursuant to Ra'avad, damages are not recoverable.[27] While a minority of decisors align themselves with Ra'avad's posture, most authorities, including *Shulhan Arukh* which cites Rambam's ruling, agree with the view of Rambam.[28] The rationales for imposing responsibility for *hezek* suggested by the authorities include the immediacy and direct nature of the harm,[29] the jilted and injured party's reliance on the *mazik* (the one who caused the damages), the injured party's unwillingness to accept the risk of loss,[30] and the fact that punitive damages generally are imposed for prevalent occurrences such as broken engagements.[31]

On the one hand, the responsibility for the consequences of broken engagements can be grounded in the category of *hezek*. On the other hand, the *halakhot* of *hiyuvim*, as we have shown, invalidate relief from a breach of a promise to marry. Yet, the *halakhot* of *hiyuvim*, as we will explain, propose invoking an *umdana* (that is, assessed expectation of an individual) which will result in awarding damages to the plaintiff in a breach-of-promise suit. A promise to perform a future action such as a promise to marry is recognized if it has induced reliance on the part of the promisee. Reliance transpires when a promisee, presuming that a nuptial promise will be honored, takes action he or she would otherwise not have taken, or refrains from taking action he or she would otherwise have taken.[32] In effect, a breach of the promise to marry generates a

---

27. This understanding of the debate rests upon two premises. First, though the dispute focuses on reimbursement for the outlay for a wedding party, the stated positions relate to compensation for all engagement and wedding-related expenses. Second, though the controversy centers on a betrothed woman who reneges on her commitment to marry the man who betroths her, clearly the import of Rambam's and Ra'avad's words is that it extends to a situation where a man or woman break off a *shiddukh*. Whether this controversy may be applied to a couple who performed a marriage ceremony (*hupah ve-kiddushin*), see *Teshuvot Pnei Yitzhak* 6, *EH* 4.

28. *SA EH* 50:3 and the sources cited supra n. 24–25. Interestingly enough, though there are seemingly self-contradictory rules in Rambam's *Mishneh Torah* and there have been attempts to resolve these contradictions (see *Otzar ha-Poskim EH* 50:3, section 24:1 and *Pithei Hoshen, Nezikin,* 3:26, n. 63) yet most *Poskim* endorse his opinion.

29. *Bah, SA EH* 50; *Sha'ar Mishpat HM* 386:1; *Kuntres Aharon,* Marriage 50:4; *Teshuvot Ein Yitzhak* 68:20; *Ohr Sameah, Zekhiyah and Matanah* 6:24; *PDR* 3:18, 32; 57, 62.

30. *Magid Mishneh, MT, Zekhiyah and Matanah* 6:24; *PDR* 3:18, 31.

31. *Helkat Mehokeik, SA EH* 50:10.

32. See this writer's, "The theory of 'efficient breach': A Jewish law perspective," ed. A. Levine, *The Oxford Handbook of Judaism and Economics,* Oxford, 2010, 340.

claim due the fact that the promisee had relied to his detriment on the promisor's initial willingness to marry the prospective mate.

Invoking a variety of contexts in which a reliance-based liability is operative, such as the *halakhot* of sales, labor relations and civil procedure, Israeli *battei din* have contended that detrimental reliance by the promisee serves as grounds for recovery under the *halakhot* of *hiyuvim*.[33] For example, suppose a plaintiff summons a defendant to appear before a *beit din*, and the defendant initially agrees to appear, but later changes his mind. Since the defendant changed his mind, he must indemnify the plaintiff for all the expenses incurred. Although there is no formal agreement between them, given the plaintiff's reliance on the defendant's promise to appear, any outlay of expenses associated with this claim is to be reimbursed by the defendant.[34]

Similarly, the *battei din* have concluded that a nuptial promise that induces detrimental reliance by the promisor is grounds for recovery of expenses should the promise be breached. The promisor who is the defendant who induced the reliance is to be viewed like an *arev*, a loan guarantor who pays the creditor in the event that the debtor defaults on the loan.[35]

Alternatively, it may be claimed that the issue of awarding damages for a breach of a nuptial promise is to be viewed through the prism of the community's social norms, the *nohag* in the community. Whereas the reliance-based approach views the affianced couple as entering into an agreement in isolation, this model views the agreement against the

---

33. *PDR* 3:18, 30–31; *Beit Din for Monetary Matters and Verification of Jewishness of the Chief Rabbinate*, supra n. 25, at 207.

34. *Teshuvot Maharam of Rothenberg*, Prague ed., 496; *Teshuvot ha-Rosh* 73:5. Cf. *Teshuvot Tashbetz* 3:165, *Bi'ur ha-Gra SA HM* 14:5; *Netivot ha-Mishpat HM* 232:10, *Teshuvot Havot Yair* 168, *Teshuvot Beit Yitzhak EH* 110 and *Imrei Binah, Shoftim* 21 understand this rule to fall under the *halakhot* of *nezek*. Whether the recovery of expenses incurred is viewed as *garmi* [direct damage] and therefore liability ensues or as *grama* [indirect damage] and the defendant is exempt from responsibility is a matter of dispute. See *Bi'ur ha-Gra*, op. cit.; *Teshuvot ha-Rashba* 1:940; *Teshuvot ha-Radvaz* 2:763.

35. *PDR* 3:57, 62; *Beit Din for Monetary Matters and Verification of Jewishness of the Chief Rabbinate*, supra n. 25, at 208–209. For earlier authorities subscribing to this line of reasoning, see *Teshuvot Maharash* 4:78; *Teshuvot Bnei Binyamin* 30.

Relying upon Rabbi Isser Zalman Meltzer's understanding of Rambam's view (See *Even ha-Azel, Zekhiyah* and *Matanah* 6:24), a *beit din* concluded that the *Halakhah* of *arev* provides the reasoning for his opinion. See *PDR*, op. cit. Whether in fact this suggestion is a cogent interpretation of Rambam's view is an open question and beyond the scope of our presentation.

background of the social code of conduct that governs such agreements: that is, the group's general conduct, expectations and acceptance of certain practices.

Rabbi Shimon bar Tzemah Duran endorsing this approach and offering his interpretation of Rambam's posture notes that in fifteenth century North Africa it was customary in various communities that certain expenditures were advanced in anticipation of an impending wedding. Consequently, if a breach of a nuptial promise happened, it was customary to reimburse the aggrieved party for these expenses. However, if the aggrieved party incurred additional expenses which were beyond the accepted social practice, the promise breaker was exempt from payment.[36]

Rabbi Moshe Zacuto (known by the acronym: Ramaz) describes a rather different scenario. He relates that in seventeenth century Italy engagements lasted one to two years in order to "test the waters" and attempt to ascertain the future stability of the relationship. Engagements were frequently broken off, gifts were returned and each party would withdraw from the relationship with no responsibility for the other side's incurred expenses. Given the existence of this social practice, Rabbi Zacuto affirms the decision of a *beit din* in the town of Mantua which declined to award reimbursement of expenses to those who incurred financial loss by a broken nuptial promise.[37]

For both Ramaz and Tashbetz an *umdana* is being deployed, in Ramaz's nomenclature – "*omed hada'at.*" In other words, the relationship of parties is being governed by *nohag*. Despite the fact that a promise to marry is an agreement as to a future action and thus by definition a *davar she'ein bo mamash*, nevertheless the parties' intent to follow social practice is presumed. Therefore, the agreement is enforceable.

At first glance, one might think that invoking this *umdana* points to a reliance-based theory of obligation to pay for pre-wedding expenses and returning of engagement gifts. The import of the *umdana* is typically expressed in terms of the 'reasonableness' of the expectations of the parties, who expect *nohag* to be adhered to. Since most members of the community abide by these norms, one can reasonably assume that it is more likely than not that any given individual in that community will do so as well. In effect, these expectations result in the promisee's reliance on the promise in taking action. As such, seemingly employing an

---

36. *Teshuvot Tashbetz* 2:166. See also *Sefer ha-Mikneh*, appendix 50:4; *Teshuvot Halikhot Yisrael* 25.

37. *Teshuvot Ramaz EH* 2. For others who subscribed to this approach, see *Teshuvot Maharashdam EH* 176; *Teshuvot Hayyim Sha'al* 10–11.

umdana seems to reflect the reliance approach. But there is, in actuality, a difference between the two approaches. The reliance-based perspective focuses on the obligatory nature of the **agreement**; the *umdana* approach seeks to distill **the intent of the parties** from social practice.[38]

Let us now revisit Professor Schereschewsky's position regarding the recovery of engagement gifts and pre-wedding expenditures due to a breach of a nuptial promise. In his opinion, the existence of an obligation between the parties based on the invoking of an *umdana* mandates compensations for the gifts and expenditures.

Clearly, the sources he cites support his conclusion regarding the recovery of gifts.[39] In the absence of a contrary expression of intent, gifts made in contemplation of marriage, typified by the engagement ring, but also including gifts between the affianced couple and gifts given to the engaged couple by third parties, may be recovered if marriage does not ensue, regardless of which party is at fault with regard to termination of the engagement. Employing the logic of *umdana*, an engagement gift is, by implication, a conditional gift title which does not become absolute until the marriage transpires. Whereas Tashbetz and Ramaz invoke an *umdana* grounded in the practices of the parties' communities, the presumed intent referred here concerning engagement gifts is based upon the parties' subjective wishes.

The following picturesque metaphor, suggested by an American judge, is equally apt as a characterization of the *halakhic* view that engagement gifts, absent intentions to the contrary, are implicitly conditioned on marriage.

Describing the conditional nature of an engagement gift, the court notes:[40]

> A gift given by a man to a woman on condition that she embark on the sea of matrimony with him is no different from a gift based on the condition that the donee sail on any other sea. If after receiving the provisional gift, the donee refuses to leave the harbor – if the anchor of contractual performance sticks in

---

38. P. Atiyah, "Contracts, promises and the law of obligations," in *Essays on Contracts*, Oxford, 1986, 13.

39. Supra n. 6.

40. *Pavlicic v. Vogtsberger*, 390 Pa. 502, 136 A. 2d 127,130 (1957). Though conditional marriage clearly departs from the paradigmatic model of marriage, which is not conditional, some courts have concurred with this court's conclusion. See *Piccininni v. Hajus*, 429 A. 2d 886 (Conn. 1980); *Ferraro v. Singh*, 495 A. 2d 946 (Pa. Super. Ct. 1985); *Brown v. Thomas*, 379 N.W. 2d 868 (Wis. App. 1985).

the sands of irresolution and procrastination – the gift must be restored to the donor.

However, Professor Schereschewsky's claim that damages for pre-wedding expenditures are to be awarded to the breach-of-promise plaintiff on the basis of an obligation established via the avenue of *umdana* is not substantiated by the sources he cites. In fact, all these sources in question address the issue of recovery of **gifts**.[41]

At this juncture, a brief comparison of the *halakhic* and American legal traditions will be helpful. The common law recognized a right to submit a claim, combining elements of both contract and tort for a breach of a promise to marry. In the United States, during the colonial period and the nineteenth century, courts recognized this cause for action. At the time, marriages, particularly among the wealthy, were often arranged and negotiated by families on the basis of the financial and economic considerations. Damages included those for mental anguish, humiliation, pre-wedding expenses and a woman's subsequent loss of marketability.[42] But by the late nineteenth century, this claim had become the subject of much criticism. Indeed, by the 1930's, twenty-five states had enacted legislation, colloquially known as "anti heart balm" statutes, abolishing the common law action for breach of the promise to marry. Other states placed limits on this cause of action.[43] This trend has continued to the present with only a few states currently permitting breach of promise actions.[44] Despite the non-recognition of the breach of the nuptial promise, tort law continues to allow potential spouses to sue each other for intentional infliction of emotional stress and negligence. Contract law has permitted the recovery of gifts in certain situations.[45]

Whereas, American law, much like Roman and French law, now

---

41. See supra n. 6.

42. N. Feinsinger, "Legislative attack on heart balm," 33 *Mich. L. Rev.* 984 (1935).

43. H. Clark, *The Law of Domestic Relations in the United States*, St. Paul: Minn.: 1968, 2, 12; Feinsinger, supra n. 42, at 979; Note, "Heart balm statutes and deceit actions," 83 *Mich. L. Rev.* 1770, 1770–1771, (1985).

44. *Boyd v. Boyd*, 39 Cal. Rptr. 400 (Ct. App. 1964); *Piccininni v. Hajus*, supra n. 40; *Aronow v. Silver*, 538 A. 2d 851 (N.J. Super Ct. Ch. Division 1987); *Bruno v. Guerra* 549 N.Y.S. 2d 925 (Sup. Ct. 1990); D. Abrams et. al., *Contemporary Family Law* 683, 2nd ed. 2009.

45. L. Belleau, "Farewell to heart balm doctrines and the tender years presumption, hello to the genderless family," 24 *Journal of the American Academy of Matrimonial Lawyers*, 365, 376 (2012). Deceit for fraudulent purposes is recognized as a cause of action. See *Piccininni v. Hajus*, supra n. 40, at 888–889; *Jackson v. Brown*, 904 P. 2d 685, 687 (Utah 1995).

deems recognition of such an action to be clearly out of step with societal mores which value individual autonomy, "freedom to marry," and the right to change one's mind without incurring liability for one's decision,[46] additional public policy considerations have been mentioned for the passage of the anti-heart balm statutes. The courts and the legal literature have raised three main criticisms of the breach of a promise to marry as a cause of action: (1) it can be used for extortion and blackmail; (2) it is subject to abuse by juries that, having extensive discretion, may award excessive damages for embarrassment and humiliation; (3) damage awards unjustly permit recovery for loss of expected economic and social position.

In *Halakhah*, the focus is quite different. In various medieval Jewish communities,[47] and certain segments of contemporary Orthodox Jewry,[48] promising to marry is considered almost tantamount to marriage and thus virtually inviolate. Professor Ya'akov Katz described the import of *shiddukhin* in medieval times as follows:[49]

> The signing of the betrothal document (*shtar tenaim*) did not create matrimonial ties . . . But, in practice, the document contained guarantees of sufficient substance to warrant regarding the future of the couple as entirely settled upon it being signed, no less than upon entering into actual betrothal (*kiddushin* – AYW). In the first place, each party undertook to pay a heavy forfeit for violating the agreement – generally half the amount of the dowry. Second, and more important, the undertaking involved the acceptance of a ban regarded as "a ban of the *kehillot*," i.e. as a decree of the Early Sages, on anyone who violated the betrothal terms and injured the good name of the other family.

The seriousness of the bond forged by the *shiddukhin* document was supported by public opinion which frowned upon its cancellation. Those who violated such an agreement without receiving a dispensation from a competent *beit din* suffered serious consequences. Not only did

46. Shifman, supra n. 1 at n. 37; C. McCormick, *Handbook on the law of damages*, St. Paul: Minn. 407 (1935); *Standard v. Bolin*, 88 Wash. 2d 614, 617–19, 565 P. 2d 94, 96–97 (1977).

47. *Otzar ha-Poskim EH* 50:3, sections 24–26; Kanarfogel, supra n. 1, at 34–35.

48. Shifman, supra n. 1, at 128

49. J. Katz, *Tradition and Crisis*, N.Y., 1961, 137–138. See also A. Grossman, *The early sages of Ashkenaz* (Hebrew), Jerusalem, 1981, 137; idem, *Pious and rebellious, Jewish women in medieval Europe*, Jerusalem, 2003, 88–97.

they have to pay the incurred losses, but they would be held in contempt, lessening their prospects for entering into an appropriate match subsequently. The writing and signing of the *shtar tenaim* as well as the institution of "the ban of the communities" extended well beyond the medieval period and in many circles continues to be observed, precisely as described by Professor Katz, until the twentieth century.[50] On the other hand, in certain Babylonian communities during Gaonic times and in certain fifteenth century communities in North Africa and seventeenth century Italian Jewish enclaves, broken engagements were as we noted a fact of life acknowledged by the authorities of the day.[51]

For communities that must deal with the issue of broken engagements, *Halakhah* has devised solutions in accordance with its own inner logic. While there is usually a period during which withdrawing from an engagement does not cause too much harm, the harm may become more extensive the longer one waits to break the engagement. As the wedding date draws near and in many Torah observant communities the span of time between *shiddukhin* and the wedding is short, the expenses incurred in anticipation of the wedding increase quickly. It thus behooves someone having second thoughts about an impending marriage to discuss these doubts with his/her prospective spouse as soon as possible. Imposing liability serves the social goals of preventing procrastination and promoting responsibility, honesty and forthrightness. Knowledge that one may be liable for monetary losses for a broken engagement is an incentive to take the promise to marry seriously, in accordance with the verse, "The remnant of Yisrael shall not do iniquity, nor speak lies."[52]

---

50. *Darkhei Moshe, Tur EH* 3; *Beit Shmuel, SA EH* 51:10; *Teshuvot Noda be-Yehudah*, Mahadura Kama, *YD* 68; *Teshuvot Maharsham* 4:154.

Regarding communal enactments, see Y. Schepansky, *The Takanot of Israel: Communal Ordinances* (Hebrew), N.Y.: 1993, 544–547. For an offering of explanations for the efficacy of communal legislation regarding engagement agreements that fail to meet the requirements of an enforceable *halakhic* duty, see Y. Kaplan, "Communal autonomy vis-à-vis the limitations of Jewish private law," (Hebrew), 25 *Mishpatim* 377 (1995).

51. *Otzar ha-Geonim, Bava Kama* 224; text supra accompanying notes 36–37. Whether two thirds or half of the wedding expenses are to be reimbursed is a matter of dispute. See *Otzar ha-Poskim EH* 50:3, sections 24:2, 27.

52. *Tzephaniah* 3:13. See *Pesahim* 91a.

Chapter 4

A parent's decision to withhold medical treatment from children: A study in competing analogies

A RANGE OF CASES in American law that has gained increasing prominence during the last thirty years centers upon the parental responsibility to provide medical treatment for children. Interestingly enough, the Talmud is reticent regarding this issue. However, post-Talmudic authorities have suggested that the *halakhot* (Jewish laws) dealing with criminal omissions, norms of *tzedakah* (loosely translated: charity) and the child support obligation may serve as indigenous *halakhic* categories for addressing this issue. Implicit in their suggestion of the relevancy of these *halakhot* for our matter is the implicit assumption that one can extend the rules governing criminal omission, *tzedakah* and child support which are applicable to one set of fact patterns to our fact pattern (i.e. parental neglect of a child's medical care) which are in relevant respects similar. Here, as in other realms of *Halakhah*, legists resort to the use of "reasoning by analogy".[1]

Equally significant however, are the *consequences* of adopting a particular analogical argument. Every analogical argument leads to very different results. Our issue suggests many competing analogies and therefore the yielding of different outcomes. Yet, aside from a decision rendered by an Israeli rabbinical court, all decisors who employ an analogy to resolve our matter fail to examine the consequences of adopting the particular analogical argument and/or the outcome of adopting a counter analogy.

Our study will attempt to unravel the consequences of viewing a par-

---

1. E. Shochetman, "On analogy in decision-making in *Halakhah* and the Foundations of Jewish law act" (Hebrew), 13 *Shenaton ha-Mishpat ha-Ivri* 307 (1988); this writer's, *Rabbinic Authority: The Vision and the Reality*, vol. 1, 53–57.

ent who withholds medical care as analogous to that of an individual who fails to rescue an endangered party, declines to give *tzedakah* or as a parent who neglects to support his child.

To fully understand the analogical argument suggested by *Halakhah* of criminal omissions, let us begin with a brief presentation of the position of American law.

Our issue presents a case of homicide by omission on the part of parents. This matter in American law entails three issues.[2] Firstly, a parent's legal duty to provide necessary medical attention and the imposition of criminal sanctions for failure to fulfill his duty. Furthermore, the matter involves the degree of negligence required for involuntary manslaughter and the circumstances under which an omission is deemed to proximately cause the death of the other.

Perhaps one of the most striking illustrations for denying responsibility is exemplified by the case of *Bradley v. State*.[3] In Bradley, a minor, epileptic daughter had fallen into a fire while experiencing a seizure and suffered severe burns. On religious grounds, the father refused to treat his daughter's burns with medication. Suggesting that there was no connection between the father's refusal to provide medical care and the child's eventual death, the court exonerated the defendant of manslaughter stating the following:[4]

> Whatever motive may have prompted the father in failing and refusing to provide medical attention for his severely burned daughter, such failure and refusal, however reprehensible, does not appear to be within the letter or intent of the statute making "the killing of a human being, by the act, procurement or culpable negligence of another" a felony called manslaughter. It is not claimed that the allegations and the proofs show that any "act" or "procurement" of the father caused the death of the child . . . Manifestly, the death of the child was caused by the accidental burning which the father had no part. . . .

In other words, the failure to prevent harm is to be distinguished from

---

2. *State v. Staples*, 126 Minn. 148 N.W. 283 (1914); *Craig v. State*, 220 Md. 590, 155 A. 2d 684 (1959); *Eaglen v. Eaglen*, 249 Ind. 144, 231 N.E. 2d 147 (1967); *Commonwealth v. Barnhart*, 345 Pa. Super. 10, 497 A. 2d. 616 (1985) appeal denied; Walker v. Superior Ct., 47 Calf. 3d. 112, 763 P. 2d 852, 253 Cal. Rptr. 1 (1988).

3. 79 Fla. 651, 84 So. 677 (1920).

4. Id. At 655, 84 So. At 679.

causing harm. Since the child's death was caused by the accidental burn-
ing in which the father had no part, the father did not "cause the killing
of the child."

Traditionally, common law has refused to impose a general duty to
rescue persons in peril. Nevertheless, exceptions to this rule have developed in the form of "special relationships between two individuals"
out of which duties of rescue emerge. The duty of rescue based on a
special relationship is well settled when the individual needing medical
attention is a child and the person under a duty is the parent.[5]

Does the Bradley decision imply recognition of humanitarian duties
that "the law should reflect, reinforce . . . at least the segment of shared
morality which consists in moral duties owed to others"? Rather this
ruling rejects the judgment of Lord Atkin in the classic English case of
Donohue v. Stevenson which states:[6]

> The rule that you are to love your neighbor becomes in law, you
> must not injure your neighbor; and the lawyer's question, who
> is my neighbor receives a restricted reply . . . The answer seems
> to be persons who are so closely and directly affected by my act
> that I ought reasonably to have them in contemplation as being
> so affected when I am directing my mind to acts of omission
> which we called in question.

Clearly, suggests Lord Atkin, the particular circumstances dictate that a
parent rescue his child. Neither humanhood nor parenthood as sources
for moral duties becomes the source of the legal obligation of care.
Whether a particular situation mandates a duty of care will be applied by
applying the rules of causation. Therefore, the rationale of causation is
the justification for a duty of rescue based upon "a special relationship."

Does *Halakhah* analyze a criminal omission in terms of causation
and thus insist on a causal link between omission and harm?[7] A cursory

---

5. *Commonwealth v. Breth*, 44 Pa. C. 56, (1915); *Nozza v. State*, 288 So. 2d 560
(Fla. Dist. Ct. App. 1974); *State v. Walden*, 306 N.C. 466, 293 S.E. 2d 780 (1982);
People v. Sealty, 136 Mich. App. 168, 356 N.W. 2d 614 (1984).

6. *Donohue v. Stevenson* A.C. 562 (1932).

7. Our presentation is based upon two assumptions. Firstly, in contradistinction
to some religious traditions, there is a duty to seek conventional medical care. See
generally, J. Bleich, "Ethico-*halakhic* considerations in the practice of medicine," 7
Dine Israel 87 (1976). Cf. *Teshuvot Avnei Nezer HM* 193. Secondly, the failure to
provide medical attention is an act of homicide by omission rather than an act of
homicide. See *Teshuvot Rav Pe'alim* 3:36.

reading of Talmudic discussions of homicide indicates that the concept of causation is limited to acts of criminal commission.[8]

If according to *Halakhah*, the harm the individual does not prevent from occurring cannot be regarded as a consequence of his refraining, since the required causal relation is absent, on what basis can one hold an individual responsible for his omission? Without recourse to a given causal relation, as suggested by American law, there exists in *Halakhah* a positive duty to every Jew, a duty beyond "the negative one" of not causing harm to the individual. A parent's obligation to provide medical treatment has been advanced by various authorities as an example of this generalized duty of rescue, one that extends to strangers.[9]

Seemingly, the application of this analogy to the duty of rescue is ineffective in the sense that it is a somewhat toothless tiger since the failure to rescue lacks a *halakhic* sanction on Biblical grounds.[10] Hence, a minor would have no redress and relief against a recalcitrant parent who refuses to provide medical care.[11]

Countering this objection, Professor Aaron Kirschenbaum states:[12]

> It is a fact of history that in Jewish society . . . non-prosecutable injunctions, by their sheer religious weight, were effective in their deterrent power. It would be misleading, therefore, to interpret the lack of judicial punishment in Jewish law for the innocent bystander who fails in his duty to come to the rescue

---

8. *Sanhedrin* 77a, 78a–b.

9. *Teshuvot Shoeil u-Meishiv,* Mahadura Kama, 3:140; *Teshuvot Beit Ephraim* 65; *Teshuvot Tzitz Eliezer* 15:40.

10. *Makkot* 15b; *Mishneh Torah* (hereafter: *MT*), *Rotzeiah u-Shemirat ha-Nefesh* 1:16; *Sanhedrin* 18:1–2.

11. The lack of sanction is limited to situations which mandate a rescue based upon the *halakhot* of criminal omissions. However, situations which mandate a rescue based upon the *halakhot* of *hashavat aveidah*, returning a lost object, will be subject to coercion by a *beit din*.

Nevertheless, rabbinically it is permissible to compel compliance in cases of criminal omissions. See *Teshuvot Meishiv Davar* 4:11; *Ginzei Hayyim*, Entry "M," Malkot, section 87; *Sedei Hemed*, Entry "M," Principle 106–110.

The assumption is that a minor, despite being below majority age is *"a ba'al din"* (a litigant) and therefore he may file a claim in *beit din* against the recalcitrant parent. A third party such as his appointed guardian or a guardian appointed by the *beit din* would formally represent the minor and appear in *beit din* to advance the minor's claim. See E. Shochetman, *Seder ha-Din in Beit Din ha-Rabbani* (Hebrew), Jerusalem: 5771, 207–211.

12. A. Kirschenbaum, "The 'Good Samaritan' and Jewish law," 7 *Dine Israel* 17–18 (1976).

of his fellow-man in distress as indicating that the duty is merely moral. Rather Jewish law views such failure as . . . a formal offense of inaction . . .

Echoing a similar idea, Professor Ernst Weinrib writes:[13]

To regard the Talmudic duty as moral rather than legal, however, is to misconceive the talmudic position. The duty of rescue is not merely a matter of conscience . . . Because Jewish law embodies a jurisprudence of obligation, the legal character of the duty to rescue lies in its very existence as a duty, even if its breach is not subject to sanction . . .

Halakhah is primarily a system of duties owed rather than rights possessed.[14] Hence the individual's duty of rescue by itself mandates compliance.

The duty of rescue is based upon both a positive and a negative commandment: "And you shall restore him to himself" and "Do not stand idle by the blood of your neighbor".[15] Whereas, the Biblical negative commandment biblically mandates assistance for victims in peril, the former Biblical verse deals with the restoration of lost property and it is interpreted by the *Midrash Halakhah* to encompass the restoration of an individual's body.[16] Seemingly, the positive and negative commandments are two sides of the same coin; the negative one has no intrinsic significance; it only relates to the omission of the positive, i.e. the failure to rescue and its attendant consequences for failing to comply with rescuing an individual in stress.

However, the Talmud views the provisions regulating the duty to rescue as a resolution of the interplay between a positive and a negative commandment emerging from two different spheres of *Halakhah*,

---

13. E. Weinrib, "Rescue and Restitution," 1 *S'vara* 59, 61 (1990).

14. See this writer's, "May one destroy a neighbor's property in order to save one's life?" in ed. Shmidman, *Turim: Studies in Jewish History and Literature presented to Dr. Bernard Lander*, N.Y., 2007, 331–332.

15. *Devarim* 22:2; *Vayikra* 19:16.

16. *Sifrei, Ki Te'tzei* 22:2 (ed. Finkelstein, 256). Our implicit assumption is that the *halakhot* dealing with restoration of lost property mandate a rescue even in non-life-threatening situations. See Rambam, *Commentary on the Mishnah, Nedarim* 4:4; *Hamra ve-Ha'yei Sanhedrin* 73a. Compare Schiff, "Opening a clinic in a condominium against the wishes of the other tenants," (Hebrew), in ed. Halperin, *Emek Halakhah*, 138–140, 1985.

namely the *halakhot* of the restoration of lost property and the *halakhot* of criminal omissions.[17] As the Talmud teaches us:[18]

> From where do we know that if a man sees his neighbor drowning. . . . he is bound to save him? From the verse, "Do not stand idly by the blood of your neighbor." But is it derived from this verse? Is it not rather from elsewhere? From where do we know (that one must rescue his neighbor from – AYW) the loss of himself? From the verse, "And you ought to restore him to himself." From that verse I might think that it is only a personal obligation, but that he is not bound to take the trouble of hiring men (if he cannot deliver himself – AYW); therefore, this verse teaches that he must.

If the *halakhot* dealing with the duty of rescue would have been governed exclusively by the *halakhot* of restoration of lost property, then the scope of the rescuer's involvement would have been limited to personal involvement.

The *halakhot* of criminal omissions mandate that an individual's duty in a rescue is not eclipsed by personal involvement. The rescuer, while attempting to render assistance to the endangered party, is dutybound to incur the expenditures required for the rescue effort.[19] Thus, the *halakhot* of criminal omissions serve to expand the scope of the rescuer's responsibility beyond the obligation mandated by the *halakhot* of restoring lost property. Hence the extent of parental responsibility for providing a child's medical care entails personal involvement and the incurring of financial expenditures.

Viewing the provisions regulating the duty of rescue as a resolution of the interplay between two diverse areas of *Halakhah* is reflected in post-talmudic discussions. For example, what happens if an elderly father or a father who is proficient in *Halakhah* and is capable of assisting in a rescue considers the rendering of a particular type of medical treatment undignified (e.g. dealing with a major hemorrhage of his child) and therefore declines to offer aid? Since according to the *halakhot* of resto-

---

17. *Beit Ephraim*, supra n. 9; *Teshuvot Lev Aryeh* 42; *Teshuvot Atzei ha-Levanon* 61.

18. *Sanhedrin* 73a.

19. For the extent of one's financial obligations in rescuing a party in peril, see *Teshuvot ha-Rivash* 387; *Teshuvot Havot Yair* 139; *Teshuvot Hatam Sofer, HM* 177; *Teshuvot Mishpat Kohen* 144; *Teshuvot Seridei Eish*, vol. 1, page 313.

ration of lost property, under these circumstances the person would be exempt from his duty to rescue lost property,[20] some *Poskim* conclude that he is equally exempt from the duty of rescue. On the other hand, the *halakhot* of criminal omissions would mandate a duty to rescue under these conditions.[21] Consequently, an elderly father or a father proficient in *Halakhah* would remain dutybound to provide the necessary medical care for his child.

Inasmuch as *Halakhah* encourages the duty to rescue,[22] *Halakhah*, similar to many civil legal systems, requires the rescuee to reimburse the rescuer for expenses that the rescuee would surely have authorized.[23] However, according to Tur and Rema if the rescuee is impoverished and therefore cannot shoulder the costs of the rescue operation, the rescuer is exempt from his duty.[24] As such, it would seem that a father would be exempt from providing medical assistance to his dependent child who is bereft of financial resources. Alternatively, it may be argued that the case of a financially dependent child may be an exception to the rule.[25]

Whereas, as we mentioned earlier according to American law, there is an absence of a general legal duty to rescue a person in peril,[26] and similarly there is no legal obligation to secure and return lost property.[27] Under *Halakhah*, as we have demonstrated, there exist divine imperatives to restore lost property as well as rescuing life. Moreover, as we have shown, the *halakhot* of restoration of lost property may serve as guidelines in fashioning the *halakhot* of the duty to rescue.

---

20. *Bava Metzia* 30a–b. For the varying definitions of "an elderly person," see *MT, Gezeilah ve-Aveidah*, 11:13; *Shitah Mekubetzet, Bava Metzia* 30a.

21. *Kelei Hemdah, Devarim, Ki Te'tzei*, 186–188; *Lev Aryeh*, supra n. 17.

22. In the process of a rescue operation, many *halakhic* duties may be suspended. See *Mishnah Pesahim* 3:7, *Yoma* 8:6; *MT, Shabbat* 2:1–3, 16–18. Under certain conditions, the rescuer is exempt from responsibility if he damages property. See *MT, Hovel u-Mazik* 8:14.

23. *Yad Ramah, Sanhedrin* 73b; *MT, Hovel u-Mazik* 8:4, *Ra'avad* ad. locum.; *Piskei ha-Rosh, Sanhedrin* 8:2; *Teshuvot Maharsham* 5:54; *Gilyonei ha-Shas, Bava Kama* 60b.

24. *Tur, HM* 426:1; *Rema, SA YD* 252:12.

25. *Teshuvot Maharashdam YD* 204.

26. J. Ratcliffe (ed.), *The Good Samaritan and the Law*, N.Y., 1966; E. Weinrib, "The case for a duty to rescue," 90 *Yale L. J.* 247 (1980); A. Woozley, "Duty to rescue: some thoughts on criminal liability," 69 *Virginia L.R.* 1273 (1986).

27. R. Brown, *The law of personal property*, section 3.5 at 30, 1971.

II.

A second analogical model suggested by an Israeli rabbinical court is to posit that the parental responsibility to provide necessary medical treatment involves entails the fulfillment of a *"hiyuv,"* an obligation, namely the *mitzvah* of *tzedakah*, charity.[28] In other words, should the minor's medical treatment require the expending of expenses, the parent would pay for the outlay of these expenses.

Seemingly, given the fact that *tzedakah* is *"mamon she'ein lo tov'im"*, monies without determinate plaintiffs,[29] the failure to contribute cannot be claimed and therefore litigated in a *beit din*. No potential recipient of *tzedakah* can demand anything from a donor as his due. In fact, it is subject to debate whether *tzedakah* belongs to the impoverished or to the *tzibur*, the community as an independent *halakhic* personality akin to a corporation.[30] In short, *tzedakah* does belong to any defined individual(s) and seemingly therefore a minor cannot recoup his medical expenses.

As the late Chief Rabbi of Israel, Rabbi Dr. Yitzhak Herzog elucidates:[31]

> 'Right' and its correlative 'duty', are fundamental concepts in law . . . Thus, to give a sufficiently plain illustration, if A owes money to B, the right to recover the debt is vested in B and he is in legal language the owner of the right which avails against A . . . A, on the other hand, owes a duty to B. He is the person against whom the right of B avails, and upon whom the correlative duty lies . . . That these elemental concepts are present in Jewish law is, of course, self evident. . . .

In other words, *Halakhah* posits that whenever someone has a right, it is a right held against some other individual and the latter has a corresponding duty to the right-holder.

Is the converse equally true? Is there a corresponding right when-

---

28. *Piskei Din Rabbanayim* (hereafter: *PDR*), 10:220, 224.

29. *Bava Kama* 36b, 93a; *Hullin* 130b; *MT, She'eilah u-Pikadon* 5:1; *Teshuvot ha-Rashba* 1:656, 669, 1256; 2:199; 4:63; *Teshuvot ha-Rivash* 465; *Teshuvot Tashbetz* 3:152, 303.

30. *Teshuvot ha-Rosh* 13:8; *Teshuvot ha-Radvaz* 1:261. Assuming one adopts the approach that the *tzibur* owns the *tzedakah*, we can understand the position that the *tzibur* can be plaintiff for any assets linked to public matters. See *Netivot ha-Mishpat* 301:6. *Teshuvot Pnei Yehoshua, HM* 103 disagrees.

31. I. Herzog, *The Main Institutions of Jewish Law*, London, vol. 1, 46, 1967.

ever there is a duty? *Halakhah* argues that the converse turns out to be demonstrably false. Clearly, the duty of *tzedakah* may require one to contribute to one or a *number* of determinate recipients based upon a system of priorities set down by *Halakhah*,[32] yet not one of them can claim the contribution as his right.

As the Israeli Rabbinical Court notes:[33]

> The obligation of *tzedakah* . . . is an obligation upon the indi-
> vidual, but he is not obligated to the recipient . . . There is a
> general obligation of *tzedakah* . . . without the existence of a
> creditor ("*ba'al hov*" – AYW) to whom he is duty-bound to pay
> his obligation. . . .

Yet, according to numerous authorities, the *mitzvah* of *tzedakah* is a *hov*, a debt, and it possesses many of the characteristics associated with other debts recognized by *Halakhah*. *Tzedekah* is: (1) an enforceable duty by a *beit din*,[34] (2) the evasion of *tzedakah* duty creates a *shi'bud nekhasim*, a lien upon the property of the recalcitrant donor[35] and (3) *tefisah* (lit.

---

32. *Rema, SA YD* 251:3.

33. *PDR* 1:145, 154–155.

34. *Ketuvot* 86a; *Bava Batra* 8b, *Hullin* 110b. For the scope and coercion and its basis, see *Tosafot Ketuvot* 86a; *Tosafot Bava Batra* 8b; *Yad Ramah, Bava Batra* 8b; *MT, Matenot Aneiyim* 7:10; *Teshuvot ha-Rivash* 260; *Teshuvot Maharik, shoresh* 148; *PDR* 1:145, 156. For dissenting views, see *Ba'al ha-Maor, Bava Kama* 4; *Tosafot Bava Batra* 8b in the name of Rabbeinu Tam.

35. *Yad Ramah*, supra n. 34; *Mishneh Torah*, supra n. 34; *Kesef Mishneh, MT, Nahalot* 11:11; *SA YD* 248:1; *Rema, SA EH* 71:2; *Shakh, SA YD* 148:4; *Bi'ur ha-Gra, SA YD* 245:9; *Ketzot ha-Hoshen* 39:1, 290:3 (in the name of Beit Yosef), 15; *Tumim HM* 86:3. For a dissenting view, see *Teshuvot Maharashdam YD* 166.

However, *Netivot ha-Mishpat, Bi'urim* 290:8 argues that if the *tzedakah* is due to a recitation of a *neder*, a vow taken by an individual to give *tzedakah*, such a vow will not result in *shi'bud nekhasim*. However, if a *beit din* coerces an individual to give *tzedakah*, Netivot ha-Mishpat agrees with the other authorities that the *tzedakah* obligation results in *shi'bud nekhasim*.

For creating a lien by utilizing the language of *hithayivut*, obligating to give *tzedakah* accompanied by the execution of a *kinyan* (a symbolic act to undertake a duty), see *Teshuvot Rabbi Akiva Eiger*, Mahadura Kama 146; *Ketzot ha-Hoshen* 290:3.

However, whereas regarding all debts, a *beit din* is empowered to recover the debt from the debtor's property even in the absence of the debtor, in the situation of a recalcitrant donor; a *beit din* is authorized to recover from his property only in his presence. See *SA YD* 248:1; *Beit Shmuel, SA EH* 71:6. Compare *Ran, Ketuvot* 49b; *Rema, SA EH* 71:2.

"the taking of possession" – seizure) of *tzedakah* by the impoverished is effective.[36]

However, various decisors[37] as well the above-cited Israeli Rabbinical Court decision note that *tzedakah* which is characterized as "*mamon she'ein lo tov'im*" distinguishes itself from the classical type of "*hov.*" Whereas, for example, the failure to repay a loan gives rise to a claim and the initiation of a *beit din* proceeding by a plaintiff, the evasion of one *tzedakah's* duty lacking a determinate recipient fails to give rise to a claim.

Seemingly, in our case, adopting the model of *tzedakah* as an avenue to obligate parental medical care, one cannot offer relief to a minor who wants to proceed to *beit din* against a recalcitrant parent who fails to provide him with medical treatment.

Nevertheless, despite the fact that *tzedakah* is "*mamon she'ein lo tov'im*", the Israel Rabbinical Court explains that a needy individual may approach the *beit din*, requesting that this forum, "the father of orphans,"[38] compel the donor to fulfill his *tzedakah* obligation.[39] Hence, in our case, the minor may approach a *beit din* and demand compliance from the recalcitrant parent who refuses to pay for his medical expenses.

The scope of the *tzedakah* duty is quite limited both with regard to the potential donors as well as the amounts given. Amounts of *tzedakah* were fixed as a tithe – thus limiting the potential donation. And, needless to say, the financial condition of the donor and the recipient become relevant factors. Consequently, a parent may be obligated to provide medical treatment only upon initially providing for his own needs.[40] In the case of parents without financial means, wealthy relatives must attend to his needs. If these resources are unavailable, then the communal charity chest may be tapped to provide medical care.[41] Or if the child is financially independent, there would be no duty to give *tzedakah*.[42]

---

36. *Ohr Zarua, Tzedakah* 22; *Mahaneh Ephraim, Matanah and Tzedakah* 1; *PDR* 1:145:156.

37. *Teshuvot ha-Rashba* 3:293–294; *Teshuvot Maharashdam YD* 168.

38. *Gittin* 37a; *Bava Kama* 37a.

39. *PDR* 1:145, 156. Implicit in our conclusion is that the system of priorities in the allocation of *tzedakah* as well as the obligation per se is enforceable. See Rambam, *Commentary on the Mishnah, Ketuvot* 4:6; *Mordekhai, Bava Batra* 491–493; *Teshuvot ha-Rashba* 3:292; *Teshuvot Maharam Mintz* 7, 65; *SA YD* 251:4, *Rema*, ad. locum. For dissenting views, see *Sefer Meisharim, Netiv* 23, section 5; *Sefer Hafla'ah, Ketuvot* 71:2.

40. *Shakh, SA YD* 240:5, 248:1; *Rema SA YD* 257:8.

41. *Nedarim* 65a; *SA YD* 257:8.

42. *PDR* 2:301; 7:136, 149–151.

Similarly, "a wicked recipient" would not be entitled to receive *tzedakah*.[43]

In short, adopting the paradigm of *tzedakah* for defining the parental duty of medical treatment has various *halakhic* consequences. On the one hand, the *halakhot* of criminal omissions obligate a greater number of rescuers who are dutybound to assist others in peril than those mandated to be donors by the *halakhot* of *tzedakah*. On the other hand, whereas the dominant view is that the rescuee must reimburse the rescuer for incurred expenses of the rescue operation, in numerous situations, the recipient of a donor's gift providing for medical care does not have to provide compensation for the incurring of these expenses. Yet, in accordance with *hilkhot tzedakah* there will be situations where a minor will be left bereft of medical care and become a public charge, dependent upon the community for his medical care.

III.

A third analogical paradigm suggested by a contemporary *Posek* and an Israeli Rabbinical Court[44] is that the basis for a father to provide medical care stems from his duty to provide *mezonot yeladim*, child support. To state it differently, the fact of a family relationship creates a special tie between a father and a child constituting the basis for a father's responsibility to support his children, including the provisions of medical treatment. In contrast of the models of criminal omission and *tzedakah* which focus upon the individual's duty to rescue and contribute respectively, the model of *mezonot yeladim* centers upon the father's duty to support his offspring. Adopting the *halakhot* of criminal omissions and *tzedakah*, since the obligation is directed to an individual, both father and mother are equally responsible.[45] Adopting the *halakhot* of *mezonot yeladim*, the obligation falls squarely upon the shoulders of the father qua parent. His duty exists even if he is destitute and his children are

---

43. *SA YD* 251:1, *Shakh*, ad. locum. Conversely, accepting monies from "*a mumar*," an apostate is questionable.

44. *Teshuvot Minhat Yitzhak* 6:150; *PDR* 10:219.

For an earlier discussion, addressing the situation of a father who undertook the duty to support his wife's daughter for a period of five years; it is a controversy where providing medical care is a component in his support duty. See *Tosafot Ketuvot* 50b; *Piskei ha-Rosh Ketuvot* 12:1 (end).

45. Regarding criminal omissions see *Bava Kama* 15a. Concerning a mother's *tzedakah* duty, see *Bnei Ahuvah, MT, Ishut* 21:16; *Teshuvot Yaskil Avdi* 6:28, 38; *PDR* 9:251, 263.

wealthy since the duty is grounded in the fact that he is his parent rather than due to the fact that the children require his material support.[46]

What is the basis for a father's obligation to provide medical treatment? The Israel Rabbinical Court suggests that the scope of a father's responsibility for medical treatment can be ascertained from the parameters of a husband's duty of medical care (including any expenditures associated with being ill) for his ailing wife.[47] Adopting the approach that child support stems from the duty to *mezonot isha*, spousal support,[48] the scope of the father's duty to provide medical assistance to his children will be identical with the requirements of a husband's obligation to furnish medical treatment to his wife which is a component of *mezonot ishah*.

As such, the question arises: what sort of medical attention must a husband provide for his ailing spouse? The Talmudic reply is "medical treatment without limitations."[49] As elucidated by the *Poskim* such medication is referring to a situation of a brief illness or an extended malady where there is a prior arrangement of the physician to pay a fixed

---

46. *Piskei ha-Rosh, Ketuvot* 4:14; *SA EH* 71:1, *Beit Shmuel SA EH* 71:1; *Taz SA EH* 1:2; *PDR* 2:175, 8:325, 333. On the other hand, in terms of being a parent, there exists no duty for a mother to provide support to her children. See *Magid Mishneh, MT Ishut* 21:18; *Teshuvot ha-Rashbash* 162; *Beit Hillel, SA EH* 71:1. However, in the event that the father cannot support his children, support them only partially or passes away, based upon *hilkhot tzedakah* if the mother has the financial means she is dutybound to support her children. See *Beit Meir EH* 82:5; *Pithei Teshuvah SA EH* 82:3; *Bnei Ahuvah*, supra n. 45; *Teshuvot va-Yikra Avraham EH* 17; *Teshuvot Minhat Avraham* 3:5; *PDR* 9:251, 263; File no. 619054/8, Haifa Regional Beit Din, July 28, 2016. As a *beit din* aptly notes that even if the mother is financially capable to support her children, nonetheless, it is incumbent for the father to continue to contribute to the support based upon his financial means. See File no. 466314/3, Ariel Regional Beit Din, September 8, 2016.

Obviously, there will be instances where the mother may be exempt from her *tzedakah* obligation to support her children. For example, in terms of *tzedakah* priorities, a mother is obligated to support her parents prior to supporting her offspring. See *SA YD* 251:3.

47. For the husband's duty to pay for medical expenses, see *Ketuvot* 51a; *Shibolei ha-Leket*, vol. 2, *ha-Segulah* ed. 128; *SA EH* 79:1. For a husband's duty to pay his wife's expenses relating to her medical condition such as contacting physicians and traveling expenses to and from the doctor, see *Teshuvot Teshurat Shai* 1:151.

Remitting expenses for a wife's medical condition is subsumed in the category of *mezonot ishah*. See *Rashi, Ketuvot* 51a; *Tosafot, Ketuvot* 52b; *SA EH* 69:2, 79:1; *Taz, SA EH* 79:1.

48. *Ran on Alfasi, Ketuvot* 28b; *Piskei ha-Rosh Ketuvot* 4:14 in the name of Maharam; *Bah, Tur EH* 71; *PDR* 2:65, 91; *Iggerot Moshe EH* 1:106, *YD* 1:143.

49. *Ketuvot* 52b.

amount to treat his wife in time of need.[50] Consequently, it is a father's duty to provide care for his children who experience an extended illness and/or compensation to physicians for their care.

However, what type of medical care and/or compensation must a husband provide for an ailing spouse with a brief illness ("medical treatment with limitations")? One decisor contends that this type of care is included in the husband's duty of *pidyon*, redemption of one's wife from captivity.[51] Notwithstanding those authorities who subsume medical care in the category of spousal support,[52] others maintain that there exists a *takanah*, legislation which rabbinically enjoins all medical care.[53]

Seemingly, a father ought to be exempt from furnishing this type of medical attention for his children. Since there neither exists a parental obligation of *pidyon* nor any special legislation which enjoins medical assistance, on what grounds can a minor expect to receive medical treatment for any illness? Unable to address this issue, the Israeli Rabbinical Court concludes that the models of criminal omissions and the norms of *tzedakah* are applicable.[54]

Moreover, the invoking of the model of *mezonot yeladim* is highly problematic for another reason. The premise of this paradigm is that we can distill the *halakhot* regarding medical care regarding children from the *halakhot* of medical care dealing with an ailing wife. In other words, the explicit assumption that the scope of *mezonot yeladim* is grounded in the parameters of *mezonot isha* is open to serious challenges. Admittedly, as we noted there is such an approach,[55] albeit it is a *shitat yahid*, a minority opinion, and the source for this approach is based upon the view of Ran who himself stated that he has not seen his view found amongst the *Rishonim*. As such Mishneh le-Melekh raises the possibility that Ran's invoking of such an approach was *le'halakhah* (in theory) but *ve'lo le'ma'aseh* (rather than for practical application).[56] In fact, Ran's approach fails to address many situations. Adopting Ran's approach would mean that upon the divorce or demise of the mother,

---

50. *Rashi, Ketuvot* 52b; *Shitah Mekubetzet Ketuvot* 52b; *Beit Shmuel SA EH* 79:1; *Helkat Mehokeik SA EH* 79:1.

51. *Beit Shmuel, SA EH* 79:1 in the name of Rosh; *Rabbi A. Eiger, Ketuvot* 52b in the name of Rosh.

52. See supra n. 47.

53. *Shitah Mekubetzet Ketuvot* 52b in the name of Ra'ah and Ritva; *Avnei Miluim* 79:2–3; *PDR*, supra n. 44, at 221–223.

54. *PDR*, supra n. 44, at 224.

55. See supra n. 48

56. *Mishneh le-Melekh, MT Ishut* 12:14.

the husband would be exempt from providing to his children. As we know, under such circumstances the father would remain dutybound to provide maintenance for his children.[57] In fact, in the wake of having a relationship with a single woman the father is obligated to provide support should offspring be sired from this relationship.[58] Similarly, should a wife have an incestuous relationship with a man and the child sired would be a *mamzer* (*halakhic* bastard), the father would be dutybound to support him.[59] Clearly, these situations impart corroboration to the majority view that child support is an independent duty, a paternal duty rather than being linked to spousal support.[60] Finally, in accordance to the *halakhot* of *mezonot* a father is obligated to support his children during the first six years of their life.[61] Starting with the seventh year, a father is dutybound to maintain based upon the *halakhot* of *tzedakah*.[62] As we discussed earlier, in accordance with *hilkhot tzedakah* numerous situations may arise which would exempt the parents from disbursement of funds. Nevertheless, Rabbi Moshe Feinstein contends that a child who resides at home and does not go to work until becoming married would be eligible for maintenance based upon *hilkhot mezonot*.[63] As such, until the children are in the work force, a father remains obligated in furnishing medical care.

Based upon the foregoing, it is problematic to employ *halakhot* of *mezonot yeladim* as an avenue to obligate a father in furnishing medical care for his children.

However, another model may be found within the framework of *Even ha-Ezer*, the *halakhot* dealing with family relations. Addressing the case of a father who executed an agreement of support with his daughter and son-in-law, Rabbi Dovid Feder, a nineteenth century authority, rules:[64]

---

57. *MT Ishut* 21:17; *Mishneh le-Melekh*, supra n. 56; *Ba'air Hetev, SA EH* 71:1.

58. *Teshuvot ha-Rosh* 17:7; *SA EH* 71:4. However, Rabbi Feinstein contends that even according to Ran there would exist a duty to support the sired child. See *Iggerot Moshe*, supra n. 48.

59. *Yevamot* 22a–b; *Shakh, SA HM* 87:57; *Teshuvot Mishpetei Uziel, YD Tinyana* 60–62.

60. *Shitah Mekubetzet, Ketuvot* 65b; *Piskei ha-Rosh, Ketuvot* 4; *Teshuvot ha-Rosh* 17:7; *Teshuvot Maharam of Rothenburg*, Berlin ed., 244; *Yam shel Shlomo, Ketuvot* 4; *Darkhei Moshe, Tur EH* 71; *Beit Shmuel, SA EH* 71:1; *Helkat Mehokeik, SA EH* 71:1; *Teshuvot Mishpetei Uziel, EH* 4; *PDR* 5:292, 304, 305; 7:136, 152.

61. *Mishneh le-Melekh*, supra n. 56; *Bah, Tur EH* 71.

62. *SA EH* 71:1.

63. *Iggerot Moshe*, supra n. 48.

64. *Teshuvot Radam HM* 4.

One who obligated himself to maintain his daughter and son-in-law according to the prevailing custom and the daughter became ill and died. Is the father allowed to deduct his daughter's medical expenses (which he incurred – AYW) from the obligation of support promised to his son-in-law? . . .

Since it is customary for a father to furnish for his daughter's illness during the course of the support period, when one undertakes an obligation, it is with the awareness of this custom. However, a major illness and large medical expenditures do not occur every day . . . and it does not *halakhically* constitute a *minhag* (a custom – AYW) if it happens infrequently. And one cannot suggest a proof from the custom that a father remunerates medical fees for a slight illness. . . . .

Accordingly, child support is governed by *Halakhah* and *minhag.* Since it was customary and usual for a father to furnish medical care for a brief illness which entails the incurring of minimal expenses, consequently Rabbi Feder argues that this type of medical attention constitutes a portion of his support obligation. As such, when the father obligated himself to support his daughter and son-in-law, he had in mind the coverage of minor medical expenses. Consequently, since the *minhag* did not indicate parental responsibility for expenditures relating to a major illness, therefore he had no duty to provide for such care.

Given that in contemporary times in the United States, the *minhag* is for a father to cover expenses incurred for major illnesses, conventionally covered in part by medical insurance, in accordance with this approach of establishing responsibility for medical treatment as a sub-category of *mezonot yeladim*, we leave it for *Poskim* and *battei din* to decide whether such expenses will be reimbursed.

The foregoing analysis of the case of parental neglect of medical care is illustrative of the complex and pivotal role of the analogical argument (known as a *hekesh*) in the decision-making process. We have seen the distinction between the competing analogies as well as the significant consequences in adopting a particular model for resolving this issue.

Deciding between competing analogies in our case will be the sole prerogative of the *Posek*. The relative strength of each analogical argument applicable to our case, its effectiveness and plausibility will hopefully be tested within the framework of future *halakhic* decisions.

Chapter 5

Corporal Punishment in school: A study in the interaction of *Halakhah* and American law with social morality

THE PURPOSE OF THIS essay is to present an apercu of the diverse approaches for enforcing school discipline as propounded in contemporary times by American law[1] and *Halakhah*.[2] Our comparative examination focuses upon the differences between the learned decisions among contemporary *halakhic* decisors and the rulings in contemporary American courts. Though we will allude to the relevant rules of these two legal systems, it is the jurisprudential perspective rather than the substantive content which is the primary theme.[3]

---

1. See generally Paul Proehl, "Tort Liability of teachers," 12 *Vanderbilt L. Rev.* 1449 (1959); Note, "Corporal Punishment: For School Children Only," 27 *Drake L. Rev.* 137 (1977–1978); Cynthia Sweeney, "Corporal Punishment in Public Schools: A Violation of Substantive Due Process?" 33 *Hastings L. J.* 1245 (1982); Nadine Block & Robert Fatham, "Convincing State Legislatures to Ban Corporal Punishment," 9 *Children's Legal Rights J.* 21 (1988); Jerry Parkinson "Federal Court Treatment of Corporal Punishment in Public Schools: Jurisprudence that is Literally Shocking to the Conscience," 39 *South Dakota L. Rev.* 276 (1994).

2. For a comprehensive treatment see Binyamin Shmueli, "Parental Corporal Punishment according to Mishpat Ivri – Traditional Approaches and Modern Trends" (Hebrew) 10 *Pelilim* 365 (2001).

3. Each of the *halakhic* arbiter's positions is formulated in the form of a "*teshuvah*," i.e., responsum. In our case, the various *teshuvot* are learned decisions in response to an inquiry rather than *beit din* rulings issued to litigants. Hence, our comparative study focuses upon the differences between the *learned decisions* among contemporary halakhic decisors and the *court rulings* in contemporary American law.

For defining a *teshuva* as a learned decision rather than a *beit din* ruling, i.e., *psak din*, see R. Hayyim Sans, *Teshuvot Divrei Hayyim* 2, *Hoshen Mishpat* (hereafter: HM) 56. The *halakhic* ramifications of this conceptual distinction are beyond the scope of this essay.

Secondly, the examination of certain contemporary substantive *halakhic* issues

In the 1977 American Supreme Court case *Ingraham v. Wright*, citing historical and contemporary documentation supporting the use of physical punishment in the public schools, Justice Lewis Powell Jr. concludes that "a single principle has governed the use of corporal punishment since before the American Revolution: teachers may impose reasonable but not excessive force to discipline a child."[4] This legal tradition has deepened over time and today many states continue to recognize this societal value – i.e., a teacher's right to administer reasonable force within the context of the school setting. Many states have legitimated this right by legislative enactment and by judicial decision.[5]

The question that arises is: What criteria should a societal value satisfy if it is to be figured into the calculus of a legal decision? The answer advanced by certain legal scholars is that judges should use the values that modern society wants to protect as the basis for establishing new legal norms or justifying the modification of existing norms.[6] Is the met-

---

which emerge from our presentation is beyond the scope of this essay. See text accompanying notes 30, 34 & 55.

4. *Ingraham v. Wright*, 430 U.S. 651, 661 (1977). For an excellent critique of this decision, see Irene Rosenberg, "*Ingraham v. Wright*: The Supreme Court's Whipping Boy," 78 *Columbia L. Rev.* 75 (1978).

5. 59 *American Jurisprudence* 2d Parent & Child, Section 22 (1987); 89 *Annotated Law Reports* 2d 396, 412–413 (1963) and accompanying supplements; Sweeney, *supra* note 1, at 1247, note 17; Parkinson, supra n. 1, at 279, notes 28 & 30; Dean Herman, "A Statutory Proposal to Prohibit the Infliction of Violence upon Children," 19 *Family L. Q.* 1, 13 (1985); Susan Bitensky, "Section 1983: Agent of Peace or Vehicle of Violence vs. Children," 54 *Oklahoma L. Rev.* 333, 362 (2001).

6. A norm is expressive of the idea that an individual ought to behave *halakhically* (i.e., *halakhic* norm), legally (i.e., legal norm), morally (i.e., moral norm) or socially (i.e., social norm) in a certain way. Georg von Wright, *The Varieties of Goodness* (Routledge & Kegan: New York, 1963), 157–177; Joseph Raz, *The Concept of a Legal System* (Clarendon: Oxford, 1970), 44–6, 124. Whereas, *halakhic* norms are prescriptions of a specific course of action directed by a religious legal system, legal norms are directives of a secular legal system.

For the diverse roles moral and social norms play within these two systems, see our ensuing discussion. For the court's task in implementation of the moral choices that people have made, see Joseph Raz, "Legal Principles & The Limits of Law," 81 *Yale L. J.* 823, 849 (1972); Laurence Tribe, "Structural Due Process," 10 *Harvard C.R. L. Rev.* 269, 304, 311–312 (1975); Neil MacCormick, *Legal Reasoning & Legal Theory* (Clarendon Press: Oxford, 1978), 187; Stanley Fiss, "Objectivity & Interpretation," 34 *Stanford L. Rev.* 739 (1982).

Our citation of constitutional legal scholarship is a reflection of our acceptance of the school of thought that advocates the application of common law reasoning to constitutional provisions. In other words, constitutional interpretation with suitable modifications may shed light on common law interpretation. See Frederic Schauer,

ing out of force by teachers rooted in the aspirations of the American community as a whole and can it be said to have substantial support in the community? Does the imposition of corporal punishment within the context of an educational setting constitute an infraction of a moral norm, i.e., an unnecessary act of violence? Implicit in these questions, is the underlying premise that one of the tasks of American law is to explore the extent to which actions that are perceived by the community as injurious to its social fabric should give rise to remedies at law.[7]

The main obstacle to using conventional morality to establish or amend a legal norm in a pluralistic society is that this approach assumes the existence of a social consensus about what values deserve to be protected. A pluralistic society acknowledges that individuals who have different ethnic, religious and socio-economic backgrounds may not share the same beliefs. In fact, there is no "common experience" through which one may discern a "community sense" of the propriety or impropriety of the employment of physical force in the American school setting. In 1977, the *Ingraham* court noted that "professional and public opinion is sharply divided on this issue."[8] Today, twenty six years later, contemporary opinion regarding this matter remains divided.

When we compare the legal acceptability of corporal punishment in the classroom with the view of numerous social scientists and medical experts, including those who have written extensively on the subject of child rearing and violence, we encounter a substantial gap. There are several potential harms for the imposition of physical force in the framework of an educational setting. The most obvious risk is that hitting a student may cause physiological damage to the child and may escalate into child abuse.[9] Additionally, it may give rise, during childhood, to

---

"Is the Common Law Law?," 77 *Calif. L. Rev.* 455, 470 (1989); Harry Wellington, *Interpreting the Constitution* (Yale: New Haven, 1990) 127; Laurence Tribe & Michael Dorf, *On Reading the Constitution* (Harvard: Cambridge, 1991) 114–117.

For the *locus classicus* of the approach which insists that community consensus is not self-validating, see John Rawls, *A Theory of Justice* (Harvard: Cambridge, 1971). See also, Jeremy Waldron, "Theoretical Foundations of Liberalism," 37 *Phil. Q.* 127, 144–45 (1987).

7. Joseph Raz, "Legal Rights," 4 *Oxford J. Leg. Studies* 1 (1984).

8. *Ibid.*, at 660.

9. Peter Newell, *Children are People Too: The Case Against Physical Punishment* 21–32 (1989); Irwin Hyman, *Reading, Writing, & The Hickory Stick: The Apalling Story of Physical and Psychological Abuse in American Schools* 95, 100 (1990); Murray Straus & Denise Donnelly, *Beating the Devil Out of Them* (New York: 1994) 62–63, 81; David Orentlicher, "Spanking and Other Corporal Punishment of Children by Parents Overvaluing Pain, Undervaluing Children," 35 *Houston L. Rev.* 147,

a host of psychological and behavioral disorders such as aggression,[10] antisocial behavior,[11] and loss of love and self-esteem leading to depression, increased anxiety and withdrawal.[12]

The foregoing overview of these professional findings leads to the realization that what was once considered a normal child rearing practice might now constitute abuse. Moreover, what is now viewed as normal treatment of a child may one day be considered abusive.[13] Accordingly, legal scholars argue that it is time for the federal courts to recognize contemporary standards of decency, affirm the moral norm of societal condemnation of unnecessary violence and abandon the use of force in the public schools.[14]

Implicit in this approach is the notion that social morality is capable of determining the legal norm rather than merely affecting it. Contrary to the teachings of David Hume, one may derive an "ought" from an "is."[15] The premise underlying this approach is that one can study public

---

156 (1998); Bitensky, supra n. 5, at 364.

10. Leonard Eron, "Parent-Child Interaction, Television Violence, and Aggression of Children," 37 *Am Psychology* 197, 203 (1982) and Norma Feshbach, "The Effects of Violence in Childhood," 2 J. *Clinical* (1974). Others reject the correlation between aggressiveness toward children and aggressiveness by children toward others. See Bruce Perry, "Incubated in Terror: Neurodevelopmental Factors in the Cycle of Violence" in *Children in a Violent Society* (Joy Osofsky ed. 1997), 124–126; Orentlicher, supra n. 9, at 157–158; Bitensky, supra n. 5, at 364; Herman, supra n. 5, at 33–35.

11. Straus et al., "Spanking by Parents and Subsequent Antisocial Behavior of Children," 151 *Archives of Pediatrics & Adolescent Med.* 761, 764–767 (1997); Orentlicher, supra n. 9, at 158–159.

12. Straus *et al.*, ibid., n. 11; Charles Greven, *Spare the Child: The Religious Roots of Punishment and the Psychological Impact of Physical Abuse* (New York, 1992),127–130; Orentlicher, supra n. 9, at 156–157 Bitensky, supra n. 5, at 364–365. However see David Benatar, "Corporal Punishment," 24 *Social Theory & Practice* 237, 243 (1998) critiquing Straus's conclusions that physical punishment can promote childhood depression; Bitensky, supra note 5, at n. 199.

13. Herman, supra n. 5, at 9; Straus, "Corporal Punishment by Parents" in *Debating Children's Lives* (Mason & Gambrill eds., 1994) 195, 197–203.

14. Parkinson, supra n. 1, at 310–311; Bitensky, "Spare the Rod, Embrace our Humanity: Toward a New Legal Regime Prohibiting Corporal Punishment of Children," 31 *U. Mich. J.L. Reform* 353, 464–473 (1998).

15. A.C. MacIntyre, "Hume on Is and Ought", W.D. Hudson (ed.), *The Is-Ought Question* (London, 1969); John Searle, "How to Derive Ought from Is" 73 *Philo. Rev.* 43 (1964); William Goodpaster, ed. *Perspectives on Morality: Essays of William K. Frankena* (Notre Dame: London, 1976), 133–147.

For one of the most interesting critiques of Searle's stance, see Bernard Hare, "The Promising Game" in *Theories of Ethics* ed. Phillippa Foot (Oxford University:

morals and yield prescriptive content. Moreover, these norms are representative of the "evolving standards of decency that mark the progress of a maturing society."[16] In the words of Arthur Lovejoy, there is a "tendency inherent in nature or in man to pass through a regular sequence of stages of development in past, present, and future, the latter stages being – with perhaps occasional retardations or minor retrogressions – superior to the earlier."[17] Translating Lovejoy's idea into jurisprudential terms, law is functioning properly if it is dynamically adapting to social and moral change.[18] Compliance with the norm of the meting out of corporal punishment in the school is mandated only if the social and moral consensus from which it emerged and which alone justifies its continued compliance continues to exist. Inherent in the legal rule of imposing corporal punishment in school is the notion of its possible legal abrogation when "the evolving standards of decency" warrant the legal conclusion that the continued justification of the rule no longer exists. In fact, a 1993 study noted that in the last 20 years, the number of states abolishing physical punishment in schools has increased from one to twenty-six.[19] Clearly, a trend towards its elimination has emerged.

Oxford, 1967), 115–27.

16. *Tropp v. Dulles*, 356 U.S. 86, 101 (1958). Upon the basis of this approach, the Supreme Court in *Tropp v. Dulles* was extremely cautious in not extending the eighth amendment prohibition of "cruel and unusual punishment" to encompass imposing physical force upon public school children.

17. Arthur Lovejoy & George Boas, *Primitivism and Related Ideas in Antiquity* (Baltimore, MD, 1935),1; see also J.B. Bury, *The Idea of Progress: An Inquiry into its Origin and Growth* (Dover: N.Y., 1955) 2; Charles van Doren, *The Idea of Progress* (Praeger: N.Y., 1967).

18. The classic works include Max Weber, *Economy & Society* (Roth & Wittich eds. 1968); Henry Maine, *Ancient Law* (Oxford: London, 1931); Benjamin Cardozo, *The Growth of the Law* (Yale: New Haven, 1924).

For an implicit critique of this approach, see Duncan Kennedy, "The Structure of Blackstone's Commentaries," 28 *Buffalo L. Rev.* 205 (1979) and Frances Olsen, "The Family and the Market," 96 *Harvard L. Rev.* 1497 (1983). As Ruth Macklin observes, "it is wholly uncontroversial to hold technological progress has taken place; largely uncontroversial to claim that intellectual and theoretical progress has occurred; somewhat controversial to say that aesthetic or artistic progress has taken place; and highly controversial to assert that moral progress has occurred." Macklin, "Moral Progress," 87 *Ethics* 37 (1977).

19. Nat'l Coalition to Abolish Corporal Punishment in Schools, Corporal Punishment Fact Sheet 1 (1993); Herman, supra n. 5, at 13–14; Block & Fatham, supra n. 1, at 23.

Accordingly, certain legal scholars contend that the courts should abolish the practice pursuant to the evolving standards of modern society.[20]

On the other hand, other professional studies regarding the efficacy of corporal punishment in school arrive at different conclusions. There is a widespread acceptance of parental and teacher's use of physical force in our society. In the related context of parental corporal punishment of children, data from studies conducted from the 1950's through the 1990's indicate that nearly ninety per cent of parents employ physical force upon their children. Forty nine per cent of the respondents to a national survey indicated approval of a public school teacher hitting a student.[21] As recently as 1998, Kandice Johnson, a law professor at the University of Missouri, offered cogent argumentation to preserve the parental privilege to employ force while simultaneously providing for the child's need for bodily integrity.[22] Lastly, Professor Murray Straus, who has devoted a significant portion of his career to the study of corporal punishment and its negative effects upon children, recognizes that the empirical evidence on the negative effects of force is not definitive.[23]

In sum, though there are signs that society is rejecting teacher's use of force as a right, nevertheless the issue remains unresolved. The mixed signals emerging from the professional literature indicate a collision between two norms of American social morality: one social norm endorsing the administration of physical punishment in the school, the other rejecting its continued use. When we speak of the social norms of a community, it is tempting to speak of a simple social consensus, a homogeneity of norms, one that forms an enduring and uncontroversial basis for our culture and traditions. Undoubtedly, our issue demonstrates that such an image is unrealistic, at least for a community in the modern world.

In the absence of societal consensus regarding this practice, how should the courts respond? In the absence of shared beliefs among the subcultures of our pluralistic society,[24]

---

20. Sweeney, supra 1, at 1283; Herman, supra 5, at 1; Orentlicher, supra n. 9, at 185.

21. Herman, supra n. 5, at 12; Orentlicher, supra n. 9 at 151.

22. Johnson, "Crime or Punishment: The Parental Corporal Punishment Defense – Reasonable and Necessary, or Excused Abuse," *University of Illinois L. Rev.* 413 (1998).

23. Straus, et al., "Spanking by Parents & Subsequent Antisocial Behavior of Children," 151 *Archives of Pediatrics & Adolescent Medicine* 761 (1997); Orentlicher, supra n. 9, at 160.

24. The court's task to convert conventional morality into a legal rule assumes

a court may, for example, believe that one colliding norm is regarded by the community as significantly more weighty than the other; or that one norm is waxing while the other is waning or that one norm is more congruent with applicable policy and more consistent with the body of the law than the other; or that one norm is better connected to the community's fundamental concepts of justice. Similarly, where there is a collision between a relatively general principle and a relatively specific judgment, each of which appears to have substantial social support, the court may attempt to reconcile the two by reformulating either the general principle or the specific judgment so that they are in equilibrium.[25]

In fact, for almost 150 years, American courts have heard challenges to the practice of the use of force in the public schools based on alleged violations of tort law, criminal law, state legislation and constitutional guarantees.[26] The employment of physical punishment in an educational framework, opponents argue, had a substantive basis in the applicable legal and social concepts of a bygone era, but is socially incongruent and systemically inconsistent with contemporary societal norms. However, these challenges have usually failed.[27] In effect, the law has put its weight and imprimatur behind the moral and social norms which continue to endorse this practice. Presently, the moral norm of condemning physical force lacks either the weight or the requisite social support to overturn the legal norm permitting the continuance of this practice.

---

the existence of a uniform set of beliefs about what values should be protected. Clearly, our issue shows the difficulty with adopting this approach. See Wellington, supra n. 6, at 284; John Ely, "Foreword: On Discovering Fundamental Values," 92 *Harvard L. Rev.* 5, 49–52 (1978); Andrew Lupu, "Untangling the Strands of the Fourteenth Amendment," 77 *Mich. L. Rev.* 981, 1047 (1979); Kathleen Sullivan, "Rainbow Republicanism," 97 *Yale L. J.*1713, 1722–23 (1988).

For other difficulties with this approach, see Paul Brest, "The Fundamental Rights Controversy: The Essential Contradictions of Normative Constitutional Scholarship," 90 *Yale L. J* 1063, 1083(1981).

25. Melvin Eisenberg, *The Nature of the Common Law* (Cambridge: Harvard, 1988), 19. According to Eisenberg, law is simply reflective of social and moral norms rather than moving progressively along some uniform evolutionary path toward which societies tend to move (either as a descriptive or prescriptive matter).

See also Wellington, supra n. 6, at 284–285; Michael Perry, "Abortion, The Public Morals, & the Police Power: The Ethical Function of Substantive Due Process," 23 *U.C.L.A.* 689, 716, 727–728, 730–731 (1976).

26. Sweeney, supra n.1, at 1254–1255; Orentlicher, supra n. 9, at 148.

27. See supra n. 26.

II.

How do contemporary *halakhic* arbiters resolve the issue of meting out corporal punishment to Jewish children within the context of the Jewish educational system? To unravel the varying and diametrically opposed positions, one must define their matrix and probe the meaning of the implicit *halakhic norm* underlying the decisions.

To define the content of this norm, one must turn to its source, the Talmud. What is the significance of the fact that this norm derives from the Talmud? One of the systemic assumptions of the *halakhic* process is the authoritative nature of the Talmud's rulings. These dicta are binding upon the Jewish community and every arbiter, in every generation, is compelled to render his decision in accordance with them.[28] Accordingly, this norm in the Talmud will assume authoritativeness in the mind of the arbiter.

The Talmud provides a clear and uncontested position regarding our issue. If a teacher inadvertently causes a mishap during the administration of physical punishment resulting in harm being done to the young student, is he exempt from criminal liability? Is the student entitled to monetary compensation (i.e., *nezek*)? Though a Jew is liable for intentional, negligent and accidental damage caused to his fellow Jew,[29] nevertheless the teacher-student relationship is an exception to this rule. As the Talmud instructs, a teacher who strikes a student inadvertently injuring him or causing his death is exempt from paying damages or criminal punishment, respectively. The rationale offered in the Talmud is that the educator is *"engaging in a mitzvah."*[30]

---

28. For the authoritativeness of Talmudic rulings dating from the Geonic period to contemporary times, see *Teshuvot Geonim*, Harkavy ed., no. 349; Rabbi Avraham Ibn Daud *Sefer ha-Kabbalah*, ed. Cohen (JPS: Philadelphia, 1967), 59; *Rambam, Introduction to the Mishneh Torah*, Mossad ha-Rav Kook ed., 11; Rabbi Moshe Schick, *Teshuvot Maharam Schick, Yoreh De'ah* (hereafter; *YD*)115:3; Rabbi Elhanan Wasserman, *Kovetz Shiurim*, vol. 2, 82; Wasserman, *Kovetz Inyanim*, 194–195,199; Rabbi Avraham Karelitz, *Kovetz Iggerot Hazon Ish* vol. 1, Letter 15; Rabbi Ovadia Yosef, *Teshuvot Yabia Omer 2, Even ha-Ezer* (hereafter; *EH*) 7.

29. *Bava Kama* 26a–27b. Though the focus of our presentation is upon developing the position of contemporary authorities regarding our topic, nevertheless, in our endnotes we will allude to earlier decisors who affirm the Talmudic norm.

Some decisors maintain that in certain cases of accidental damage, the injured party has no cause of action. See *Tosafot Bava Kama* 27b; Rabbi Shabbetai Rappaport, *Shakh, Shulhan Arukh* (hereafter: *SA) HM* 378: 2.

30. *Makot* 8b. See *Mishneh Torah* (hereafter: *MT*), *Hilkhot Deot* 6:10; *MT, Hilkhot Rotzeiah u-Shemirat ha-Nefesh* 5:6; *Hasdei David, Tosefta Bava Kama* 9:11;

The Talmud adds a crucial caveat. The teacher who administers reasonable corporal punishment is exempt from liability. However, the teacher who employs excessive force is criminally liable and damages will be awarded to the injured party.[31]

Into what conceptual-axiological framework does the practice of teacher-imposed corporal punishment fit? Is it a one dimensional act or does it involve a tense and dialectical action? The Talmudic posture, reminiscent of a Tosefta's ruling,[32] reflects a polarity, the balancing of two commandments. On one hand, there is recognition of the legitimate goal of educating children. An educator, engaging in the commandment of *"hinnukh"* (i.e., education)[33] or *"tokhahah"*[34] (i.e., reproof) may em-

---

Rabbi Yehezkel Abramsky, *Hazon Yehezkel, Bava Kama* 9:11; R. Eliyahu of Vilna, *Mishlei* 13:24; Rabbi Ya'akov Reicher, *Teshuvot Shevut Ya'akov, HM* 3:140; Rabbi Joseph Franco, *Teshuvot Sha'arei Rahamin, HM* 7; Rabbi Gershon Koblenetz, *Teshuvot Kiryat Hannah* 22.

Others reject *"mitzvah"* as the underlying rationale for a teacher's exemption from liability. See *Teshuvot Ramatz, HM Hashmatot* 11.

31. *Ketuvot* 50a; *Gittin* 31a, 36a; *Bava Batra* 21a; *Makot* 16b; *Bekhorot* 46a; *Yerushalmi Moed Katan* 3:1. See MT, *Hilkhot Talmud Torah* 2:2; Rabbi Yosef Karo, *SA, YD* 245:9. For termination of teacher's employment due to meting out unreasonable punishment of students, see *Teshuvot Geonim, Geonica*, part 2, p. 119.

32. *Tosefta Bava Kama* 9:11.

33. *Rashi, Makot* 8a; *Mei'ri, Bet ha-Behirah, Makot* 8a; *MT Hilkhot Deot* 6:10; Rabbi Aaron ha-Levi, *Sefer ha-Hinnukh, Mitzvah* 595.

34. *Makot* 8b. *Tosafot, Makkot* 8b; *Hiddushei ha-Ramban, Makkot* 8b. Does a teacher's obligation to mete out corporal punishment stem from his educational role or in his capacity as a committed Jew discharging a duty to prevent other fellow Jews from transgressing *Halakhah*? If the teacher's exemption is based upon the *mitzvah* of *"tokhahah,"* according to certain decisors, every Jew is allowed to administer physical punishment in order to prevent a Jew from committing a transgression (*"le-afrushei me-isura"*). See Rabbi Asher b. Yehiel, *Piskei ha-Rosh Bava Kama* 3:13; Rabbi Shlomo Luria, *Yam Shel Shlomo, Bava Kama* 3:9; Rabbi Mordecai Jaffe; *Levush, SA, HM* 421:13; *Teshuvot Maharam Lublin* 13; Rabbi Refael Hazzan, *Teshuvot Hikekei Lev, Orah Hayyim* 19. Compare Rabbi Aryeh Heller, *Ketzot, Meshovev Netivot, HM* 3:1; Rabbi Meir ha-Kohen, *Ohr Sameah, Hilkhot Mamrim* 4:3; Rabbi Naftali Berlin, *Ha'amek She'elah* 27.

However, according to other authorities, only a Jew who stands in a relationship to the transgressor (e.g., spouses) can employ such punishment. See Rabbi Yisrael Isserlein, *Teshuvot Terumat ha-Deshen* 218; Rabbi Moshe Isserles, *Rema, SA HM* 421:1. This conclusion will apply equally by analogy to the teacher-student relationship. See *Shevut Ya'akov,* supra note 30.

Whether there exists a contemporary *halakhic* obligation to secure compliance to *mitzvot* through the use of physical coercion is beyond the scope of this presentation.

ploy force as a legitimate means to promote the welfare of a child.[35] On the other hand, the Talmud must reckon with the general prohibition against "*habalah*," i.e., wounding.[36] In effect, the *halakhic* norm of the allowance of the employment of force in an educational setting is an illustration of privileged battery, involving a "*mattir*," a suspension of the prohibition of *habalah*.[37] In the absence of the Talmud's legitimating category of the educator's performance of a *mitzvah*, the prohibition of *habalah* is operative. The "dialectical pull" or tension between the two *mitzvot* is great, for the "breakdown of the equilibrium" is always an imminent possibility. Accordingly, if the use of force is to express the anger or frustration of the teacher rather than for purposes of the child's behavioral modification, the act falls under the rubric of *habalah*.[38]

Halakhically, how does one understand this Talmudic posture? A contemporary Torah scholar, Rabbi Dr. Neriah Gutel, suggests that the normative recognition of reasonable corporal punishment by an educator is expressive of the decision making principle "*aseh doheh lo ta'aseh*" – i.e., when a positive and a negative duty are in conflict and one or the other must be transgressed, priority is accorded to the fulfillment of the positive commandment.[39] Though Rabbi Gutel does not convey to us his reasoning for invoking this principle, the teaching of Rabbi Shaul Nathanson is quite instructive in understanding Rabbi Gutel's position. According to Rabbi Nathanson,[40] the Jew who while perform-

---

35. In *Makot* 8b, there emerges the dictum of Rabah which introduces a ruling that seems to be at variance with the accepted norm outlined in our presentation. According to Rabah, corporal punishment serves as a means of educating studious children. See *Iggerot Moshe, YD* 2:103; Rabbi Hayyim Sonnenfeld, *Teshuvot Shalmat Hayyim* 352; Rabbi Avraham ha-Levi, *Teshuvot Even Hain*, p.246.

36. *Bava Kama* 90b; *Sanhedrin* 58b.

37. R. J. David Bleich, "Privileged Battery," 27 *Tradition* (Spring 1993) 72, 73; Shmueli, supra n. 2, at 382–386; Yehiel Kaplan, "The New Trend in Corporal Punishment of Children for Educational Reasons" (Hebrew), 3 *Kiryat Hamishpat* 447, 478 (2003).

38. See supra n. 36; *Nishmat Avraham* 3: HM 424:7.

39. N. Gutel, "He Who Spares his Stick, Hates his Son" (Hebrew), *Shana b'Shana* 169, 180(5762). Rabbi Gutel's exact words are that "every permissive assault . . . is akin . . ." to this principle.

For another contemporary solution, see Rabbi Yitzhak Weiss, *Teshuvot Minhat Yitzhak* 3:105.

40. *Teshuvot Shoeil u-Meishiv*, Mahadura Tinyana, 1:95.

For other rationales for this principle see *Ramban al ha-Torah, Shemot* 20:8 and R. Hayyim Medini *Sedei Hemed, Kelalim, Ma'arekhet* 70, *Kelal* 41. Although the Rashba does not invoke the principle of "*aseh doheh lo ta'aseh*" in explaining the basis for a teacher's exemption from liability in our situation, nevertheless, he

ing a positive commandment simultaneously transgresses a negative commandment, does not intend to rebel against the *devar Hashem* but rather desires to discharge a positive commandment. Accordingly, there is no *halakhic* infraction. The *halakhic* weight accorded to a positive commandment which will suspend a negative commandment resonates in other areas of social interrelationships. As Rabbi Elhanan Wasserman observes,[41] "All the prohibitions between man and his fellow man are only prohibited if they entail wanton destruction . . . all these prohibitions are permitted for a beneficial purpose. . . ." In our situation, the *educator's intent* transforms a prohibited act of *habalah* into a defined and regulated performance serving the educational goals of the Jewish community.

How does one define the parameters of this performance? The tension between these two commandments, *hinnukh* and *habalah*, involves a quest for equilibrium which results in the talmudic articulation of a norm that essentially sanctions the use of reasonable and moderate force within the educational setting.[42] Is it a mandatory norm, i.e., a *hovah*? Clearly, our analysis suggests that the talmudic norm of the practice of moderate corporal punishment in the school is permissive and hence discretionary, i.e., *reshut*.[43] In short, it is a *permissive norm*, in the sense that it is serves as an exception to the general prohibition against battery. Secondly, it is a *discretionary norm*. Though physical punishment is al-

---

similarly observes: ". . . these matters are simple: he intends to fulfill a *mitzvah* . . . and everything follows the motivation. . . ." (Rabbi Shlomo ben Aderet, *Teshuvot ha-Rashba* 1:534).

41. Rabbi Wasserman, *Kovetz He'arot*, Yevamot 70. A similar opinion is also advanced by Rabbi Sherman, 16 *Tehumin* 160, 164 (5756) and 20 *Tehumin* 353, 362 (5760), who cites this view as earlier expressed by R. Wasserman. Cf., however, the *Meiri, Beit ha-Behirah, Bava Batra* 16a, *R. Yonah, Sha'arei Teshuvah* 3:85, and others who persuasively argue that there are exceptions to this principle. Cf. Hatam Sofer, *Kovetz ha-Teshuvot* 7.

For the role of "*motivation*" in the non-applicability of the prohibition of *habalah* in other matters, see *SA HM* 421:13; Rabbi Yehoshua Falk, *Sma, SA HM* 421:28; *Yam Shel Shlomo, Bava Kama* 3:27; Rabbi Abraham Borenstein, *Teshuvot Avnei Nezer, YD* 321; *Iggerot Moshe, HM* 1: 103, 2:66; Rabbi Mordekai Breisch, *Teshuvot Helkat Ya'akov* 3:11; *Teshuvot Minhat Yitzhak* 6:105; Rabbi Menashe Klein, *Teshuvot Mishneh Halakhot* 4:246–247; Rabbi Shlomo Z. Urbach, *Nishmat Avraham YD* 349: 3–4.

42. See supra n. 31.

43. The Talmudic terminology is "*muttar*" (permitted). See *Makkot* 8b. In fact, in subsequent generations, the terminology of "*muttar*" and "*rashai*" (allowed) is utilized. *MT, Hilkhot Deot* 6:1; *Terumat ha-Deshen*, supra note 34; *Hikekei Lev*, supra note 34; *Sedei Hemed, Kelalim, Ma'arekhet 6, Kelal 26*, subsection 14, s.v. *od katav*.

lowed in the classroom under certain prescribed conditions, a teacher is not mandated to employ force with his students.

Having defined the dialectical structure, and permissive and discretionary nature of this Talmudic norm, we now can focus our attention upon the varying contemporary approaches which reflect a case study in the exercise of *halakhic discretion*. Discretion is the authority accorded by the *halakhic* system to each and every arbiter to choose among different possible solutions, each of the alternatives being legitimate. It is not being claimed that an arbiter is sometimes free to decide on the basis of a whim or bias. Neither is it being advanced that an arbiter is ever totally free from the control of authoritative standards and prescribed canons of interpretation of the *halakhic* decision making process which limit his discretion. Rather the claim is that the resolution of our issue is predicated upon the presence of a number of options, each of which will be legitimate in the framework of the system. Where discretion exists, it is as though the system is announcing to the decisor, "I have determined the contours of this talmudic norm (i.e., reasonable force in the school is permitted). From here on, it is for you, the arbiter, to determine the applicability of the Talmudic norm, for I, the system, allow you, the arbiter, to choose."[44]

In our scenario, we have observed that the system defines the norm of the employment of physical punishment in the classroom as discretionary. In effect, the arbiter stands before two normative possibilities. The arbiter can either direct the teacher to utilize reasonable force in the classroom or instruct the teacher to refrain from using force. Each directive would be legitimate and would accord with the nature and the dictates of the Talmudic norm.

How did the various contemporary decisors resolve our issue? For

---

44. For the suggested conceptual framework for defining judicial discretion, see Aharon Barak, *Judicial Discretion* (Yale: New Haven, 1989), 7–15. Discretion presupposes a zone of possibilities, each of which is legitimate in the context of the system. In our case, the arbiter may choose either to refrain from endorsing corporal punishment or may sanction the use of reasonable force in the classroom. Beyond this zone of legitimacy, the arbiter has no *judicial* discretion.

Nevertheless, to promote the use of nonviolent methods of school discipline in society, a decisor is *legislatively* empowered based upon *"lemigdar milta"* (lit., to safeguard the matter) to award medical expenses to an injured student in cases of the teacher's employment of reasonable force. See *Shevut Ya'akov*, supra note 30; *Teshuvot Orhot Yosher* 2, HM 7.

Rabbi Moshe Feinstein, prior to employing physical force, teachers ought to ask themselves these questions.[45]

1. What is my intent in administering this type of force?
2. To what am I responding?
3. What did the student do?
4. Can this form of punishment resolve the situation?
5. Do I have any alternatives?

In short, three factors are relevant: the educator's intent in administering corporal punishment, the nature of the force, and the circumstances surrounding the situation.

The above questions delineate the broad parameters which determine the reasonableness of imposing corporal punishment. First, Rabbi Feinstein contends, teachers can use physical punishment if their intention is to control, train or educate the student through the use of force.[46] In fact, there is evidence on record in the secular professional literature that physical force per se is not harmful and is effective under certain conditions.[47] However, if the administration of force is to express anger or frustration toward the student rather than motivated for educational reasons, Rabbi Feinstein concludes that the educator will be criminally liable for any assault.[48] Second, the nature of force utilized and the number of times the student is struck become relevant considerations in determining the reasonableness of the punishment being employed.[49] In fact, the scope of the teacher's privilege to use disciplinary force is more limited than the parental privilege.[50] Third, the student's age, physical condition, and developmental level ought to be factored into the equation.[51] Finally, for Rabbi Feinstein, the strongest argument against the use of force is the availability of alternative methods of educational discipline. The administration of force is a last resort

----

45. The series of five questions has been constructed by this writer based upon Rabbi Feinstein's standard for school discipline as set forth in his responsa.

46. *Iggerot Moshe EH* 3:40; *YD* 2:103, 106.

47. Orentlicher, supra n. 9, at 159; Herman, supra n. 5, at 27. For recent studies demonstrating positive results from spanking, see *Pediatrics* 98:4, October 1996, Supplement.

48. For his recognition of the permissive nature of the norm and the articulation of the standard, see *Iggerot Moshe, YD* 1: 140; 2:103; *EH* 4:68.

49. *Iggerot Moshe, YD* 3:76; 4:30.

50. *Ibid.,* 1:140; 4:30; *EH* 4:68.

51. *Ibid.,* 1:140; 2:8; 4:30.

in disciplining a student.[52] Misbehavior can be prevented by appropriate verbal responses. For Rabbi Feinstein, communications to the student must be consistent with the teacher's feelings. If teachers say one thing but convey something different with their tone or facial expressions, then the child receives a mixed message that is confusing. A teacher should communicate his message in a sincere and warm manner.[53]

Focusing upon Talmudic dicta, reviewing and appraising all the arguments marshaled by his predecessors and then arriving at a cogent and persuasive position, Rabbi Feinstein defines the parameters of this Talmudic norm.[54] His position reflects an articulation of a standard that essentially defines the often thin line between acceptable and improper physical punishment and requires the use of force to be moderate rather than excessive. If implemented properly and only as a last resort, this standard provides a viable defense to teachers who use inconsequential force.[55] However, a teacher's privilege does not extend to instances of abuse or assault charges.[56]

A diametrically opposing position is suggested by Rabbi Hayyim David Halevy. Rabbi Halevy writes:[57]

... everything is dependent upon the educational character of the individual, the locale, societal conditions and the like, and the use of physical force for education, even though it is *halakhically* permitted, may not achieve its purpose.

For Rabbi Halevy, "societal conditions" can be invoked as a factor in rendering a decision. If these conditions reflect a disapproval of the use of force in an educational setting, Rabbi Halevy posits, *Halakhah* ought to reflect the societal consensus regarding this matter.

Interestingly, Rabbi Samson Raphael Hirsch, a nineteenth century arbiter and educator, arrives at a similar conclusion, albeit from a different perspective. He observes:[58]

---

52. *Ibid.,* 1:140.

53. *Ibid.,* 4:30.

54. See his responsa cited in notes 46–53. Additionally, see "Responsa of Rabbi Moshe Feinstein" in Eli Munk, *Reward and Punishment in Education* (Hebrew), (Hamesorah: Bnei Brak, 5742), 107–110; *Iggerot Moshe, HM,* 1:3.

55. *Iggerot Moshe, YD* 1:140. Whether the teacher would be liable based upon other *halakhic* principles such as *"dina d'malkhuta dina"* (lit. the law of the kingship is the law) is beyond the scope of this presentation.

56. *Iggerot Moshe, EH* 4:68; *YD* 4:30.

57. Halevy, *Aseh Lekha Rav* 1:76. See also, Halevy, *Kitzur Shulhan Arukh Mekor Hayyim,* Shaar 6, Chapter 126, subsection 14; *Mekor Hayyim ha-Shalem,* vol. 5, 251:20. See Shmueli, supra n. 2, at n. 218.

58. Hirsch, *Yesodot ha-Hinnukh* (Netzah: Tel Aviv, 1948) 2:65. See Shmueli supra

We will be the last ones to recommend corporal punishment and we do not tend to agree with the opinion that a teacher who does not know how to control ongoing incidents in the school without meting out physical force is the appropriate teacher. This matter especially applies to parents. If the child conditions himself to his parental criticism due to his fear of the potential use of force . . . his ethical impulse will be compromised and will fail to be attentive to his teacher's directives. . . .

For Rabbi Hirsch, tolerance for corporal punishment is a highly problematic stance. The practice impairs the *halakhic* sensitivity of the child. Utilizing his intellectual perceptions and without recourse to empirical evidence which indicates that the imposition of force promotes immoral behavior,[59] Rabbi Hirsch opts for nonviolent alternatives for educating children. Both Rabbi Hirsch and Rabbi Halevy fail to endorse the employment of physical force in the classroom. Whereas for Rabbi Hirsch, the power of the intellect (i.e., *sevara*) serves as the grounds for rendering his decision, Rabbi Halevy utilizes societal reality as a factor in his *halakhic* calculus. In effect, the system allows each arbiter to choose between competing rationales (e.g., *sevara* vs. social realia) as grounds for declining to invoke the talmudic norm.

Is Rabbi Halevy's approach innovative? It is important to recognize that this line of reasoning was adopted over seven hundred years ago, by Rabbi Asher b. Yehiel (known by the acronym: Rosh) and Rabbi Moshe b. Nahman (known by the acronym: Ramban). As the Ramban observes:[60] "Every man smites his son and strikes his student"; and the Rosh notes:[61] "In the manner that young children are physically punished and are pulled by their ears." In short, as Rabbi Gutel concludes, for both the Rosh and the Ramban, social realia serve as admissible data for arriving at a *halakhic* decision.[62] Since, in their respective communities, the administration of force in the classroom was prevalent, therefore, these arbiters approved of the practice. On the other hand, due to the fact

---

n. 2, at n. 223. For a similar conclusion advanced in the name of R. Hayyim Volozhin, see Rabbi Yitzhak Levy, 17 *Tehumin* 157, 158 (5757).

Though the focus of our essay is on the position of contemporary decisors, nevertheless, we have briefly focused on the views of earlier decisors such as Rabbi Hirsch, Rabbi Asher b. Yehiel and Rabbi Moshe b. Nahman in order to compare R. Halevy's posture with their positions. See text accompanying notes 58, 60 & 61.

59. Orentlicher, supra n. 9, at 158–159.
60. *Milhamot ha-Shem, Bava Kama* 87b.
61. *Piskei ha-Rosh, Moed Katan* 3:94.
62. Gutel, supra n. 39, at 174.

that the practice is socially incongruent with his times, Rabbi Halevy opposes the continuance of this practice.

III.

Our comparative examination of *Halakhah* and American law merits analysis in defining the role that social and moral norms must satisfy in each legal system if they are to figure in the calculus of judicial reasoning concerning an educator's employment of force in school.

American law has put its weight behind the social norm which continues to endorse this practice. The original social reality that gave rise to the legal norm, and upon which basis alone the norm continues to be defended, remains the underlying matrix of the legal norm. Presently, in the mind of the American courts, the social norm of condemning ostensibly unnecessary acts of violence either is incongruent with applicable policy or lacks the requisite social support to overturn the legal norm sanctioning the continuance of the practice. In the future, courts may take the lead by overturning this legal norm and establishing a new legal rule reflective of a changed social reality. For American law, the legal norm is predicated upon a given social reality. In the words of a contemporary scholar, "Legal norms are primary expressions of and means of reproducing the 'shared values' that function as the integrating glue in liberal societies, orienting everyone's highly differentiated tasks toward a set of common social purposes."[63] In short, the American legal system posits that this extralegal source is legally significant. Social realia are determinative in defining the content of a legal norm.

How do *halakhic* authorities understand the role of societal conditions in rendering a decision regarding this practice? Is community consensus self-validating? Are the Rosh's and Ramban's rulings simply a reflection of a particular historical situation, namely medieval societal approval of corporal punishment in school? Is Rabbi Halevy's decision a legitimatization of a trend emerging from a particular cultural-socio context, i.e., contemporary communal disapproval of the use of physical punishment? Are the *halakhic* rulings regarding this matter contingent upon time and place, varying with the vicissitudes of historic exigencies and changing value perceptions? Does a particular arbiter's decision reflect an abrogation of a preexisting *halakhic* norm?

Upon careful analysis, our presentation would hardly call for such an unwarranted conclusion. Our examination indicates that the *halakhic*

---

63. Robert Gordon, "Critical Legal Histories," 36 *Stanford L. Rev.* 57, 93 (1984).

applicability or non-applicability of this practice is an issue resolved by a *decisor* rather than predetermined by socio-cultural reality. Secondly, it is the function of the *halakhic* system to provide the arbiter with normative guidance for addressing life situations. *Halakhah* responds to the challenge in accordance with its own inner, immanent logic, on its own terms and on the basis of the prescribed methods, procedures, and canons of interpretation of its decision making process.

In our case, the Talmudic norm is an *a priori* category posited by the system. It is the function of this norm to provide guidance. In our issue at bar, the Talmudic norm is discretionary. The norm assumes pivotal significance allowing for two normative possibilities: the employment or rejection of the practice of utilizing reasonable force within the framework of the classroom. Since inherently the norm is non-mandatory, the system allows the arbiter to decide whether to invoke the norm or not.

As we have shown, the grounds for the applicability or non-applicability of the talmudic norm among contemporary decisors are varied. Rejecting logic as a justification for refusing to invoke the norm, Rabbi Halevy asserts that social realia are admissible data and serve as the grounds for refraining from applying the norm. On the other hand, according to Rabbi Feinstein and other contemporary decisors,[64] given that the legitimacy of the use of moderate punishment in school is pursuant to the talmudic norm, buttressed by their understanding of the *halakhic* canons of interpretation and prooftexts regarding our issue – then in the absence of the efficacy of nonviolent alternatives for disciplining children, moderate force by the teacher is permitted in the classroom. In sum, for both arbiters the norm allows for varied and diametrically opposed positions. Throughout the decision making process the norm has neither been amended nor abrogated. It remains authoritative, offering guidance to each arbiter to arrive at his particular decision.

Hopefully, our study reflects an insight attributed to Rabbi Samson Raphael Hirsch. In homiletic fashion, Rabbi Hirsch interprets the question "Have you established prescribed times for Torah?" (*Shabbat* 31a) in the following manner: Prior to entering the world-to-come, every Jew will be asked whether he has shaped the Torah to the times or the times to the Torah. Indeed, the Talmud's unequivocal response is that a Jew's responsibility is to shape the times by the Torah.

---

64. *Mishnah Berurah, SA Orah Hayyim* 343:1 & 551:103; Rabbi Avraham Sherman, 16 *Tehumin* 160 (5756); Shmueli, supra n. 2, at 418–419, n.190.

Note: Parental corporal punishment

The suggestion has been advanced (see Gutel, supra n. 39, at 183–187) that the controversy between Rabbi Yehiel Weinberg (*Teshuvot Seridei Esh* 3:95) and Rabbi Eliyahu Dessler *(Mikhtav me-Eliyahu*, Bnei Brak, 5724, 3:360–362) hinges upon the acceptability of factoring modern psychological findings into a *halakhic* decision.

According to Rabbi Weinberg, these data are relevant considerations in arriving at a decision. However, for Rabbi Dessler, only "the words of *Hazal, rishonim* and *minhagei Yisrael*" (lit. the words of our Sages, early decisors and Jewish customs) serve as ingredients in rendering a decision.

A careful reading of their positions leads us to a very different conclusion. Pursuant to the *halakhic* norm, parents are permitted to employ force upon young children. However, there is a prohibition to impose this type of punishment upon older children (*Moed Katan* 17a; for an exhaustive list of authorities who subscribe to this Talmudic norm, see *Even Hain*, supra n. 35, at 217–223).

In his responsum, dealing with a delusional older child (15–16 years) possessed by legerdemain, Rabbi Weinberg advises the parents to follow modern pedagogical directives and employ nonviolent forms of discipline to modify their son's behavior. Clearly, Rabbi Weinberg's mention of professional findings was simply advanced in order to show the psychological soundness of the *preexisting halakhic* norm which prohibits the use of force with older children. His use of psychology is expository, i.e., to probe the profundities of the norm.

Similarly, in his discussion dealing with the privilege of employing force with young children, Rabbi Dessler argues vehemently for legitimating the practice of corporal punishment based upon the teachings of the Jewish tradition. (In addition to Rabbi Dessler's reliance on the teachings of the Gra and Luzzato, there are ample aggadic sources which embrace his position; see *Even Hain*, supra n. 35, at 250.) Here again, the decisor is utilizing the wisdom of our *halakhic* ethical traditions rather than modern psychological data *for heuristic purposes* to explain the cogency of the *halakhic* norm. Neither Rabbi Dessler nor Rabbi Weinberg is addressing our question of the admissibility of non-*halakhic* sources as a *factor* in rendering a decision.

**Note: 5749 *"Kol Koreh"* of Israel's Chief Rabbinate regarding
             Parental Corporal Punishment**

On the fourth day of Adar 1 5749, the former Chief Rabbis of Israel,
Rabbi Abraham Shapiro and Rabbi Mordechai Eliyahu issued the following *"kol koreh"* (i.e., proclamation):

   In the last few years, there have been numerous reported incidents
of physical punishment of children and even physical abuse. . . . We
shudder that the phenomenon is occurring among our Jewish brethren;
that parents and adults will exploit their power and their family position against babies and young children . . . those parents who encounter
difficulties in child-rearing and therefore resort to force and emotional
abuse should turn to counseling for proper guidance . . . in child rearing.

(Z. Heilbaron, 46 *Safra le-Saifa*, 79, 92[5754], Kaplan, supra n. 37, at
n.149.)

Chapter 6

Child Custody: A Comparative Analysis

THE PURPOSE OF THIS presentation is to give an apercu of the varying approaches for the disposition of child custody cases developed by American law during this past thirty years and the Rabbinical Courts of Israel (hereafter: the *Beit Din*),[1] a contemporary repository of the sources of *Halakhah*.

Though there will be occasion to allude to the substantive content of American law,[2] and the norms of *Halakhah*,[3] it is the jurisprudential perspective rather the substantive content which is the primary theme.

1.   American law

A parent's relationship to his child may be viewed as a status carrying

---

1. This study is based upon the published decisions of the Rabbinical Courts of Israel (*Piskei Din* – hereafter: *PDR*), volumes 1 through 22 as well as the decisions which appear on the website of the Israeli Rabbinical Courts through March 2017. All these *battei din* operate under the aegis of Israel's Chief Rabbinate.

2. See H. Foster and D. Freed, "Child custody," 39 *N.Y.U.L.R.* 423 (1964); H. Foster and D. Freed, eds., *Current Developments in Child Custody*, Law Journal Seminars-Press, N.Y., 1978; D. Chambers, "Rethinking the substantive rules for child-custody disputes in divorce," 83 *Michigan L. Rev.* 8 (1984); J. Atkinson, "Criteria for deciding child custody in the trial and the appellate courts," 18 *Family Law Q.* 1 (1984); M. Grossberg, *A Judgment of Solomon: The D'Hauteville Case And Legal Experience in Antebellum America*, Cambridge, 1996.

3. For an overview, see B.Z. Schereschewsky, *Dinei Mishpahah* (Hebrew), Jerusalem, 1993, 397–409; E. Shochetman, "The essence of the principles governing the custody of children in *Halakhah*," (Hebrew) in M. Elon, ed. 5 *Shenaton ha-Mishpat ha-Ivri* 285 (5738); Y. Gilat, "Is the best interest of the child the determining factor in a parental conflict regarding custody of their child?," (Hebrew), 8 *Mehkarei Mishpat* 297 (1980); idem, "The role of religio-*halakhic* factors in custody and rearing disputes," (Hebrew), 16 *Dinei Yisrael* 133 (1991–1992); M. Katz, "Warburg's view of the approach of the Israeli rabbinical courts to child custody and support," *Yale Law School, Honor's Thesis (1992)*.

with it certain responsibilities and duties owed to the child with reference to care, education and support. When a family breaks up through death, divorce, separation, child neglect or abandonment, the individual who performs most of the parental functions, who lives and cares for the child is said to have custody of the child, even though someone else may exercise some other parental rights and obligations.[4]

In determining a custody dispute between natural parents and proceedings involving a natural parent and a third party, American courts have frequently based their decisions on two doctrines. The first of these doctrines, which may be called "the parental right" theory,[5] establishes that natural parents unless declared unfit have a right to custody of their children upon the severing of marital ties.[6] The parental doctrine is justified based upon the assumption that a natural parent will most adequately fulfill the child's needs.[7]

Other American courts recognize that the question is not one of the rights of parents or others to custody but the right of the child[8] and of the state to place the child in an environment most conductive to its welfare.[9] While it is generally proper and fitting that a parent should have custody of a child, this is only true to the extent that it will be conducive to the child's welfare. Consequently, custody may be taken away from either or both parents if the welfare of the child demands such action.

---

4. *R. Pound,* "Individual interests involved in domestic relations," *14 Michigan L. Rev.* 177 (1916).

5. For the historical antecedents of this doctrine in early common law, see W. Blackstone, *Commentaries on the Laws of England,* vol. 1, 453; F. Pollock and F. Maitland, *History of English Law,* 2nd ed. 1899. This doctrine was frequently invoked during the 1940's in the California courts. See, e.g. *In re Hampton's Estate,* 55 Cal. App. 2d 543, 131 P. 2d 564 (1942); *Roche v. Roche,* 25 Cal. 2d 141,152 P. 2d 999 (1944); *Shea v. Shea,* 100 Cal. App. 2d 60, 223 P. 2d 32, 34 (1950). During the 1960's, other courts continued to employ this doctrine despite trenchant dissenting opinions. See e.g., *Raymond v. Cotner,* 175 Neb. 158, 120 N.W. 2d 892 (1963); *In re Mathers,* 371 Mich. 516, 124 N.W. 2d 678 (1963).

6. *Jones v. Darnall,* 103 Ind. 569, 2 N.E. 229 (1885); *Everett v. Barry* 127 Colo. 34, 251 P. 2d 826 (1953); *Pickett v. Farrow,* 340 S.W. 2d 462 (Ky. 1960).

7. *Ross v. Pick,* 199 Md. 341, 86 A. 2d 463 (1952); *Smith v. Jones,* 275 Ala. 148, 153 So. 2d 226 (1963).

8. For a review of arguments in favor of rights for children, see M. Roberts, "Parent and child conflict: between liberty and responsibility," 10 *N.D. J.L. Ethics and Pub. Policy,* 485 (1996); L. Teitelbaum. "Foreword: The meaning of rights of Children," 10 *N.M.L. Rev.* 235 (1980); B. Woodhouse, "Children's Rights," *University of Pa. Law School, Public Law and Legal Theory Research Paper series,* March 2000.

9. *Chapsky v. Wood,* 26 Kansas 650 (1881); *Finlay v. Finlay,* 240 N.Y. 429, 148 N.E. 624 (1925).

This does not mean however, that a child may be taken away from the warmth and security of the place he knows as home merely because the child will be given better economic, social and educational conditions elsewhere. An extreme interpretation of this doctrine known as "the best interests of the child" doctrine could eventually lead to a redistribution of the entire minor population among "the fitter" members of the community, a policy the courts have declined to implement.[10]

Before "the best interests of the child" doctrine comes into play, some event or behavior must have terminated the parental right to custody. The natural parents possess a prior right only to be forfeited by separation from their child over a long period of time, by abandonment, neglect or gross unfitness as parents.[11] Consequently, poverty of the parent is itself no sign of unfitness, and the fact that another party may be financially more qualified to assume custody of the child is irrelevant.[12]

Seemingly, the conflict between these two basic doctrines (parental rights v. best interests of the child) is more an issue of semantics than substance, more apparent than real,[13] since even those courts which apply "the best interests of the child" doctrine firmly support the thesis that one of the most significant determining factors as to what constitutes the child's welfare is custody by his natural parents.[14] Since both doctrines seek the same basic objective from two different perspectives, it seems to make little difference whether the termination of parental rights is rationalized in terms of the child's best interests or parental unfitness. Consequently, some courts and legal commentators equate the two doctrines.[15]

---

10. *Lacher v. Venus*, 177 Wis. 558,571, 188 N.W. 613, 618 (1922); *Baumann v. Baumann*, 169 Nebraska 805, 101 N.W. 2d 192, 195 (1960).

11. H. Foster, "Adoption and child custody: Best interest of the child?" 22 *Buffalo L. Rev.* 1 (1972).

12. *Chapsky v. Wood*, supra n. 9; *In re White*, 54 Cal. App. 2d 637, 129 P. 2d. 617 (1950). Although the relative financial conditions of the contesting parties are not usually determinative of the right to custody, the father's inability to provide the minimum needs for the child's well-being may be a significant factor in awarding custody to a third party. See *Lancey v. Shelley*, 232 Iowa 178, 2 N.W. 2d 781 (1942); *Comm. Ex. Rel. Lucchette v. Lucchette*, 166 Pa. Super 530, 72 A. 2d 617 (1950).

13. Q. Johnstone, "Child custody," 1 *Kansas L. Rev.* 37, 42, 47 (1952); H. Clark, *Law of Domestic Relations*, St. Paul, West, 1968, 592.

14. *Brown v. Dewitt*, 320 Mich. 156, 30 N.W. 2d 818 (1948); *Ross v. Pick*, supra n. 7; *In re custody of Hampton J. Adams Co.* 84 Pa. Ct. C.P. (1963).

15. *Application of Vallimont*, 182 Kansas 334, 321 P. 2d 190 (1958); *Giacopelli v. Florence Cr. Herden Home*, 16 Ill. 2d 556, 158 N.E. 2d 613 (1959); See supra n. 13; 42 *American Jurisprudence*, 2d, Infants, sections 53–54.

Of course, the two approaches are not necessarily at variance with each other. Certainly, no court likes to think that its decision undermines the child's best interests; but the rationalization should be distinguished from the rule of the case. The fact that the courts themselves frequently go to great lengths to show that in a given case the affirmation of a parental right to the child does not undermine the child's best interests, in effect implies that these two approaches may lead to different outcomes.

To focus best upon the practical differences between these two doctrines, one must distinguish between custody proceedings involving natural parents and custody contests between a natural parent and a third party.

The last century saw the demise of the common law notion that a father had a right to custody of his child, and now statutes have been enacted in state legislatures that the place the mother and the father on an equal footing.[16] Nevertheless, a paradoxical situation developed. The legal rights of the father to custody of the child which were abrogated by the various legislatures were only replaced by a judicial recognition of the rights of the mother to custody. Despite the equalization statutes, if everything is equal and in the absence of compelling reasons of maternal unfitness, until approximately 35 to 40 years ago, the courts have usually awarded custody to the mother, particularly children of tender years.[17]

Whereas a former strict application of the parental right approach would result in an automatic preference for the father assuming he is fit, until the late 1970's and early 1980's preference was accorded to the mother assuming she is fit. Though few would disagree that there is psychological data to legitimate the preference, commonly known as the tender years presumption to operate in favor of the mother,[18] the blind acceptance of this shibboleth ignores the empirical data demonstrating that "mothering" may be a function independent of the gender of the individual performing it.[19]

16. J. Madden, *Person and Domestic Relations*, St. Paul, West, 1931, 369–372.

17. R. Drinan, "The rights of children in modern American family law," 2 *Journal of Family L.* 101,102 (1962). See also, A. Roth, "The tender years presumption in child custody disputes," 15 *Journal of Family L.* 423–434 (1977) who collects cases from some 37 states which adopt this presumption, often despite the existence of "equalization statutes" passed by various state legislatures.

18. J. Madden, "Persons and domestic relations studies to the future development of the laws governing the settlement of interparental child custody disputes," 11 *Journal of Family L.* 557 (1971).

19. L. Yarrow, "Maternal deprivation: toward an empirical and conceptual reevaluation," 58 *Psychological Bulletin* 459, 475–479 (1961); J. Levine, *Who will raise*

Adopting the perspective of the best interests approach would require the courts to make a full scale inquiry into the relevant data concerning the child's actual welfare. In fact, with the rejection of the tender years presumption by the courts and state legislatures in favor of either awarding physical custody to the father or by incorporating what is called joint custody or shared parenting,[20] the child best interests doctrine was employed to make an in-depth inquiry to arrive at the best parenting arrangements.

Undoubtedly, custody proceedings involving a natural parent and a third party offer the greatest opportunity for separation of parent-oriented factors from child-oriented factors in custody dispositions. The importance of the nuclear family and the traumatic effect on children separated from their parents, particularly their mother, is supported not only by common experience but by a vast literature in the area of child psychology and psychiatry.[21] Consequently, many courts who adopt the best interests of the child approach conclude that in a contest between a natural parent and a third party, the child's welfare requires an award to a parent.[22]

2.   *Halakhah*

In order to present the approaches of the Rabbinical Courts of Israel to child custody proceedings, it is necessary to compare the position of American law and *Halakhah* concerning the relationship of child custody to child support.

When a family breaks up, due to death, divorce, separation or child abandonment, the various elements of the custody relationship have to be dealt with separately by the courts. Thus, one parent may exercise certain rights and have certain obligations vis-à-vis the child despite the

---

the children? New options for fathers (and mothers), 1976.

20. J. Paradise, "The disparity between men and women in custody disputes: Is joint custody the answer to everyone's problems?" 72 *St. John's Law Rev.* 517, 528–529 (2012). By 2013, thirty-six states authorized shared parenting, either by presumption, preference or by adopting it via statute. See "Chart 2: Custody criteria," 46 *Family Law Q.*, 524–527 (2013).

21. R. Patton and L. Gardner, *Growth, failure and maternal deprivation*, 81–84, 1963; J. Bowlby, *Child care and the growth of love* (1973).

22. *Brown v. Dewitt*, 320 Mich. 156, 30 N.W. 2d 818 (1946); *Ross v. Pick*, supra n. 7; In re Custody of Hampton J. *Adams Co.*, 84 Pa. Ct. C.P. (1963); Foster and Freed, supra n. 2.

fact that custody of the child has been awarded to the other party or a third party.

If a parent did not have custody of his child would this be tantamount to absolving the parent from his legal duty of child support? Is the legal duty of support given in reciprocation (i.e. in exchange) for the parental right to custody? Consequently, if in a divorce decree, custody is awarded to the mother, is the father who is obligated to support his child, exempt from his duty?

Invoking the principle of reciprocity, common law[23] and early twentieth century American law[24] exempt the father from child support,[25] upon awarding custody to the mother. The prerequisite for invoking this principle of reciprocity is the recognition of a parental right to custody, i.e. the parental right doctrine. The best interests approach which imparts recognition to the child's right logically excludes the invoking of this principle of reciprocity.

Whereas common law and early twentieth century American law argue that the parental duty of support is in exchange for the parental right to custody, generally speaking *Halakhah* contends that *mezonot yeladim*, child support, is determined independently of any formula of reciprocity.[26] According to the majority authorities, a father is primarily liable for child support by virtue of his paternity,[27] irrespective

---

23. J. Bishop, *Marriage and Divorce*, section 557 6th ed., 1881; F. Schouler, *Marriage, divorce and separation and domestic relations*, section 752, 6th ed., 1921.

24. See cases cited in Note, 42 *Harvard L. Rev.* 112 (1928). By the 1960's, the duty of child support has been determined independently and consequently American courts have ordered fathers to pay child support regardless of the fact that custody may have been awarded to the mother. See Clark, supra n. 13, at 400, n. 26.

25. Though in the past, the father has been held liable for child support it should, however, be noted that recent cases and statute law have placed parents on parity with regard to support. See 51 *Annual Survey of Law, N.Y.U.* 378 (1976); L. Weitzman, "Recent developments in child support cases," 179 *NY Law J.* 1, 1978.

26. Schereschewsky, supra n. 3, at 375–379.

27. *Shitah Mekubetzet, Ketuvot* 65b; *Piskei ha-Rosh, Ketuvot* 4; *Teshuvot Maharam of Rothenburg*, Berlin ed., 244; *Yam shel Shlomo, Ketuvot* 4; *Teshuvot Mishpetei Uziel, EH* 4; *PDR* 5:292, 304, 305; 7:136, 152.

A contrasting approach and supported by some authorities was expressed by Rabbi Nissim ben Reuven who is of the opinion that a father's support obligation stems from his duty to support his wife. *Ran on Alfasi, Ketuvot* 5; *Melekhet Shlomo, Ketuvot* 4:6; *Iggerot Moshe, EH* 106.

Though a plain reading of *MT, Ishut* 12:14 would seem to show that Rambam espouses Ran's view (see *Mishneh le-Melekh, MT Ishut* 12:14), yet, in this author's consultation with Rabbi Yosef B. Soloveitchik, he disagreed with such an interpretation. For understanding Rambam's position, see *Teshuvot Tashbetz* 2:138; *Avnei*

of whether the marriage has been terminated by death[28] or divorce, or whether the child was born as a *mamzer*, due to an incestuous relationship.[29] Acknowledging that the father's duty to support his child is by virtue of his paternity, the *Beit Din*, in numerous decisions rules that the child is entitled to paternal support even if in a given situation custody has been awarded to the mother.[30] Furthermore, even if a wife is found guilty of conduct which justifies divorce, the husband remains obligated to support his child.[31] Similarly, the fact that the mother has custody of his child will not entitle the father to refuse to pay for his son's education.[32] Thus, in resolving matters dealing with the parental duty of support of a child and child custody, the *Beit Din* is more concerned with the resolution of a human problem than with spinning out a symmetrical pattern of duties and rights based upon the principle of reciprocity.

Since the doctrine of reciprocity, as we discussed earlier, is based upon a parental right approach to custody, does the *Beit Din's* rejection of this doctrine imply a rejection of the parental right approach? Without addressing all the aspects governing the parent-child relationship, one example will suffice to illustrate that the reciprocity principle acknowledging a parental right perspective is operative in other realms.

According to *Halakhah*, the finds of a son belongs to the father in consideration for the support given to the child.[33] The father is entitled to the finds though the child is of age (i.e. beyond the age he is obligated to maintain him) provided that the child is his dependent. But if the child is not supported by him, the finds belong to the child, even though the child is not of age.[34] Invoking the *halakhic* rule "for their hand (i.e.

Miluim EH 61; *PDR* 7:136, 144–145.

However, there are decisors who maintain that Ran did not view his posture as a guide for arriving at practical decisions. See *Mishneh le-Melekh*, op. cit.; *Avnei Miluim*, op. cit.; *Teshuvot Maharam of Lublin* 79.

For a third approach towards defining the father's obligation of child support, see *PDR* 2:65, 90–91.

28. *SA EH* 82:7 and commentaries ad. locum, *SA EH* 61:1, 4; *Teshuvot ha-Rashbash* 168; *PDR* 2:65, 91.

29. *PDR* 1:145, 154; 7:136, 144, 146, 152.

30. *PDR* 1:55, 61–62, 161, 163; 7:10, 21–22.

31. *PDR* 1:55, 61, 147, 159.

32. *PDR* 2:298, 303; 7:10, 21, 22.

33. *Bava Metzia* 12a–b; *Yerushalmi, Ketuvot* 6:1; *Tosafot Bava Metzia* 12b; *SA HM* 270:2.

34. Whereas the finds of a daughter belong to the father even if the daughter is financially independent. See supra n. 33. See also, *Rashi, Ketuvot* 47a, *Bava Metzia* 12a; *Tosafot Ketuvot* 47b.

the minors' – AYW) is like his hand (the father's – AYW),"[35] certain decisors maintain that a son's earnings equally belong to the father.[36] In other words, the formula of reciprocity is applicable both with regard to a son's earnings as well as to his finds. Though the *Beit Din* has not rendered a ruling regarding a son's earnings, the *Beit Din* invokes the reciprocity principle regarding a son's finds,[37] acknowledging in effect a parental right perspective.

As such, the *Beit Din* recognizes the rule that a father's entitlement to his son's finds was given in consideration of the father's duty of child support while simultaneously rejecting the notion that the parental right of custody was given in consideration of the father's duty of child support. Why is the reciprocity formula invoked in one matter and rejected in another?

Despite the fact that we have not conducted a comprehensive and systematic examination into all the aspects governing the parent-child relationship, we can offer the following rationale for understanding the *Beit Din's* posture and ultimately for defining the majority approach being adopted in resolving custody contests.

Though a child's finds and earnings belong to the father, torts committed by a parent vis-à-vis his minor child are actionable.[38] To allow

---

35. *Mishnah Ma'aser Sheni* 4:4; *Mishnah Eruvin* 7:6.

36. *Tosafot Eruvin* 79b; *Tosafot Gittin* 64b; *Tosafot Bava Metzia* 12b. For a contrasting opinion, see *Shitah Mekubetzet Bava Metzia* 12b. For an examination of both opinions, see *SA OH* 366:10 and HM 270:2 and commentaries ad. locum.

37. *PDR* 3:329, 331–332.

38. *Tosefta Bava Kama* 9:8–11; *Bava Metzia* 87a–b. Though a father possesses no right to sell his son (see *Teshuvot Hatam Sofer HM* 111; *Teshuvot Mishpetei Uziel EH* 91; *Even ha-Azel, Avadim* 8:19; *Hashukei Hemed Bava Kama* 100a in the name of Rabbi Elyashiv; *PDR* 1:145, 157 (Rabbi Goldschmidt's opinion); S. Daichovsky, "Ownership of Fertilized Eggs," (Hebrew), 22 *Tehumin* 404, 406), a poverty-stricken father may deliver his daughter into bondage. Nonetheless, whereas a slave is the personal property of its master, the daughter as a bondswoman is a legal person endowed with rights and duties bound by *Halakhah* to render service to a third party. See *Mekhilta de-R. Yishmael,* Horowitz-Rabin ed., 247; *Sifra, va-Yikra* 25:43; *Kiddushin* 20a.

Moreover, a father could only sell her to a person with whom or with whose son a marriage could be consummated. Though according to certain *Poskim* this union does not require a daughter's consent, the master or son did not own her. On the contrary, the standards of a monogamous relationship were applicable and *halakhically* speaking she is entitled to all the rights of a married woman. See *MT, Avadim* 4:8; *Kesef Mishneh*, ad. locum.; *Tosafot Kiddushin* 5a. This institution did not exist after 70 C.E. and possibly was suspended as early as the Second Commonwealth. See B. Cohen, *Roman and Jewish Law*, N. Y., 1961, 159–278, 772–777; M. Elon, *Herut*

even parents *halakhic* rights over children beyond paternalistic motivations,[39] would imply a sanction to a relationship of possessive rights vis-à-vis another individual; a relationship though enforced by Roman law that is alien to *Halakhah*.[40]

A review of some of the *Beit Din* decisions will demonstrate that a father has a right, albeit not a proprietary one, in his children, both sons and daughters.[41] Following in a well-trodden *mesorah*, albeit a minority view, a mother has a *zekhut*, a right vis-à-vis the father to have custody of her children if their best interests dictate such an arrangement.[42] However, a mother is not obligated to employ the right and therefore she does not have to accept custody of her children. She may send them to their father and he may not refuse to accept them and should he file against her in a *beit din* he will not succeed in his claim to transfer custody to the mother.[43]

---

ha-Perat be-Darkhei Geviyah hov be-Mishpat ha-Ivri, (Hebrew) 1–17, 1964; E. Urbach, "The laws regarding slavery as a source for the social history of the period of the Second Temple, the Mishnah and the Talmud," (Hebrew), 23 *Tzion* 141, (1960).

For the proscription for a *beit din* to sell a slave to a non-Jew due the fact that a *beit din* does not own the slave, see *MT Avadim* 1:3; *Hiddushei Maharit, Kiddushin* 14b; M. Amiel, *le-Heker Midot ha-Halakhah*, 2, Midah 17.49. See also, *MT, Avadim* 4:10; *Beit ha-Behirah, Kiddushin* 16a.

39. A father's right to give his minor daughter in marriage does not reflect the notion of *patria potestas* (lit. the power of a father). A primary consideration uppermost in the minds of the authorities which dictated the sanction of child marriages was the protection of the young against child abuse, particularly the desire to protect the chastity of young girls. See A. Freimann, *Seder Kiddushin ve-Nissu'in*, Jerusalem, 1945; I. Agus, *The Heroic Age of Franco-German Jewry*, N.Y., 1969; J. Katz, "Marriage and sexual life among Jews at the close of the Middle Ages" (Hebrew), 10 *Tzion* 21, 24 (1945); E. Kanarfogel, "Rabbinic Conceptions of Marriage and Matchmaking in Christian Europe," ed. E. Baumgarten, et al. *Entangled Historians: Knowledge, Authority and Jewish Culture in the 13*th *Century*, Philadelphia 2017, 27–31.

40. A. Rabello, "*Patria potestas* in Roman and Jewish Law" (Hebrew), 5 *Dinei Yisrael* 85 (1974).

41. *PDR* 1:65, 76; 4:93, 94–95; 12:139, 141–143; 13:17, 21, 26–27, 335, 338.

42. *Teshuvot Geonim*, Harkavy ed. 553; *Halakhot Gedolot* 2:250; *Teshuvot Ri Megas* 71; Rabbeinu Yeruham, *Sefer Toldot Adam ve-Havah*, 23:3; *Helkat Mehokeik, SA EH* 82:10; *Teshuvot ha-Mabit* 1:165; *Teshuvot Darkhei Noam EH* 26, 38, 40; *Teshuvot Minhat Yitzhak* 7:113; *Teshuvot le-Horot Natan*, 3, *EH* 87–89; *Teshuvot Tzitz Eliezer* 16:44; Gilat, supra n. 3; Katz, supra n. 3.

Though a master can neither sell nor give a Jewish maidservant, for the purposes of establishing a family, her father is permitted to sell her. See *MT Avadim* 4:10, 13.

43. Rambam, *Perush ha-Mishnayot on Ketuvot*, 12:1; *MT, Ishut* 21:18; *Magid Mishneh*, ad. locum.; *Teshuvot Tashbetz* 3:144; *Tur EH* 82; *SA EH* 82:8; *Helkat Mehokeik, SA EH* 82:12.

The ramification of a father's right to custody is found in a series of the *Beit Din's* decisions. For example, the *Beit Din* authoritatively cites Rambam's view[44] that if the boy above the age of six should desire to remain with his mother without his father's consent; the father is entitled to refuse to pay his maintenance.[45] As Rabbi Yosef Kapah states:[46]

> Parents are not inanimate objects. Also, parents are composed by a body and soul and have feelings. And a mother has a natural right to find emotional satisfaction to caress her children. Parents have the right to receive emotional satisfaction to see their children grow and develop properly . . . And in Shulhan Arukh EH 82:7 it states that after attaining six years a father can say if he does not live with me I will not support him and recently the Beit Din ha-Gadol exempted a father from maintaining his daughter who declared that she does not want to see her father and does not tolerate him. . . .

A Haifa Regional Beit Din rules that a father was entitled to withhold support from a daughter who refused to allow her father visitation privileges.[47] The decision was appealed to the Beit Din ha-Rabbani ha-Gadol which agrees with the lower *beit din's* decision and, implicitly following Rabbi Dovid ben Zimra's view,[48] states a different rationale:[49]

> According to *Halakhah*, the genealogy of children is traced to the father, as it is written "To their families to their male ancestors," and the father's family is called a family and not the mother's family. Therefore, he (the father – AYW) is obligated in supporting them and raising them. As such he has the full

---

Compare Rabbi Tzvi Gartner's view that the mother as well as the father have equal rights of custody in their children. See T. Gartner, "In the matter of the authority of *beit din* to judge child custody," (Hebrew), 7 *Yeshurun*, 499, 508 (5760). A review of the sources cited supra in notes 42–43 contradict his position. Notwithstanding the situation where both parents are irreligious where each parent has an equal right to mold the moral character of their child (see *PDR* 13:335, 338), in other cases his view requires deliberation.

44. *MT, Ishut* 21:18.

45. *PDR* 2:298, 303, 13:17.

46. *Beit Din Me'yuhad* 1/81, *Nagar v. Nagar*, PD 38 (1), 412. See also *PDR* 9:251, 262 (Rabbi Kapah's opinion).

47. *PDR* 13:3.

48. *Teshuvot ha-Radvaz* 3:851.

49. *PDR* 13:17, 20.

right to demand that they be raised by him and benefit from all of what is involved. . . . However, the rabbis were concerned with the children's best interests and found it proper to annul the father's custodial right . . . and establish that a son be with his mother until the age of six and the daughter would always remain with her mother. . . . However, in doing this the father was not deprived of his basic rights regarding his children which encompass continuing ties between him (the father – AYW) and them (the children – AYW) during the time they were in their mother's custody. . . .

To state it differently, implicitly following an earlier ruling of the *Beit Din*,[50] even if custody has been awarded to the mother, implicitly following earlier rulings,[51] the Beit Din ha-Rabbani ha-Gadol argues that a father has the basic right to be granted visitation privileges.[52] Consequently, the mother is proscribed from moving away to another place which preempts the father from visiting his child.[53]

Finally, it is unsurprising where a father questions the actual paternity of the child that the *Beit Din* refuses to direct a daughter to visit her father.[54]

In sum, there are *Beit Din* judgments which espouse the parental right to custody.

On the other hand, there is no question of parental rights in custody proceedings, the majority view of the *Beit Din* explains.[55] Lest one misconstrues the Talmudic rule that "the daughter remains with her mother regardless of her age" or that "the son is with his father after the age of six" as connoting the sanction of possessive rights, the *Beit Din* reaffirms the words of a sixteenth century legist, Rabbi Shmuel de Medina who opines that custody situations focus upon "the rights of the child" rather than the rights of the parents.[56]

---

50. *PDR* 12:129, 141.

51. *PDR* 9:251, 259; 12:129, 141.

52. For viewing these privileges as a quasi-custody right see Katz, supra n. 3, at 12, 18.

53. *PDR* 4:93, 94–95. Therefore, it is unsurprising that a mother is proscribed from taking her son below the age of six to another country since the father is unable to perform certain basic Torah educational rearing responsibilities with him. See *Teshuvot Noda be-Yehudah*, Mahadura Tinyana *EH* 89.

54. *PDR* 1:145, 157.

55. *Teshuvot Ateret Devorah EH* 1:42.

56. *Teshuvot Maharashdam EH* 123. PDR 1:65, 75, 145, 157; 3:353, 358, 4:66,

In fact, by focusing upon the child's right, in effect the *Beit Din* is dealing with the parental duty to provide proper care to his child rather than a parental right. *Halakhah*, similar to other religious legal systems, is primarily a system of duties owed, rather than rights possessed.[57] Consequently, the primary legal category in custody proceedings is the "*hiyuv,*" i.e. the individual's duty rather than his prerogative. If the doctrine of the logical correlativity of rights and duties assert that every duty entails the existence of a correlative right,[58] then in custody cases, corresponding to the parental duty of child care is the right of the child to be provided with proper care. Therefore, lest one focus exclusively on parental rights, the *Beit Din* focuses upon the child's right.[59]

Though the majority of the *battei din* reject the parental right doctrine, one could seemingly argue that the *Beit Din* accepts the best interests of the child approach, developed by American law which recognizes the child's right to proper care. And yet, though in both American law (a right-based system[60]) and *Halakhah* (a duty-based system), corresponding to the parental duty of child care there exists a child's right to be provided with proper care, it is important to distinguish which is derivative from which.[61]

There is a difference between the idea that a parent has a duty to provide a proper home because the child has a right to receive proper care and the notion that the child has a right to be provided with a proper home because the father is duty-bound to provide proper care. In the first instance where one is dealing with a right-based theory, one justifies the duty by pointing to the right; if one requires justification, it is *the right* that one must justify. Consequently, the best interests of the child

---

332; 11:366, 368; 13:338. File no. 0849-23-1, Haifa Regional Beit Din, November 10, 2004; File 586034/4, Haifa Regional Beit Din, January 16,2011; File no. 293094/5, Netanya Regional Beit Din, February 2, 2011; File no. 842473/1, Tel Aviv-Yaffo Regional Beit Din, September 6, 2011; File no. 586034-4, Haifa Regional Beit Din, November 23,2011; File no. 1037916/3, Be'air Sheva Regional Beit Din, December 2, 2015; File no. 1073383/1, Beit Din ha-Rabbani ha-Gadol, June 28, 2016; File no. 1086472/1, Beit Din ha-Rabbani ha-Gadol, December 20, 2016; File no. 1089963/8, Netanya Regional Beit Din, August 17,2017.

57. See this writer's, "May one destroy a neighbor's property in order to save one's life?" in ed. M. Shmidman, *Turim: Studies in Jewish history and Literature: Presented to Dr. Bernard Lander*, N.Y., 2007, 331–332.

58. I. Herzog, *The Main Institutions of Jewish Law*, London, 1946, vol. 1, 46.

59. See supra n. 56.

60. M. Glendon, *Rights-Talk: The impoverishment of political discourse*, N.Y., 1991.

61. R. Dworkin, *Taking rights seriously*, Cambridge, 1977, 171.

doctrine, a by-product of a right-based system, the focus is on *the child's right*, whereas in *Halakhah*, the focus is on the *parental duty* of care.[62]

Furthermore, there is a difference in emphasis between the neglect of duty and the interference with a right. To focus upon duties and their breach is to concentrate necessarily upon the person who has the duty; it is to invoke criteria by which to make moral assessments of his conduct. Rights, on the other hand, call attention to the injury inflicted; to the fact that the possessor of the right is adversely affected by the action.[63] Here, adopting the perspective of the child's best interests approach propounded by American courts, the individual at the center is the child who benefits from the parent's compliance. In *Halakhah*, the individual at the center is the parent who is complying with the will of Hashem. As stated by the *Beit Din*:[64]

> Here we have only duties from one side, the father who is obligated to support his child and is obligated to supervise and care for him.

Though both parents may assume the duty for the care and welfare of their children which would result in joint custody or what is called shared parenting,[65] however frequently the involved parties fail to be mutually agreeable to such an arrangement. Consequently, adopting the *mesorah* of those *Poskim* who espouse "*tovat ha-yeled*" (the child's best interests), the beneficiary of the parental duty as the guideline to resolve custody battles,[66] the *Beit Din* employs rules which result in either child

---

62. It is somewhat strange that the *Beit Din* (see supra n. 56) focuses upon the child's right rather than the parental duty. However, clearly the validation of the child's right is grounded in the parent's duty to provide proper care for his children. In fact, *Beit Din* will sometimes stress both the right of a child along with the parental duty. See *PDR* 1:145, 158.

63. Focusing upon "the harm principle" traces itself back to the liberal morality of John Stuart Mill and the possessive individualism of Thomas Hobbes and receives its classical legal expression in Austinian jurisprudence. See J. Mill, *On Liberty*, N.Y., 1956, 99–100.; Macpherson, *The political theory of possessive individualism: Hobbes to Locke*, Oxford: England, 1962; J. Austin, *Lectures on jurisprudence*, London, 1879. See also, J. Feinberg, *Harm to others*, Oxford, N.Y., 1984, idem, *Offense to others*, Oxford, N.Y., 1985.

64. *PDR* 1:145, 158.

65. Physical and legal custody would be shared by both parents. For its *halakhic* recognition, see File no. 995674/8, Haifa Regional Beit Din, November 23, 2016.

66. *Teshuvot ha-Rashba ha-Meyuhasot le-Ramban* 38; *Teshuvot ha-Rosh* 82:3; *Teshuvot Maharam me-Padua* 53; *Teshuvot ha-Mabit* 2:62; *Rema, SA EH* 82:7;

placement, usually with the father who is the natural guardian of his children[67] or the mother who is the appointed guardian of her children.[68]

In the case of a son below the age of six, the rule of thumb adopted by the majority of authorities is that the welfare of the child of tender years is normally best served by placing him with his mother with the understanding that the father is entitled to visit his son to fulfill his educational responsibilities vis-à-vis his child.[69] Above the age of six, the son must live with his father, since at this age the child requires intensive Torah educational guidance. Assuming the father is non-observant, there would be still grounds for child placement with his father who can teach him secular education.[70] Following in the footsteps of Rabbi Yitzhak of Vilna,[71] in the event that the father delegates his educational responsibility to a yeshiva to teach his son, then *Beit Din* rules that the son may be placed with the mother assuming it is in the child's best interests.[72] Notwithstanding certain *Poskim* who give custody to the father,[73] the *Beit Din* rule is that regardless of her age, the daughter remains with the mother to be instructed in the ways of moral propriety.[74] In other

---

Teshuvot ha-Radvaz 1:127, 156 (Cf. *Radvaz*, supra n. 48); *Beit Shmuel, SA EH* 82:10; *Helkat Mehokeik, SA EH* 82:10; *Teshuvot Darkhei Noam EH* 26; *Teshuvot Mishpetei Shmuel* 90; *Pithei Teshuvah, SA EH* 82:7.

67. *Teshuvot ha-Rosh* 87:1, 96:2; *Rema, SA HM* 285:5; *Sma, SA HM* 285:33.

68. See supra text accompanying notes 42–43. See also, *SA HM* 290:1–2.

69. *MT, Ishut* 21:17; *Magid Mishneh*, ad. locum.; *Derishah Tur EH* 82:2; *SA EH* 82:7. Cf. *Toldot Adom ve-Havah, Sefer Havah, Netiv* 23, vol. 3; *Ra'avad, MT Ishut* 21:17.

70. *PDR* 13:3, 12. On the other hand, if the father acts immorally, there would be grounds to place the child with his mother. See *PDR* 4:332, 335–336, 8:354, 362. Placing a child with a nonobservant parent raises issues of the minor child eating nonkosher food and transgressing the Shabbat. See *Tosafot Shabbat* 121a; *Yam shel Shlomo, Yevamot* 14:7; *Teshuvot Re'em* 79–80; *Teshuvot ha-Radvaz* 5:1432; *Teshuvot Hatam Sofer OH* 83; *Teshuvot Ahiezer* 3:81; *Teshuvot Pri Yitzhak* 1:12

71. For the manuscript of his ruling which is found in *Zera Anashim*, see Avraham Dovid, 49 *Kiryat Sefer* 557 (5729).

72. *PDR* 7:10, 17. Since today a father's educational responsibility is delegated to educational institutions, consequently the practice is that Israeli rabbinical courts is to give custody of a boy to his mother provided she is a fit parent. See *PDR* 21:260, 263.

73. *Rashi, Ketuvot* 102b, s.v. *zot omeret*; *Piskei ha-Rosh Ketuvot* 12:4 in the name of "*yesh omrim*"; *Teshuvot Ri Megas* 71.

74. File no. 0849-23-1, Haifa Regional Beit Din, November 10, 2004; File no. 293094/5, Netanya Regional Beit Din, February 2, 2011; File no. 842473/1, Tel Aviv-Yaffo Regional Beit Din, September 6, 2011; File no. 586034-4, Haifa Regional Beit Din, November 23,2011; File no. 1037916/3, Be'air Sheva Regional Beit Din, December 2, 2015; File no. 1086472/1, Beit Din ha-Rabbani ha-Gadol, December 20, 2016.

words, despite the fact that a father has a duty to educate his daughter,[75] nonetheless the mother's ability to inculcate certain values trumps the father's obligation and the daughter remains with the mother. Even if the mother moves away to another city and in effect the move preempts the daughter's (as well as the son's) accessibility, such a move is recognized provided it is in the child's best interests.[76]

Whereas in other areas of man's activities, *Halakhah* enforces duties by a system of civil law and a plaintiff asserts rights against individuals who fail to comply with their *halakhic* duties, in resolving conflicting parental claims, the *Beit Din* as "the father of the orphans" intervenes on behalf of the child. Whether one assumes that the *Beit Din's* intervention is legitimated by the general authority entrusted to them to engage in enacting *takanot* (legislation),[77] or whether one assumes it is based upon the binding force of *minhag* (custom),[78] the implication is that the *dayan* does not merely apply the existing rules of child custody to cases in doubt but in situations lacking any clear precedent, the *dayan* acts in a legislative capacity or based upon custom. Does this mean that a *dayan* is free to arrive at decisions uncontrolled by authoritative standards?

Presumably such a conclusion is forthcoming. For example, if it is proven that the father of a seven year old son is not carrying out the duties of fatherhood properly, the *Beit Din* is empowered to entrust the child to his mother.[79] Furthermore, in other Israeli decisions, the *Beit Din* would have permitted a daughter to reside in the United States, despite the inaccessibility of the father who resides in *Eretz Yisrael*.[80] His inaccessibility may preclude him from exercising his rights vis-à-vis his child. Seemingly, the *Beit Din* is acting arbitrarily.

The crucial question is what happens when the *Beit Din* determines that no rule is applicable in a particular case and the *dayan* wishes to overrule a rule? There is no doubt that the rules established by the

---

Precedent for this position can be found in *MT, Ishut* 21:16–18; *Teshuvot ha-Rashbash* 202; *Tur EH* 82:7.

75. See *Rashi, Pesahim* 88a; *Tosafot Yeshanim Yoma* 82a; *Magen Avraham, SA OH* 343:1; *Mahatzit ha-Shekel*, ad. locum.

76. *Teshuvot Maharbil* 1:58; Beit Din ha-Rabbani ha-Gadol, supra n. 56. Seemingly, *Maharshdam*, supra n. 56 disagrees with this view, however see *Teshuvot Nofet Tzufim EH* 91 and *Teshuvot Darkhei Noam EH* 38.

77. *Rashba*, supra n. 66; *Mishpetei Shmuel*, supra n. 66; *Maharashdam*, supra n. 56; *PDR* 2:162, 170–171; 4:93, 95, 97, 108; Y. Goldberg, 9 *Shurat ha-Din* 94, (5745).

78. *Teshuvot Maharashdam EH* 308.

79. See supra n.70.

80. *PDR* 7:3, 8; Beit Din ha-Rabbani ha-Gadol, supra n. 56. Cf. *PDR* 4:93, 95.

Poskim find authoritative support in the *Beit Din's* decisions.[81] For example, psychiatric findings will be considered by the *Beit Din* in order to arrive at a reasonable assessment of the physical, mental and moral well-being of the child whose custody is at issue. However, whereas a *Beit Din* will accept the testimony of a psychologist who testifies that "in light of the particular circumstances, the seven year old boy should remain with his mother"; it will reject a testimony that states "the natural needs of a seven year old son are to be with his mother."[82] Whereas, the former testimony is valid testimony and conveys to the *Beit Din* that the rule that a son above the age of six is to be with his father is rebuttable in the particular case, the latter testimony conveys the establishment of a new rule.

The fact that a rule may be rebuttable given the particular circumstances of the case indicates that the *dayan's* decision does not merely entail the mechanical application of a rule. Resolving custody cases in *Halakhah* involves more that the formal application of rules.[83] In fact, the *Beit Din* points out these rules are *hazakot*, presumptions.[84] Moreover, the application of these rules is controlled by a principle. Whereas a rule attaches a definite consequence to a detailed state of facts, a principle prescribes highly unspecific actions.[85] It is in accordance with this usage of the terms, that we can speak of a principle underlying a certain rule, determining its scope and justifying exceptions to it.

It is indeed a principle which is most energetically at work here, carrying weight in resolving custody cases by the *Beit Din*. On numerous instances, the *Beit Din* states that the operative principle here is the

---

81. *PDR* 1:55, 61, 145, 157; supra n. 74–75, 78.

82. *PDR* 3:353, 360. Moreover, in contradistinction to whether a sick person ought to fast on Yom Kippur becomes a question which is resolved by a physician, in a matter of child custody, it is the *beit din* rather than the prognosis of a health care professional which will determine the disposition of the child. In other words, a *beit din* may seek the advice of the professional but in the final analysis the final arbiter will be the rabbinic authority. See *PDR* 11:153,161; File no. 0849-23-1, Haifa Regional Beit Din, November 10, 2004.

83. Ibid.

84. *PDR* 1:55, 61, 145, 157.

85. For the usage of these two terms in American law, see Dworkin, supra n. 61, at 14–80; J. Raz, "Legal principles and the limits of the law," 81 *Yale L. J.* 81 (1972).

consideration of the material, social, spiritual and educational interests of the child.[86] The principle stands behind every rule.[87]

The extent to which the principle of *"tovat ha-yeled"* is utilized for different purposes can be seen by a brief review of some of the decisions of the *Beit Din*. Perhaps the most extensive and conservative function of a principle is to interpret rules. Consequently, in one situation the *Beit Din* contends that the child's welfare is the underlying rationale which lies at the base of the rules of custody disposition.[88] As an efficient principle, it imparts coherence of a purpose to a realm of *Halakhah*, namely custody arrangements by explaining the rules in accordance with one principle and thus demonstrating that we are not dealing with a mere collection of rules.

Secondly, through the medium of the application of the principle, the scope of the rules may be widened. No rule can be formulated in such a way that no situations can arise in which its application is open to question. Therefore, "non-standard cases" will emerge requiring the exercise of judicial discretion via the invoking the principle of *tovat ha-yeled*.

For example, if in a given situation, the father's psychological instability prevents him from fulfilling his educational responsibilities towards his son, the *Beit Din* states it is incumbent upon a third party or an educational institution to receive custody of the child.[89] However other *battei din* have refused to authorize an educational institution to assume the father's duties.[90] Given these circumstances, the son remained with his mother. To state it differently, here the *Beit Din* acknowledges the operation of *tovat ha-yeled* as a vehicle to interpret the rule but felt that the principle does not encompass extending the rule that a father has

---

86. *PDR* 1:55, 61, 65, 75, 173, 178; 2:3, 8; 3:353, 358; 4:66, 74, 332, 334; 11:172, 173, 366, 368, 369; 18:103, 106. File no. 1-23-2950, Beit Din ha-Rabbani ha-Gadol, June 17, 2004; File no. 0849-23-1, supra n. 82; File 586034/4, Haifa Regional Beit Din, January 16,2011; File no. 842473/1, Tel Aviv-Yaffo Regional Beit Din, September 6, 2011; File no. 586034-4, Haifa Regional Beit Din, November 23, 2011; File no. 586034/4, Haifa Regional Beit Din, July 25, 2012; File 1073383/1, Beit Din ha-Rabbani ha-Gadol, June 28, 2016; File no. 995674/8, Haifa Regional Beit Din, November 23, 2016; Beit Din ha-Rabbani ha-Gadol, supra n. 74; File no. 868053/4, Be'air Sheva Regional Beit Din, February 22, 2017; File no. 970523/9, Yerushalayim Regional Beit Din, February 26,2017; File no. 1089963/8, Netanya Regional Beit Din, August 17,2017.

87. Though the principle is operative in a *teshuvah* of Gaonim (see *Otzar ha-Geonim, Ketuvot* 102b, 359–360), its precise formulation is given a few hundred years later. See *Rashba*, supra n.66.

88. *PDR* 1:55, 61.

89. *PDR* 1:65, 75; 2:298, 303; 4:66, 74.

90. *PDR* 4:66, 74.

custody of his son who is above the age of six to an institution becoming *locus parentis*, assuming certain parental responsibilities.

What happens where there is a conflict of rules? On one hand, there is a rule that every son above the age of six is placed with his father; and on the other hand, there is a rule that the child's wishes are a relevant factor in his own placement. If the child is old enough to form an intelligent judgment about his custody and his judgment has not been tainted by the provocation and instigation of a parent, his wishes will be respected by the *Beit Din*.[91] His wishes will be respected both with regard to visitation arrangements[92] as well as the choice of the institution for Yeshiva schooling.[93] These series of ruling regarding the child's wishes are based upon *tovat ha-yeled*.[94]

Since the principle of *tovat ha-yeled* is more general than the rules, in cases where the *Beit Din* ascertains that the application of the existing rule would undermine the principle, the *Beit Din* arrives at a decision without recourse to the rule. For example, although the rule of custody dictates that a boy above the age of six ought to remain with his father; considerations of *tovat ha-yeled* will be the determining factor. Consequently, a son above the age of six will remain with his mother who is providing a Torah education rather than be placed with a father who is exhibiting schizophrenic tendencies.[95] In another case the *Beit Din* awarded custody to an adulterous mother since the father's behavior manifested an unwillingness to raise and educate his older son.[96] In another situation, the *Beit Din* recognizes that a father may develop a psychological-affectionate relationship equivalent to that of the mother and consequently, the father retains custody of the young child.[97] Finally,

---

91. *PDR* 1:55, 61; 2:298, 300–301; 4:332, 333. This position is based upon *Helkat Mehokeik, SA EH* 82:9; *Teshuvot Mahari ibn Lev* 1:74 in the name of Rambam; *Teshuvot Maharam Alsheikh* 38 in the name of Rambam.

92. *PDR* 1:145, 158.

93. *PDR* 7:10, 15–16.

94. *PDR* 1:145, 158. Just as we found that psychological testimony is admissible regarding custody disposition (see supra text accompanying n. 80), similarly, in the ascertaining of the child's wishes, the *Beit Din* utilizes the services of third parties such as health care professionals. See A. Shaki, "Aspects of the laws of child custody – with emphasis in applying the principle of the child's best interests" (Hebrew), 10 *Iyunei Mishpat* 5, 9, n. 25, 22–23 (5744).

95. *PDR* 1:65, 76.

96. *PDR* 1:55, 63.

97. *PDR* 1:173, 176. The dissenting opinion in this case accepted the grounds for the majority decision but argued that a psychological relationship with the father had never developed. See *PDR* 1:173, 177–178.

as we mentioned that according to Rambam should a boy above the age of six desire to remain with his mother, his father is entitled to refuse to pay his support,[98] the *Beit Din* concludes that if the child's best interests dictate that he remain with his mother, under such circumstances, the father will remain obligated to maintain his son.[99] In the aforementioned cases, the principle of *tovat ha-yeled* serves as the grounds for the *Beit Din's* decisions.

Though *tovat ha-yeled* may provide the basis for resolving cases without application of the rules, serve as a vehicle to interpret rules, be employed as grounds for exceptions to the rules and serve as a means to reconcile conflicts between rules of custody, nevertheless, on certain occasions, the *Beit Din* observes that this principle may be overridden by a principle from another sphere of *Halakhah*. For example, what happens if a father desires that his seven year old daughter settle with him in *Eretz Yisrael*? On one hand, there is a rule that "a man may compel his entire household to settle in the land of *Eretz Yisrael*"[100] which reflects the divine commandment incumbent upon each individual Jew to settle in *Eretz Yisrael*. On the other hand, the child's welfare dictates that the daughter remains with her mother. By placing the daughter in her father's custody we advance the *mitzvah* of settling in *Eretz Yisrael* and by placing the daughter with the mother we serve the child's best interests. One *Beit Din* decides that fulfilling the *mitzvah* was paramount and the other rules that the child's welfare overrides the *mitzvah*.[101]

The position that the *Beit Din* is free to act arbitrarily in custody cases is vigorously challenged by the above cases. To argue that a *beit din* is free to reach a decision uncontrolled by authoritative standards is to fail to attend to the interplay of rules and principles operating in these cases. Certainly, our presentation suggests that there is more than one solution to a problem and different *battei din* may arrive at different conclusions. There will be instances where one panel will widen the scope of a rule whereas another panel will argue for a strict reading of the rule.[102] Secondly, *tovat ha-yeled* may be subject to varying interpretations.[103]

In conclusion, the interplay between a rule and a principle in custody cases reflects how a panel will attempt to resolve a case based upon the

---

98. Supra n. 44.
99. *PDR* 1:55, 61–62, 161, 163; 7:10, 34. Cf. *PDR* 2:298, 303; 13:17.
100. *Ketuvot* 110b.
101. *PDR* 7:3, 8; 1:103.
102. *PDR* 4:66, 74.
103. *PDR* 1:173.

child's best interests perspective. On the other hand, for those *battei din* who espouse the approach of the parental right to custody, in the final analysis their determination may at times reflect the child's best interests such as proscribing a mother's right to move to another country lest the father's visitation privileges will be extinguished.[104] Moreover, assuming a father's visitation privileges is a paternal right;[105] he must be accorded the exercise of his right in the case of a son below the age of six and a daughter regardless of her age.[106] In effect, said conclusion comports with the child's best interests to see and develop a relationship with both his parents. As Rabbi Uriel Lavi, *av beit din* (presiding *dayan*) of Yerushalayim Beit Din aptly notes, the difference between the two approaches is only in *theory*. Except for a situation where a son above the age of six refuses to live with his father,[107] *in practice* the child's best interests will always override paternal rights.[108]

We can sharpen our comparison of the dynamics of the child custody decision making process as propounded by *Halakhah* and American law by introducing the framework suggested by a contemporary scholar of American family law. He distinguishes between a judge's discretion and the application of rules.

The history of the law considers many antinomies and therefore must reckon with the opposing values emerging from these antinomies. One of them is the story of an unremitting struggle between rules and discretion. The tension between these two approaches to legal problems continues to pervade and perplex the law today. Perhaps nowhere is that tension more pronounced and more troubling than in family law.[109]

As we have shown in American law, rules which embodied paternal and maternal presumptions regarding child placement have been replaced by a judicial determination of who is the fit custodial parent by invoking a child best interest standard which is composed of various factors. In effect, broad discretion is placed in the hands of the judge.[110]

---

104. *PDR* 13:17, 20.

105. See infra n. 102; *PDR* 4:93, 95.

106. *PDR* 9:251, 259; 12:129, 141.

107. In such a situation, in accordance with the parental right doctrine, the father will be exempt from paying support. On the other hand, in pursuance to *tovat ha-yeled* approach, under such circumstances, the father will have to continue to pay child support.

108. *Ateret Devorah*, supra n. 55, at 283.

109. Carl Schneider, "The tension between rules and discretion in family law: A report and reflection," 27 *Family Law* Quarterly, 229 (1993).

110. Academic criticism has emerged which argues that the standard is too

The history of American custody law reflects a paradigmatic shift from rules to discretion.

On the other hand, in the *halakhah* of child custody we are not confronted with the stark choice: discretion or rules. Our study has demonstrated that we are encountering the *dayan's* search for the right mix of rules and discretion as embodied in the principle of *"tovat ha-yeled".*

After having analyzed the varying perspectives underlying the treatment of child custody cases by *Halakhah* and American law, we hope to have avoided Santayana's reproach that comparison "is the expedient of those who cannot reach the heart of the things compared."[111]

---

vague and therefore indeterminate to serve as a guideline for the judge. See R. Mnookin, "Child custody adjudication: judicial functions in the face of indeterminacy," 39 *Law & Contemporary Problems,* Summer 1975,226,227; D. Chambers, "Rethinking the substantive rules for custody disputes in divorce," 83 *Mich. L. Rev.* 477, 487–489 (1984); A. Charlow, "Awarding custody: The best interests of the child and other fictions," 5 *Yale L. & Policy Rev.* 267, 269–73, 281–83 (1987); J. Elster, " Solomonic judgments: against the best interest of the child, "53 *U. Chi. L. Rev.* 1 (1987); M. Garrison, "How do judges decide divorce cases? An empirical analysis of discretionary decisionmaking," 74 *N.C.L. Rev.* 401, 411–412 (1996). Some authorities have contended that rules should supplement the child best interest standard. See R. Uviller, "Fathers' rights and feminism: The maternal presumption revisited," 1 *Harv. Women's L.J.,* 130 (1978); M. Minow, "Consider the consequences," 84 *Michigan L. Rev.* 900, 908 (1986); C. Schneider, "Discretion, rules and law: Child custody and the UMDA's best-interest standard," 89 *Mich. L. Rev.* 2215, 2219–25 (1991); E. Scott, "Pluralism, parental preference, and child custody," 80 *California L. Rev.* 615 (1992); M. Brinig, "Substantive parenting arrangements in the USA: Unpacking the policy choices," 27 *Child & Family Law Q.* 3 (2015).

111. G. Santayana, *Character and Opinion in the United States,* N.Y., 1921, 166.

Chapter 7

A man receives an improper *heter nissuin* (*halakhic* permission to remarry) without giving his first wife a *get* – Relief via the execution of a *"get zikui"*

ACCORDING TO *HALAKHAH*, DISSOLUTION of the matrimonial bond requires the voluntary agreement of both spouses; failure of one spouse to agree to the divorce action precludes the execution of the divorce. Coercing a recalcitrant husband to grant a *get* ("a *get me'useh*") produces a divorce that is arguably invalid according to the majority of *Poskim*. Nonetheless, in the absence of a *beit din* obligating him to give a *get*, there exists no *halakhic* impediment for a husband to stipulate that his consent at the time of the *seder ha-get* (execution of a Jewish writ of divorce) is dependent upon his wife's compliance with certain conditions, a form of divorce known as *gerushin al tenai* (a conditional divorce).[1] In contemporary times, numerous Israeli *dayanim* will allow a wife to appease her *get* recalcitrant husband by offering material inducement.[2]

For many years, our Torah observant community has encountered, both here and abroad, situations where a recalcitrant husband chooses to condition the giving of a *get* upon receiving certain benefits such as receiving monetary remuneration from his wife, receiving custody of a child, or having certain issues related to the end of marriage resolved in a *beit din*.[3] Let me share three cases that I have encountered in recent

---

1. Mishnah *Gittin* 7:5–9; *SA EH* 29:7, 143:1.

2. *PDR* 16:271, 275–276. For further discussion demonstrating that such an arrangement does not run afoul of the strictures of a *get me'useh*, see this writer's, *Rabbinic Authority*, vol. 3, 56, n. 3. For a divorcee's relief from the consequences of an exploitative divorce agreement, see this writer's *Rabbinic Authority*, vol. 3, 97–133.

3. See this writer's *Rabbinic Authority*, vol. 3, 55–81.

years. One husband would give a *get* on the condition that he would receive one million dollars from his wife who has been an *agunah* now for over a decade. In another situation, despite the fact that there was a financial prenuptial agreement which stated that the wife owned her one million dollar home, the husband conditioned the giving of the *get* upon being able to revisit in *beit din* whether in fact the home belonged to her. To date, this woman has been an *agunah* for over six years. Finally, a wife filed suit in civil court in order to address the matter of custody of their children. Though the husband consented to have this matter resolved in civil court, nonetheless, once the court awarded custody to his wife, he conditioned the giving of the *get* upon his wife's readiness to revisit the parenting arrangements in *beit din*.

The common denominator of these three cases is that all three wives refused to comply with their husband's requests and therefore they still cannot remarry due to the fact that a *get* failed to be given to them by their respective husbands. Furthermore, in two of the cases, the husbands received a *heter nissuin* (permission to remarry) from a *beit din* which requires that a *get* be deposited at the *beit din* which would be given to the wife if she complied with her husband's requests. Subsequently, both husbands remarried without giving a *get* to their first wife. In the third case, the husband has threatened to proceed for a *heter nissuin* should his wife refuse to accede to his request to revisit the parenting arrangements in *beit din*.[4]

Despite the fact that there has been a *minhag* (the custom) in Ashkenazic communities dating back to over four hundred years ago to refrain from implementing *gerushin al tenai*,[5] a practice has reared its head where husbands condition the giving of the *get* upon a wife's compliance with certain requests.[6] With the existence of this *minhag*, *get* recalcitrant husbands in certain instances have enlisted the assistance of *battei din* in order to receive a *heter nissuin*. Given the particular circumstances surrounding these two cases, the issuance of a *heter nissuin* by the two *battei din* is, to say the least, *halakhically* problematic.

Let's begin by first presenting the rudimentary *halakhot* governing the initiation of a divorce action. (1) A *get* is the husband's possession

---

4. In a fourth instance, a *get* recalcitrant husband was prepared . . . *nissuin* (permission to remarry), however his prospective wife told him that she wouldn't marry him unless he gave a *get* to his wife. He relented and gave a *get* to his wife and subsequently the prospective wife changed her mind and did not marry him.

5. *Levush EH* 145:10; *Arukh ha-Shulhan EH* 147:11.

6. See supra n. 4.

and a *get* must be given by the husband *be'ratzon* (voluntarily).[7] (2) In the text of the *get*, it must be clear that the husband is severing the marital relationship.[8] (3) The *get* must be written for the wife, (*le'shemah*).[9] (4) The husband or a *sofer* (scribe) at the husband's directive must write the *get* and the witnesses who will attest to the execution of the *get* must have heard the husband's directive to sign the *get*.[10] (5) The husband or his agent must deliver the *get* to his wife.[11] (6) The wife must voluntarily accept the *get*.[12]

Seemingly, given that the husband hasn't communicated instructions to write a *get*, and the witnesses have not heard the husband's directive to sign the *get*, there would be no basis for a *beit din* writing a *get* for the wife. Moreover, the absence of a husband's instructions to write a *get* precludes the fulfilling the requirement of *le-shemah*.[13] In fact, numerous contemporary authorities, including but not limited to Rabbi Moshe Farbstein and Rabbi Yitzhak Yosef, have invalidated a third party's writing of a *get* if there was no prior authorization given by the husband.[14]

---

7. *Beit Yosef EH* 134 in the name of Tashbetz; *Tur EH* 120:1; *SA EH* 134:1–3, 5; *Netivot ha-Mishpat HM* 205:1; *Teshuvot Hemdat Shlomo HM* 13; *Hazon Ish EH* 99:1; *Shiurei ha-Grah ha-Levi* (stencil), page 239. Whether a husband must declare "I want to give a *get*" see *Ohr Sameah, Gerushin* 2:20, *Mamrim* 4:3; *Teshuvot Radakh* 9:11; *Teshuvot Shoeil u-Meishiv,* Mahadura 6, 55; *Teshuvot Avnei Tzedek* 8; *Teshuvot Havot Yair* 55.

8. *MT, Gerushin* 1:1, 3; *Teshuvot ha-Rosh* 45 (end); *SA EH* 141:16–17, 126:8.

9. *MT, Gerushin* 1:1; *SA EH* 120:4, 131:1, 16–17; *Helkat Mehokeik SA EH* 120:9, 123:1; *Beit Shmuel, SA EH* 141:27.

10. *Tur* and *Beit Yosef EH* 120; *SA EH* 120:1, 4; *Hazon Ish EH* 83:15; *Iggerot Moshe EH* 1:116. Whether a written directive by the husband suffices or one must hear the husband's voice, see *Piskei ha-Rosh Gittin* 6:30; *Pithei Teshuvah SA EH* 120:18; *Teshuvot Maharim Brisk* 32; *Teshuvot Beit Ephraim EH* 80; *Teshuvot Maharsham* 3: 352 (5), 5:44; *Teshuvot Minhat Shlomo* 1:58; *Iggerot Moshe*, op. cit.

Whether the husband is required to give the parchment and ink to the *sofer* and if he fails to provide these materials is the validity of the *get* a question, see *Sefer ha-Terumot* 131; *Levush* 120:1; *Teshuvot Tzemah Tzedek EH* 150; *Teshuvot Yabia Omer* 3, *EH* 25.

11. *SA EH* 140:1.

12. *Teshuvot ha-Rosh* 42:1; *Rema, SA EH* 119:6.

13. *Tosafot Gittin* 22b; *Hiddushei ha-Rashba, Gittin* 23a; *Ran* on *Rif, Gittin* 11a; *Teshuvot Devar Yehoshua* 4:43.

14. Letter of Rabbi Moshe Farbstein to Dayan Uriel Lavi dated Sivan 5774 (letter on file with author); letter of Rabbi Yitzhak Yosef to Dayan Lavi dated 16 Heshvan 5774 (letter on file with author). See also Mishnat Yosef, Tevet 5776, 26–29, 88–116, 302–321.

Moreover, the fact that the husband refuses to give a *get* seemingly undercuts the propriety of a third party giving a *get*.[15]

However, there are other *Poskim* who disagree with the above positions. The emerging question is whether there are grounds for a *beit din* to issue a *get zikui* in the event that a husband remarries a second wife without giving a *get* to his first wife. *Zakhin le'adam she-lo be-fanav* (conferring a benefit upon a person in his absence) allows for a third party to perform an act that affects a person, without his knowledge, as long as that act comes within the rubric of "a benefit" for him. For example, if a debtor has only one creditor, then a friend of the creditor may seize the property on behalf of the creditor.[16] Or if a husband desires to give his wife a *get* but she refuses to accept it, it may be a benefit to become divorced under certain conditions and the *get* is executed in her absence and without her prior authorization.[17] The common denominator in these two cases is that we are invoking the concept of *zakhin le'adam she-lo be-fanav*.

The issue is whether *zakhin* applies when we take something away from an individual. For example, if an individual neglected to sell his *hametz* on the eve of *Pesah* and the *hametz* potentially would lose its value,[18] can a friend sell it prior to *Pesah* on behalf of his friend? Or, in our situation where a husband refuses to give a *get* to his wife and yet receives permission to remarry, can a *beit din* give it to her despite her husband's protestations? In both of these scenarios, the person who owns the *hametz* and the husband who is *get* recalcitrant will be deprived of something or someone respectively, due to the action of another. To state it differently, we know there is a rule of *zakhin le'adam she-lo be-fanav*, can we equally confer benefits involving *zakhin mei'adam she-lo be-fanav* (hereafter: *zakhin*)?

Admittedly, throughout various passages of the Talmud, commentaries, *teshuvot* (responsa) and *sifrei psak* (restatements of *Halakhah*) such as Shulhan Arukh, one finds *zakhin* being applied in circumstances where a benefit is being conferred rather than being taken away from an individual.[19] However, there are a few passages in the Talmud as well as discussions amongst the *Poskim* which recognize that *zakhin* is equally

---

15. For a contrary view, see *Rabbinic Authority*, vol. 3, 196–198.

16. *SA HM* 105.

17. See *Rabbinic Authority*, vol. 3, 178–186.

18. The loss of value would be due to the fact that it one is forbidden to derive any benefit from *hametz* which is owned by a Jew during *Pesah* (i.e, not sold to a non-Jew prior to *Pesah*) even after *Pesah*.

19. *Encyclopedia Talmudit*, vol. 12, 135–198.

operative in situations where one takes something from an individual. For example, a passage in Tractate *Pesahim* teaches us:[20]

> There was an incident with a man who deposited for safekeeping a full bag of *hametz* . . . But when the eve of *Pesah* arrived, mice penetrated it and the *hametz* was leaking out. He approached a rabbi and asked what he should do. At the first hour, he told him "wait", second hour he told him "wait" . . . at the fifth hour, he told him "proceed to the market and sell it . . . to a non-Jew."

Since the fifth hour was the last hour that the owner of the *hametz* could benefit from his foodstuffs, the rabbi instructed the man to sell it to a non-Jew before *Pesah*, because with the arrival of *Pesah* the *hametz* would be prohibited to the owner and thus the owner would lose the *hametz*.

Notwithstanding Ketzot ha-Hoshen, Mirkevet ha-Mishneh and a few other authorities, the majority of *Poskim*, including but not limited to Tosafot, Rabbis Moshe ben Nahman, Nissim of Gerondi, Yisrael Isserelin, Yosef Karo, Moshe Issereles, David ben Shmuel ha-Levi, Avraham Gumbiner, Moshe Sofer, Yitzhak Elhanan Spektor, Avraham Tzvi Eisenstadt, Meir Eisenstadt, Hayyim Ozer Grodzensky, Avraham Karelitz, Shimon Shkop, Shalom Schwadron, Avraham Kook, Eliezer Shach, Shlomo Z. Urbach, Moshe Feinstein, and Uriel Lavi argue that the concept of *zakhin* encompasses matters where one takes away something from someone.[21]

The question is whether there is a basis for invoking *zakhin mei-adam* in the context of divorce cases. In effect, may one take a *get* from the husband (who has remarried without a proper *heter nissuin*) without his consent and give it to his first wife? In light of Ramban's position we do encounter grounds for validating a *get zikui* in a situation where the

---

20. *Pesahim* 13a.

21. *Teshuvot Seridei Eish* 3:25 (3) in the name of *Tosafot Yevamot* 113a; *Hiddushei ha-Ramban, Gittin* 52a; *Ran,* ad. locum.; *Teshuvot Terumat ha-Deshen* 1188; *SA OH* 443:2; *Rema SA YD* 328:3; *Taz,* ad. locum. subsection 2; *Magen Avraham SA OH* 558:3; *Teshuvot Hatam Sofer EH* 1:11, 2:43; *Teshuvot Be'air Yitzhak OH* 1 (5); *Pithei Teshuvah SA YD* 320:6; *Teshuvot Panim Meirot* 2:52; *Teshuvot Ahiezer* 1:28 (15); *Hazon Ish, EH* 49:10; *Hiddushei Rabbi Shimon, Kiddushin* 19; *Teshuvot Maharsham* 2:103; *Teshuvot Mishpat Kohen* 150; *Avi Ezri,* Mahadura Tinyana, *Terumot* 4:3; *Teshuvot Minhat Shlomo,* Mahadura Tinyana 107; *Iggerot Moshe EH* 1:117; File no. 861974/2, Tzfat Regional Beit Din, May 20, 2014. Cf. *Ketzot ha-Hoshen* 243:8; *Mirkevet ha-Mishneh, Gerushin* 6:3.

husband did not provide instructions to give a *get*. Upon a review of his position,[22] we encounter an apparent self-contradiction in his words. On one hand, should there be a husband's letter directing the *sofer* to write a *get*, in pursuance to Ramban, he would be in compliance with the requirement of *le-shemah*. On the other hand, Ramban contends that the *sofer* must have received explicit verbal instructions from the husband to prepare the *get*. Resolving this seeming contradiction, Rabbi Feinstein argues that Ramban's view is that it must be crystal clear that the husband wants to initiate the process of divorce, i.e. *le-shemah*. The presumption is that a wife is *lav le-gerushin omedet* (that she is not destined to be divorced) and therefore there is a requirement of *le-shemah*.[23] Consequently, if the husband communicates verbal instructions to the scribe or writes a letter that he wants the *sofer* to draft a *get*, his intentions are clear and the *le-shemah* condition is obtained.[24] To state it differently, Ramban is concerned with verifiability that in fact the husband desires to initiate the divorce process rather than that the husband must initiate the process of mandating the writing of the *get*.

Based upon Rabbi Feinstein's understanding of Ramban, in the context of *zakhin*, where the husband is absent, the *sofer* is receiving a directive from the *beit din* to draft the bill of divorce and is well aware that this procedure is being implemented to benefit the husband. In other words, without a husband's directive to initiate the process, the *get* is a *hov*. However, if there is an absolute unmitigated benefit, divorce is no longer a *hov*. As such, despite the absence of the husband's instructions, based upon Rabbi Feinstein's elucidation of Ramban's view, the requirement of *le-shemah* is in effect being verified via the rule of *zakhin*. Following in the footsteps of Rabbi Akiva Eiger and Hazon Ish, in the words of Rabbi Herzog:[25]

---

22. *Hiddushei ha-Ramban, Gittin* 23a (*hashmatot*).

23. Following in the footsteps of *Tosafot, Zevahim* 2b, Ramban rules that the requirement of *le-shemah* is to ensure that the wife is "*le-gerushin omedet.*"

24. *Iggerot Moshe, EH* 1:116, 119. See also Rabbi Goldberg's affirmation of Ramban's posture (as well as validating the propriety of a *get zikui*). See Rabbi Zalman N. Goldberg, "Agency and conferring benefit in *kiddushin, get* and undertaking obligations," (Hebrew), 1 *Le-Ma'an Da'at* 61, Elul 5774.

25. *Hiddushei Rabbi Akiva Eiger, Bava Metzia* 22a; *Hazon Ish EH* 86:1–2; *Teshuvot Heikhal Yitzhak EH* 2:54. See also, *Miluei Even* 29.

In accordance with *Tosafot Gittin* 72a, *s.v. kolo; Teshuvot Avnei Nezer EH* 156:9 and *Hiddushei Rabbi Shimon Shkop, Gittin* 7 (11–12) who argue that with the employment of *zakhin* one can instruct the scribe and witnesses in place of the husband. Cf. O. Weiss, *Minhat Asher, Kiddushin* 47.

> Since it is a clear benefit for her, the *get* will not be a nullity due
> to the fact that the husband did not instruct . . . it is as if the
> husband is in front of us and commands . . .

Numerous *Poskim* arrive at the same conclusion, contending that either
zakhin preempts the need for a husband's instructions to the scribe and
the witnesses, or the requirement of *le'shemah* is in effect being accom-
plished through her status of "*le-gerushin omedet.*"[26]

The question is whether a *gilui da'at* (an expression of one's opinion)
must have been articulated by the husband prior to executing a *get zikui*.
Generally, in matters of *kiddushin* for one to invoke *zakhin*, there must be
a *gilui da'at* from the beneficiary that he desires the conferral of the benefit.[27] Does this requirement extend to matters of divorce? For example,
if a husband is insistent that he appoint a *shaliah le-holakhah* (an agent
who will deliver a *get* to his wife) or actually appointed a *shaliah*, can a
third party invoke *zakhin* and give a get to his wife? Notwithstanding
some authorities who reject the employment of *zakhin* under such circumstances,[28] and others who mandate a *gilui da'at* prior to invoking of
zakhin,[29] Rabbis Y. Elyashiv and Z. P. Frank argue that one can benefit
a husband even if the party conferring the benefit was not appointed as
"the agent for delivery."[30] Rabbis Yehiel Weinberg, Karelitz, and Feinstein
conclude that *zakhin* is effective even without a husband's *gilui da'at* that
he desires to give a *get* to his wife, provided that there is an absolute benefit for the husband.[31] Moreover, when dealing with a husband who is a
shoteh (mentally dysfunctional in accordance with *halakhic* criteria), a
husband's *gilui da'at* to give a *get* prior to becoming a *shoteh* is irrelevant
in establishing the husband's benefit.[32] According to these authorities,
the same conclusion would equally apply in our situation. Namely, there

---

26. See *Rabbinic Authority*, vol. 3, 194, n. 79.

27. *Piskei ha-Rosh, Kiddushin* 2:7; *Ketzot ha-Hoshen* 382:2; *Teshuvot Ahiezer* 1:28
(16–17).

28. *Teshuvot Be'air Yitzhak OH* 1 (5); *Teshuvot Zekan Aharon* 1:95; *Teshuvot
Maharsham* 6:136.

29. *Teshuvot Hatam Sofer EH* 2:43; *Mirkevet ha-Mishneh* in the name of Rabbi
Krotosyn, *Gerushin* 6:3; *Teshuvot Ahiezer* 1:28; *Dvar Halakhah, miluim* 93, 122; *Devarim Ahadim* 45; *Teshuvot Beit Avi EH* 157 (17); *Teshuvot Minhat Yitzhak* 1:48–49.

30. *Teshuvot Heikhal Yitzhak EH* 2:55 in the name of Rabbi Elyashiv; *Kovetz
Teshuvot* 1:77; *Teshuvot Har Tzvi EH* 2:155.

31. *Teshuvot Seridei Esh* 90 (32); *Hazon Ish EH* 49:10; *Iggerot Moshe EH* 1:117.

32. *Get Pashut* 121:10; *Hazon Ish EH* 49:10, 86:3.

would be no requirement of a husband's *gilui da'at* before establishing the husband's benefit in giving the *get*.

How ought the *zekhut* (privilege) to give a *get* be defined? Rabbi Eliyahu Mizrachi of sixteenth century Constantinople, Turkey, addresses the case of a husband who was apprehensive that he would soon die and his wife would be obligated to engage in *yibum* (levirate marriage) with his apostate brother. To forestall this possibility, he wanted to divorce his wife prior to his demise. Since his wife was unavailable at that time, the husband appointed a third party to confer the benefit of a *get* upon her. Given that it is a *zekhut* that she would not marry her brother-in-law who is an apostate, Rabbi Mizrachi opines that she is divorced via *zakhin*. And even if she desired to marry him via *yibum*, she would remain divorced despite her objections because it is in her benefit to be "saved from sin."[33] A similar definition of the concept of *zekhut* is offered in contemporary times by Rabbi Z. Nehemiah Goldberg who offers as an example of a husband's *zekhut* if he is obligated to pay spousal support and engage in conjugal relations and unable to fulfill his *halakhic* marital duties due to the fact that he is in a vegetative state.[34] To state it differently, for Rabbis Mizrachi, Goldberg and Moshe Bula,[35] *zekhut* is defined by *halakhic* criteria.

Some *Poskim*, including Rabbi Dovid ha-Kohen of Corfu, argue that *zekhut* is defined by the subjective wishes of the beneficiary of the *zekhut*.[36] So for example, if in fact the wife wants to remain married to her apostate brother-in-law, invoking *zakhin* would be ineffective.[37] On the other hand, there are other authorities who subscribe to the posture of Rabbis Mizrachi and Goldberg by sanctioning the implementation of *zakhin* concerning an apostate or an adulterous wife who refuses to receive a *get* due to the fact that *zekhut hanefesh* (spiritual benefit) mandates that such an individual be "saved from sin" and the wife ought to be divorced from her spouse.[38]

A case where *zakhin* was applicable despite a husband's protest may be found in a letter authored by Rabbi Elyashiv in September 1954, sent to Rabbi Y. Herzog in 1959, and subsequently (around 1990) this letter

---

33. *Teshuvot Re'em* 68.

34. See Goldberg, supra n. 24, at 66.

35. M. Bula, *Zekhut Moshe* 7.

36. *Teshuvot Radakh, bayit* 9, *heder* 12; *Teshuvot Rabbi Akiva Eiger Hadashot* (Budapest 5698) 3:79; *Teshuvot Pnei Moshe* 1:33; *Teshuvot She'erit Yisrael EH* 5, *Kuntres Heter Agunah*.

37. *Radakh*, supra n. 36.

38. See *Rabbinic Authority*, vol. 3, 179–180, notes 17–19, 182–183, notes 27–29.

was incorporated into volume one of his *Kovetz Teshuvot*, his rulings.[39] Addressing the case of an *agunah* whose husband was living behind the Iron Curtain and in all probability remarried due to the enforced separation from his wife, relying explicitly upon a decision of Rabbi Yitzhak Elhanan Spektor and implicitly following the *mesorah* of Rabbi Mizrachi and other authorities,[40] Rabbi Elyashiv rules that the accrued benefit of "saving him from sin" may serve as grounds to employ *zakhin* even if the husband "stands and screams," even if the husband would fail to recognize "the spiritual good," the *zekhut* not to be in violation of the *herem* (excommunication) against polygamy.[41] In fact, Rabbi Elyashiv's proof that *get zikui* will be operative even in the wake of a husband's objection is learnt from the case of an apostate wife who refuses to receive a *get*.[42]

Despite the disparity between the biblical prohibition of adultery and the rabbinic ban against polygamy, Rabbi Elyashiv nevertheless released the woman from "*igun*." Lest one challenge the soundness of this *psak*, notwithstanding that there are authorities who claim bigamy is a rabbinic violation,[43] there are decisors who contend that transgressing the *herem* entails a biblical violation.[44] Even if it is open to debate whether the *herem* is operative after the fifth millennium (1240 CE), it may be viewed as a *minhag* (custom)[45] and it must be seen through the lens of a *neder* (vow) which is grounded biblically.[46] As such, implementing a *get zikui* ought to be effective.

However, other authorities such as Rabbi Yitzhak Yosef and the late Dayan H. Shlomo Sha'anan (in conversation with this author) disagree with our understanding (as well as others[47]) of the position of Rabbi Elyashiv. In their mind, *zakhin* is operative in Rabbi Elyashiv's case due to the fact that the husband appointed an agent though he subsequently passed away. As such it is clear that in fact the husband expressed an interest in giving a *get* to his wife. Had the husband failed to designate an

---

39. *Heikhal Yitzhak*, supra n. 30; *Kovetz Teshuvot*, supra n. 30.

40. See supra text accompanying notes 34–35, 39.

41. *Teshuvot Ein Yitzhak EH* 1:46; *Kovetz Teshuvot*, supra n. 30, subsection 11.

42. See *Rabbinic Authority*, vol. 3, 181, notes 21–22.

43. *Teshuvot ha-Ran* 38; *Teshuvot Noda be-Yehudah EH* 33, 77; *Teshuvot Hakham Tzvi* 117; *Teshuvot Maharam Schick EH* 4; *Teshuvot Maharsham* 1:21.

In fact, it is for this reason that Dayan Tzion Boaron refused (in an oral communication with this author) to accept the *psak* of Rabbi Elyashiv.

44. *Teshuvot Avodat ha-Gershuni* 53; *Teshuvot Divrei Rivot* 305; *Teshuvot Hatam Sofer EH* 1:2; *Teshuvot Divrei Hayyim*, vol. 2, *EH* 14.

45. *Darkhei Moshe Tur EH* 1:12, *Rema SA EH* 1:10.

46. *Otzar ha-Poskim EH* 1 (76).

47. Tzfat Regional Beit Din, supra n. 21.

agent, in their minds Rabbi Elyashiv would have refrained from invoking *zakhin*.[48]

Firstly, there is no indication from the context of Rabbi Elyashiv's ruling in subsection 11 of his *teshuvah* (responsum) that in fact he was addressing the case of a husband who had appointed an agent. Moreover, even if we would be dealing with this scenario, numerous *Poskim* contend that under such conditions once the agent dies there is no basis to employ *zakhin*.[49] Finally, in subsection 13 of the *teshuvah* Rabbi Elyashiv stresses that a *get* can be given either by the avenue of agency or via a *zekhut gamur*, an absolute unmitigated benefit.

Clearly even if one would adopt the minority view's interpretation of Rabbi Elyashiv's ruling that there is a basis to employ *zakhin* provided there was an appointment of an agent even if he subsequently died,[50] nonetheless, in a matter of *igun*, we would follow the majority opinion which would result in a leniency, namely the deploying of a *get zikui* in the circumstances where a *get* recalcitrant husband is transgressing the *herem* of Rabbeinu Gershom by engaging in a bigamous relationship based upon an improper *heter nissuin*.

Our foregoing presentation of the propriety of executing a *get zikui* for a husband who is transgressing the *herem* of Rabbeinu Gershom by marrying a second woman without giving a *get* to his first wife rests upon the following foundations:

1. *Zakhin mei-adam she-lo be-fanav* is operative in accordance with the rule of *zakhin le'adam she-lo be-fanav*.
2. The *mezakeh*, the one conferring the benefit such as a *beit din*[51] will communicate to the scribe that the husband ought to be divorced from his wife and the *beit din* will inform the witnesses that they ought to sign the *get* which has been prepared by the scribe. As such the *le-shemah* requirement is fulfilled.
3. The *mezakeh* is empowered to give the *get* to the wife.[52]
4. *Zakhin* will be effective even without the husband's prior *gilui da'at*

---

48. *Mishnat Yosef*, supra n. 14, 33; *Teshuvot ha-Rishon le-Tzion EH* 25.

49. *She'erit Yisrael*, supra n. 36; *Teshuvot Maharash Engel* 7:187; *Teshuvot Seridei Esh* 1:90; *Teshuvot Heikhal Yitzhak EH* 2:64; *Teshuvot Minhat Yitzhak* 1:48 (4). See M. Wygoda with H. Zafri, *Agency*, 787–788.

50. *Dvar Halakhah, miluim* 93, 122 in the name of Rabbi Meir Arik; *Iggerot Moshe EH* 1:117.

51. *Nekudot ha-Kessef YD* 305:10; *Pnei Yehoshua, Kiddushin* 42b, *Ketuvot* 11a; *Teshuvot Oneg Yom Tov, YD* 110; *Teshuvot Be'air Yitzhak, OH* 1:6.

52. *Birkat Shmuel, Kiddushin* 10 and 15 in the name of Rabbi Hayyim Soloveitchik; *Teshuvot Ahiezer* 1:29 (4).

that he desires to be divorced and/or despite the husband's objections.

5. One may employ *zakhin* provided there is a *zekhut gamur* to the husband that he ought to be divorced.

6. *Zekhut* may be defined by *halakhic* criteria rather than the subjective wishes of the husband, namely an absolute spiritual benefit such as the avoidance of sin.

Despite the fact that every foundation presented above was and continues to this very day to be fraught with *halakhic* controversy, we have shown here as well as elsewhere that there are authorities who will execute a *get zikui* under certain circumstances.[53] A review of the above six foundations shows that *zakhin* is a **halakhic fiction** that, if certain conditions are obtained, in effect empowers the *mezakeh* to accomplish whatever *Halakhah* mandates as the husband's responsibility vis-à-vis his involvement in the *get* process.

In the wake of contemporary instances where a husband receives an improper *heter nissuin* and proceeds to remarry a second wife without giving a *get* to his first wife, there is a *mesorah* (a tradition) of Rabbi Yosef Elyashiv, a renowned Torah scholar for Ashkenazic Jewry as well as a ruling handed down by Rabbi Shlomo Kahana which endorses these foundations and thus facilitates the execution of a *get zikui*, which in the process conveys a *zekhut*, namely a husband's avoidance of sin.[54]

Deciding *le-halakhah* (on a theoretical plane) as well as *le'ma'aseh* (as a practical judgment) between the competing arguments regarding the readiness to recognize the institution of *zakhin* as a means to save a husband from sin while simultaneously saving a wife from *igun* becomes the province of the *posek*, the decisor.

---

53. See *Rabbinic Authority*, vol. 3, 177–211.

54. Shlomo Kahana, *Sefer ha-Yovel Karnot Tzadik* in honor of Rabbi Menahem Schneersohn, 253, 255.

II Rabbinic Authority
The Reality

Chapter 8

Introduction

EXPLICITLY OR IMPLICITLY RELYING upon an Israeli *beit din* decision authored over thirty years ago,[1] a string of decisions have been handed down recently by three *battei din* (rabbinical courts) which are under the network of the Rabbanut, Israel's Chief Rabbinate (hereafter: Israeli *battei din*), which rule that in a situation of an *agunah* there is a well-trodden *mesorah*, tradition, that a *beit din* is empowered to coerce the husband to give a *get*.[2] In a case where a husband has opted out of the marriage by moving away from his spouse and by refraining from complying with his marital duties such as engaging in conjugal relations and providing material support for his wife and/or family, a situation of *"igun"* has been created by his refusal to give a *get*. Invoking *Rishonim* (early Jewish legal authorities) and *Aharonim* (later Jewish legal authorities) alike,[3] these *battei din* contend that under such conditions a *beit din* is empowered to coerce this husband to give a *get*.

---

1. *PDR* 13:264, 267–274 (= *Teshuvot Lev Aryeh* 23).

2. File no. 578173/1, Haifa Regional Beit Din, October 28, 2013; File no. 1066559/1, Yerushalayim Regional Beit Din, October 30, 2016 which can be accessed in *ha-Din ve-ha-Dayan* 45; File no. 865704/1, Tzfat Regional Beit Din, May 8, 2017.

According to some authorities, the issuance of a *get* coercion ruling results in the creation of a duty to heed the words of Torah scholars. See *Tosafot Rid, Gittin* 88b; *Teshuvot ha-Rid* 22; *Ohr Zarua* 1:754; *Kefiyah be-Get*, 20, 152–153. To state it differently, the issuance of a compulsory order is grounded in the *halakhah* of complying with a directive of a Torah scholar as well as the *halakhot* dealing with *gittin*.

3. *Teshuvot ha-Rosh* 32:9, 43:8,13; *Hiddushei ha-Ramban,Yevamot* 64a (second reply); *Teshuvot ha-Rashba* 1:693; *Teshuvot Maharam Alshakar* 73 in the name of Rosh; *Teshuvot Tashbetz* 2:68; *Rabbeinu Nissim on Rif, Kiddushin* 28a ("*kofin al midat Sedom*" – we coerce a *get* when a person acts improperly") *Teshuvot Maharhash* 4:49 in the name of Rashba; *Shitah Mekubetzet Ketuvot* 64a in the name of Ra'ah and Ritva, *Teshuvot ha-Rashbash* 46,383; *Teshuvot Ein Yitzhak* 2:62; *Teshuvot Maharashdam EH* 64 in the name of Maharam of Padua; *Tur SA EH* 154; *Rema SA EH* 154:3; *SA EH* 154:8–9; *Beit Shmuel, SA EH* 154:21; *Gevurat Anashim* 28.48 ("*ikar le'dina*");

Hokhmat Shlomo EH 154:21 in the name of *Rema EH* 154:21; *Teshuvot ha-Mabit* 1:76; *Teshuvot Avnei Nezer EH* 238:20; R. Amar, *Teshuvot Devar Shmuel EH* 44; *Teshuvot Zekan Aharon* 149; *Teshuvot Hakham Tzvi* 1, 31; *Hiddushei Hatam Sofer, Nedarim* 90a; Rabbi A. Eiger, *Derush ve-Hiddush*, 91(compare with his conclusion recorded on 91b) (Vilna ed.); *Teshuvot Nofet Tzufim* 116; *Pnei Yehoshua Ketuvot* 64 in the name of Rambam; *Hazon Ish EH* 108:11.

In File no. 847350/3, op. cit, argues *Dayan* U. Lavi that one of the cases for coercing a *get* is when a husband moves to another country and in effect he deprives his wife of intimate relations. To buttress his conclusion he invokes various rabbinic sources including the position of Rabbeinu Yeruham (*Sefer Meisharim*, Netiv 23, Helek 8) that if a couple is separated for a year and there are no hopes for marital reconciliation, a husband who is *get* recalcitrant ought to be coerced in giving it. See further, this writer's *Rabbinic Authority*, vol. 2, 203–208. In other words, should the circumstances require it; R. Lavi mandates *get* coercion regardless of whether a husband is living in another country or whether he is living separate from his wife in the same town. The common denominator in both scenarios is that the absence of conjugal relations and may we add the potential for the commission of sin propels the acute need to execute a *get* and as such dissolve the marital ties. Implicit in his conclusion is that Rabbeinu Yeruham is mandating *get* coercion as a practical solution to the problem of *igun.*

The same conclusion ought to equally apply to Rabbi Hayyim Pelagi's ruling (*Teshuvot Hayyim ve-Shalom* 2:35,112) that an eighteen month marital separation with no prospects for *shalom bayit,* marital reconciliation requires the imposition of *get* coercion should the husband refuse to give a *get.* Whether Rabbi Pelagi's holding refers to the meting out of actual physical coercion or only verbal persuasion is subject to debate amongst the Israeli rabbinical courts. See *PDR* 7:111–133, 11:206, 9:211–213, 12:206, 13:360, 362, 15:158–161.

The implicit conclusion in Rabbi Lavi's decision is that extended marital separation with its attendant absence of intimate relations (and sometimes spousal support) may serve as the sole justification rather than a *senif* (supporting argument) for the imposition of *get* coercion. In fact, there are recent decisions which subscribe to this position. See *Ateret Devorah* 2:89; File no. 523426/2, Haifa Regional Beit Din, September 1, 2014; File no. 849440/19, Tel Aviv-Yaffo Regional Beit Din, July 14, 2015; File no. 965579/2, Netanya Regional Beit Din, July 23, 2015; File no. 940783/13, Haifa Regional Beit Din, November 30, 2015; File no. 936936/2, Tel Aviv-Yaffo Regional Beit Din, December 5, 2016. In fact, centuries earlier, Beit Yosef concurs with Rabbeinu Yeruham that extended separation with no prospects for reconciliation can be grounds for *get* coercion even if the wife is unable to advance an *ilat gerushin,* a ground for divorce. See *Beit Yosef, Tur, EH* 77(end) s.v. *afeilu nidah*; Rabbi A. Eiger, *Derush ve-Hiddush*, Ketavim, 91. For additional earlier authorities who endorse Rabbeinu Yeruham's posture, see *Iyunim be-Mishpat EH* 262–266.

Cf. *Teshuvot ha-Rosh* 43:3, *Teshuvot ha-Rashba ha-Meyuhusot le-Ramban* 138, *Teshuvot ha-Rivash* 127, *Teshuvot Tashbetz* 2:8; *SA EH* 154:5, *Teshuvot ha-Radvaz* 4:1331; and *Bi'ur ha-Gra SA EH* 154:48, 50 and *Teshuvot Hakham Tzvi* 1 who contend that *get* coercion is applicable only in the cases explicitly stated in the Mishneh and Talmud that one can coerce a *get.* Since a husband's abandonment of his wife with the attendant consequences of the absence of intimate relations and providing support by moving to another country is neither mentioned in the Mishnah nor in

Seemingly, this ruling may address the *agunah* problem at least for the Jews who reside in *Eretz Yisrael*. As we know, in 1953, the *Knesset*, the Israeli parliament in the wake of a rabbinical court's determination that a husband be compelled to grant his wife a *get*, passed legislation which directed the district court upon application of the attorney general to imprison the recalcitrant spouse.[4] Clearly, the effectiveness of this solution to deal with the *agunah* problem is open to question due to the fact that despite the prolonged Israeli incarceration, Yihye Avraham, who refused to free his wife from the chains of "*igun*," died in jail after being imprisoned there for decades.[5] Or more recently, Tzviya Gorodetski, whose husband has been in prison for the last 17 years as he continues to refuse to give her a *get* as mandated by Israeli *battei din*. Nonetheless, in many instances the threat of or actual incarceration may serve as an incentive for a husband to give a *get*. The ineffectiveness of the solution of imprisonment to address the *agunah* problem in every instance is highlighted by two recent *battei din* decisions which rule that individuals incarcerated due to *get* recalcitrance may be viewed by Israeli criminal law as criminals and therefore subject to additional sanctions, sanctions which will not run afoul of the strictures of "*get me'useh*", a

---

the Talmud as grounds for *get* coercion, therefore there is no foundation to coerce a *get* under such circumstances. The assumption of this position is that the wife can decide whether to follow him and therefore coercion is inapplicable. However, if in fact the husband's departure is reflective of a marital breakdown and the prospects of marital reconciliation are nonexistent seemingly the above cited *Poskim* would concur that there are grounds for *get* coercion. However, since these authorities (except *Teshuvot ha-Rosh* 43:8, 13) insist that *get* coercion is only applicable to the instances mentioned in the Mishnah and Talmud; seemingly they would still remain steadfast in their posture to reject *get* coercion under such circumstances. However, if a couple is living separately and the woman has not received her *get*, some contend that the aforementioned authorities would agree that *get* coercion ought to be sanctioned. See *Teshuvot Zekan Aharon* 149. *Hakham Tzvi*, op. cit. contends that an *igun* situation ought to mandate a compulsion order.

For an additional reason why there ought to be grounds for a compulsory order of the *get* where there has been prolonged separation of the couple and there is an absence of conjugal relations is the concern that the wife may begin to live a life of promiscuity. For the factoring of this reason as grounds for a husband to give a *get*, see *Hayyim ve-Shalom*,op. cit.; *Teshuvot Masat Binyamin* 44; *Teshuvot Maharashdam* 56; *Teshuvot Hikekei Lev EH* 57; *Teshuvot Yabia Omer* 3, *EH* 20.

4. Rabbinical Courts Jurisdiction Law (Marriage and Divorce), 5713–1953, section 6.

5. See C.A. 220/67, 164/67, *Attorney General v. Yihye and Ora Avraham*, (1968), P.D. 22(1)29.

coerced *get*.[6] In fact, as noted in the *dayan's* dissenting opinion in one of these recent rulings,[7] if incarceration was ineffective during a span of seventeen years, being labeled a criminal with its attendant legal consequences such as mandating harsher conditions during his incarceration serves as no guarantee that a *get* will be forthcoming in the future from the husband.

The issue is whether other Israeli *battei din* will endorse these rulings that *igun* may serve as the basis for coercing a *get*? Firstly, as we know, a *get* must be executed with the consent of both the husband and wife. Should a husband refuse to give a *get*, a *beit din* cannot coerce him lest we create a situation of a *"get me'useh"*, a coerced writ of Jewish divorce. Should the wife remarry under such circumstances and should she sire a child from this relationship the offspring would be a *mamzer* (a *halakhic* bastard) due to the fact that the wife is still considered married to her first husband. In the event a *get* recalcitrant husband will be threatened with incarceration or be imprisoned and decides to give a *get* in order to avoid imprisonment, in pursuance to certain authorities the execution of *get* under such conditions would be null and void.[8] Yet there are some decisors who either argue that imprisonment is an indirect form of coercion and therefore it is *halakhically* permitted or that the conditions of incarceration nowadays are less severe than the ones found in earlier times and as such this measure is not to be viewed as form of coercion.[9]

Even if the consensus of other *battei din* is to align themselves with the posture that imprisonment of a recalcitrant husband does not create a *get me'useh*, we leave open the question whether the presence of *igun* as the singular ground for mandating *get* coercion would be acceptable in the eyes of most Israeli *battei din*.

To fully understand the significance of the aforementioned three Israeli *battei din* rulings both for the *Golah*, Diaspora as well as *Eretz Yisrael*, we need to briefly present some of the basic elements of *halakhic* divorce law. Whether a husband is *obligated* to give a *get* generally speaking hinges upon whether there exists an *ilat gerushin*, a ground for divorce. The *ilot gerushin* may be subdivided into two categories.

---

6. File no. 622918/9, Yerushalayim Regional Beit Din, May 29, 2017; File no. 846913/2, Haifa Regional Beit Din, June 12, 2017.

7. Yerushalayim Regional Beit Din, supra n. 6.

8. *Teshuvot ha-Rashba* 2:276; *Teshuvot ha-Rivash* 232; *Teshuvot Maharik shoresh* 63; *Teshuvot Masat Binyamin* 22; *Arukh ha-Shulhan EH* 134:22.

9. *Teshuvot ha-Radvaz* 4:157; *Teshuvot Kol Mevaser* 1:83; *Teshuvot Heikhal Yitzhak, EH* 1:1; *Teshuvot Yabia Omer* 3, *EH* 20 (35). For judgments which sanction indirect coercion, see this writer's *Rabbinic Authority*, vol. 1, 142–156.

One type of an *ilah* may relate to the inability of a wife to have conjugal relations with her husband due to the fact that he is afflicted by a contagious and/or dangerous disease or by dint of her revulsion of his body odor which is linked to his occupation.[10] On the other hand, a husband's inappropriate behavior may serve as a justification for divorce. For example, spousal rape, refusal to cohabitate with his wife, physical and/or emotional divorce of his wife, or refusal to financially support her may serve under certain conditions as a claim for coercing or obligating a husband to give a *get*.[11]

The question arises whether a couple who has separated for either one year[12] or for eighteen months[13] with no prospects for *shalom bayit*, marital reconciliation, can a *beit din* coerce or obligate the husband to give a *get* or is a *beit din* order to coerce or obligate a *get* limited to a party demonstrating that there exists an *ilat gerushin*? Though there are a few earlier authorities who either obligate (*le'hayev*) or are willing to coerce a *get* (*le'kefyat get*) under such circumstances,[14] nevertheless it remains a dispute amongst contemporary *rabbis* and *dayanim* whether you can obligate much less coerce a *get* under such conditions where there is no *ilat gerushin*.[15] Nonetheless, in the wake of no prospects for marital reconciliation there are *Poskim* who would sanction a *beit din's* right to render a judgment of "*mitzvah le-garesh*", a duty to divorce [16] in

---

10. *Ketuvot* 77a; *Yevamot* 65b.

11. *SA EH* 76:1,154:1, 6; *Rema, SA EH* 154:3.

12. Rabbeinu Yeruham, *Sefer Meisharim, Netiv* 23, *Helek* 8.

13. *Teshuvot Hayyim ve-Shalom* 2:35,112; *Iggerot Moshe* 4, *YD* 4 (15).

14. See supra notes 12–13.

15. For a list of some contemporary *dayanim* who would recognize grounds to obligate a *get* under these circumstances, see this writer's *Rabbinic Authority*, vol. 2, 206.

For decisors who contend that "a dead marriage of prolonged separation" *per se* will not serve as grounds to obligate a husband to give a *get*, see *Teshuvot Divrei Malkiel* 3:144–145; Y. Herzog, *Pesakim u-Ketavim* 7:124, 8:169; *Teshuvot Divrei Shmuel* 3:145; *Teshuvot Tzitz Eliezer* 6:2, 17:52, 67; *PDR* 1:162, 9:200, 211–213 (Rabbi S. Goren's opinion), 13:360, 362; File no. 4827-21-2, Beit Din ha-Rabbani ha-Gadol, July 3, 2005; File no. 059133397-21-1, Beit Din ha-Rabbani ha-Gadol, December 25, 2007 which can be found in *ha-Din ve-ha-Dayan* 18; File no. 288169/3, Netanya Regional Beit Din, October 20, 2010; File no. 982961/1, Netanya Regional Beit Din, August 9, 2016.

16. In other words, given that there is a concern for a *get me'useh* and therefore the *beit din* refrains from issuing a compulsion order or a decision to obligate a *get*, the *beit din* directs the husband to fulfill his duty to Hashem, God to divorce his wife. See Y. Herzog, "Apprehensions concerning an enforced *get*," (Hebrew) 1 *Hadarom* 4(1957) .

order to eliminate an *igun* situation.[17] Rendering such a judgment would allow a *beit din* to direct the community to initiate *harhakot*, measures which isolate religiously, socially and economically the *get* recalcitrant husband from the fellow Jews in his community.[18] On the other hand, in the wake of an extended separation as well as the absence of a husband's compliance with his marital duties, under such circumstances the afore-mentioned three Israeli *beit* din panels [as well as some others] would coerce a husband to give a *get*.

That being said, what are the prospects for an Israeli *dayan* who serves in the network of *battei din* under Israel's Chief Rabbinate to accept the aforementioned three recent rulings which coerce a *get* in the case of an *agunah* which would result in the husband's incarceration should he fail to comply with the *beit din's* order?[19] Even if the particular *dayan* subscribes to the view that "a dead marriage of prolonged separation" serves as a basis for a *beit din* to obligate a *get*, will he equally mandate *get* coercion under such conditions? Given that there are authorities who refuse to coerce under such conditions, one would expect that there is a concern for a *get me'useh* since there is no unanimity amongst the *Poskim* to sanction *get* coercion under these circumstances.In their mind, the presence of *halakhic* controversy regarding to imposing *get* coercion when a couple separates for an extended period of time and a husband's failure to comply with his marital duties preempts any fu-ture arbiter or *beit din* to mandate *get* coercion.[20] As we have shown elsewhere,[21] generally speaking Israeli *battei din* have refrained from rendering compulsory order judgments regarding matters dealing with *ilot gerushin* and would expect the adoption of an identical stance con-cerning the impropriety of rendering *get* coercion due to a situation of *igun*. In sum, despite the recent rulings regarding *get* coercion in the situation of *igun*, we leave as an open question whether these decisions will resonate with many of the other *dayanim*.Nothwithstanding some *Poskim* as well as a few contemporary Israeli *battei din* who have issued

---

17. *Beit Yosef, Tur EH* 154 in the name of Tashbetz; *Iggerot Moshe YD* 4:15(2).

18. See this writer's *Rabbinic Authority*, vol. 3, 291–293.

19. See supra n. 2

20. *Teshuvot ha-Rosh* 43:3; *Tur EH* 154 in the name of Rosh; *Rema SA EH* 154:21; *Darkhei Moshe, Tur SA* 154:14; *Teshuvot Maharbil* 3, 3:120; *Teshuvot Hatam Sofer EH* 1:116; *Gevurat Anashim* 45; *PDR* 2:188,193, 3:220,222,4:164,166. To understand the reason that one generally requires a *halakhic* consensus concerning coercing a *get* as a precondition to the imposition of *get* coercion by a *beit din*, see infra text accompanying n. 28 and this writer's *Rabbinic Authority*, vol. 3, 34–43.

21. See this writer's *Rabbinic Authority*, vol. 3, 43–54.

compulsion orders in the wake of extended marital separation and the attendant lack of prospects for marital reconciliation,[22] a *get* recalcitrant husband who has been separated from his wife for at least a year and has refused to provide for his wife and/or their children generally speaking does not await the possibility that an Israeli *beit din* may coerce him to give a *get* resulting in his imprisonment should he fail to comply with the *beit din's* judgment.

Nonetheless, this well-trodden *mesorah* that sanctions *get* coercion in the case of an *agunah*[23] may be significant regarding the ability of a *beit din* to void a marriage, in particular concerning the Jewish communities in the Diaspora. *Halakhah* has been characterized by many as *"torat hayyim,"* a teaching of life, and therefore dating back to the times of the Mishnah and Talmud, *Halakhah* has furnished the grounds for obligating or coercing a husband to give a *get* to his wife. With the issuance of these divorce judgments, it seems that the *beit din's* authority has been quite effective in ensuring *get* compliance both in Mishnaic and Talmudic times as well as in the Middle Ages. (Absent any historical studies regarding this matter, we are positing this conclusion.) As such, we can understand that there were very few medieval *halakhic* discussions of voiding a marriage by invalidating the propriety of the wedding ceremony, by invoking the techniques the techniques of *"kiddushei ta'ut"* (loosely translated: a mistaken marriage) and *"umdana demukhah"* (loosely translated: a major inference expressed by one person – hereafter: *umdana*) or by employing a *sefek sefeika de'dina* in order to void a marriage.[24]

However, if we fast forward to the age of Enlightenment and modern times where many civil governments refrained from allowing the Jewish communities to physically coerce Jewish husbands to give a *get,* we begin to learn from studying the *teshuvot*, the responsa, that there were increased instances of *bittul kiddushin*, voiding a marriage. In the wake of the absence of being able to apply coercive measures against a *get* recalcitrant husband for a few centuries, it is of no surprise to learn that some authorities teach us that under certain conditions the techniques of *kiddushei ta'ut* (loosely translated: a mistaken marriage) and *umdana*

---

22. See supra notes 3 and 15.

23. See supra notes 2–3.

24. For earlier discussions of these techniques, see this writer's *Rabbinic Authority*, vol. 3, 134–176, 231–269, 294–327. Additionally, see infra chapter 8.

(a wife's expectation in the marriage) ought to be applied by rabbinic authorities.[25]

Accordingly, the consequence of a judgment to compel the giving of a *get* means that *shotim* (flogging) as per certain decisors, social shunning such as imposition of a *herem* (excommunication) or imprisonment under certain conditions may be utilized to facilitate obedience to the *beit din's* directive. In the event that these methods as well as others would be unsuccessful or could not be used legally (and therefore *halakhically* is proscribed) then these authorities argue that one can investigate the merits of being *mevateil* the *kiddushin*, voiding the marriage. Clearly, in their opinion should a *beit din* arrive at a judgment which obligates a *get* which means that the husband will be verbally persuaded to give a *get* or a ruling which deems it is a *mitzvah*, a duty to give a *get* or it is recommended to give a *get*, then a *beit din* can pursue the possibility of being *mevateil* the *kiddushin*. As Rabbi Feinstein and others have pointed out one cannot pursue that avenue unless the *beit din* has tried to convince the husband to give a *get* by issuing one of the four types of divorce judgments which has been mentioned. See Mesorat Moshe (attributed to Rabbi Feinstein) 1, 419(5778). In all of our decisions presented in this

---

25. *Teshuvot Maharam of Rothenberg*, Cremona ed. 77 in the name of Ra'avyah; *Teshuvot Ein Yitzhak 1, EH* 24, Anaf 6, 38–39; *Teshuvot Devar Eliyahu* 48; *Iggerot Moshe EH* 1:79–80, 3:43 (end), 4:52; *Teshuvot Har Tzvi EH* 2:181; *Teshuvot Yabia Omer* 9, *EH* 38; *Tzal'ot ha-Bayit* 6; *Teshuvot Shoeil u-Meishiv*, Mahadura Kama 198; *Teshuvot Noda be-Yehudah*, Mahadura Kama *EH* 88, Mahadura Tinyana *EH* 80(end),135.

Implicit in this approach is that a scenario of *kiddushei ta'ut* inexorably leads to the conclusion that *get* coercion is the *halakhic* remedy. See *Beit Shmuel SA EH* 154:2. However, whereas Beit Shmuel fails to advance the argument that in the absence of being able to mete out coercion one may void the marriage (see *Har Tzvi*, op. cit. and *Kovetz Teshuvot* 4:152 in the name of the Beit Shmuel), in the wake of the absence of *get* coercion, the aforesaid *Poskim* endorse under certain conditions the solution of voiding a marriage.

The fact that the permissibility of invoking *kiddushei ta'ut* is contingent upon the absence of being able to apply coercive measures today should not be understood to communicate to other *Poskim* that Rabbi Feinstein, Rabbi Frank and the others will refrain from being *mevateil kiddushin* when *get* coercion is inapplicable. A reading of their responsa will indicate otherwise. For example, claims Rabbi Feinstein that a husband who fails to disclose prior to his marriage that he is gay or refuses to have children there are grounds to void the marriage based upon *kiddushei ta'ut* without examining the issue through the lens of whether this *ilat gerushin* of exhibiting *shoteh* (*halakhically* mentally dysfunctional) conduct is subject to *get* coercion. See *Iggerot Moshe EH* 4:13,113. To state it differently, in arriving at their respective judgments, various arguments were advanced in order to void a marriage. The matter of *get* coercion was not necessarily one of them.

chapter prior to deliberating whether there was a basis to void a marriage we obligated a *get* and in certain instances we directed the community to religiously, socially and economically isolate the husband should he fail to give a *get* to his wife. Namely we invoked *harhakot* (the isolating measures) of Rabbeinu Tam vis-à-vis the *get* recalcitrant husband.

Should a *beit din* issue a compulsion order to give a *get* but the husband still remained steadfast in terms of *get* recalcitrance or due to legal constraints a *beit din* was unable to render such a divorce judgment, nonetheless the fact that there were grounds to issue a compulsion order is *halakhically* significant. The import of coercing a *get*, as noted by Hagahot Maimoniyot, Ishut 25:1 and Teshuvot Heikhal Yitzhak 1:1 is that the husband's behavior which serves as the cause for coercion is to be categorized as either "grave" or entails "an injustice to the woman". In other words, a husband's failure to disclose this major defect gives credence to the wife's plea that this marriage ought to be deemed as a *mekah ta'ut*, a mistaken transaction and therefore a *beit din* may contend under certain conditions that a *get* ought to be coerced. Conversely, if a *beit din* decides that there is no basis to compel a *get*, the inference to be drawn is that the wife is capable of living with a husband who has a particular flaw which does not rise to the level of a mum *gadol*, a major defect. As such we understood the importance of ascertaining whether in fact there were grounds to void a marriage based upon *kiddushei ta'ut* which is predicated upon *makeh ta'ut* by investigating whether the husband's behavior would be an *ilat gerushin* which would be subject to *get* coercion.

To state it differently, the question of whether one may void a marriage, in accordance with these decisors who contend that the presence of a *mum gadol* justifies the issuance of a compulsion order,[26] entails a

---

26. See the opinions of Rabbi Yoel Sirkes, Shmuel Phoebus and and Rabbi Y. Elhanan Spektor as presented in File no. 870175/4, Haifa Regional Beit Din, December 29, 2014.

In our *beit din* decisions found in this chapter, we have adopted this approach. Consequently, we have invoked the decisors who mandated *get* coercion as relief in dealing with a particular *ilat gerushin*. In the absence of the ability to employ such relief under certain conditions we have been *mevateil* the *kiddushin*, voided the marriage. Given that generally speaking whether *get* coercion is an appropriate solution is frequently subject to debate, we have addressed below the propriety of endorsing the view that *get* coercion is to be sanctioned to the exclusion of others who oppose compulsion orders as an avenue of relief. See infra text accompanying notes 29–33.

Those aforesaid authorities who investigate the merits of voiding a marriage through the prism of the propriety of *get* coercion, how do they relate to the threshold question whether the *ilat gerushin* may be coerced by a *beit din* or not? To state it differently, if the *ilat gerushin* is subject to *get* coercion then one may investigate whether there are grounds to void the marriage due to the inability to compel the husband to give a *get.* On the other hand if the *ila* is not subject to *get* coercion an arbiter is proscribed from deliberating whether the conditions have been obtained in order to void the marriage, As such, the merits of voiding the marriage will be investigated through the prism of the appropriateness of compelling a *get* or not.

In some of the cases which we present in this chapter we are relying upon a *me'ut ha-Poskim* (a few authorities) who or a minority view that would coerce a *get.* Such a conclusion undermines the rule that if the majority of authorities coerce a *get,* one still must factor into consideration the minority opinion who refrains from coercing a *get* in order to avoid the strictures of a *get me'useh.*[27] Consequently, in a particular situation where there exists a minority view which prohibits *get* coercion, the rendering of a compulsion order would not be sanctioned by numerous authorities.[28] On the other hand, should the majority view

---

Talmudic presumption of *"tav le'meitav tan do mi-le-meitav armalu"* (lit. translated: better to live as two than to live alone)? Do they agree with Rabbi Y. Spektor that the aforementioned *hazakah,* presumption is inapplicable if one **cannot** coerce a *get?* See *Teshuvot Shoeil u-Meishiv,* Mahadura Kama 176. Clearly, Rabbi Y. Spektor and others concur with Rabbi Nathanson's position. *See Teshuvot Ein Yitzhak 1, EH 24(41); Teshuvot Birkat Retzeh 107; Teshuvot Ahiezer 27(4); Teshuvot She'eilot Moshe EH 2(59); Teshuvot Da'at Mordekhai 2:1; Iggerot Moshe EH 1:79.*

27. See supra text accompanying n. 20. Implicit in our presentation (text accompanying notes 28–29) is that the concept of *"da'at me'ut"* (a minority view) encompasses a view held by *me'ut ha-Poskim* or by one arbiter.

28. See *Tosafot, Yevamot* 64a, s.v. *yotzi; Tur EH* 154 in the name of *Piskei ha-Rosh, Yevamot* 6:11; *Rema,* supra n. 20; *Teshuvot Binyamin Ze'ev* 88; *Teshuvot Maharashdam YD* 146; *Teshuvot Re'em* 1:14; *Hatam Sofer,* supra n. 20; *Get Pashut,* Kelal 5(end); *Teshuvot Devar Yehoshua* 3, *EH* 30; *Teshuvot Sha'arei De'ah* 1:119 in the name of Ran. Cf. *SA EH* 154:21.In his ruling, he first states the majority opinion and then states as a *"yesh omrim"* (some say) the minority view. In accordance to Rabbi Malakhi ha-Kohen, when Shulhan Aruch formulates his ruling in such a fashion, it means that he is aligning himself with the first opinion, namely the view of the majority that imposition of *get* coercion is permissible. See *Yad Malakhi, Kelalei ha-Shulhan Aruch* 17.

The implicit assumption in our presentation is that the *halakhic* rule *"aharei rabbim le-hatot"* (follow the majority) applies not only if the authorities have debated the issue fact to face such as in a *beit din* proceeding but equally pertains to an intergenerational *halakhic* controversy. See *Teshuvot ha-Ran* 51; *SA EH* 154:21,*Rema,* ad. locum.; *Get Pashut, Kelal 1 in the name of Maharik, Mahara Sasson and Marharlbah; Teshuvot Ein Yitzhak 2, EH 2, 62; Teshuvot Mahariz Enzel 88; Teshuvot Hatan*

permit *get* coercion, in the case of emergency and a *igun* situation, one may rely upon their opinion and impose upon a husband to give a *get*.[29]

Clearly based upon the foregoing in non-*igun* situations frequently there would be no grounds to compel the giving of a *get*.

However, upon further reflection, there are two additional approaches which we have adopted which implicitly reject the aforementioned *mesorah* that the absence of *halakhic* unanimity regarding an issue preempts the possibility for an arbiter or a *beit din* to coerce a husband to give a *get*. Firstly, in a case where there are a few *ilot gerushin* such as a husband's refusal to provide support, being *"oveir al dat Yehudit,"* (transgressing the Jewish religion) and engaging in spousal battery, one is permitted to join all these *ilot gerushin* (grounds for divorce) together and coerce a *get*.[30]

Sofer EH 59; *Teshuvot Oneg Yom Tov* 168; *Teshuvot Devar Yehoshua* 3:30; *PDR* 4:166 (R. Elyashiv's opinion).

On the other hand, there are *Poskim* who may rely upon a minority view in order to coerce a *get*. For the basis for such an approach, see infra text accompanying notes 30 and 32.

29. In the wake of an emergency (*be-di'avad – post facto*) or a situation of *igun*, we may follow the majority opinion and impose *get* coercion. See *Teshuvot Ein Yitzhak* 2, *EH* 72, Hashmatot 63; *Beit Yosef, Tur EH* 147; *Teshuvot Beit Yosef,* Yibum 2 (*halitzah*); *Get Pashut,* Kelal 6 (end); *Teshuvot Oneg Yom Tov* 168; *Teshuvot Hayyim ve-Shalom* 1 *EH* 35; *Teshuvot Mahariz Enzel* 88; *PDR* 4:164,166 (Rabbi Elyashiv's opinion) = *Kovetz Teshuvot* 2:83. Cf. *Gevurat Anashim* 45.

30. For the propriety of joining different *ilot gerushin* (**in non-*igun* situations**) in order to permit a *beit din* to arrive at a judgment of *get* coercion, see *Teshuvot ha-Rosh* 35:1; *Teshuvot Beit Yosef,* Yibum 2; *Teshuvot ha-Rema* 96 in the name of Rabbi E. Ashkenazi; *Teshuvot Ne'eman Shmuel* 66; *Teshuvot Ein Yitzhak* 2, *EH* 35; *Teshuvot Hatan Sofer* 59; *Teshuvot Heikhal Yitzhak EH* 1:2, 3; *Hazon Ish EH* 69(23); *Teshuvot Yabia Omer* 3, *EH* 20(34); *Teshuvot Ateret Shlomo* 1:4(10); *PDR* 1:38, 3:12–13, 8:126; File no. 467862/1, Netanya Regional Beit Din, January 16,2011.

Conceptually, the above approach is based upon the fact that there is a *safek*, a doubt whether there are grounds to coerce a *get* which means we are dealing with a *safek d'oraita* (a biblical doubt) regarding the status of being an *eishet ish*, a married woman. In accordance to some decisors we can nullify the prohibition of *eishet ish* (the status of a married woman) if an arbiter or *beit din* can demonstrate that there is a *sefeik sefeika* (a double doubt) regarding what the *Halakhah* ought to be concerning this biblical matter.See *Sedei Hemed*, Get 30(6) and infra text accompanying n. 42. As such joining more than one *ilat gerushin* which is grounds for *get* coercion with at least one other which equally serves as a basis for a compulsion order one creates at least two *halakhic* doubts, a *sefeik sefeika* in a *d'oraita* matter of the prohibition of *eishet ish*. However, argues Rabbi Moshe Ibn Haviv that if the majority of decisors contend that there is no basis for *get* coercion such as in the case of spousal battery then a *safek* fails to emerge and consequently one cannot join this *ilat gerushin* with

Furthermore, in contradistinction to Rabbi Moshe Sofer's opinion and others,[31] even if there are authorities who refuse to coerce a *get*, one is obligated to comply with the rulings of the contemporary *beit din* or arbiter should there be a mandate for *get* coercion.[32] For example whether a particular *ilat gerushin* such as a husband who engages in spousal rape or battery is subject to *get* coercion is generally speaking the

---

another. See *Get Pashut* 120(26). On the other hand, should *me'ut ha-Poskim* (a few decisors) rather than a minority view of one mandate *get coercion*, then we can join *ilot gerushin*. Therefore, given that *me'ut ha-Poskim* sanction *get* coercion for example in the case of spousal battery, a *safek* has been created and should it be joined with another *ilat gerushin* which is subject to *get* coercion a compulsion order is permitted. See Rabbi Landau, *Sefer Safek Melakhim*, 11:67 and infra chapter 8e.

Furthermore, we should note that there are authorities who will join even an *ilat gerushin* which is subject to compulsion by dint of a **minority opinion which has been rejected by *halakhic* authorities** to another *ilat gerushin* which is subject to *get* coercion. On the other hand, a minority opinion which has been not subject to *halakhic* debate and deliberation will not be construed as creating a *safek*. See *Teshuvot Zivhei Tzedek* 2, 35:158; *Teshuvot Me'il Shmuel* 11(end).In fact, numerous *Poskim* who implement the *sefek sefeika de'dina* to trump the *hezkat eishet ish* (the status of a married woman) do not qualify that the *safek* must emerge from a dispute where the opinions are *shaqul*, equally balanced with each other. As such, even if there is a debate where a minority view mandates that a particular *ilat gerushin* is subject to compulsion and normative *Halakhah* rejects this minority opinion a bonified *safek* emerges which may be joined to another *safek* emerging from another *ilat gerushin*. See infra n. 44. For additional *Poskim* who affirm the effectiveness of the *sefek sefeika de'dina* under these circumstances, see *Teshuvot Yabia Omer* 7, EH 6 (5–7).

Cf. others who contend that the *beit din* procedure of joining *ilot gerushin* in order to coerce a *get* is permitted on the condition that we are dealing with **an *igun* situation**. See *Sedei Hemed Ma'arekhet Get*, 30:6.

Therefore, as we explained in light of the fact that *get* coercion is an unavailable *halakhic* remedy in the *Golah*, consequently under certain conditions we may void the marriage.For cases where we have advanced more than one well-established *ilat gerushin* (ground for divorce) to mete out *get* coercion, we have followed the above *mesorah*,tradition. See infra chapter 8c, e and g.

Cf. others such as *Teshuvot Oneg Yom Tov* 167 and *Teshuvot Havot Da'at* 110 who argue that since we are dealing with permitting a prohibition of *eishet ish*, a married woman in the case of *sefek sefeika* on biblical grounds we are required to act stringently and therefore refrained from employing a *sefek sefeika* to trump *hezkat eishet ish*.

31. See supra text accompanying n. 20.

32. See *Teshuvot Ein Yitzhak* 2, EH 35; *Sedei Hemed, Gerushin* 1:15; *Heikhal Yitzhak EH* 1:2; *Teshuvot Har Tzvi EH* 2:183:7. Alternatively, in the wake of a husband's recalcitrance to abide by a *beit din's* decision to *obligate* him to give a *get* to his wife, a *beit din* is empowered to *coerce* him to give a *get* due to his failure to abide by "the words of Torah scholars," i.e. complying with a *beit din's* ruling. See *Teshuvot Yaskil Avdi* 6, *EH* 96.

subject of *halakhic* debate. Therefore, even if the contemporary arbiter's posture does not reflect the view of others who reject *get* coercion under such circumstances, his ruling does not run afoul of the strictures of a *get me'useh* provided that his position is grounded in an earlier *Posek's* view that mandates *get* coercion in such a situation. Another example where one can rely upon a contemporary ruling is where a husband fails to disclose a *mum gadol*, a major defect prior to the marriage and his conduct is deemed a case of *kiddushei ta'ut* which generates a situation of a *safek kiddushin* (loosely translated: a doubtful marriage on rabbinic grounds[33]) which in pursuance to certain decisors mandates that the *beit din* issue a compulsion order regarding the giving of the *get*.[34] To state

---

33. The concept of *safek kiddushin* is not a by-product of the application of the rule *"safek d'oraita le-humra"* (concerning a biblical matter we rule stringently) and consequently we coerce or obligate a *get* on biblical grounds should the couple desire to become divorced. The implication of this notion of *safek kiddushin* is that we reinstate the original *hazakah*, the presumption namely that the woman is now construed as a *penuyah*, a single woman. In other words, should a *safek* pertaining to the *kiddushin* emerge, from a biblical perspective she is viewed as a *penuyah* and she may remarry without receiving a *get* from her husband. However due to the fact that we are dealing with a *devar she'be'ervah* (lit: a matter of sexuality) on *rabbinic* grounds *Halakhah* mandates that she receive a *get* from her husband before she is permitted to remarry. See *Ran*, on Alfasi, *Kiddushin* 5b; *Teshuvot Maharashdam EH* 11,207; *Teshuvot Maharit* 1:138; *Teshuvot Maharik*, shoresh 169; R. Amarlieo, *Teshuvot Kerem Shlomo EH* 24(end). Cf. *Teshuvot Mahari ibn Lev* 1:17; *Pri Megadim YD* 110 (end) Kelalei Sefek Sefeika.

Moreover, in the event there is a case of *kiddushei ta'ut*, there emerges the *hezkat penuyah* biblically and we are not concerned rabbinically for *devar she'be'ervah* and she is free to remarry without receiving a *get* from her husband. See *Teshuvot Maharsham* 8:239; R. Boaron, *Teshuvot Sha'arei Tzion* 3, *EH* 4:5. Cf. other *Poskim* who contend that in a case of *kiddushei ta'ut* there are grounds only to coerce the husband to give a *get*. Voiding the marriage is not an option. See *Beit Shmuel SA EH* 154:2; *PDR* 1:65, 74 (R. Elyashiv's opinion).

For the definition of a *devar she'be'ervah* as either referring to any testimony that will change the status of the person in terms of a prohibition, is linked to a matter of incest or relates to permission to remarry or become divorced, see R. Shkop, *Sha'arei Yosher*, Sha'ar 1, Chapter 10, *Teshuvot Rabbi Akiva Eiger* 124–125 and *Iggerot Moshe YD* 227:5.

34. *Teshuvot Maharam of Rothenberg*, Cremona ed. 77 in the name of Ra'avyah; *Ohr Zarua* 761 in the name of Rabbeinu Simha; *Teshuvot Maharah Ohr Zarua* 126 in the name of Ramah,170; *Sefer Beit ha-Behirah, Kiddushin* 65a; *Kesef Mishneh, MT, Ishut* 4:6; *Teshuvot Maharil Diskin*, Pesakim 48; *Teshuvot Maharashdam EH* 12 in the name of Rashba.

Cf. See *Shitah Mekubezet, Ketuvot* 72b in the name of Rivash and Maharit; *Teshuvot ha-Rashbash* 574; *Teshuvot ha-Radvaz* 1115; *Teshuvot Mahari ibn Lev* 1:18; *Hazon Ish, Ketuvot* 69:23.

it differently, even though there are others who disagree and advance the opinion that there is no basis for *get* coercion for a *safek kiddushin* such as a case of *kiddushei ta'ut*,[35] nonetheless since the contemporary arbiter rules in accordance to the opposing view his judgment does not run afoul of the strictures of a *get me'useh*.

In short, a contemporary arbiter's or *beit din's* ruling which will mandate *get* coercion either concerning an *ilat gerushin* or in a case of *kiddushei ta'ut* will suffice in order to avoid creating a *get me'useh*.[36]In the event there is a basis to apply coercion in a particular case, given that in modern times we cannot implement coercive measures in the Diaspora there may be grounds under certain conditions to void the marriage based upon *kiddushei ta'ut* [37]and/or *umdana*.[38]

In the wake of the three Israeli rulings (as well as a few others) which we cited at the beginning of our introduction to this chapter should a *beit din* encounter a case of *igun* and subscribe to the *mesorah* that we can coerce a *get* if the wife is an *agunah*, we now have another avenue to utilize to void a marriage under certain conditions. In other words, *under certain conditions rabbinic authorities are not only voiding a mar-*

According to Beit Shmuel, there is a *safek kiddushin* which requires *get* coercion in a case of *kiddushei ta'ut* on the condition that the husband *intentionally* failed to disclose a *mum gadol* prior to the marriage. See *Beit Shmuel SA EH* 154:2,117:24. Cf. *Beit Shmuel SA EH* 48:2.

35. *Teshuvot Maharshal* 25 in the name of Rashba; *Teshuvot Lehem Rav* 24; *Teshuvot Maharshakh* 1:22 in the name of Rabbi Bassan; *Teshuvot Divrei Rivot* 378.

36. See infra cases 8d and 8h.Clearly, endorsing this *mesorah*, tradition would equally serve as the grounds for imposing *get* coercion in infra chapter 8c, e, f and g.

Whether one requires a *beit din* composed of three arbiters or one arbiter to coerce a *get* is subject to dispute. See this writer's *Rabbinic Authority*, vol. 3, 12, n. 3.

37. Interestingly enough, in a case of *kiddushei ta'ut* where one does not require a *get* but authorities have decided to be stringent and mandated one, some authorities claim that one can apply *get* coercion. See *Ohr Zarua, Teshuvot* 360–361; *Teshuvot Avnei Nezer EH* 176:7 in the name of Rosh, Rivash and Maharit.

In short, for those authorities who require that *get* coercion be a prerequisite prior to engaging in voiding a marriage (see supra text accompanying n. 25) the grounds for the the coercion can either be due to the fact that the particular *ilat gerushin* or a combination of *ilot gerushin* dictate *get* coercion (see supra notes 30 and 32).

Alternatively, It may be contingent upon the position that the situation of *kiddushei ta'ut* mandates *get* coercion (as advanced by the above cited *Poskim*) or is based upon the fact that the woman is an *agunah*, namely a wife's extended separation from her husband and her husband's refusal to fulfill his duties to engage in conjugal relations and support which propels a ruling of *get* coercion (see supra text accompanying notes 1–3). See infra chapter 8f and 8g.

38. See supra text accompanying n. 25.

riage if the ilat gerushin (or a combination of ilot) dictates that coercion ought to be applied against a get recalcitrant husband or due to the fact that a case of kiddushei ta'ut generates a safek kiddushin which mandates get coercion but equally voiding the marriage may transpire should the wife become an agunah where get coercion is an impossibility.[39] In the cases presented in this chapter, all three arguments have been advanced as grounds for issuing compulsion orders against a husband.

In sum, in light of the contemporary inability to implement *get* coercion in *Eretz Yisrael* and in the *Golah*, (except for Morocco), our foregoing presentation of various cases where a marriage was voided due to deploying the means of *kiddushei ta'ut* and/or *umdana* is either due to the existence of an *ilat gerushin* claim (or the existence of more than one *ilat gerushin* in a particular case[40]) which is subject to *get* coercion, in light of the fact that we are dealing with a *safek kiddushin* and/or due to the fact that the wife is an *agunah* who is entitled that a *beit din* will impose a compulsory order upon the husband to give a *get.*[41]

In contradistinction to investigating the merits of *bittul kiddushin* by examining the *ilat gerushin* whether it justifies a compulsion order as aptly noted by *Dayan* Binyamin Be'eri argues that even if a particular *ilat gerushin* fails to permit a *beit din* to impose *get* coercion, nonetheless should the defect be a *mum gadol*, a major flaw, there may still be grounds fo voiding the marriage due to *kiddushei ta'ut.*[42]

Moreover, a review of numerous *teshuvot* will demonstrate upon addressing the merits of voiding the marriage only occasionally a *Posek* will advance argumentation that the particular *ilat gerushin* under review dictates *get* coercion.[43]

---

39. See supra text accompanying notes 1–3, 33–34.Concerning the grounds for voiding the marriage whereby the wife becomes an *agunah* and *get* coercion fails to be an option is based upon the deployment of the *umdana* "I never would have married him knowing that I would remain an *agunah* forever". See *Teshuvot Hut ha-Meshullash* 3:5; *Teshuvot Pithei She'arim, Sheilot u-Teshuvot* 32. This *umdana* has been utilized as a *senif*, a supporting argument accompanied by another reason(s) rather than as a sole justification to void the marriage. Cf. *Iggerot Moshe EH* 1:162(*halitzah*).

Additionally, if the constellation of facts in a particular case generates a *sefek sefeika de'dina* there will be a basis to void the marriage. See infra text accompanying notes 42–45.

40. See supra text accompanying n. 30.

41. See supra text accompanying notes 25–40.

42. See Haifa ruling, supra n. 26.

43. See supra n. 25. For the application of this approach see infra chapter 8d, text accompanying n. 17.

The effectiveness of the various avenues to void a marriage (i.e. *kiddushei ta'ut* and *umdana*) will be shown in the cases examined below and will be demonstrated in one of two ways: Firstly, we will show based upon a scrutiny of the facts the ability of a *beit din* to apply a particular technique to void the marriage. Prior to arriving at this conclusion, we will demonstrate that there is a basis to impose *get* coercion for the particular *ilat gerushin* under consideration and/or advance argumentation that the particular *ila* serves as a ground for being *mevateil kiddushin* despite the fact that it is not subject to *get* coercion.

Secondly, in advancing a *mesorah* which instructs us that even though there are *Poskim* who reject the implementation of one or all of these techniques to be *mevateil kiddushin*, void the marriage; yet depending upon the facts of the case we may still be able to void the marriage by factoring the opposition's stance into arriving at a *psak din*, a decision to voiding the marriage.

How does a *beit din* or a rabbinic authority void a marriage based upon recognition of those authorities who **reject** voiding it? With the establishment of a *halakhic* marriage, there emerges the *hazakah*, the presumption of an *eishet ish*, the status of a married woman which renders both spouses subject to various *issurim*, prohibitions including sexual ties to a third party. As noted by some *Poskim*, if there is *sefek sefeika*, a double doubt regarding what the *Halakhah* ought to be, one can permit certain leniencies concerning certain marital and divorce matters even though there is a *hazakah* of an *eishet ish*.[44] For example, given the circumstances of a particular case there may be a *halakhic* dispute whether one can void a marriage based upon *kiddushei ta'ut* and *umdana*. As such we have *sefek sefeika de'dina* (a double doubt what

---

44. For the effectiveness of a *sefek sefeika* in *Halakhah* to trump *hezkat eishet ish* in certain marital and divorce contexts, see M. Yerushalamski, *Teshuvot Minhat Moshe EH* 11; M. Yerushalamski, *Teshuvot Be'air Moshe, Kuntres Binyan Yerushalayim* 18. For additional sources, see infra n. 47. In effect, in a situation of *safek* (in our case a *sefek sefeika*) we do not change her original status, namely that she was a *penuyah*, a single woman. See *Pri Hadash, YD* 110, Kelalei Sefek Sefeika. For the parameters of this technique, see supra n. 30.

For the employment of a *sefek sefeika de'dina* emerging from a *pegam*, an impropriety in the marriage ceremony accompanied by circumstances which raise the phenomenon of *kiddushei ta'ut* which result in allowing a woman to remarry without receiving a *get*, see *Teshuvot Beit Av* 7, *Teshuvot Ezrat Avraham EH* 28:3.

Even though generally speaking the prohibition of *eishet ish* means that we are concerned to rule stringently (see *Tosafot Kiddushin* 50b; *Teshuvot Tashbetz* 1:130, 4:129; *Teshuvot ha-Rashba* 1:1234; *Rema, SA EH* 27:4; *Teshuvot ha-Radvaz* 4:129,7:39) nonetheless, the invoking of *sefek sefeika de'dina* trumps the *hazakah* of *eishet ish*.

the *Halakhah* ought to be). Firstly there is a *halakhic safek* whether one can employ *kiddushei ta'ut* as a vehicle to void the marriage. Secondly, there is a *halakhic safek* whether one can deploy *umdana* as a technique to void a marriage.In sum; there are two doubts *(sefek sefeika)* whether one can *halakhically* utilize these two avenues to void a marriage. In other words the two *halakhic* – legal doubts are linked to the same issue, namely to voiding a marriage.[45]

The emerging question is whether the *sefek sefeika de'dina* will be grounds to void the marriage and thus transforms the wife from a *hezkat eishet ish* (presumptively a married woman) to a *hezkat penuyah* (presumptively a single woman) where a *get* will not be required on rabbinic grounds ? Nothwithstanding some authorities who contend that she continues to retain her *hezkat eishit* either due to the fact that *sefek sefeika de'dina* is ineffective to nullify the *hazakah* or they reject in principle that there is a *sefek* concerning voiding a marriage,[46] implicit in the above approach is their alignment with numerous *Poskim* who argue that in fact a *sefek sefeika de'dina* reinstates the original *hazakah* of being a single woman.[47]

---

45. *Kereti u-Feleti*, Beit Hasafek. Cf. *Shakh, SA YD* 110:11–13. On the other hand, claims Rabbi Yosef Ibn Lev that one can employ *sefek sefeika de'dina* regarding two different issues. See *Teshuvot Mahari ibn Lev* 3:41.

46. For those who reject *sefek sefeika de'dina* as a vehicle to void a marriage, see *Tosafot Bava Batra* 23b in the name of Rashbam; *Mishneh le-Melekh,Tumat Tzara'at* 2:1; *Avnei Milluim* 27:8(18); *Knesset ha-Gedolah, YD* 18, Hagahot ha-Tur 3, 28, Hagahot ha-Tur 3; *Pri Megadim, YD* 384:18; *Sha'arei Yosher*, Sha'ar 2, Perek 9.

On the other hand, due to the fact that the Talmud, Rambam, Tur and Shulhan Aruch do not sanction voiding a marriage, contends Rabbi Yosef Henkin that one cannot even state that there is a *safek* of *kiddushei ta'ut*. See Perushei Ibra, 43. Consequently, if in a particular case there is a *sefek* if one implements an *umdana*, one cannot argue that there is a second *sefek* regarding *kiddushei ta'ut* and therefore void the marriage. In the eyes of Rabbi Henkin there can never be a *sefek* concerning *kiddushei ta'ut*. To state it differently, in accordance to the Talmud and the classical restatements of *Halakhah*, for Rabbi Henkin a wife requires a *get me'd'oraita* (biblically) in a case of divorce including a situation of *kiddushei ta'ut*.

Alternatively, there may be no *safek* due to the fact that the *sefek sefeika de'dina* may be inapplicable where the particular *halakhic* dispute in question entails a majority opinion that is stringent. See supra n. 30.

47. *Teshuvot Oneg Yom Tov* 142 in the name of Rambam,70; *Ran, Kiddushin* 5b; *Teshuvot Torat Hesed of Lublin, OH* 15:4; *Teshuvot Hikrei Lev, YD* 1:111; *Teshuvot Rabbi Akiva Eiger*, Mahadura Kama 36; *Teshuvot Maharit EH* 18,138; *Tumim* 34:27; *Teshuvot ha-Mabit* 1:49; *Teshuvot Ranah* 1:68; *Get Pashut, Gittin* 129 (13); *Teshuvot Beit Yitzhak EH* 1:92 (end); *Teshuvot Ein Yitzhak EH* 1:38, 62:12,2:25; Rabbi Landau, *Sefer Sefeikot Melakhim*, 10:9; *Teshuvot Heikhal Yitzhak* 1 *EH*, 2:9; *Teshuvot Yabia Omer* 7, *EH* 6:5–8, 8, *EH* 3 (16), 9, *EH* 20(4); File no. 1126792/1, Netanya Regional

Consequently, in regard to *bittul kiddushin*, voiding a marriage we are invoking the *mesorah*, the tradition that a *sefek sefeika de'dina* regarding what the *Halakhah* ought to be is effective to trump a *hezkat eishet ish*. For example in case 8c there is a controversy whether *kiddushei ta'ut* is a valid technique to void a marriage.[48] As such, there emerges a *safek*, a doubt whether voiding a marriage in such a fashion is *halakhically* proper. Moreover, there is a second *safek* in that case whether there are grounds to void a marriage based upon the deployment of an *umdana*.[49] Given that in an *igun* situation, we are dealing with the inability of authorities to procure *get* compliance, therefore under such circumstances we must characterize the matter as a *bedi'avad*, a *post-facto* situation and we must seek a *halakhic* solution.[50] In light of the aforementioned *mesorah*, when there exists a *sefek sefeika de'dina* whether certain techniques may be implemented to void a marriage, the *sefek sefeika* is effective against the *hezkat eishet ish* and the wife has a *hezekat penuyah*. Therefore under certain conditions the marriage may be voided such as we ruled in case 8c.

In short, as we will read in this chapter there are four techniques which can be implemented under certain conditions (e.g. an *igun* situation) and in light of certain facts may serve to be *mevateil kiddushin*, void a marriage: *the presence of a sefek sefeika de'dina, discovering a pegam, a halakhic impropriety in the seder kidddushin ve'nissuin, the marriage ceremony, a husband who intentionally or unintentionally engages in misrepresentation and/or fails to disclose prior to marriage a major defect ("kiddushei ta'ut"), and a major expectation that the wife desired at the time of the marriage ("umdana demukhah") which failed to materialize during the course of the marriage.*

Beit Din, October 1, 2017.

Others contend that generally speaking one cannot validate the employment of a *sefek sefeika de'dina* (see supra n. 46); however, in a case of *igun* it is permissible. See *Minhat Moshe*, op. cit. in the name of Radal. Some claim that the deployment of this double doubt is contingent upon the fact that the *halakhic* controversy is evenly balanced between the authorities, namely some are lenient and others are stringent. However if the majority of *Poskim* argue stringently one cannot utilize the *sefek sefeika*. See *Get Pashut* 120(26). See further supra n. 30.

48. See this writer's *Rabbinic Authority*, vol. 3, 140, n. 8, 141, n. 10.

49. See infra chapter 8c notes 40 and 53 and infra chapter 8f notes 29, 47–48.

50. *Rema, SA EH* 169:12; *Teshuvot Masat Binyamin* 44, 98; *Helkat Mehokeik SA EH* 17:31; *Pithei Teshuvah SA EH* 17: 72; *Teshuvot Re'em* 1:36; *Teshuvot Sha'arei Tzion EH* 2:15. The aforementioned *mesorah* is predicated equally upon circumstances which were viewed as a *bedi'avad* situation. See *Minhat Moshe and Be'air Moshe,* supra n. 44.

Finally, whether a decision which voids a marriage requires an endorsement of "a second opinion(s)" is a subject of controversy. As we analyzed elsewhere,[51] though there are a few renown and well respected *Aharonim* (later decisors) such as Maharam of Lublin, Rabbi Hayyim Ozer Grodzinsky, Rabbi Avraham K. Shapiro, and Rabbi Michal Epstein who mandate such a requirement inorder to avoid in the words of *Dayan* Avraham Sherman the transgression of "the *issur* of *eishit eish* (the prohibition of a married woman to marry another Jewish man – AYW) and to avoid the proliferation of bastards",[52] the majority of *Poskim* view it as a *nohag*, a practice which centuries earlier addressed the classical *agunah* whose husband's whereabouts are unknown and subsequently in contemporary times was adopted by some authorities in dealing with marriage and divorce in general and voiding a marriage in particular. Finally, should a *Posek* issue a ruling entailing the voiding a marriage which is contingent upon receiving outside rabbinic approval, clearly as authorities have noted that another *Posek* may rely upon this ruling even if the decision does not receive approval.[53]

---

51. See this writer's *Rabbinic Authority*, vol. 3, 256–262.

52. File no. 6122-21-1, Beit Din ha-Rabbani ha-Gadol, May 10, 2009. See also, A. Sherman, "The authority of *gedolei ha-dor* in matters of personal status," (Hebrew) 30 *Tehumin* 163 (5770).

53. *Teshuvot Hikekei Lev EH* 57; *Teshuvot Ohel Yitzhak Hasid YD* 16; *Teshuvot Yabia Omer* 5, *EH* 18(8).

A. THE VALIDITY OF THE MARRIAGE OF A JEWISH WOMAN TO A *MUMAR*, AN APOSTATE.

The facts of the case

At the hearing, Judy began her presentation by stating that during the one and a half years of knowing Michael, he was a successful day trader. He was happy and fun to be with and quite bright. Judy as well as her children of her first marriage loved to be with him. Shortly before she married him, Judy entered into Michael's home and found him acting strangely. He told her that he had taken a sleeping pill called Ambien which can produce some bizarre side effects. He promised never to take it anymore. During the period that she knew him, he never told her about any medication that he was taking. However, shortly before the wedding, Michael did mention that he had suffered from depression years ago but presently neither was depressed nor taking medication for it. After Michael's disclosure, she felt that she would be able to handle the situation and proceeded to marry him.

A few months into the marriage, Michael began to exhibit signs of depression. He would lie on the recliner all day and do nothing, frequently sleeping during the daytime. At that time, he lost significant sums of money in the market which led him to be further depressed and dysfunctional. He was dirty and would wear dirty clothes during the day. Upon Judy's return from work, she found the house a wreck. Suddenly, he would cry and exhibit unwarranted outbursts of anger. There were various types of pills including anti-depressants which were prescribed for him in 2012 and 2013. Judy did not know whether his erratic behavior was caused by taking the medications or by refusing to take the medications. Judy had never observed such behavior during their period of engagement.

In contrast to Judy's presentation, Michael responded to her claim statement by informing us in writing that he admitted to being predisposed to depression and had adult attention deficit disorder and was on disability due to his depression. In Michael's words, "My depression and lack of career ambition were part of our ongoing conversation starting not long after we began being in each other's lives well into our marriage." In fact, Michael contends that Judy escorted him to a doctor where the physician informed her that he was suffering from depression. Moreover, whereas, at the hearing Judy told us that they were dating for a one and half years prior to their marriage, Michael wrote in an e-mail during the summer of 2015 *(me'siach lefe tumo* – innocently) that they were in a relationship for six and half years and recently wrote they were "in a relationship for nearly six years," and in certain periods when her children were with her first husband who said in his words "we practically lived with each other." Moreover, he wrote that they were together for three and a half years and Michael alleges that Judy insists it was 2.5 years. Upon reading Michael's reply to her claim statement, Judy informed us that she knew Michael for four and a half years and argued that she had no idea (as well as no experience) of the ramifications of someone who suffers from manic depression and therefore chose to marry him.

Implicitly concurring with Michael's representation, a health care professional who provided therapy to Judy told us that she was "emotionally compromised" and therefore was unable to discern that he was acting in an abnormal fashion.

Finally, Judy alleges that prior to the wedding Michael transgressed the Shabbat, did not observe the laws of *kashruth* and had fights with him when he brought nonkosher food into the house. Her allegation concerning his Shabbat transgression was corroborated by six individuals, his consumption of nonkosher food was corroborated by two individuals, and two of Judy's friends informed us that he was respectful of Judy's right to keep a kosher home, though one of the two women admitted to us that the respect may have disappeared with their deteriorating marriage. One individual who knows Michael for over two decades witnessed on innumerable occasions Michael being *"mehalail Shabbat"* by driving his car, digging and planting in his front lawn, and occasionally mowing his grass on Shabbat. Two neighbors who knew him for over a decade have seen Michael leaving his house in a car as well as mowing his lawn on Shabbat. Another individual told us that after the family Shabbat lunch meal was finished; Michael would proceed to engage in planting in his backyard. Another individual told us that sometimes he would sit at the Shabbat lunch table and sometimes would get up and go to work at his computer. A third individual as well as one of the two individuals mentioned above observed him many times coming out of his car with bags from McDonald's which led them to believe that he doesn't keep kosher.

Contrary to the above representation, Michael insists that out of respect for his wife, he never brought non-kosher food into their home. Such a representation implicitly tells us that in fact he consumed non-kosher food. Michael resided in the midst of an Orthodox Jewish community for 25 years and on his own block, over 75% of the block was composed of Orthodox Jewish families, and thus more than ten Orthodox adult Jewish males who reside in the community know of his violation of Shabbat. For decades, every Shabbat the Orthodox Jews who lived in the neighborhood, including some who were next door neighbors, were privy to his public conduct. In fact, one of his neighbors claims that Michael intentionally waited for him to pass his house prior to engaging in his non-Shabbat activities. Two neighbors told us that a few individuals attempted to influence Michael "to change his ways" but it was to no avail.

His non-Orthodox Jewish lifestyle dates back to his family upbringing. His parents were in principle against the practice of any religion and only civilly married. He never received any Jewish education including Talmud Torah classes and never had a *bar mitzvah*. All his siblings and many of his cousins intermarried. Whether Michael wanted to cremate his father upon his demise or in fact had bought a plot in a Jewish cemetery for his father years before meeting Judy is subject to a difference of opinion between the couple. However, Judy additionally mentioned that her mother-in-law was cremated by Michael and this representation went unchallenged by Michael. Michael was an opponent of any organized religion and in his wife's words, "on most days he did not believe in God." Even on Rosh Hashanah and Yom Kippur he did not attend synagogue services. As one individual told us, in the few times that he attended a synagogue service, Michael came in wearing shorts. When his neighbor who was a Chabad rabbi persuaded him to a don a pair of *tefillin*, Judy informed us that he allegedly thought the incident was humorous. One Orthodox Jew, one Orthodox rabbi and one Orthodox Jewish woman told us that Michael is very bright and an intellectual and read various books in philosophy dealing with religion and philosophically became an atheist or "almost an atheist" who engaged in philosophical discussions for the sake of advancing his position rather than being open to hear contradictory views to his avowed position for the sake of changing his position. In short, their presentation corroborates Judy's representation. Moreover, in his reply to Judy's claim statement, Michael did not challenge Judy's presentation of him as an individual who rejects religion! Though Michael seemingly was prepared to have their matters be resolved in a local *beit din* rather than this *beit din* which was located hundreds of miles away from Illinois, however at the end of the day, he never pursued their matters in a *beit din*. Moreover, Judy summoned him regarding his claims against her to a local *beit din* and he refused to appear. In our estimation, his ideological opposition against organized religion in general and resolving issues in a religious forum such as a *beit din* in particular and/or his discomfort to appear in an Orthodox Jewish forum given his lifestyle may serve as the reason (or reasons) for his unwillingness to proceed to a *beit din*.

If one reads closely Michael's response to Judy's written claim statement one can discern that his lack of religiosity in general and its ideological underpinnings in particular are not in dispute. As an attorney, his reply to Judy's claim statement was nuanced. He mentions that he respected the religious practices of others who entered his home; a representation confirmed by two women who were guests at his home, but he did not challenge Judy's representation regarding his individual lack of observance. Michael tries to deflect Judy's representation about him by stating that some of her representations were "half-truths" which may be correct and that she was not observant at all times, but the basic representation advanced by Judy which was corroborated by three individuals is that he was an atheist or almost an atheist is not challenged by Michael. In fact, he writes that publicly "my lifestyle was no secret" and "Judy did not expect me to change lifelong habits." In fact, we asked three Torah observant men and one Torah observant woman whether one could categorize Michael as *"a tinok shenishbah bein hagoyim"* (loosely translated: a baby who was raised by non-Jews) due to his lack of exposure to Jewish education and religious upbringing and his exposure to the prevailing values of society, they unanimously and emphatically said "absolutely not."

We have issued a *psak din* which obligates Michael to give a *get* to Judy. However, he continues to refuse to give a *get* alleging that the *get* will be only forthcoming once Judy pays some outstanding monetary debts to him.

Consequently, given his refusal to give a *get* we are now addressing whether there is grounds to void the marriage.

Discussion

1.   *KIDDUSHEI TA'UT* — AN ERROR IN THE MARRIAGE

The initial question which emerges from Judy's presentation and Michael's reply to the claim statement is there grounds for Judy to argue that prior to the marriage she didn't realize the severity of Michael's depression and therefore having discovered only after their marriage, she has the right to state: "I never would have married him, had I known the extent of the severity of his psychological disorder"?

Prior to invoking the technique of *"kiddushei ta'ut"* to void a marriage and claim there was an error in the creation of the marriage, three pre-conditions must have been obtained:[1]

(1) The husband's defect must be a major one ("*a mum gadol*") such as sexual impotency, refusing to have children, mental dysfunction, homosexuality and/or engaging in a crime. All of the aforementioned examples have been characterized by one or numerous authorities as a *mum gadol*. Clearly, as Rabbi Hayyim Berlin and Rabbi Shalom Messas note, one must be concerned with "the slippery slope," lest a decisor allow an insignificant flaw such as a husband's periodic outbursts of anger, being a spendthrift or stinginess as grounds to void a marriage.[2]

The issue is whether having depression is to be labeled "*a mum gadol*." Michael was prescribed medications (which sometimes were allegedly taken and sometimes not) which were for patients who have a major depressive disorder and anxiety disorder. Based upon the anti-depressant medication which was in the home as well as the symptoms described, three health care professionals concluded that he had a major psychological disorder.[3]

(2) The wife must be unaware of the defect prior to the marriage and must discover it only after the marriage.

Upon reviewing Judy's presentation, one finds discrepancies between what was told to us at hearing and what Michael wrote as a response to

---

1. We will only address two of those conditions. Regarding the third condition, see infra. n. 13.

2. *Teshuvot Nishmat Hayyim* 87 (126); *Teshuvot Shemesh u-Magen* 3, *EH* 27.

3. For *Poskim* who voided a marriage based upon a husband's psychological disorder, see *Teshuvot Har Tzvi EH* 2:180; *Iggerot Moshe EH* 1:80, *Teshuvot Maharsham* 6:159 (with an additional supporting argument to void the marriage), 6:160; *Teshuvot Mishpetei Uziel* 5:57 (with an additional supporting argument to void the marriage), File no. 870175/4, Haifa Regional Beit Din, December 29, 2014.

Clearly, from a *halakhic* evidentiary perspective, we may require a health care professional who actually met Michael and submitted a diagnosis that he suffered from severe depression. Without such a diagnosis there would be no basis to void the marriage. Our reliance here upon the opinion of health care professionals who never met is simply being utilized for our presentation here and should not be construed as a valid proof that in fact we could void this marriage without a conventional health care professional's diagnosis of the husband. In fact, this marriage was voided on different grounds as we will explain.

her claim statement and her reply to his representation. For example, during the hearing (as well as in a telephone conversation prior to the hearing) she represented to us that knowledge of his disorder was only discovered shortly prior to the marriage and at that time he was healthy. However, based upon the written exchange between Michael and her, her representation now is that she had no idea (as well as no experience) of the ramifications of someone who suffers from manic depression and therefore chose to marry him. In other words, she knew for a long time about his disorder but did not observe the severe symptoms of having depression.[4]

Implicit in this representation is that during the four and half years or six years she knew him she did not observe him suffering from manic depression. Usually, we are dealing with a situation where a husband fails to disclose intentionally or unintentionally that he has a psychological disorder. And therefore, assuming other conditions are obtained, one can void the marriage based upon *kiddushei ta'ut*, an error in the marriage.

However, in our case we are dealing with an awareness of the *mum gadol*. Subsequently, a few years into the marriage, his psychological condition allegedly deteriorated and she exclaimed, "Had I known that his condition would degenerate, I never would have married him." Whereas prior to the marriage she felt that she would be able to handle the situation, the depth and severity of the disorder now preempts that possibility.

Rabbi Yosef Karo rules:[5]

> A man who is mentally dysfunctional on a daily basis and his wife says, "my father in the time of his stress married me off and I thought I would be able to deal with the matter. Now, I realize that he is mentally dysfunctional and I fear that in his rage he will kill me." [In such a case] we don't coerce him to give a *get*.

Despite the fact that the wife's situation is life-threatening, Rabbi Karo does not sanction *get* coercion! Explaining the rationale for this ruling, Gaon of Vilna states:[6]

---

4. This representation contradicts her earlier claim that she only found out about his depression shortly before the marriage.

5. *Shulhan Arukh* (hereafter: *SA*) *Even ha-Ezer* (hereafter: *EH*) 154:5.

6. *Bi'ur ha-Gra, SA EH* 154:17.

Since she knew, we do not say that "she thought she could handle the situation. . . ."

To state it differently, a wife cannot initially claim that she thought she would be capable of dealing with her husband's condition and now realizes that she can't deal with it. Therefore, we do not coerce a *get*. In fact, Rabbi Yehuda Litwin contends that in a situation which entails a mental disorder which changes "from time to time" we do assume that a wife accepts the situation.[7]

Nonetheless, many *Poskim* disagree with the aforementioned views.

Even though she knew that her prospective husband had skin boils prior to the marriage and she accepted this defect in the form of a *tenai* (a condition to the marriage), nonetheless the students of Rabbeinu Yonah note:[8]

> Except for a husband who has skin boils (*mukeh shehin*) that she can say "now I am unable to deal with it since daily the sickness becomes more severe". . . .

In other words, her change of heart regarding her ability to live with a husband who was afflicted with boils would trump her *tenai* and *get* coercion is permissible.

The question is what is the reason why the persistence and the sudden severity of a husband's skin boils which emerges after the onset of the marriage ought to undermine the *tenai?* Addressing a young woman who was dysfunctional the majority of the time and exhibited moments of sanity only portions of the time prior to the marriage and subsequently became a *shotah* (*halakhically* mentally dysfunctional), R. Aryeh Leibush Horowitz in *Teshuvot Harei Besamim*, Mahadura Tinyana 72 observes:

Accepting a *mum* only is applicable if the condition remains the same. However, the degree of mental dysfunction changes from one period to the next; therefore he accepted the situation in her condition that she was in prior to the marriage; and the insanities that emerged afterwards he could not tolerate and therefore one cannot say that he accepted it.

On the basis of this reasoning, R. Horowitz lifted the *herem* of Rabbeinu Gershom, which prohibits a husband to give a *get* against his wife's wishes, and permitted him to remarry.

The notion that the depth and severity of a medical condition may change for the worse is also noted regarding a wife who had epilepsy by

7. *Teshuvot Sha'arei De'ah* 171.
8. *Shitah Mekubetzet, Ketuvot* 77a.

Rabbi Moshe Trani[9] and regarding a wife who exhibited a neurological and cerebral disease by Rabbi Meir Arik.[10] As such, should there be a behavioral change, a prior statement that he accepts the situation may be discounted. Consequently, these authorities allowed the husband to remarry without the wife receiving her *get*.

All the aforesaid rulings deal with grave defects concerning a wife; it is open to debate whether we could apply the same conclusion regarding the flaws of a husband. In recent years, two Israeli rabbinical courts apply this conclusion dealing with a wife's defects to a husband's flaws and state that such a conclusion is acceptable among the *Poskim*.[11]

Based upon the foregoing, seemingly there ought to be grounds to void the marriage even though prior to the marriage Judy neither fully comprehended nor experienced the severe symptoms of Michael's disorder. However, based upon the cumulative evidence submitted to this panel which indicates discrepancies in Judy's representation of the train of events prior to her marriage as well as the panel's assessment that it is highly unlikely that for four and half years or six years prior to the marriage that Judy was unaware of Michael's manic depression. In other words, prior to the marriage the symptoms of his disorder were "full-blown" in her presence.[12] But as the health care professional testified to us she was "emotionally compromised" and therefore she was unable to discern that he was acting in an abnormal fashion.

As such, there would be no basis for voiding the marriage utilizing the tool of *kiddushei ta'ut*.[13]

---

9. *Teshuvot ha-Mabit* 3:212.

10. *Teshuvot Imrei Yosher* 2:119.

11. *Piskei Din Rabbanayim* (hereafter: *PDR*) 21:279, 283; 17 *Shurat ha-Din* 123 (5770).

12. In contemporary times, at least two *battei din* arrived at the same conclusion that a wife cannot hide her disorder from her husband when the man and woman knew each other and lived with each other prior to the marriage. *PDR* 13:43; File no. 818315/7, Be'air Sheva Regional Beit Din, September 21, 2015.

13. Given that in accordance to her presentation, she experienced *for the first time* the symptoms of manic depression a few months into the marriage and chose to remain in the marriage for approximately two additional years rather than immediately bolt the marriage, we would have had to address whether in fact there would be a basis to void the marriage. However, this panel accepted the representation that the severity of the illness manifested itself years *prior* to the marriage; therefore there was no presence of a *mum gadol* which would void the marriage. Consequently, we were not required to address the issue of the lapse of time of Judy's becoming aware of her manic state and her decision to leave the marriage and whether she in fact accepted his condition and as such as there would be no basis to void the marriage.

2.   THE VALIDITY OF A *KIDDUSHIN* PERFORMED BY A
          MUMAR

Based upon the foregoing, prior to the wedding Michael was in principle against practicing any religion, nonobservant in terms of *Halakhah*,
transgressed the Shabbat and did not keep kosher. The question is
whether his behavior impacted upon the validity of the *kiddushin*, the
act of *halakhic* engagement and ultimately the validity of his marriage to
Judy? In other words, is an individual who violates the Shabbat publicly
to be labeled a *"mumar"* and if the answer is in the affirmative we must
then address whether *kiddushin* with such a person is valid.

The threshold question is whether the definition of a *mumar* is
limited to an apostate, somebody who leaves Judaism and engages in
hamarat dat, converts to another religion. Clearly, the Talmud distinguishes between a *mumar* who in practice disavows the entire Torah
("*mumar le'khol ha'torah kulah*") and in effect disavows being a member
of the covenant faith community or rebels against one sin ("*mumar
le'aveirah ahat*").[14] One example of a "*mumar le'khol ha'torah kulah*"
is a Jew who publicly desecrates the Shabbat.[15] Another distinction is
established between a *mumar* who engages in sin due to principled opposition ("*le-hakh'is*") or out of convenience ("*le'taivon*") and therefore
commits the sin.[16] Unlike the apostate Jew, the common denominator of
all these types of *mumarim* is that they have not converted to another
religion.[17] However,on the other hand, these individuals have ideological
opposition to perform a particular divine commandment or the entire
spectrum of *mitzvot*.

The question is whether a Jew who publicly violates the Shabbat is
viewed as a *mumar*. In order to be deemed a public violator of Shabbat
notwithstanding that there are some authorities who mandate that ten
Orthodox Jewish males have to attest that they observed him publicly
transgressing the Shabbat,[18] many *Poskim* only require that ten Orthodox

---

14. *Hullin* 4b–5a.

15. *Hullin* 5a.

16. *Hullin* 4a.

17. So, for example whether there is a requirement of *halitzah* from an apostate
levir or equally from a Jew who rejected the entire Torah or a Jew who publicly
violated the Shabbat is open to debate. See *Mordekhai, Yevamot* 4:107 in the name of
the Gaonim and variant views recorded in *Teshuvot Yabia Omer* 9, *EH* 36:6.

18. *Hagahot Rabbi Akiva Eiger, Yoreh De'ah* (hereafter: *YD*) 264; *Teshuvot Binyan
Tzion* 1:64; *Teshuvot Hatam Sofer YD* 120; *Teshuvot Yehudah Ya'aleh, YD* 50.

Jewish males were aware that he violates the Shabbat.[19] Moreover, given that Michael worked the land on Shabbat,[20] even the *shitat yahid*, the minority opinion who argues that only such an individual is deemed a public transgressor of Shabbat would agree in our case that he is deemed a violator.[21]

Given that more than ten Orthodox Jewish males would attest to the fact that Michael publicly violated the Shabbat,therefore he ought to be classified as a public transgressor of the Shabbat (and as such a *mumar*), the issue is whether being *mekadesh*, consecrating and designating a woman as his wife was valid? In accordance to the majority of *Poskim*, his *kiddushin* is valid *me'doraita*, biblically.[22] However there are a few authorities, who invalidate the *kiddushin*, view it valid *me'derabbanan*, on a rabbinic level or argue that such *kiddushin* is "*a safek kiddushin*," a *kiddushin* which is *halakhically* in doubt.[23]

Finally, in reply to the question whether due to his lack of religious upbringing and being deprived of a Jewish education and conforming to the norms and values of the society in which he lives Michael is to be labeled "*a tinok shenishbah bein hagoyim*"? As we mentioned earlier in our rendition of the facts of this case, three Torah observant men and one Torah observant woman unanimously and emphatically said "absolutely not." As noted by Michael's own admission he was in principle ideologically opposed to practicing any religion. He was an atheist.

Addressing the case of a husband whose maternal grandparents were *mumarim* and were married in a Christian church and he himself was "*a tinok shenishbah bein hagoyim*" who while serving in the army was intentionally transgressing various sins in a loathsome and repugnant

---

19. *Shakh, SA YD* 157:4; *Ba'air Hetev, SA YD* 157:3 (Cf. *Ba'air Hetev, SA YD* 2:15); *Teshuvot Maharam Schick, OH* 128; *Teshuvot Tzemah Tzedek, EH* 259; Rabbi Algazi, *Kehillat Ya'akov* 696; *Sedei Hemed Hashalem, Ma'arekhet ha-peh, Kelal* 16 in the name of Rashba, Tashbetz, Radvaz and Pri Megadim.

20. Mowing the lawn (improves the growth of the grass) as well as digging and planting constitute "*avodat karka*," working the land.

21. *Beit Yosef Tur EH* 44 in the name of Ittur; *Teshuvot Lev Hayyim OH* 175 in the name of Ittur.

22. *Orhot Hayyim, Kiddushin*, page 55 in the name of Rashi; *Mishneh Torah, Ishut* 4:15; *Sefer ha-Ittur, Kiddushin; Ohr Zarua, Yibum* and *Kiddushin* 604; *Teshuvot ha-Rashba* 1162; *Teshuvot Tashbetz* 3:47; *Teshuvot Terumat ha-Deshen* 219; *Tur EH* 44; *SA, EH* 44:9; *Teshuvot Noda be-Yehudah, Mahadura Tinyana EH* 80.

23. *Mordekhai Yevamot* 4:107 in the name of Rabbi Shimshon regarding a *yavam* who is a *mumar; Ittur, Hilkhot Kiddushin* in the name of *yesh omrim; Tur*, supra n. 21 in the name of "*yesh omrim*"; *Teshuvot Mahari Mintz* 12; *Teshuvot Maharashdam EH* 10 as well as in the name of Rambam and Semag; *Levush Mordekhai* 64.

fashion including failing to observe the Shabbat, Rabbi Yitzhak Weiss of the twentieth century rules:[24]

> There are four views regarding a *mumar* who was *mekadesh*: One, that the *kiddushin* is recognized biblically. Second, that the *kiddushin* is invalid. Third, it is a doubtful *kiddushin*. Fourth, it is *kiddushin* which is valid on a rabbinic level. And delve into Maharsham . . . who investigated if one should join those who contend that the *kiddushin* is valid only rabbinically. And he wrote that since the majority of *Poskim* rule that such *kiddushin* is to be recognized biblically, one cannot rule leniently for only this reason. But he joined this doubt to a second doubt that is more frequent and results in leniency. . . . Where one doubt is more frequent and results in leniency, we join a second doubt that more frequently results in stringency. . . .

In short, one can invoke a *sefek sefeika* (a double doubt) in the context of the presence of apostasy in the husband's family and thereby void the *kiddushin* of the *mumar*. To state it differently, given that Rabbi Weiss aligns himself with the position that in contemporary times a Jew who intentionally is a transgressor and is repulsed by the performance of *mitzvot* including publically transgressing the Shabbat is to be subsumed in the category of *"a tinok shenishbah bein hagoyim"* [25]consequently the husband is not to be identified as a *mumar*. Such a person can only be a *mumar* if apostacy to another religion existed in his family.

Seemingly, given the absence of an actual conversion to another religion in Michael's family preempts the possibility of deploying the *sefek sefeika*. However, upon further thought, it is a distinct possibility that Rabbi Weiss ought to agree to the employment of the *sefek sefeika* under our circumstances where the husband was in principle opposed to practicing any religion. He is a *"mumar le'khol ha'Torah kulah"*, an apostate to the entire Torah generally and every religion in particular. Moreover, Michael's parents were equally against all religions and scoffed at those adherents who observed them. In fact, they were civilly married due to

---

24. *Teshuvot Minhat Yitzhak* 3:107.

25. *Teshuvot Minhat Yitzhak* 1:10. Since the fact pattern of Rabbi Weiss's *teshuvah* (responsum) deals with a husband who intentionally is a sinner and relates in a loathsome manner to acting religiously, it is somewhat difficult to accept the notion that this is an example in Rabbi Weiss's mind of *"a tinok shenishbah bein hagoyim"* who has failed to be exposed Jewish education and a religious upbring.

their ideological opposition to adopting any religious life style much less the norms of Judaism. Such an upbringing as well as Michael's personal lifestyle and ideological perspective regarding religion may be equivalent in the eyes of Rabbi Weiss as a Jewish couple who have married in a Christian church. As such, in accordance to Rabbi Weiss there ought to be grounds to void the marriage based upon the invoking of a *sefek sefeika*.

On the other hand, an earlier position authored by Rabbi Schwadron of nineteenth century Galicia leads to the same results.

Addressing the validity of *kiddushin* of a *mumar* who publicly transgresses the Shabbat, Rabbi Schwadron opines:[26]

> Concerning a *mumar* who was *mekadesh* a woman there are a few authorities who claim the *kiddushin* is valid rabbinically even though the majority of *Poskim* are stringent, nevertheless there is "a double doubt" to be lenient . . . When one doubt is more frequent to result in leniency we "join it" to a second doubt though it is more frequent to result in stringency . . . and the presumption of being a married woman is voided, see Maharit, vol. 1 section 138 that one rules leniently in *sefek sefeika* (double doubt) of *kiddushin*. . . . However it seems it is unclear whether in fact he was a Shabbat transgressor at the time of the marriage and if he became a *mumar* afterwards, the two doubts did not emerge simultaneously and therefore we cannot be lenient due to a double doubt.

Lest one argue that in contemporary times Maharsham considers a public transgressor of Shabbat as *"a tinok shenishbah bein hagoyim"* and as such he would not be deemed a *mumar,* in another ruling, relying upon the view of Rabbi Ya'akov Ettlinger he states that if it is clear that he knows the *halakhot* of Shabbat and yet has the audacity to transgress them in front of ten Torah observant Jewish males, in the words of the Maharsham he is a *mumar gamur* and one is prohibited from drinking his wine.[27] Based upon the cumulative evidence submitted to this panel, the defendant's behavior labels him as a *mumar gamur,* an absolute apostate.[28]

In other words, in accordance with his posture, one may invoke a *sefek*

---

26. *Teshuvot Maharsham* 2:110.
27. *Teshuvot Maharsham* 1:121.
28. See infra n. 30.

sefeika as a vehicle to void the marriage when dealing with a *mumar*, a public transgressor of a Shabbat.[29]

Therefore, in our case where it is clear that prior to the marriage Michael was a *mumar*, namely a public transgressor of Shabbat and an atheist [30] therefore based upon the aforesaid *sefek sefeika* we may invalidate the act of *kiddushin*.[31]

To state it differently, given that the majority of renowned *Poskim* validate the *kiddushin* of a *mumar*, concludes Rabbi Moshe Feinstein that one cannot invoke the technique of *sefek sefeika* in order to arrive at a lenient position and void the marriage.[32] As such, Rabbi Feinstein in our case would have been unwilling to void the marriage. However, we are relying upon the positions of Maharsham and Minhat Yitzhak

---

29. As noted by Maharsham, his conclusion is in accordance with Maharit who argues that in case of a *sefek sefeika* involving *kiddushin*, one may rule leniently. See *Teshuvot Maharit* 1:138(end).In his particular case, since it wasn't clear that in fact the husband was a *mumar* who violated the Shabbat publicly, therefore the *sefek sefeika* could not be utilized in order to void the marriage.

30. Notwithstanding Rabbis Kook, Henkin, Y. Weiss and others who argue that in contemporary times, a *mumar* is limited to one who is an apostate rather than a public transgressor of Shabbat (see *Teshuvot Da'at Kohen* 153; *Perushei Ibra* 5:5 and *Teshuvot Minhat Yitzhak* 3:107), nonetheless Judy's description of him, as well as the statements of third parties which were all given "*ma'se'ach le'fee tumah*," lit. speaking with innocence, corresponds to the earlier *halakhic* rulings which dealt with a *mumar* who violated publicly the Shabbat which was accompanied by a principled rejection of the binding authority of *Halakhah* as well as any established religious authority. Finally, though Michael challenged certain facets of Judy's depiction of him, Michael did not question Judy's representation of him regarding his principled rejection of religion in general and the Jewish religion in particular.

Our conclusion is based on the ruling of Rabbi Ya'akov Ettlinger and Rabbi Shalom Schwadron. Even though they contend that today a public transgressor of Shabbat cannot be categorized as a *mumar*, nevertheless, if the individual rejects *mitzvot* including being a public desecrator of Shabbat for ideological reasons rather than for economic reasons, he is "comparable to an absolute *mumar*." See Y. Ettlinger, *Minhat Ani*, Jerusalem, 1963, 91a; *Teshuvot Binyan Tzion ha-Hadashot* 23; *Maharsham*, supra n. 27.

31. *Teshuvot Avnei ha-Ephod* 15 suggests that "the double doubt" entails the fact that the majority of authorities claim that the *kiddushin* of a *mumar* is rabbinic and the minority argues it is biblically valid; we may invalidate the marriage based upon "a double doubt." With all due respect, a review of the rulings regarding this matter will indicate the converse, namely the majority of decisors argue the *kiddushin* is recognized biblically and the minority validates it on rabbinic grounds. See *Teshuvot Beit Yitzhak* 1:25; *Teshuvot Maharsham* 2:110. Hence, Avnei ha-Ephod's suggestion to void the marriage of a *mumar* lacks foundation.

32. *Iggerot Moshe EH* 4:83. Additionally, see *Teshuvot Noda be-Yehudah, EH* Mahadura Tinyana 80; *Pithei Teshuvah SA EH* 44:9 in the name of Noda be-Yehudah.

who are prepared to deploy the tool of *sefek sefeika* in order to void the marriage of a *mumar*.[33]

Implicit in the opinions of Rabbis Schwadron and Weiss is that the definition of a *mumar* is not limited to a Jew who converted to another religion as has been propounded by other authorities;[34] rather a Jew who is *"a tinok shenishbah bein hagoyim"* who intentionally violates prohibitions including transgressing the Shabbat publicly and mocks *mitzvot* may be equally identified as a *mumar*.[35] On the basis of these authorities, we assume that Michael is to be viewed as a *mumar*. As such, his *kiddushin* is invalid.

Based upon the foregoing; Judy is free to remarry any Jewish man other than a *Kohen*, without receiving a *get*.

---

33. For the grounds to rely upon a *shitat yahid* (a minority view) or *me'ut ha-Poskim* (a minority of authorities) that the *kiddushin* performed a *mumar* is invalid, see this writer's *Rabbinic Authority*, vol. 3, 252–256.

Furthermore, *Sefer ha-Ittur, Kiddushin* cites in his words *"earlier teshuvot"* which rule that the *kiddushin* performed by a *mumar* is invalid and as explained by *Teshuvot Maharashdam EH* 10, the reason that *Tur EH* 44 cites this position is because such a view is significant *Halakhah le'ma'aseh* (practical ruling). As such, the employment of *sefek sefeika* by Rabbis Schwadron and Weiss is predicated in part by the factoring into consideration this early position which predates Rabbi Yitzhak ben Abba Mari of Marseilles, France who lived in the twelfth century, the author of the Sefer ha-Ittur.

34. *Teshuvot She'eilat Ya'avetz* 32; *Teshuvot Mitzpeh Aryeh Tinyana* 19; *Teshuvot Hatam Sofer* 2:73, 6:56; *Teshuvot Avnei Nezer* 223; *Teshuvot Be'air Esek* 76.

35. *Teshuvot be-Zail ha-Hokhmah* 1:51(2); *Hazon Ish, EH* 118:5; *Teshuvot Kokhav me-Ya'akov* 41; *Teshuvot Yabia Omer* 9, *EH* 36:6–7; *Teshuvot Sha'arei Tzion* 2, *EH* 20 (7).

B.   A HUSBAND WHO IS INFECTED WITH HIV

During the Fall of 2008, the couple married in accordance with *Halakhah*. Four years later, Avraham informed Esther that they would be getting divorced and at that time he left the marital home. During the last three and a half years, Esther attempted to receive her *get* from Avraham but until now he has refused to give his wife her *get* unless he would receive $100,000. There were settlement negotiations but at the end the negotiations fell apart. To this date, despite the fact that we obligated a *get*, a *get* was not forthcoming.

It was clear to Esther that Avraham would continue to refuse giving a *get* but requested from the panel whether there would be grounds to void the marriage based upon the fact that she contracted from her spouse a sexually transmitted disease called human papilloma virus (hereafter: HPV). Women usually discover that they have HPV when they have a Pap smear. Esther visited her doctor for her annual physical exam soon after she married and her doctor informed her that her Pap smear results were irregular. After testing, her physician told her that she had HPV. There are approximately 100 types of HPV; some cause cervical cancer, some generate genital warts and others are subclinical and there are no recognizable symptoms. After further testing, Esther found that the HPV that was transmitted by Avraham was harmless and that it would disappear in a few years. Given the fact that Esther alleges she never had intercourse with any other man except Avraham,[1] she knew that the HPV could only have been sexually transmitted by Avraham. Upon inquiry, Avraham told her that he had intimate relations with another woman prior to marriage. Despite the fact that Esther's doctor counseled her to refrain from having relations with Avraham, she continued to engage in conjugal relations. In effect, though she was infecting herself again and again every time she cohabitated with him, Esther, who was in love with Avraham, allegedly continued to engage in conjugal relations in order to keep her husband happy. Had she known prior to the marriage that he had HPV she never would have married him. In other words, Esther is contending that her husband's failure to

---

1. Since as the panel determined there was no basis for voiding the marriage based upon "*kiddushei ta'ut*" (see infra condition no. 3), there is no need to address the *halakhic* trustworthiness of her statement that in fact Avraham transmitted the HPV and she had relations only with Avraham.

disclose, intentionally or unintentionally,[2] that he had HPV is grounds to void her marriage and therefore she is free to remarry without receiving a *get* from Avraham.

Discussion

Before determining whether there is a basis to argue that there is "*a mum gadol*," a major flaw which Avraham failed to disclose and may serve as a reason to void the marriage, the threshold question is whether there are grounds to coerce a *get* due to a sexually transmitted disease by the husband. Specifically, we will address this issue through the prism of a husband who contracted AIDS and transmitted HIV to his spouse.

1. GROUNDS FOR *GET* COERCION DUE TO A SEXUALLY
    TRANSMITTED DISEASE BY THE HUSBAND

The grounds for compelling the issuance of a *get* due to matters such as physical defects are mentioned in the Talmud.[3] After the close of the Talmud, the question arises whether a *beit din* may compel a husband to give a *get* to his wife in circumstances not specified in the Talmud. May a *beit din* compel a *get* if a husband has infected his wife with a sexually transmitted disease, a disease which is not mentioned in the Talmud? Is the list a closed list or can we expand the list based upon *medameh milta le-milta*,[4] utilizing analogical reasoning? This question is subject to much debate among the *Poskim*.

However, even if an authority claims that the list in the Talmud is a closed list, one should refrain from assuming that there will be no situation (or situations) where the *Posek* will refuse to coerce a *get* in a new case. For example, on one hand, addressing the situation of a mentally dysfunctional husband, Rabbi Asher ben Yehiel, known by the acronym: Rosh, refuses to sanction *get* coercion due to the fact that this disorder is not cited in the Talmud.[5] Yet, on the other hand, when dealing with an epileptic wife Rosh permits *get* coercion.[6] This seeming contradiction

---

2. Currently, there is no test for HPV for men.
3. *Ketuvot* 63b, 76a, 77a–b; *Yevamot* 65b.
4. See this writer's *Rabbinic Authority*, vol. 1, 53–57.
5. *Teshuvot ha-Rosh* 43:3.
6. *Teshuvot ha-Rosh* 42:1.

between the two rulings is addressed by Rabbi Moshe Yisrael who notes
who notes:[7]

> ... when Rosh states that one should not add to the cases men-
> tioned in ha-Madir (referring to a *perek* in Ketuvot – AYW)
> that does not mean that there are no situations where there are
> grounds for coercion. But rather what is meant, that one should
> not add unless a case is like those mentioned ...

In other words, if we can engage in *medameh milta le-milta* (analogical reasoning) then we may add other situations where *get* coercion
is permissible. Consequently, though a particular dangerous disease is
absent from the list, nevertheless since there is mention in the Talmud
that a husband who has skin boils is a basis for *get* coercion similarly one
can invoke another dangerous malady. And Rosh's view is not "a lone
ranger." There are numerous *Poskim* who will coerce a *get* in situations
of a husband who is infected by a dangerous disease. Some authorities
will require that in fact the disease is a danger to the wife should she be
exposed to it and some will mandate an additional requirement that the
wife cannot tolerate living with a husband who has succumbed to such a
disease.[8] Consequently, as such it is unsurprising that today, contemporary authorities would coerce a *get* if a husband had AIDS and infected
his wife with HIV.[9]

However, as noted by some authorities, should the disease fail to pose
a danger, there would be no basis to obligate the husband to give a *get*.[10]

2.   *KIDDUSHEI TA'UT* (LIT. A MISTAKEN BETROTHAL,
         LOOSELY TRANSLATED AS A MISTAKEN MARRIAGE)

Given that today, at least in the *Golah*, the Diaspora, we legally and
therefore *halakhically* aren't empowered to coerce a *get*, some *Poskim*
such as Rabbi Y. Elhanan Spektor, Eliyahu Klatzkin, Tzvi P. Frank and
Moshe Feinstein argue that one must seek whether the conditions are

---

7. *Teshuvot Mas'at Moshe* 1, *EH* 17. See also, *Teshuvot Maharam Gavison* 10.

8. *Teshuvot Re'em* in *Teshuvot Sefer Amukim* 19; *Teshuvot Maharit* 2, *EH* 14;
Teshuvot Divrei Rivot 402; *Maharam Gavison*, supra n. 7; *Teshuvot Maharitz* 229.

9. *Teshuvot Mishneh Halakhot* 17:46; *Teshuvot Ateret Devorah EH* 2:90.

10. *Mordekhai, Ketuvot* 7:201; *Teshuvot Hatam Sofer EH* 2:116; *Teshuvot Devar
Yehoshua* 3:30.

ripe that enable a *Posek* to void a marriage based upon *kiddushei ta'ut* in a situation where a *get* will not be given.[11]

Prior to a *beit din* invoking the tool of *kiddushei ta'ut* to void a marriage retroactively and claim there was an error in the creation of the marriage, three preconditions must have been obtained:

(1) The husband's defect must be a major one (a *mum gadol*) such as sexual impotency, refusing to have children, insanity, homosexuality, apostasy, a marital expectation communicated by the prospective husband prior to the marriage which turns out to be a misrepresentation, or engaging in criminal behavior such as business fraud, a flaw which must have been preexisting prior to the onset of the marriage. All of the aforementioned examples of a husband's flaws have been characterized by one or more *Poskim* as a *mum gadol*. Whether a particular defect serves as a major defect and therefore grounds for voiding a marriage is subject to the discretion of the *beit din*.

The emerging issue from ths case is whether transmitting sexual disease to a wife which is infectious and therefore entails danger to the spouse, is that disease to be labeled "*a mum gadol*"? Addressing the situation of a husband infected with AIDS, though initially Rabbi Menashe Klein writes that given that the STD emerged after the marriage and there was no corroborating evidence that in fact the disease existed prior to the marriage, one might infer that if in fact supporting evidence would have been produced, assuming other conditions would have been obtained, R. Klein would conclude that there are grounds to engage in *bittul kiddushin*, voiding the marriage. However, it is clear from his subsequent argumentation that in fact he is in principle opposed to invoking "*kiddushei ta'ut*" as a vehicle to void any marriage.[12]

However, *Dayan* Shalom Messas and Rabbi Avraham Shulsinger rule that having been infected with AIDS, the HIV is a *mum gadol*.[13] Seemingly, one may argue that there is the Talmudic statement "one who is performing a *mitzvah* will never experience anything bad." As such, in our case Esther should not be concerned about becoming infected with HPV during cohabitation and therefore one cannot classify this STD as "*a mum gadol*."

The implicit assumption here is that the wife is performing a *mitzvah*

---

11. *Teshuvot Ein Yitzhak* 1, *EH* 24; *Teshuvot Devar Eliyahu* 48; *Teshuvot Har Tzvi EH* 2:181; *Iggerot Moshe EH* 1:79.

12. *Mishneh Halakhot*, supra n. 9.

13. *Teshuvot Shemesh u-Magen* 4, *EH* 100; *Teshuvot Be'air Sarim* 5:49.

by engaging in intercourse. Clearly, a wife is exempt from the biblical *mitzvah* of *p'ru ur'vu*, "increase and multiply",[14] however according to some *Poskim* it is incumbent upon her to fulfill two rabbinic duties, namely " *la-shevet*", "populating the world"[15] and "*la-erev*," "in the evening do not withhold your hand from planting"[16].[17] Without addressing the difference between these two *mitzvot*, suffice it to say that there is an obligation incumbent upon the wife to promote procreation beyond the statutory requirement of a son and daughter which is mandated by the *mitzvah* of *p'ru ur'vu*.[18] In fact, some *Poskim* reproved families who had only two children.[19] Others claim that she performs a *mitzvah* due to the fact that she assists him in fulfilling the duty of *p'ru ur'vu*.[20]

Notwithstanding that Rabbi Shulsinger raises doubts whether fulfilling the *mitzvah* of "*la-shevet*" and "*la-erev*" would rise to the level of "one who is performing a *mitzvah* will never experience anything bad,"[21] nonetheless there are other *Poskim* who would reject the applicability of this statement. For these authorities, it is applicable only to a disease which has been labeled as "*seguli*" such as "*a ru'ah ra'ah*," an evil spirit or "*minhag shedim*," the practice of demons.[22] On the other hand, diseases which are "*derekh ha-teva*," which transpire naturally, may potentially affect a person even if he/she is engaged in the performance of a *mitzvah*. And in cases where harm is a frequent occurrence, one cannot invoke "the agents who perform a *mitzvah* are not harmed."[23]

Notwithstanding some authorities who argue that "one who is performing a *mitzvah* will never experience anything bad" is applicable to diseases linked to the natural order,[24] some *Poskim* disagree.[25] In short, HIV is to be viewed as "*a mum gadol*" because despite the fact that a wife may be performing a *mitzvah* by engaging in intimate relations, such *halakhic* behavior will not protect her from contracting STD.

---

14. *Bereshit* 9:1, 7.

15. *Yeshayahu* 45:18.

16. *Kohelet* 11:6.

17. *Tosafot Shabbat* 110b, s.v. *ve'ha'tanya*.; *Atzei Arazim* 1:2; *Beit Shmuel, SA EH* 1:2; *Teshuvot Hatam Sofer EH* 1:20.

18. *Perush ha-Ramban al ha-Torah, Bereshit* 9:7.

19. *Teshuvot Helkat Ya'akov* 2:11; *Teshuvot Melameid le'Ho'eil* 3:18.

20. *Hiddushei ha-Ran, Kiddushin* 41a.

21. *Be'air Sarim*, supra n. 13.

22. *Rashi, Hullin* 107b; *Tosafot Yoma* 77b; *Rashi, Ta'anit* 20b.

23. *Be'air Sarim*, supra n. 13.

24. *Teshuvot Beit She'arim* 350, *Teshuvot Hatam Sofer* 1, *EH* 130; *Teshuvot Hakham Tzvi* 1.

25. *Teshuvot Divrei Malkiel* 2:53 (6); *Hakham Tzvi* supra n. 24.

Now let us address our situation. Clearly, based upon the battery of testing the type of HPV which infected Esther was harmless and therefore cannot be classified as "*a mum gadol.*" Yet, since a woman may contract multiple types of HPV from the same man, it is in the realm of possibility that Avraham may have been infected equally with HPV6, HPV16 or HPV18, STDs which have been known to significantly increase the risk of cervical cancer. Despite her physician's advice to refrain from having sexual relations with him, she continued to be intimate with him. Given that there exists the possibility that sometime in the future he may transmit one of these high-risk HPV's to Esther resulting in the potential to cause cervical cancer to Esther, having HPV16 or HPV18 falls into the category of "*a safek sakanah,*" a possible danger to life, and we would view it as a potential *mum gadol.*

A source that in a situation of "*safek sakanah,*" one is obligated to coerce a *get* may be found in the words of Rabbi Shmuel Vital who addresses the case of a wife who was afflicted with leprosy.[26]

> Even though we find daily occurrences that men who are lepers sleep with wives who are healthy and are not infected by these males, and some men who are healthy who sleep with women who are lepers and do not become infected by these women. One should know that temperaments vary – there is a type which infects and there is another type which does not infect ... And the same applies to the disease of leprosy and the like. One person may be infected and another person isn't infected. And possibly this man may be one of the men who becomes infected, and we are more stringent with danger, and a man does not live in the same basket with a snake.

And similarly, we should arrive at the same conclusion in our case. There are different types of HPV. There are some which are harmless and others which are harmful. And possibly in the future Avraham will be transmitting an HPV which is dangerous. Consequently, just as *get* coercion should be applied regarding the wife who is afflicted with leprosy, similarly in our situation.

Rabbi Elhanan Spektor stresses the identical point and rules that if there exists a doubt whether a particular malady is to be classified in the

---

26. *Teshuvot Be'air Mayyim Hayyim* 7.

category of an infectious and dangerous disease, then a *get* ought to be coerced.[27]

Therefore, there we may view this future, possibly virulent HPV as a situation of "*safek sakanah*" and therefore it is a major flaw. Given that *get* coercion is not an option; the voiding of a marriage may be possibility.

(2) The wife must be unaware of the *mum* prior to the inception of the marriage and only discovered it after the marriage.

Based upon Esther's statement,[28] we find that she only became aware of the STD after the onset of the marriage.

(3) Finally, upon a wife's awareness of this major latent defect, she must decide to leave the marriage. Whether she has to bolt the marriage immediately or may choose to remain for a period of time due to certain reasons is open to *halakhic* controversy.

In light of the facts in our case, we may refrain from staking out a position regarding this debate. Given that she continued to have conjugal relations with him, "*savrah ve-kiblah*" – she accepted the possibility that in the future she may be infected with a high-profile HPV and therefore she cannot contend that there was an error in the marriage. Secondly, at the end of the day, Avraham divorced her. As such, due to her decision to stay with the marriage including having intimate relations with Avraham one cannot contend that the possibility of an endangerment by a virulent HPV may serve as grounds to void the marriage based upon "*kiddushei ta'ut.*" Based upon the foregoing, there exist no grounds to void the marriage.

Secondly, in addition to classifying this matter as a *mum gadol*, the fact that he failed to disclose it prior to their marriage is an act of deceit and in accordance to Rosh as well as Rema such behavior serves as grounds to coerce a *get*.[29] Here again, given that *get* coercion is not an option;

---

27. *Teshuvot Ein Yitzhak EH* 2:35, anaf 7, subsection 7.

28. Since as the panel determined there was no basis for voiding the marriage based upon "*kiddushei ta'ut*" (see infra condition no. 3), we had no reason to perform due diligence by requesting of Esther to produce supporting documentation that in fact she was infected by HPV.

29. *Teshuvot ha-Rosh* 35:2, Rema, *SA EH* 77: 3; *Teshuvot Divrei Malkiel* 3:100. See *Beit Shmuel SA EH* 117:11, 24 who arrives at the same conclusion where a wife misrepresents herself to her prospective spouse prior to the marriage. In pursuance to Beit Shmuel, such behavior constitutes an act of deceit even if the husband's *mum*, defect is a minor one. Others argue that if the wife is a *shoteh*, *halakhically* mentally dysfunctional and therefore she unintentionallly engaged in misrepresentation, there

the voiding of a marriage may be possibility in a situation of deceit and misrepresentation.[30] In other words, the grounds would be based upon the fact that the husband acted improperly (*"kiddushin she'lo ke'hogen"*) that he failed to disclose that he was infected with a sexually transmitted disease.[31] Here again, despite her awareness of being potentially infected since she remained married to Avraham, there would be no basis to void the marriage.

As we mentioned at the beginning of our *psak din*, decision we obligated Avraham to give a *get* to Esther.

---

would be no basis to imposing *get* coercion. See *Teshuvot Divrei Malkiel* 3, *EH* 100.

In fact, some argue that one can define the contours of what constitutes a husband's flaw in order to invoke *kiddushei ta'ut* from the nature and scope of a wife's major defect. See this writer's *Rabbinic Authority*, vol. 3, 151–152. For another case study of a husband's misrepresentation prior to the marriage to his prospective wife, see this writer's *Rabbinic Authority*, vol. 3, 294–305.

On the other hand, there are other *Poskim* who claim that a husband's misrepresentation prior to the marriage may serve as an avenue to void the marriage provided that the wife stipulated a *tenai*, a condition that the time of the *kiddushin* that she was marrying him assuming (for example) that he was a *kohen* or a wealthy person and in the aftermath during the marriage she discovers that he is *Levi* or poor respectively. See *Teshuvot Tashbetz* 1:130; *Teshuvot Hatam Sofer EH* 2:82; *Teshuvot Rav Pe'alim* 1, *EH* 8. In the absence of such a *tenai*, despite the act of deceit initiated by the husband prior to the marriage the wife remains married.

Furthermore, others argue that one cannot rely upon *Rosh*, op. cit and *Rema*, op. cit who mandate *get* coercion in dealing with a misrepresentation relating to the performance of the act of *kiddushin*. Here we are addressing a husband who engaged in an act of deceit by failing to inform his prospective wife prior to their marriage that in the future she may be infected with HIV, namely a *mum gadol*, a major defect. Given these circumstances there is a distinct possibility that Rosh and Rema would refrain from imposing *get* coercion. See *Hafla'ah*, Kuntres Aharon 117(end); *Hazon Ish, Ketuvot* 69(33); *Teshuvot Galya Massekhet* 8.

30. *Hatam Sofer,* supra n. 29; Rabbi Y. Weinberg, *Hamaor,* Tishrei 5757.

31. For the classification of this situation as *"kiddushin she'lo ke'hogen"* rather than as an example of *kiddushei ta'ut*, see PDR 10:241, 247.

C.   A HUSBAND WITH AN INABILITY TO COPULATE

Sara Kramer vs. David Kramer

On April 1, 2016, Sara Kramer of Seattle, Washington submitted a request to the *beit din* to be *mevatel* her *kiddushin*, to void her marriage due to the fact that her husband, David refused to give her a *get*. Despite the fact that we obligated him to give a *get* on July 2, 2015, until today, David continues to refuse to give a *get* to *Sara*.

In light of the arguments submitted by Sara during our *beit din* hearing, we were aware of our concern that the inability to have a *get* executed may lead to *tarbut ra'ah*, loosely translated as infidelity. Centuries ago, Rabbi Hayyim Pelagi warns that if a married couple separate and the *beit din* sees no hope for reconciliation and *shalom bayit*, a *get* ought to be executed lest the couple engage in sin.[1] And given the breakdown of the nuclear family unit and laxity in moral standards in contemporary times, Rabbi O. Yosef claims:[2]

> Today . . . in the free world where each man acts in accordance to his perception of what is proper and *hutzpah* is pervasive in the world and experience shows that when wives leave their husbands . . . without giving them a *get* they live with other men and they have no shame . . . and *mamzerim* abound in the world.

In light of the fact that the couple separated in September 2014 and there are no prospects for marital reconciliation, a *get* has not been forthcoming, and there is concern for sinning, we must address whether there are grounds for *bittul kiddushin*.

The focus of our deliberation centers upon the wife's argument regarding her husband's refusal to engage in conjugal relations. In her presentation to this panel, she claims that her husband was incapable of copulate, namely an inability to maintain an erection while engaging in conjugal relations. Additionally, generally there existed no intimate relations between her and her husband and that the husband desired to engage only in anal sex.[3]

---

1. *Teshuvot Hayyim ve-Shalom* 2: 35,112.

2. *Teshuvot Yabia Omer* 3, *Even ha-Ezer* (hereafter: *EH*) 18 (13).

3. Despite the fact that *Nitva* was absent from the *beit din* proceeding and we are well aware that there is "a presumption that a wife will not be impudent in

I.   *Kiddushei Ta'ut* (lit. A mistaken betrothal, loosely translated as a mistaken marriage)

Prior to invoking the tool of *kiddushei ta'ut* to void a marriage retroactively and claim there was an error in the creation of the marriage, three preconditions must have been obtained:

(1) The husband's defect must be a major one (a *mum gadol*) such as sexual impotency, refusing to have children, insanity, homosexuality, apostasy, a marital expectation communicated by the prospective husband prior to the marriage which turns out to be a misrepresentation, engaging in criminal behavior such as business fraud or exposing one's mate to a contagious disease such as syphilis or HIV, a flaw which must have been preexisting prior to the onset of the marriage. All of the aforementioned examples of a husband's flaws have been characterized by one or more *Poskim* as a *mum gadol*. Whether a particular defect serves as major defect and therefore grounds for voiding a marriage is subject to the discretion of the *beit din*.

Though to the best of our knowledge there are no extant *teshuvot* dealing with a husband's inability to copulate where *Poskim* have voided marriages, there are numerous rulings where a husband who is sexually impotent may be labeled a *mum gadol* and may be grounds to void the marriage. Notwithstanding some decisors who claim that one is proscribed from voiding *kiddushin* of a sexually impotent husband,[4] there are *Poskim* who sanction voiding a marriage in such a situation.[5]

---

the presence of her husband" (*Ketuvot* 23a; *SA EH* 17:2, 100:10), consequently we should not give credence to some of *Tova'at's* allegations which were advanced in his absence. For one of the *halakhic* reasons which permit us to accept the trustworthiness of some of her claims such as the lack of intimacy and his inability to copulate, see *Teshuvot ha-Rashba* 1:628; *Teshuvot ha-Rosh* 43:5; *Rema SA EH* 154:7; *Teshuvot Mas'at Binyamin* 1:126; *Gevurat Anashim* 5–6, 67; *Bi'ur ha-Gra, SA EH* 17:12; *Teshuvot Nivhar mi-Kesef EH* 45; *Teshuvot Yabia Omer* 4, *EH* 11 (5). See infra, Chapter 8e, n. 2.

Secondly, should a wife allege that her husband refuses to have relations with her, we trust her as we would trust her if she claims he is impotent. See *Teshuvot ha-Rosh* 43:5; *Rema SA EH* 154:7.Cf. *MT. Ishut* 14:16; *SA EH* 77:4; *Taz SA EH* 154:6.

4. *Teshuvot Da'at Sofer* 49; *Teshuvot Tzemah Tzedek*, 2:312; *Teshuvot Beit Avi* 2–3, 135, *Teshuvot Hayyim ve-Shalom* 2:6.

5. *Teshuvot Ein Yitzhak* 1 *EH* 24, anaf 6(25) (*halitzah* case); *Teshuvot Maharsham*, 3:15; *Teshuvot Devar Eliyahu*, 48; *Iggerot Moshe EH* 1:79; *Teshuvot Har Tzvi*, *EH* 2:181; *Hazon Yehezkel on Masekhet Zevahim*, *EH* 8; *Teshuvot Yabia Omer* 7, *EH* 7 in

Additionally, in accordance with some authorities,[6] one may rely *le'ma'aseh* (in practice) upon those authorities who voided marriages in this situation *le'halakhah ve'lo le'ma'aseh* (in theory but not in practice).[7]

Moreover, addressing the grounds for a release from *halitzah*[8] due to

---

the name of Atzei Arazim, ha-Mikneh and Tiv Kiddushin.

6. *Sedei Hemed ha-Shalem* (*Kelalei ha-Poskim* 17); *Teshuvot Yabia Omer* 3, *EH* 18.

In two different rulings, contends Rabbi Kook that one cannot void the marriage based upon the husband's failure to disclosre prior to the onset of the marriage that he was sexually impotent or had an inability to copulate. Among the arguments that were advanced for his posture was his understanding that the *hazakah* (presumption) of "*tav le'meitav tan do mi-le-meitav armalu*" is applicable even under such conditions. See *Teshuvot Ezrat Kohen EH* 4, 44. For a brief discussion of the *hazakah*, see infra text accompanying n. 24.

7. *Teshuvot Havot Yair* 221; *Teshuvot Ein Yitzhak 1 EH* 24.

8. A husband who dies without having a child there is a duty upon his brother to marry his sister-in-law known as fulfilling the obligation of *yibum*. However, normative *Halakhah* mandates a ceremony entitled *halitzah* where the brother-in-law (known as a *levir*) renounces his duty to marry his sister-in-law (known as the *yevamah*) and releases her to marry anyone of her own choosing. See *Rema SA EH* 1.

Our purpose of citing the ruling of Rabbi Spektor is in order to cull from his *teshuvah* an approach for defining impotence as a *mum gadol*. Whether one can utilize the *halitzah* ruling to conclude that one can equally void the marriage of a husband who is impotent is open to much debate. Even though a *shomeret yavam* (a widow awaiting her deceased husband's brother to perform *halitzah*) is biblically prohibited to anyone else and her status is not as stringent as the status of a married woman who is biblically prohibited to anyone else, one may nonetheless apply *halitzah* rulings to marriage cases in matters of *kiddushei ta'ut*. See *Yevamot* 119a (Rava's dictum); *Teshuvot Terumat ha-Deshen* 250; *Teshuvot Noda be-Yehudah*, Mahadura Tinyana *EH* 66 (end) and compare with *Mahadura Kama Orah Hayyim* 21; *Hazon Yehezkel*, supra n. 5; *Teshuvot Har Tzvi*, *EH* 1:95, 99. In fact, in addressing cases dealing with voiding marriages, contemporary *Poskim* (as well as earlier decisors) relied upon *halitzah* rulings as a precedent to void a marriage. See *Iggerot Moshe EH* 3:48; File no. 1-14-1393, Yerushalayim Regional Beit Din, March 5, 2003; File no. 870175/4, Haifa Regional Beit Din, December 29, 2014. We adopted this approach.

Cf. *Teshuvot Torat Hesed OH* 29 and *Teshuvot Rabaz* 88 (3) who would reject such an application of *halitzah* rulings to marriage situations in light of the stringency of the status of a married woman.It would seem that Rabbi Spektor subscribes to their position. See infra n. 9, *Ein Yitzhak*.

Moreover, claims Rabbi Spektor that the marriage is voided but there is requirement of a *get le'humra*, the giving of a *get* as a stringency on rabbinic grounds. See *Ein Yitzhak*, supra n. 7, at subsection 39.Consequently, we are unable to utilize this ruling as a basis for voiding the marriage in our case.Let us note that Rabbi Feinstein contends that since Rabbi Spektor mandated a *get le'humra* as a secondary conclusion to his ruling ("*od yesh lo'mar*") therefore he actually had a doubt whether in fact a *get* really was required. See *Iggerot Moshe EH* 1:79.

a missing levir (brother-in-law) upon a wife's discovery after marriage that her husband is sexually impotent, Rabbi Spektor writes:[9]

> In truth, . . . this is a major defect to void a marriage as Beit Yosef . . . writes in the name of Rashba that this flaw, that one cannot engage in intercourse at all, we know why a bridge enters the wedding canopy . . . and we coerce him to free her . . . we see that this is severe flaw because the majority are particular about this . . . and the *Halakhah* like all defects . . . is that it depends on the agreement of the citizenry as it is elucidated in Hoshen Mishpat 232:6 and therefore we coerce in regard to this defect . . .

To state it differently, the combination of invoking the *sevara* (*halakhic* logic) that "we all know why a bride enters the wedding canopy" and *omaid ha-da'at*, a person's expectations that certain flaws like impotency void a couple's agreement to marry, propels Rabbi Spektor to arrive at the conclusion that there are grounds to free her without performing *halitzah*.

On the other hand, addressing the grounds for voiding a marriage where the wife discovers after marriage that her husband is sexually impotent, Rabbi Feinstein advances a different rationale:[10]

> Since it is clear and straightforward that he isn't capable to engage in intercourse which is a primary component of intimate relations for this is the reason why a bride enters the wedding canopy (embarks upon marriage – AYW) and the Torah identifies it as "*innui*" (torment – AYW) . . . and if in matters regarding which one doesn't decide to become married . . . one cannot refrain from giving her (maintenance and clothing – AYW). . . . Therefore, it is clear that an individual who is not capable of intercourse is the greater defect . . . and one does not have to bring proofs for this. . . .

In other words, Rabbi Feinstein's line of reasoning equally applies to our situation of a couple who sired a child yet the husband is unable to copulate. Just as a husband's sexual impotence creates a situation of "*innui*"

---

9. *Ein Yitzhak*, supra n. 7 at subsection 38. However, in dealing with a *get* recalcitrant husband who is impotent, concludes Rabbi Spektor that there would be no grounds to void a marriage. See *Teshuvot Be'air Yitzhak* 4:3.

10. *Iggerot Moshe*, supra n. 5.

(tormentation) for the wife, similarly a husband's inability to copulate engenders pain for the wife. Responding to a case where a husband was unable to sustain an erection (in the words of the wife – he entered and ... his organ (penis – AYW) died"), Rabbi Dovid ibn Zimra (*Teshuvot ha-Radvaz* 4: 1188) rules that the husband failed to fulfill the *mitzvah* of *onah* and caused her pain. As we know generally speaking (except for *shifah harufah* – a maidservant with whom her owner has intercourse), entry of the crown of the penis into the vagina which is known as *har'arah* doesn't suffice to comply with the duty of *onah*. See *Radvaz*, op. cit; *Teshuvot Maharsham* 5:48.

In short, implicitly following Rabbi Yosef Karo and Rema,[11] the above is summed up in Shakh's following formulation:[12]

> And if she claims that her husband does not sleep with her and does not engage in intercourse with her, the *Halakhah* is identical to the *Halakhah* when a wife claims that her husband is impotent.

Just as Rabbi Yosef Karo and Shakh argue that a husband refraining from having conjugal relations is *halakhically* equivalent to being sexually impotent, similarly the inability to copulate is to be treated like sexual impotence. Just as sexual impotence prevents a husband from performing his duty of "*onah*," intimate relations, similarly, the inability to copulate undermines this duty of conjugal relations and engenders pain.[13]

Given the *halakhic* equivalence of the inability to copulate to sexual impotence, consequently there ought to be grounds to coerce a husband to give a *get*, similar to a case of sexual impotence.[14] In fact, Rabbi

---

11. *SA EH* 76:13, 154:7; *Rema, SA EH* 154:7.

12. *Gevurat Anashim* 1. See also, *Gevurat Anashim* 54.

13. *Ba'air Hetev SA EH* 46:1 and *Pithei Teshuvah SA EH* 46:1 in the name of *Teshuvot ha-Radvaz* 4:1188 (118); *Sha'ar ha-Melekh, Issurei Biah* 3:15; *Knesset ha-Gedolah, ha-Gahot Tur* 154:39; M. Azulai on *Levush EH* 154:18; *PDR* 4:326, 328(Rabbis Nissim, Elyashiv and Zolty); 10:82,87.

14. For authorities who will coerce a *get* in the case of impotence under certain conditions, see *Teshuvot ha-Rid* 79; *Teshuvot ha-Rosh* 43:5 in the name of Ritzva; *Teshuvot ha-Rashba* 1:1236, 1255; *Teshuvot ha-Rashba ha-Meyuhosot le-Ramban* 139, 141; *SA EH* 154:7; *Teshuvot Maharashdam EH* 103; *Teshuvot Ein Yitzhak* 2, *EH* 34 (5) in the name of the majority of *Poskim*; *Tur EH* 77, 154; *PDR* 5:129, 131; 9:94, 96 (Rabbis Unterman, Elyashiv and Yisraeli); *Teshuvot Dibrot Eliyahu* 5:67.

Cf. other decisors who mandate that a wife's plea for divorce due to a husband's competency must be accompanied by a plea that she wants to have children in order for an arbiter to coerce a get. See *Teshuvot ha-Rosh* 43:2.

Yoshiyahu Pinto mandated *get* coercion in a case where a husband was unable to copulate.[15] Given the fact that today, outside of *Eretz Yisrael* and Morocco, the civil authorities will not enforce a *beit din's* directive to coerce a *get*, Rabbis Spektor, Klatzkin, Feinstein, Tzvi P. Frank, O. Yosef and others state there is a need to implement *kiddushei ta'ut* should the circumstances dictate that type of solution.[16] As such, we view a husband's inability to copulate as "a *mum gadol*."

Seemingly, our conclusion that the inability to copulate constitutes a major defect is insufficient to void the marriage. One of the reasons the decisors chose to refrain from voiding the marriage was that there were prospects that the husband would be cured and then ready to engage in relations with his wife.[17]

Moreover, we have assumed until now that the husband was either obligated to give a *get* or ought to be coerced to give a *get*. Nonetheless, since treating the problem with medication may have solved the problem, under such circumstances there would be no duty to give a *get*.[18] If there is no foundation to obligate a *get* in our case, *a fortiori* there was no basis for *get* coercion and as such there is clearly no basis to void the marriage!

We have three replies to this position. Firstly, according to Rabbi Yitzhak Kolitz, albeit expressing a minority view will obligate a *get* even if the husband has yet to seek medical assistance.[19]

Secondly, Rabbi Tzvi Pesah Frank teaches us the following:[20]

> This concern that he may be cured applies to the *Halakhah* of coercing him to free her. In this context, one must distinguish

---

15. *Nivhar mi-Kesef*, supra n. 3. Cf. some *battei din* that will only *obligate* a *get* when dealing with a husband who is unable to copulate. See, File no. 3878-1, Ashdod Regional Beit Din, July 14, 2013; File no. 867976-1, Tiberias Regional Beit Din, March 7, 2016.

16. *Teshuvot Maharam of Rothenberg*, Cremona ed. 77 in the name of Ra'avyah; *Beit Yitzhak*, supra n. 7; *Teshuvot Devar Eliyahu* 48; *Iggerot Moshe EH* 1:79–80, 3:43 (end), 4:52; *Teshuvot Har Tzvi EH* 2:181; *Teshuvot Yabia Omer* 9, *EH* 38.

17. *Teshuvot Tashbetz* 1:1; *Teshuvot ha-Rivash* 127; *Teshuvot Be'air Yitzhak, EH* 4 (2); *Teshuvot Da'at Sofer* 49 in the name of Havot Ya'ir; *Teshuvot Maharsham* 3:16; *Teshuvot Ezrat Kohen EH* 4.

18. *Teshuvot Noda be-Yehudah*, Mahadura Tinyana *EH* 89; *PDR* 12:103, 118, 121–122 (Rabbis O. Yosef's and E. Waldenberg's opinions); File no. 38781-2, Ashdod Regional Beit Din, July 14, 2013.

19. See *PDR* 12:115–116. For the propriety of resolving cases of *igun* based upon a minority opinion, see this writer's *Rabbinic Authority*, vol. 3, 239–262.

20. *Har Tzvi*, supra n. 16.

between a permanent flaw and a temporary flaw where our Sages did not say we coerce a *get* when there are prospects of improvement. However when dealing with a mistaken transaction since it is dependent upon human expectations and the expectation is that a person does not want to enter a situation where there is a doubt (whether the person will be cured – AYW). . . .

In contradistinction to Rabbi Menahem Schneersohn who contends that the issue of curability is a factor in *kiddushei ta'ut* as well as concerning *get* coercion,[21] Rabbi Frank claims this factor of curability only relates to whether one coerces a *get*. In our case, if the wife would have been aware of this flaw and that it may not be curable; clearly she would not have married him.

The husband refused to avail himself of medical assistance. It was the husband's responsibility to seek help.[22] In the event that the husband refuses to be cured, following implicitly the *mesorah* of others,[23] as Ra'avyah and Rabbi Stern argue, the Talmudic *hazakah* (presumption) of "*tav le'meitav tan do mi-le-meitav armalu*" (lit. translated: better to live as two than to live alone)[24] is inapplicable.[25] As such, under these circumstances *bittul kiddushin* is applicable.[26]

As noted by Rabbi Avraham Yudlovich, David's failure to engage in conjugal relations is a breach of an implicit condition of the marriage in general and an explicit condition of the *ketubah*, the marriage agreement in particular.As such, in a case of *igun* the marriage may be voided based upon *kiddushei ta'ut*.[27]

---

21. *Teshuvot Tzemah Tzedek*, 2:312 (2).

22. *Helkat Mehokeik, SA EH* 76:18.

23. *Ein Yitzhak*, supra n. 7 relying upon *Havot Yair*, supra n. 7; *Teshuvot Iggerot Moshe EH* 1:79. For other *teshuvot* which address whether the *hazakah* applies to major defects of the husband, see *Teshuvot Shevut Ya'akov* 1:101; *Teshuvot Hut ha-Meshullash* 3:3; *Iggerot Moshe EH* 3:48, 4:113; *Teshuvot Yabia Omer* 7, *EH* 7.

24. *Yevamot* 118b; *Ketuvot* 75a; *Kiddushin* 7a, 41a; *Bava Kama* 110b–111a.

25. *Teshuvot Maharam of Rothenberg*, Cremona ed. 77 in the name of Ra'avyah; *Teshuvot ha-Shavit*, 7:20. Cf. *Ezrat Kohen*, supra n. 17.

26. In effect, Rabbi Stern is in agreement with a contemporary *Posek*, Rabbi Frank that curability will not preempt the possibility of voiding a marriage.See *Teshuvot Har Tzvi EH* 2:181. However others such as Rabbi Shalom Schwadron disagree with this position. See *Teshuvot Maharsham* 6:160.

27. *Teshuvot Beit Av, Ezrat Avraham*, 27 (2). However, we should note that even if a *ketubah* would not be executed a husband's marital duties such as *onah* is construed as a *tenai beit din* (loosely translated: a *halakhic* duty) and consequently is an *obligato ex lege*. See *MT, Ishut* 12:1, 5; *Tur EH* 79; *SA EH* 79:1; *Helkat Mehokeik SA*

(2) The wife must be unaware of the defect prior to the inception of the marriage and only discovered it after the marriage. On the other hand, if for example, during the marriage a husband commits adultery or contracts Alzheimer's, though both may be characterized as a *mum gadol* that significantly impairs the matrimonial relationship, nevertheless since the conduct or disease respectively occurred after the onset of the marriage there would be no grounds for a wife's claim that the marriage was consummated in error.

Based upon the cumulative evidence submitted, we find that Sara became aware of her husband's inability to copulate after the onset of the marriage.

Lest one challenge our conclusion based upon the fact that there is no proof that in fact this *mum* preexisted the marriage and therefore we should follow Rabbi Aharon Walkin's ruling that one is proscribed from voiding the marriage based upon "*kiddushei ta'ut*" when it isn't clear that sexual impotence preexisted the marriage,[28] we must respectfully disagree.

In contradistinction to Rabbi Walkin's posture, a review of the *teshuvot*, rulings dealing with impotence and which explore the possibility to void the marriage via the vehicle of *kiddushei ta'ut* only inquire whether there is medical testimony or documentation if the husband was impotent after the marriage was executed or if the wife still was a virgin.[29] There is an implicit premise in the aforementioned *teshuvot* that the flaw existed prior to the marriage. Addressing a case where there was no proof that prior to the marriage the husband was sexually impotent, Mahariz Enzel rules that we invoke the *hazakah*, the presumption that in fact he was impotent prior to the marriage![30] Therefore, in our case, even though no proof was submitted that demonstrated that his disorder of being unable to copulate existed prior to the marriage this should not preclude this panel from voiding the marriage. Moreover, though generally if a wife is aware of a husband's major flaw prior to the marriage, there would be no grounds to subsequently void the marriage,

---

EH 79:1; *Taz, SA EH* 69:1 in the name of Tur.

28. *Teshuvot Zekan Aharon*, 2:104.

29. *Teshuvot Beit Avi*, 2–3:135; *Teshuvot Beit Av*, 7:14; *Devar Eliyahu*, supra n. 16; *Teshuvot Hayyim ve-Shalom*, 2:6; *Teshuvot Maharsham* 3:16; *Iggerot Moshe EH* 3:45, 48, 4:52.

30. *Teshuvot Mahariz Enzel* 35, s.v. *omnam*. See also, *Hiddushei ha-Ramban, Yevamot* 2b; *Iggerot Moshe EH* 3: 45, 49, *EH* 4:113. See also this writer's *Rabbinic Authority,* vol. 3, 138, n. 4 (end), 154–156, n. 45.

in a situation where he is sexually impotent and the wife is aware of the defect prior to the marriage, the marriage could be voided subsequently because of the inability to sire children. [31] Consequently, based upon invoking "*medameh milta le-milta*" (analogical reasoning) we conclude that the inability to copulate is an impediment to engaging in conjugal relations and therefore even if Sara would have known about his defect prior to their marriage, there would be a basis to subsequently void the marriage.

Lest one challenge our conclusion that the husband was unaware prior to his marriage of his inability to copulate therefore since his failure to disclose this *mum* to his wife was unintentional therefore we cannot invoke *kiddushei ta'ut* in order to void their marriage, we disagree. Nothwithstanding that there exist authorities who would refrain from employing the technique of *kiddushei ta'ut* under these conditions,[32] other *Poskim* disagree and contend that this avenue to engage in *bittul kiddushin* will equally apply regardless if the husband intentionally or unintentionally failed to disclose the *mum* to his wife prior to the marriage.[33]

(3) Finally, upon a wife's awareness of the major latent defect, she must decide to leave the marriage. Regarding this condition, whether she must immediately leave the marriage or not is subject to debate. Though in accordance with certain *Poskim*,[34] upon discovery of a major latent defect one must bolt the marriage immediately or refrain from remaining in the marriage for an extended period of time, nonetheless, in pursuance to Rabbi Moshe Feinstein and others who argue that she may continue to live with him provided she offers a reasonable explanation.[35]

---

31. Shaul ben Tzvi Hirsh, *Teshuvot Besamim Rosh* 340; D. Weinfeld, *Teshuvot Doveiv Meisharim* 1:77. Cf. *Havot Yair*, supra n. 7.

32. Rabbi Perlmutter, *Teshuvot Even Shoham EH* 57; *Teshuvot Rav Pe'alim* 1, *EH* 8.

33. *Teshuvot Sha'arei Tzion* 2, *EH* 20 (22–25) in the name of Tosafot, Ran, Tur and Rema.

34. *Tur* and *Beit Yosef EH* 154; *Teshuvot Maharik, shoresh* 24; *Teshuvot R. Akiva Eiger*, Mahadura Tinyana, 56.

In fact, should a woman fail to disclose a *mum*, defect prior to the marriage, should the man discover the flaw after the marriage, he is obligated to bolt the marriage immediately. Otherwise, the marriage is valid. See *Beit Shmuel, SA EH* 117:19. According to the aforesaid position, the same conclusion ought to be applied to a wife's discovery of her husband's latent defects after the onset of the marriage.

35. *Iggerot Moshe EH* 3:45 ("*ta'am hagun*" or "*tirutzim nekhonim*"), 48, 4:113; *PDR* 1:5, 11–12. See this writer's *Rabbinic Authority*, vol. 3, 136–139.

Consequently, in our situation, the couple married in July 2010. The defect was discovered in August–September of 2011 and she left the marital home during September 2014. In pursuance to the first approach, one cannot void the marriage since it seems she accepted the fact that he had a flaw (*"savrah ve-kiblah"*) given that she only left almost three years after her discovery.

The compelling question is why did she discover her husband's disorder of the inability to ejaculate only after one year and a half of marriage? Secondly, upon discovery of the defect why did she remain married to him? Why did she wait three years before separating from him?

In response to our first question, let's cite an excerpt from *Dayan* Tzion Boaron's ruling.[36] Dealing with a husband who was mentally dysfunctional, Rabbi Boaron describes the wife's mindset prior to discovering that her husband was suffering from a mental disorder in the following fashion:

> And one should not conclude that since she lived with him for seven years and gave birth to two children, she observed the defect and forgave him (*"mehilah"*). That is not the case. When dealing with such matters a person cannot understand the nature of the disease until much time has elapsed since sometimes due to her love for him she rationalizes his anger and temper and his agitated condition as being transient and she longs and hopes that the situation will improve. In particular, a person who takes medication regularly, there are times when he is content and silent. . . . One cannot say one observes and one is appeased as written in Maharsham . . . when he was asked about a couple who lived together for over 14 years. Since episodes of mental dysfunctionality occur from time to time and a man hopes to be cured and therefore . . . one cannot speak of seeing and being appeased.

In our case, when Sara married David she was 19 years old and, in her own words, "naïve." It was only in August 2011, a year and a half after her marriage commenced that she began to understand partially what was transpiring in her bedroom. And only after conversing with her girlfriend did she fully understand that her husband had a serious problem, namely an inability to copulate.

After she recognized "the situation," she did not leave him because

---

36. *Teshuvot Sha'arei Tzion* 3, *EH* 4.

he promised that he would seek medical help for his problem. Rabbi Boaron argues that sometimes it takes time to be educated to what is transpiring in front of one's eyes and one cannot say "she observed and was appeased" because in Rabbi Boaron's scenario the mentally impaired husband was taking medication. A fortiori in our case where it took time for Sara to comprehend what was happening and even after she came to the realization of what she was dealing with nonetheless her husband refused to take medication one cannot say "she observed and was appeased"! After a brief time, she realized that all his promises to seek medical assistance would never materialize, nonetheless she remained in the marital home due to the fact she apparently had no money to pay for the rent as well as ongoing domestic expenses. As Rabbi Feinstein rules in a situation where a wife has "a ta'am hagun," a proper reason or "tirutzim nekhonim" reasonable explanations to remain with her husband,[37] one may remain despite his major defect.[38] Finally, after three years, upon being able to address her financial matters, she left him due to his inability to copulate and for her to live with him intimately. Rather than bolt the marriage immediately, the wife should wait and see if the situation may be curable.[39] Unknowingly, as we mentioned in our first decision Sara was following the view of some Poskim that one waits two or three years hoping that a cure would be found.[40]

Let us summarize our presentation by citing from Dayan Boaron's aforementioned teshuvah dealing with a mentally dysfunctional husband.

> We find that in our case that the kiddushin have been under-mined certainly in terms of the hazakah that a person is not appeased with such a defect . . . and there is omeid ha-da'at (a clear expectation – AYW) that if she had known about the dis-

---

37. Iggerot Moshe, EH, 3:45

38. The rationale for Sara to remain with her husband due to being financially incapable at this point in her life to leave him is memorialized in various halakhot. For example, as Tosafot Bava Kama 110b, s.v de'adateia de'hahi notes becoming divorced is a "hov", a debt to the wife since spousal support among other monetary privileges is lost. See also Teshuvot Hatam Sofer EH 2:131; Iggerot Moshe EH 1:148.

39. Tur EH 76; Derishah, Tur, EH 76:6; Helkat Mehokeik, SA EH 76:18; Beit Shmuel SA EH 76:17; Teshuvot Noda-be-Yehudah, Mahadura Tinyana, EH 89; Teshuvot Mateh Avraham 11.

40. Teshuvot Maharashdam EH 103 in the name of Teshuvot Maharlbah 33; PDR 12:100, 122 (R. O. Yosef's opinion).

ease prior to the marriage surely she would not have consented to marry him.

In accordance with the *halakhic* thinking of Rabbi Boaron, there is a presumption that a wife will not appease herself by living with a husband who has problems with copulation and there is a clear expectation that if she knew about what would occur "in the bedroom" during the marriage, she never would have married a husband who possessed such a major defect.

2. *Umdana* – A wife's assessed expectations of the marriage

The question is whether a husband's abstention from conjugal relations may serve as grounds to void a marriage.

There is a duty upon a husband to have conjugal relations with his wife. Whereas according to some authorities the obligation is derived from the Biblical word in Shemot 21:10 "*she'erah* . . . he shall not diminish" or "*ve'onatah* he shall not diminish,"[41] others derive the duty by logical inference. Elaborating upon this position, Rabbi Naftali T. Berlin states:[42]

> Reason informs us that (the husband) is so bound . . . as everyone knows, for this purpose that a bride enters into marriage. . . . Hence if he denies her sexual ties, she is deprived of her right.

When dealing with monetary matters, generally speaking, *Halakhah* allows individuals including prospective spouses to determine their own monetary relationships, provided that the arrangement complies with a proper form, i.e., *kinyan*, and is not violative of any prohibitions such as theft or the interdict against taking *ribbit* (*halakhic* interest).[43]

On the other hand, a husband is proscribed from preparing a prenuptial agreement which releases himself from his duty to perform conjugal relations[44] due to the fact that such abstention from relations engenders "*tza'ar*," pain for his wife and/or is understood as entailing "the *ikar*

---

41. *Mekhilta de R. Yishmael Mishpatim* 3, (ed. Horowitz-Rabin).

42. *Birkat ha-Netziv, Mekhilta*, supra n. 41.

43. *Kiddushin* 19b; *SA, EH* 38:5; *SA, HM* 291:17; *Beit Yosef, Tur HM* 305:4; *SA, HM* 305:4; *Rema, SA HM* 344:1.

44. *Hiddushei ha-Ramban, Bava Batra* 126b, s.v. *harei zu mekudeshet.*

Alternatively, it is viewed as *mehilah*, waiving her right to engaging in relations. See *Shitah Mekubetzet, Ketuvot* 56a in the name of Rashba.

ha-nissuin", the essence of marriage.[45] Notwithstanding the view of Talmud Yerushalmi and a few decisors,[46] adopting the Talmud Bavli's position,[47] the majority of *Poskim* invalidate such a condition due to the fact that it is "*matneh al mah sha-katuv ba-Torah,*" it is a stipulation in variance to the Torah.[48]

In short, the performance of "*onah*" is one of the foundations of a *halakhic* marriage and consequently a husband cannot decide to unilaterally opt out of it.[49]

The obligations and rights between a husband and wife emerge from the establishment of marriage regardless of whether the parties put these duties and rights into writing and regardless if they spoke about them. One of the husband's duties is to provide "*onah,*" the engagement in intimate relations.[50] Here we are not referring to creating a family

---

45. *Rashi, Kiddushin* 19b; *Ramban,* supra n. 44; *Ramban, Sefer ha-Zekhut, Ketuvot* 26 (on Rif).

46. *Talmud Yerushalmi, Ketuvot* 5:7 and *Bava Metzia* 7:7; *Hiddushei ha-Ritva, Kiddushin* 19b, *Bava Metzia* 51a and *Bava Batra* 126b; *Mordekhai Ketuvot* 213 and *Bava Metzia* 369.

47. *Ketuvot* 56a, *Kiddushin* 19b, *Bava Metzia* 94a.

48. *Rashi, Ketuvot* 56a; *Rashbam, Bava Batra* 126b; *Ramban,* supra n. 44; *MT, Ishut* 12:7; *Tur EH* 38:12–13; *SA* and *Rema EH* 38:5.

49. Though if a wife requests (or possibly sets a condition) before the marriage (or possibly during the marriage) that her husband refrain from performing *onah,* assuming the husband has fulfilled the *mitzvah* of having children, there are authorities who will validate this arrangement (see *MT, Ishut* 15:1, *SA EH* 76:6; *Mishneh le-Melekh, MT Ishut* 6:10; *Perishah, Tur EH* 76:17; *Hagahot Rabbi Akiva Eiger, SA EH* 76:1; *Teshuvot Shoeil u-Meishiv* 3:108), clearly in our case no such arrangement was advanced by Sara.

50. *Mishneh Torah* (hereafter: *MT*), *Ishut* 12:1, *Piskei ha-Rosh, Ketuvot* 5:32; *SA EH* 69:1, 154:3; *Bi'ur ha-Gra SA EH* 154:7.

As some authorities argue there are two elements in this "*shi'bud*" (loosely translated: servitude) being bound to his wife. Firstly, *onah* entails engaging in conjugal relations. Secondly, the husband is bound to engage in *kirvat ba'sar,* caressing such as kissing and hugging his wife. Should he refuse to engage in sexual relations with his spouse and assuming certain conditions are obtained he is deemed a *moreid* (rebellious) and the wife may request her *get.* See *Piskei ha-Rosh, Ketuvot* 62:29; *Bah, Tur EH* 76. Should a husband refuse to caress his spouse, he is deemed a "*moreid.*" See *Teshuvot Mahaneh Hayyim* 2, *EH* 41 (end); *Teshuvot Yaskil Avdi* 6 *EH* 106(1).As such, the wife may request a *get* and should he refuse to give it, a *beit din* may compel him to give one. See *SA EH* 77:1.

For the factoring of "*kiruv ba'sar*" regarding the voiding of a marriage and the issue of *mamzerut* (*halakhic* bastardy), see *Teshuvot Shevut Ya'akov* 1:101; *Teshuvot Ein Yitzhak* 1, *EH* 24, Anaf 4, subsection 34; *Teshuvot Minhat Yitzhak* 7:122. See also *Teshuvot Ktav Sofer EH* 102(end).

but rather engaging in sexual relations. The husband's performance of the imperative of *onah* applies even if his wife gave birth to children in a former marriage or from him.[51] A husband's failure to perform *onah* places him in the category of "a *moreid*," a rebellious husband and we coerce a *get* even without forewarning him.[52]

In short, Sara is arguing that had she known that there would be no conjugal relations she never would have married him. In effect, she is advancing an *umdana*. In contradistinction to *kiddushei ta'ut* which as we have demonstrated focuses upon a husband's flaw prior to the marriage, namely the existence of a preexisting grave flaw in the husband's physiology or behavior which if failed to be disclosed may under certain conditions be grounds to void a marriage (*bittul kiddushin*), *umdana* deals with an event (or events) which transpires *after* the inception of marriage. For example, "had I known that my husband would have become a *mumar* (an apostate Jew), become a criminal or would have become mentally dysfunctional during our years of marriage I never would have married him" may serve as illustrations of a wife invoking an *umdana demukhah*, a major inference from assessed expectations (hereafter: *umdana*) which if proven may serve as grounds to void a marriage without the giving of a *get*.[53]

---

51. *Teshuvot ha-Rosh* 43:5; *Tur* and *Beit Yosef EH* 154; *SA EH* 154:7; *PDR* 1:55, 59; 10:104.

52. *SA EH* 77:1; Rabbi E. Lehrman, *Devar Eliyahu* 73. Other decisors such as *Teshuvot ha-Rosh* 43:10 and *Hazon Ish EH* 108:13 require a forewarning.

53. For examples of various *umdanot* which serve as a basis to void a marriage, see *Tosafot, Ketuvot* 47b,s.v. *shelo*; *Teshuvot Maharam of Rothenburg* Prague ed., 1022; *Teshuvot Noda be-Yehudah*, Mahadura Kama *EH* 88, Mahadura Tinyana *EH* 80 (end),135; *Teshuvot Beit ha-Levi* 3:3; *Teshuvot Hesed le-Avraham*, Mahadura Tinyana *EH* 55; *Teshuvot Radakh*, Bayit 9; *Teshuvat Torat Hesed EH* 26; *Teshuvot She'eilot Moshe EH* 2 (*halitzah*); *Teshuvot Zikhron Yehonatan* 1, *YD* 5; *Teshuvot Avnei Hefetz* 30; *Teshuvot Sha'arei Ezra* 4, *EH* 26; *Teshuvot Meishivat Nefesh EH* 73–77; *Teshuvot Maharsham* 7:95 (a matter of a wife's being mentally dysfunctional); D. Meisels, *Teshuvot Radad, EH* 40; *Iggerot Moshe EH* 4:121; *Teshuvot Har Tzvi EH* 2:133. Whether an *umdana* may serve as the sole avenue to void a marriage or as a *senif*, a supporting argument to void a marriage is subject to debate.

For our conceptual distinction between *kiddushei ta'ut* and *umdana*, see *Teshuvot Ohr Sameah* 2:29; *She'eilot Moshe, op. cit.*; *Zikhron Yehonatan*, op. cit. For authorities who invoke *umdana* as a technique to void a marriage, see *Poskim* cited above.

It is important to stress that *umdana* has been employed in the *teshuvot* even regarding *kiddushei ta'ut* where the defect emerged *after* the onset of the *kiddushin* but did not exist prior to the *kiddushin*. In other words, concerning *kiddushei ta'ut*, once the major latent defect has been identified, some *Poskim* will employ the *umdana* by stating "had she known prior to the marriage about this major defect she

The question is whether a husband's unwillingness to engage in sexual relations rises to the level of an *umdana demukhah*, a major inference from assessed expectations for his wife. If in fact in this case, we are

---

never would have married him." Or even if the defect transpired *after* the marriage such as a husband living with another woman or becoming an apostate there is an *umdana gedolah*, a major expectation that she never would have married him. These would be examples of *kiddushei ta'ut* due to the fact that these situations are analyzed within the context of the *halakhot* of *mekah ta'ut*, the laws of a mistaken transaction where an *umdana gedolah*, a major expectation may nullify a transaction. As such these cases are viewed within the prism of *kiddushei ta'ut*. See *Rema, SA HM* 207:4; *Bi'ur ha-Gra SA HM* 207:14; *Teshuvot Noda be-Yehudah*, Mahadura Kama *YD* 69; *Teshuvot Radakh* 9. See further *Zikhron Yehonatan*, op. cit.; this writer's *Rabbinic Authority*, vol. 3, 158, n. 49.

Cf. *Tosafot Ketuvot* 47b, s.v. *shelo*.

In effect this is the position propounded by Rabbi Refael Shlomo Daichovsky, a retired *dayan* from the Beit Din ha-Rabbani ha-Gadol. Addressing the situation of a Yemenite man who married two women while living in Yemen and subsequently moves to *Eretz Yisrael*, Rabbi Daichovsky states the following:

The entire subject of defects is linked to the opinion of people and their absence of mental readiness to accept a deplorable situation regarding their spouse . . . A defect is not limited to the realm of individual physiology; also a behavioral defect such as being a pimp (*ro'eh zonoth*) would obligate the giving of a *get*. . . . In the western world it is degradation for the woman "to share her bed" with another woman. And a husband who would marry a second wife would be obligated a *get* not only because of the *herem* of Rabbeinu Gershom (the prohibition against bigamy – AYW) but also due to the degradation and the defect that is involved (in this second marriage – AYW) . . . Here (in *Eretz Yisrael* – AYW) the matter is a major embarassment and it should be viewed as a *mum gadol* (a major defect – AYW). . . . See File no. 1-22-1510, Beit Din ha-Rabbani ha-Gadol, September 7, 2004.

Though the definitional guidance for understanding the nature of a *mum* was presented by *Dayan* Daichovsky within the context of obligating the giving of a *get*, we can apply it to *kiddushei ta'ut* one of the techniques of voiding a marriage. Usually, when employing *kiddushei ta'ut*, we are dealing with a husband who fails to disclose to his wife prior to their marriage that he has a *mum gadol*, a major flaw. Here in the case of the Beit Din ha-Rabbani ha-Gadol we are dealing with behavior which occurred during the marriage of the first wife, namely her husband decided to marry a second wife. Despite the fact that one cannot contend that this behavior preexisted the first marriage yet as we mentioned earlier it may be viewed as an example of *kiddushei ta'ut* based upon invoking the *umdana* "*ada'ata dehakhi lo kidshah nafshah*". In other words, the *umdana* is "had she known that her husband would have married a second woman without giving her a *get*, she never would have married him". See *Sefer Mesorat Moshe*, vol. 1, 419. The implicit assumption is that *umdana* is viewed as a *ta'ut*. See Ra'avyah, *Teshuvot u-Be'urei Sugyot*, 1032; *Teshuvot Me'il Tzedakah* 2.

For an earlier discussion of this type of *umdana* in the context of *kiddushei ta'ut*, see *Zikhron Yehonatan*, op. cit. at subsection 17.

dealing with *an umdana demukhah,* according to many *Poskim,* the assessed expectation of one person suffices in order to void a commercial transaction and according to certain *Poskim* under certain conditions we can invoke an *umdana* in order to void a marriage or eliminate the need for a *halitzah.* [54]

This *umdana* of marriage of *"ada'ata dehakhi lo kidshah nafshah"*(lit. with this understanding she never would have married him) is to be understood as an implicit condition to the marriage.[55] In other words, in our case, given that the husband here failed to have intimate relations he is an undermining a *tenai,* a condition to the marriage and therefore we may invoke the *umdana "ada'ata dehakhi lo kidshah nafshah."* Moreover, in accordance with Rabbi Moshe Rozin one may invoke this *umdana* (on this understanding she did not betroth[56] him) as a vehicle to void the marriage in a situation where conjugal relations are being withheld by a husband.[57]

This *umdana* "contemplates" that under certain conditions the wife expects that she will be able to exit the marriage if her spouse acts improperly. As some *Poskim* point out, prior to invoking the *umdana* one must be assured that there exists no basis to coerce the husband to give a *get.*[58] If *get* coercion is a distinct possibility, her marriage may be dissolved by *get* coercion due to her husband's failure to perform *onah* and therefore there would be no basis for invoking an *umdana.*

If *Tova'at* had been residing in *Eretz Yisrael* where *get* coercion is an option, albeit employed on a limited basis, the marriage may have been dissolved by *get* coercion. And in pursuance to certain *Poskim,* in light of the option of *get* coercion, Sara may have been unable to invoke the *umdana.* However, today outside of *Eretz Yisrael,* where Sara resides, there is no *beit din* which is legally and thus *halakhically* empowered to

---

54. *Mordekhai, Yevamot* 4:29; *Teshuvot She'ailat Yitzhak,* 174, 186 (R. Stern's opinion); *Teshuvot Noda be-Yehudah,* Mahadura Kama, *YD* 69; *Mahadura Kama EH* 88; *Teshuvot Ohel Moshe* 1:62, Mahadura Tlitai 123; *Beit Meir, Tzal'ot ha-Bayit* 6; *Teshuvot She'eilot Moshe EH* 2 (4); R.Y. Frankel, *Derekh Yesharah, be-Din Halitzah* in the name of R. Feinstein; *Iggerot Moshe EH* 4:121; *Teshuvot Sha'arei Ezra* 4:26. For the basis of utilizing *halitzah* rulings to void a marriage, see this writer's *Rabbinic Authority,* vol. 3, 154, n. 44.

55. *Teshuvot Binyamin Ze'ev* 71; *Teshuvot Terumat ha-Deshen* 223; Rabbi Shkop, *Sha'arei Yosher* 5:18. For understanding this *umdana* as a *"ta'ut,"* an error, see *Me'il Tzedakah,* supra n. 53.

56. The word betrothal may be loosely translated as she did not marry him.

57. *Teshuvot She'eilot Moshe EH* 2 (28).

58. Rabbi Meir Posner, *Tzal'ot ha-Bayit* 6; *Zikhron Yehonatan,* supra n.53; *Teshuvot Shoeil u-Meishiv,* Mahadura Kama 198.

coerce a husband to give a *get*. Consequently, in the absence of the ability to coerce David to give a *get*, based upon the submitted facts we may employ the *umdana* due to his failure to have relations with his wife.

Based upon the foregoing presentation and the cumulative evidence submitted to this *beit din*, notwithstanding contrary views recorded in some *teshuvot* which reject the deployment of *umdana* as a means to void a marriage,[59] following a *mesorah* to which we alluded to earlier in our presentation,[60] we find that our analysis of the *umdana, ada'ata de-hakhi lo kidshah nafshah* which may be invoked concerning the absence of marital relations on most occasions provides the grounds for freeing the *Tova'at* from her marriage without the giving of a *get*.

In sum, we are voiding this marriage due to the husband's incapability of copulating during intercourse based upon "*kiddushei ta'ut*" and his unwillingness to engage in conjugal relations based upon the invoking of an "*umdana.*"

To state it differently, with the establishment of a *halakhic* marriage, there emerges the *hazakah*, the presumption of an *eishet ish*, a married woman which renders both spouses subject to various *issurim*, prohibitions including sexual ties to a third party. As noted by some *Poskim*, if there is *sefek sefeika me'doraita de'dina*, a double doubt regarding what the *Halakhah* ought to be, one can permit certain leniencies concerning certain marital and divorce matters and therefore trump the *hazakah* of an *eishet ish*.[61]

Consequently, in regard to *bittul kiddushin*, voiding a marriage we are

---

59. *Teshuvot Avodat ha-Gershuni* 35; *Teshuvot Beit Yitzhak* 1:106; *Teshuvot Heikhal Yitzhak EH* 2:25; File no. 861974/1, Tzfat Regional Beit Din, January 21, 2013 (Rabbi Y. Ariel's opinion).

In accordance with their view, invoking the *umdana* creates a situation of a *safek kiddushin*, a doubtful *kiddushin*, and for some *Poskim* such as *Teshuvot Maharbil* 1:17 one should refrain from being more lenient in *kiddushei safek* than a doubtful divorce. Nonetheless, *Teshuvot Maharik, shoresh* 171, *Pri Hadash, YD* 110 (end) dealing with *Sefek Sefeika, Teshuvot Maharsham*, vol. 8, *EH* 239, *Teshuvot Sha'arei Tzion* 3, *EH* 4, 22–24 and others follow the view of Ran in first chapter of Tractate Kiddushin that *safek kiddushin* creates a *hezkat penuyah*, a presumption of a single woman *me'deoraita*, on a Biblical level, and the rabbis ruled stringently due to the prohibition of *eishet ish* and therefore she requires a *get*.

60. See supra n. 53.

61. For the effectiveness of a *sefek sefeika* in *Halakhah* to trump *hezkat eishet ish* in certain marital and divorce contexts, see M. Yerushalamski, *Teshuvat Minhat Moshe EH* 11; M. Yerushalamski, *Teshuvot Be'air Moshe, Kuntres Binyan Yerusha-layim* 18; *Teshuvot Yabia Omer* 7, *EH* 6(5–7), 8, *EH* 3(16), 9, *EH* 20(4). See supra Introduction, text accompanying notes 44–47.

invoking the *mesorah*, the tradition that a *sefek sefeika de'dina* is effective to trump a *hezkat eishet ish*. In our case, there is a controversy whether *kiddushei ta'ut* is a valid technique to void a marriage. [62] As such, there emerges a *safek*, a doubt whether voiding a marriage in such a fashion is *halakhically* proper. Moreover, there is a second *safek* whether there are grounds to void a marriage based upon the deployment of an *umdana*.[63] In light of the aforementioned *mesorah*, when there exists a *sefek sefeika* whether a certain technique may be implemented to void a marriage, the *sefek sefeika* is effective against the *hezkat eishet ish* and therefore under certain conditions the marriage may be voided.

Based upon the foregoing presentation, Sara is free to remarry, even a *Kohen*, without a *get*.

---

62. See this writer's *Rabbinic Authority*, vol. 3, 140, n. 8, 141, n. 10.
63. See supra notes 53 and 59.

D.   A HUSBAND WHO SUFFERS FROM A DELUSIONAL JEALOUSY DISORDER AND ENGAGES IN SPOUSAL RAPE

The facts of the case

The couple was married in 2004 according to *Halakhah*. Over a period of eleven years, they had three children. Four to five years into the marriage, Miriam (hereafter: *Tova'at* – the plaintiff) read Yosef (hereafter: *Nitva's* – defendant's) text messages that he sent to other women such as "thank you for last night" and once overheard him having a lengthy telephone conversation with a woman. As a result of these events, *Tova'at* confronted him regarding these liaisons and conversations and he became very angry. Subsequent to this conversation, in October 2012, he accused her of sleeping with other men including his cousins, her brother-in-law, his brother-in-law, the kosher store owner and other men she did not know. These accusations did not subside and her siblings, when asked, "what can you say about their marriage," their immediate reply focused upon his allegations of the *Tova'at's* cheating. These were allegations because *Nitva* was never able to corroborate that such behavior occurred. Nevertheless, *Nitva's* accusations abounded about his wife. If he saw a tissue or napkin, he thought she was throwing away sperm. He would arrange the pillows at night and if they were not perfectly arranged the way he left them, he accused her of bringing over a man. Due to her alleged cheating, he would keep her in their home and not let her leave. A few times, he stalked her, recorded her conversations on the home and cell phones, and put GPS on her phone. He installed cameras in and outside of the house in order to monitor *Tova'at's* activities. From time to time, he had hallucinations which made life difficult for the couple. With the onset of his allegations of cheating, *Nitva* began to engage numerous times in emotional and physical abuse including spousal rape, even during the time that she was a *nidah*, her menstrual period. . With the onset of the abuse, she became afraid of him and scared of falling asleep. Her children were frightened and their grades in school dropped. *Nitva* made her swear on a *sefer* Torah in the synagogue that she was faithful to him.

Upon observing some of this behavior, *Nitva's* parents took him to a psychiatrist and the diagnosis given was that he had "delusional jealousy disorder." *Tova'at* submitted to us a bottle of medicine dated December 2, 2012, which states that a psychiatrist prescribed for *Nitva* a medicine known as risperidone which is antipsychotic medication and prescribed for people suffering from delusional jealousy disorder.[1] It is a psychiatric phenomenon in which an individual has a delusional belief that his spouse is being unfaithful. Individuals who suffer from a jealousy disorder, but who fail to experience delusions will not fit the diagnostic criteria for this type of a disorder. Some of the symptoms of this disorder include interrogating the spouse's phone calls, accusing one's spouse of looking or giving attention to other men, questioning the partner's conduct, claiming the partner is engaging in an affair, and engaging in verbal, emotional, and physical abuse. *Tova'at's* representation of his conduct confirms the psychiatrist's diagnosis.[2] Delusional jealousy has received increasing attention from the psychiatric community in the last twenty-five years due to its link with subsequent aggression, especially as directed toward spouses.[3]

Though *Nitva* went for therapy a few times between the end of November 2012 until January or February 2013, *Nitva* refused to continue the counseling because he felt that "*Tova'at* was the problem, not him" (his approximate words). *Nitva* started to take medication for his disorder in December 2012 but ceased taking the medication because *Nitva* claimed "that *Tova'at* was the problem, not him." In reply to our question to members of her family, "what can you tell us about their marriage?" their response was that *Nitva* continuously claims that *Tova'at* is cheating but he has never brought any evidence to support such accusations.

Given that the situation failed to improve, *Nitva's* parents suggested to their daughter-in-law to leave him. In June 2014, the couple separated. Given that the marital situation had deteriorated already in October 2012, the *Beit Din* asked her – "why did she wait until June 2014 to bolt the marriage?" Her reply was she had tried to save the marriage for her children and herself and her in-laws were supportive of her mission, but at the end of the day, she realized (and her in-laws agreed) that there were no prospects "to turn the clock backwards" to restore her husband to psychological normalcy and therefore she separated from him. Her reasons for divorce were because of the emotional abuse, physical abuse

---

1. See J. Arturo Silver, et al, "The dangerousness of persons with delusional disorder," 26 *J Am Acad. Psychiatry L.* 607, 609 (1998).

2. Despite the fact that *Nitva* was absent from the various *beit din* proceedings there are *halakhic* grounds to conduct the *beit din* hearing in his absence. Moreover, we implemented certain *halakhic* procedures in order to corroborate the veracity of the wife's allegations. See supra Chapter 8c, n. 3.

3. Silver, et al supra n. 1.

and spousal rape perpetrated by *Nitva*. On various occasions she warned *Nitva* to cease from abusing her sexually, physically and emotionally. Though *Nitva* hit her a few times, she refrained from reporting these incidents to the police. However, on November 27, 2013, *Tova'at* reported an incident to the police and from that time onwards, she had a full order of protection which was subsequently reissued on June 30, 2015, and recently on July 8, 2016. Though in May 2014, *Nitva* was allowed to return to the marital home, the abuse did not subside and a month later the couple separated.

The *Tova'at* does not want to return to him under any circumstances and since the separation transpired over two years ago, she is requesting her *get*. Though various local rabbis have attempted to persuade him to give a *get* and over a year ago, we obligated him to give a *get*,[4] nonetheless he remains recalcitrant and alleges that he will give the *get* provided that *Tova'at* waives her right to approximately $20,000 of unpaid child support payments, discontinues all civil actions such as claims for continuing child support as well as having the order of protection withdrawn.

Tova'at refuses to comply with his demands and consequently *Nitva* refuses to give a *get*. Therefore, we now have to address whether there are grounds to engage in *bittul kiddushin*, loosely translated as voiding the marriage.

Discussion

The threshold question is whether a person exhibiting delusional jealousy disorder falls into the *halakhic* category of a *shoteh* (*halakhically* mentally dysfunctional)? The Tosefta and Talmud define four characteristics of a *shoteh*: one who goes out alone at night, he who spends the night in a cemetery, one who tears his clothes and one who loses what is given to him.[5] Notwithstanding Rabbeinu Simhah, Rabbi Avigdor, Rabbi Moshe Sofer in the name of Rashba, Rabbi Yosef Steinhardt, Rabbi Schneersohn and Sanzer Rov who claim that the list is closed,[6] Hakhmei

---

4. For a discussion of the decision, see this writer'a *Rabbinic Authority*, vol. 3, 284–293.

5. *Tosefta Terumot* 1:3; *Hagigah* 3b. For a fourth type of behavior which is deemed *shoteh*-like conduct, see *Hagigah*, ibid.

6. *Teshuvot ha-Rashba* 1:765, 4:201; *Beit Yosef, Tur EH* 119 in the name of Rabbeinu Simhah; *Teshuvot Maharik, shoresh* 19 in the name of Rabbi Avigdor; *Teshuvot Hatam Sofer EH* 2:24 in the name of Rashba; *Teshuvot Zikhron Yosef* 10; *Teshuvot Tzemah Tzedek, EH* 153; *Teshuvot Divrei Hayyim EH* 53, 74. See also *Teshuvot ha-Rivash* 20; *Teshuvot Tashbetz* 2:132; *Shakh SA YD* 1:24; *Taz SA YD* 1:12.

Provencia, Rambam, Mahari Weil, Tur, Shulhan Arukh, Rema and others rule that the list is not exhaustive of *shoteh* conduct and therefore a person can be classified as a *shoteh* even if his behavior was not one of the four characteristics of a *shoteh* as enumerated in the Talmud.[7]

Adopting the latter approach, the question is whether exhibiting delusional jealousy disorder reflects *shoteh*-like behavior. Individuals with delusional disorder are afflicted with the symptom of "being out of touch with reality." This behavior may parallel the concept of *shoteh le-davar ehad*, insane concerning one matter while remaining lucid in other matters of his behavior. As the Lomzer Rov teaches us the individual who is *itim halim, ittim shoteh* (sometimes sane and sometimes psychotic) experiences moments when he is completely normal and other times when he is abnormal. On the other hand, *shoteh le-davar ehad* is continuously delusional in one area and acts normal in other areas.[8]

In accordance with various *Poskim shoteh le-davar ehad* is halakhically viewed as a *shoteh*.[9] Numerous *Poskim* argue that the psychotic

7.　See *Teshuvot Hakhmei Provencia* 57; *Mishneh Torah* (hereafter: *MT*), *Edut* 3:3; *Teshuvot Mahari Weil* 52; *Tur HM* 35; *SA YD* 1:5, *HM* 35:8 (Cf. *YD* 1:5); *Darkhei Moshe ha-Arukh Tur EH* 119:5, 121; *Sma, SA HM* 35:21; *Beit Shmuel, SA EH* 121:9; *Torat Gittin* 121:5. It is debated whether Rambam would deem an individual a *shoteh* when exhibiting behavior which is not one of the four characteristics mentioned in the Talmud only with regard to submitting testimony or in all other realms. See Rabbi Yehezkel Landau, *Ohr ha-Yashar* 30; *Teshuvot Ba'al ha-Tanya* 25; *Zikhron Yosef*, supra n. 6; *Tevuot Shor* 1:29.

8.　*Teshuvot Divrei Malkiel* 3:137; Professor Yisrael Strauss, "The *shoteh* and psychosis in *Halakhah* with contemporary clinical application" (Hebrew), *Kenas ha-Dayanim*, 267, 273 (5774). Cf. *Tzemah Tzedek*, supra n. 6 who argues that the two concepts are not identical.

9.　*Tzemah Tzedek*, supra n. 6; *Teshuvot Oneg Yom Tov* 153; *Teshuvot Beit Yitzhak EH* 2:6; *Teshuvot Helkat Yoav* 1:20; *Zikhron Yosef*, supra n. 6; *Teshuvot Mishnat Rabbi Aharon* 53; *Iggerot Moshe EH* 120:2. Cf. Rabbi Moshe Sofer who contends that whether a *shoteh le-davar ehad* is viewed as a *shoteh* is a *safek*, a matter of doubt and requires further clinical and *halakhic* inquiry. See *Teshuvot Hatam Sofer EH* 2:2.

But an individual who is *shoteh le-davar ehad* is viewed as normal in other areas such as consummating a marriage or divorcing a wife. See *Teshuvot Maharit EH* 2:16; *Teshuvot Nefesh Hayah EH* 27; *Tzemah Tzedek*, supra n. 6; *Iggerot Moshe EH* 1:120, 4:97. Cf. *Torat Gittin* 121 (end); *Rabbi Landau*, supra n. 7; *Ohr Gadol* 27 in the name of *Sha'agat Aryeh*.

Cf. others who deem him as a *shoteh* even when he acts normally in other matters. See *Hakhmei Provencia* supra n. 7 in the name of Rabbi Kimhi; *Oneg Yom Tov*, op. cit.; *Beit Yitzhak*, op. cit.; *Teshuvot Divrei Hayyim*, 2 *EH* 74; *Mishnat Rabbi Aharon*, op. cit.; *Zikhron Yosef*, supra n. 6. Some of these authorities such as Rabbi Kimhi arrived at their ruling based upon the fact that one cannot diagnose their other behavior. In the event that a professional assessment can be arrived at that

behavior must have occurred at least three times in order to label him a *shoteh*.[10]

Based upon the foregoing *halakhic* analysis as well as the cumulative evidence submitted to this panel, the behavior of an individual exhibiting delusional jealousy disorder is the conduct of a *shoteh* for two reasons: Firstly, such behavior is subsumed in the category of *shoteh le-davar ehad* and secondly the recurrence of this psychotic conduct[11] more than three times labels him as a *shoteh*. Pursuing the view of Tosafot that mandates that there must have been an assessment that in fact he is a *shoteh le-davar ehad*,[12] Yosef was diagnosed by a health care professional with this disorder and therefore Yosef is deemed a *shoteh* only with regard to his recurring conduct which is symptomatic of his delusional jealousy disorder.

The question is whether one may void a marriage entails a threshold issue whether the *ilat gerushin* (grounds for divorce) may be coerced by a *beit din* or not?[13] To state it differently, in pursuance to this *mesorah*, if the *ilat gerushin* is subject to *get* coercion then one may investigate whether there are grounds to void the marriage. On the other hand if the *ila* is not subject to *get* coercion an arbiter is proscribed from deliberating whether the conditions have been obtained in order to void the marriage.

Consequently, based upon presentation the emerging question is whether there is a basis to coerce him to give a *get* due to his mental disorder which was not symptomatic of the *shoteh*-like behavior as outlined in Talmud Hagigah?[14] Given these circumstances, clearly there are *Poskim* who would be unwilling to coerce a *get*. [15]Consequently, in the

---

the person acts normally in other areas of life, then he would be deemed normal in regard to these matters.

10. *Teshuvot Maharam ben Barukh* 455; *Pri Megadim YD* 1:23; *Sha'agat Aryeh, Ohr ha-Yashar* 28–31; *Teshuvot Beit Ephraim EH* 89; *Zikhron Yosef*, supra n. 6.

11. In accordance with Rabbi Landau's position the articulation of words is insufficient to establish a person as a *shoteh*. See *Pithei Teshuvah, SA EH* 121:3 in the name of Maharim; *Rabbi Landau*, supra n. 7, *Beit Ephraim*, supra n. 10.

12. *Tosafot, Gittin* 70b, s.v. *hatam*. See also Hazan, *Teshuvot Yehaveh Da'at* 2:16.

13. Prior to entertaining the merits of voiding a marriage based upon *umdana* (see infra text accompanying notes 14–19) argue some authorities that the *ilat gerushin*, grounds for divorce must be subject to get coercion.See *Tzal'ot ha-Bayit* 6; *Teshuvot Shoeil u-Meishiv*, Mahadura Kama 198; *Teshuvot Noda be-Yehudah*, Mahadura Tinyana *EH* 80.

14. See text supra accompanying n. 5.

15. *Teshuvot Marshash EH* 33; *Teshuvot Makom Shmuel* 82; *Teshuvot Binyan Olam EH* 3; *Teshuvot Beit Shlomo EH* 95; Rabbi Y. Kohen, *Teshuvot Divrei Yosef EH*

pursuance of the above *mesorah*, tradition there would be no basis to deliberate from the perspective of the husband's mental condition upon the merits of voiding this marriage.However, there are other decisors such as Rabbi Moshe Feinstein and Rabbi Tzvi P. Frank for have voided marriages where the husband exhibited *shoteh*-like conduct which did not reflect necessarily the Talmudic criteria of what constitutes such behavior. [16]

Alternatively, as aptly noted by *Dayan* Binyamin Be'eri who gave his endorsement of a recent Haifa Beit Din ruling (which is the longest extant *teshuvah*, responsum dealing with *kiddushei ta'ut* ever written) argues that even if a particular *ilat gerushin* fails to permit a *beit din* to impose *get* coercion, nonetheless there may still be grounds fo voiding the marriage due to *kiddushei ta'ut*.[17] Moreover, a review of numerous *teshuvot*, responsa will demonstrate that it is unusual that a *Posek* will advance argumentation that the particular *ilat gerushin* under review dictates *get* coercion prior to addressing the merits of voiding the marriage.

In contradistinction to *kiddushei ta'ut* which focuses upon an event prior to the marriage, namely the existence of preexisting grave flaw in the husband's physiology or behavior which if failed to be disclosed may under certain conditions be grounds to void a marriage (*bittul kiddushin*), *umdana* deals with an event (or events) which transpires after the inception of marriage. In the Talmud and subsequent *mefarshim* (commentaries) and *teshuvot* (responsa), it is known as – "*ada'ata dehakhi lo kidshah nafshah*" (on this understanding she did not betroth[18] him). For example, "had I known that my husband would have become a *mumar* (an apostate Jew), become a criminal or would have become mentally dysfunctional during our years of marriage I never would have married him" may serve as illustrations of a wife invoking an *umdana demukhah*, a major inference from assessed expectations (hereafter: *umdana*) which if proven may serve grounds to void a marriage without the giving of a *get*.[19]

5.

16. *Iggerot Moshe EH* 1:80; *Teshuvot Har Tzvi EH* 2:180.

17. See File no. 870175/4, Haifa Regional Beit Din, December 29, 2014.

18. The *umdana* may be loosely translated as she would not have married him.

19. For examples of various *umdanot* which serve as a basis to void a marriage, see *Tosafot Ketuvot* 47b, s.v. *shelo*; *Teshuvot Maharam of Rothenburg* Prague ed., 1022; *Teshuvot Noda be-Yehudah*, Mahadura Kama *EH* 88, Mahadura Tinyana *EH* 80(end), 135; *Teshuvot Beit ha-Levi* 3:3; *Teshuvot Hesed le-Avraham*, Mahadura Tinyana, *EH* 55; *Teshuvot Torat Hesed, EH* 26; *Teshuvot Radakh, Bayit* 9; *Teshuvot*

Based upon the cumulative evidence submitted to this panel at our hearings which occurred in the summers of 2015 and 2016, it is clear that *Nitva* was suffering from delusional jealousy disorder. The question is whether "had she known that her husband would have developed delusional jealousy disorder during her years of marriage she never would have married him" may be advanced on her behalf by the *beit din* as grounds to void their marriage? In other words, can we employ the *umdana* – "ada'ata dehakhi lo kidshah nafshah" (lit. on this understanding, she never would have married him") in order to void the marriage?

Addressing the situation of a mentally dysfunctional wife, Rabbi Tzvi Pesah Frank argues that living with a *shoteh*, a spouse who is mentally impaired and is viewed *halakhically* as a *shoteh* is an illustration of the Talmudic observation "one does not live together with a snake in the same basket."[20] As Talmud Yevamot 112b explains the reason it has been *halakhically* legislated that marriage cannot be consummated by a *shoteh* is because "one does not live together with a snake in the same basket." Consequently, addressing the case of a mentally impaired husband who is hospitalized, concludes Rabbi Frank, we void the marriage based upon the *umdana* of – "ada'ata dehakhi lo kidshah nafshah."[21] Addressing the case of a mentally dysfunctional wife who is unable to receive a *get*, Rabbi Shalom Schwadron contends that one may void the marriage based upon the identical rationale of "one does not live together with a snake in the same basket."[22] Moreover, Rabbi Schwadron adds that the invoking the *umdana* means that a *tenai*, a condition of the marriage has been violated.[23]

Clearly, having to live with a spouse who exhibits the symptoms of an individual who is suffering from a delusional jealousy disorder is

---

She'eilot Moshe EH 2(*halitzah*); *Teshuvot Zikhron Yehonatan* 1, *YD* 5; *Teshuvot Avnei Hefetz* 30; *Teshuvot Sha'arei Ezra* 4 *EH* 26; *Teshuvot Divrei Malkiel* 4:100; *Teshuvot Tzvi Tiferet* 4; *Teshuvot Meishivat Nefesh EH* 73–77; *Teshuvot Divrei Hayyim* 1, *EH* 3; *Teshuvot Maharsham* 7:95 (a matter of a wife's mental dysfunction); D. Meisels, *Teshuvot Radad EH* 40; *Iggerot Moshe, EH* 1:80, 4:121; *Teshuvot Har Tzvi EH* 2:133. Whether an *umdana* may serve as the sole avenue to void a marriage or as a *senif*, a supporting argument to void a marriage is subject to debate.

20. *Teshuvot Har Tzvi EH* 1:14.

21. *Teshuvot Har Tzvi EH* 2:133.

22. The *psak*, decision, of voiding the marriage is also based upon the fact that the husband had yet fulfilled the *mitzvah* of having children and that the decision required the approval of three rabbis. The purpose of citing Maharsham's *teshuvah* is strictly for the purpose of showing how another *Posek* applies the rationale of "one does not live together with a snake in the same basket" to the case of a *shoteh*.

23. *Maharsham,* supra n. 19.

manifestly different from residing with a husband who is a conventional *shoteh*. But the net result is identical. Both marital experiences entail severe psychological disorders which evoke one to exclaim "one does not live together with a snake in the same basket."

The application of the *umdana* is not limited to the inability to live with a husband who exhibits delusional jealousy disorder. A fundamental requirement for a stable marriage is a husband's respect for his wife.[24] Our foregoing presentation of the facts conveys to this panel *Nitva's* lack of respect for his spouse. The *halakhic* imperatives of *kavod ha'beriyot* and *kavod ha'ishah* are well known and well documented and do not require any further elaboration here. What we have here is a continuing violation of the rabbinic directive "that a man ought to respect his wife more than himself and love her like himself . . . and he should not instill excessive fear and his speaking should be calm rather than be sad or angry."[25]

The lack of *Nitva's kavod*, respect, to his wife was strikingly present in their bedroom.Unlike civil law, the norms of *Halakhah* are not limited to matters of social,economic and political interaction but equally extend to how a married ought to act in their bedroom. There is a duty upon a husband to have conjugal relations with his wife. Whereas according to some authorities the obligation is derived from the Biblical word in Shemot 21:10 "*she'erah* . . . he shall not diminish" or "*ve'onatah* he shall not diminish,"[26] others derive the duty by logical inference.[27] Elaborating upon this position, Rabbi Naftali T. Berlin expounds:[28]

> Reason informs us that (the husband) is so bound . . . as everyone knows, for this purpose that a bride enters into marriage. . . . Hence if he denies her sexual ties, she is deprived of her right.

In other words, *Halakhah* recognizes the wife's right to conjugal relations and therefore the husband has a duty to provide it to her.[29] In fact,

---

24. *Ohr Zarua, Bava Kama* 161; *Teshuvot Maharam of Rothenburg*, Cremona ed., 291, Prague ed. 81; *Teshuvot ha-Rashba ha-Meyuhasot la-Ramban* 102.

25. *Mishneh Torah* (hereafter: MT), *Ishut* 16:19; *Be'air ha-Golah, SA EH* 154:10.

26. *Mekhilta de R. Yishmael Mishpatim* 3, ed. Horowitz-Rabin.

27. *Mekhilta de R. Yishmael*, supra n. 26; *Ketuvot* 48a.

28. *Birkat ha-Netziv, Mekhilta*, supra n. 26.

29. However, if the wife waives her right to engaging in intimate relations, the husband is exempt from his duty of "*onah*" provided that he has fulfilled the *mitzvah* of having children. See *Tosafot Ketuvot* in the name of R. Elhanan, *Ketuvot* 56a, s.v *harei zo; Teshuvot Tashbetz* 1:94; *MT, Ishut* 15:1; *Hiddushei ha-Ramban, Bava Batra*

for Rashba, a couple is mutually obligated one to another as result of the establishment of the marriage.[30]

Others such as Rabbi Avraham Min Hahar and Rabbi Berlin emphasize that the husband has a *kinyan* vis a-vis his wife but only with regard to sexual relations.[31]

However, although the husband's *kinyan* exists and she has a duty to engage in conjugal relations, her husband may not ravish her. As Rabbi Yosef of Trani notes, "certainly she is not subject to him incessantly when she does not desire it."[32] His words were cited subsequently by Rabbi Refael ibn Shimon. Almost two hundred years ago, there was a case reported to a *beit din* of Rabbi Refael ibn Shimon in Egypt where the husband had relations with his wife frequently during one night, leaving her tired and sleepless, and the holding of the *beit din* was that the wife was not deemed a *moredet* (a rebellious wife who refuses to engage in intercourse with her husband) and she was validated for her refusal to have intercourse.[33]

A wife may cease and desist from having relations with a husband who advances excessive demands regarding conjugal relations and she will not be deemed a *moredet* who under certain conditions may be divorced by her husband.[34]

Our presentation can be best summed up in the words found in Chapter 6 of Iggeret ha-Kodesh whose authorship is attributed to Ramban:

> When a man has relations (with his spouse) he should not do so against her will and he should not rape her; the Divine Presence does not reside in such unions . . . he should persuade her with kind and enticing words and other proper and appeasing things. . . . Rather he should awaken her and arouse with alluring words and desire as we said. In short: Before having intercourse, when a man is aroused he should make sure that his wife is enticed as well. In effect, your wife's mindset should correspond to yours.

126b; *Teshuvot Maharik, shoresh* 10 in the name of Rabbeinu Tam, *Darkhei Moshe, Tur EH* 38:8; *Beit Shmuel, SA EH* 66:6.

30. *Hiddushei ha-Rashba, Nedarim* 15b.

31. A. Min Hahar, *Perush to Nedarim* 15b; *Birkat ha-Netziv,* supra n. 26.

32. *Teshuvot Maharit* 1:5. See also, Mabit, *Kiryat Sefer, Ishut* 14.

33. *Bat Na'avat ha-Mardut* II, 2.

34. Kupfer, *Teshuvot u-Pesakim* 156; *Teshuvot Yaskil Avdi* 5:69, 6:25.

Moreover, having to experience pain as a result of being a victim of spousal rape violates what the Talmud teaches us that a wife was given to a husband "for life and not for pain."[35] Being a victim of spousal rape in and of itself entails an infraction of *Halakhah*. Being a victim of sexual abuse, *Tova'at* is an object to be exploited rather than a human being to be respected.

Contemporary *Poskim* such as Hazon Ish and Rabbi Y. Halberstam rule that rape even though generally it does not entail the meting out of force (albeit under certain circumstances it occurs but it is secondary to the actual act of rape) is a violation of *lo yosif* and therefore is an infraction of *habalah*, battery.[36]

Consequently, whether one would coerce a *get* in this case of spousal rape may be derived from how *Poskim* rule regarding coercing a *get* in the case of in battered wife. Notwithstanding that many *Poskim* reject *get* coercion in the case of a battered wife,[37] there are others who under certain conditions will issue a *psak din* of *kefiyat get*, a compulsion order.[38]

Furthermore, as we mentioned, *Nitva* was engaged in acts of emotional abuse such as prohibiting *Tova'at* from leaving their home, stalking her when she was escorted by her in-laws, recording her conversations on the home and cell phones, and putting GPS on her phone. Moreover, he installed cameras in and outside of the house in order to monitor *Tova'at's* activities. In accordance with Mishnah, Talmudim and *Poskim* under certain conditions one may coerce a *get* when a husband emotionally abuses his wife.[39]

---

35. *Ketuvot* 61a.

36. *Hazon Ish, HM* 19:2; *Teshuvot Divrei Yatziv EH* 77:3.

37. *Teshuvot ha-Rosh* 33:3; *Beit Yosef, Tur EH* 154; *Darkhei Moshe, Tur EH* 154:17; *Teshuvot ha-Radvaz* 4:157; R. Kalfon Moshe, *Teshuvot Shoeil u-Meishiv*, 4 *EH* 14; *Teshuvot Mishpat Tzedek* 1:59.

38. *Teshuvot Maharam of Rothenberg*, Cremona ed., 291–292; *Teshuvot ha-Rashba ha-Meyuhosot le-Ramban*, supra n. 24; *Rabbeinu Simhah, Ohr Zarua*, supra n. 23; *Teshuvot Tashbetz* 2:8; *Beit Yosef*, supra n. 37 in the name of Agudah; *Bi'ur ha-Gra, SA EH* 154:17; *Darkhei Moshe,Tur EH* 154:17; *Rema, EH* 154:3 in the name of "*yesh omrim*"; *Teshuvot Perah Mateh Aharon* 1:60; *Teshuvot Hatam Sofer EH* 2:60; *Teshuvot Mateh Lehem EH* 1:8; *Teshuvot Noseh ha-Ephod* 32 (15); *Teshuvot Hayyim ve-Shalom* 2:112; *Teshuvot Tzitz Eliezer* 6:42 (3); *Teshuvot Dibrot Eliyahu* 7:86–88; *Mishpatekha le-Ya'akov* 2:45; File no. 1056520/2, Tel Aviv-Yaffo Regional Beit Din, April 10, 2016.

Hazon Ish Gittin 108:14 advances the logic of *get* coercion in the case of spousal battery but is in doubt whether in fact it ought to be an option.

39. *Ketuvot* 71b–72a; *Ketuvot* 77a; *Yerushalmi Gittin* 9:10; *Teshuvot ha-Rashba ha-Meyuhosot le-Ramban*, supra n. 24; *Darkhei Moshe Tur EH* 154:17; *Tur and SA*

Noting the impropriety of emotional abuse of a spouse, argues Gaon of Vilna,[40]

> Even other matters that do not engender that much pain such as a husband who takes a *neder*, a vow that his wife should refrain from going to her father's home or to a house of mourning . . . *a fortiori* if he pains her physically.

In other words, implicitly following earlier authorities,[41] Vilna Gaon is deriving the *halakhah* of *get* coercion in the matter of spousal physical abuse from the *Halakhah* of *get* coercion in the case of spousal emotional abuse.

Finally, if *Tova'at* had been residing in *Eretz Yisrael* where *get* coercion is an option, albeit employed on a limited basis, the marriage may have been under certain conditions dissolved by *get* coercion. And in pursuance to certain *Poskim*,[42] in light of the option of *get* coercion, *Tova'at* may have been unable to invoke the *umdana*. However, today outside of *Eretz Yisrael* where *Tova'at* resides, there is no *beit din* which is legally and thus *halakhically* empowered to coerce a husband to give a *get*. Consequently, in the absence of the ability to coerce *Nitva* to give a *get*, based upon the submitted facts we may employ the *umdana* regarding *Nitva's* different acts of spousal abuse.[43] This *umdana* – "*ada'ata dehakhi lo kidshah nafshah*" is to be understood as an implicit condition to the marriage.[44] In other words, in our case, given that the husband failed to respect his wife by engaging in different forms of abuse includ-

---

EH 70:3, 154:7; *Teshuvot Maharit* 1:113; *Teshuvot Tashbetz* 2:8; *Teshuvot Binyamin Ze'ev* 88. Notwithstanding Rabbeinu Hananeil who contends that the word "*yotzi*" in some of the above sources means "obligating a *get*," we are following Tosafot who argue that the word means "coercing a *get*." See *Tosafot, Ketuvot* 70a, s.v. *yotzi*.

40. *Bi'ur ha-Gra SA EH* 154:10.

41. *Teshuvot ha-Rashba ha-Meyuhosot le-Ramban*, supra n.24; *Tashbetz*, supra n. 38; *Teshuvot Yakhin u-Boaz* 2:43.

42. Some authorities will employ *get* coercion in cases of a husband's mental disorder such as schizophrenia and epilepsy. See *Teshuvot ha-Rosh* 42:1, *Rema, SA EH* 117:1; *Teshuvot Hayyim ve-Shalom* 2:35; *Teshuvot Tzitz Eliezer*, 6:42, *Perek Aleph*. A *fortiori*, in our case of a husband who suffers from delusional jealousy disorder, there ought to be grounds for *get* coercion!

43. Rabbi Meir Posner, *Tzal'ot ha-Bayit* 6; *Zikhron Yehonatan*, supra n. 14; *Teshuvot Shoeil u-Meishiv*, Mahadura Kama 198.

44. *Teshuvot Binyamin Ze'ev* 71; *Teshuvot Terumat ha-Deshen* 223; *Rabbi Shkop, Sha'arei Yosher* 5:18. For understanding this *umdana* as a "*ta'ut*," an error, see *Teshuvot Me'il Tzedakah* 2.

ing spousal rape and emotional abuse, *Nitva* is undermining a *tenai*, an implicit condition to the marriage and therefore we may invoke the *umdana "ada'ata dehakhi lo kidshah nafshah."* Moreover, in accordance with Rabbi Moshe Rozin one may invoke this *umdana* as a vehicle to void the marriage in a situation where a husband fails to fulfill his duty of *onah*, conjugal relations in a proper *halakhic* fashion.[45]

Based upon the foregoing presentation and the cumulative evidence submitted to this *beit din*, notwithstanding contrary views which reject the deployment of *umdana* as a means to void a marriage,[46] following a *mesorah* which we alluded to at the beginning of our discussion,[47] we find that our analysis of the *umdana, ada'ata dehakhi lo kidshah nafshah* which may be invoked concerning mental dysfunction of a husband as well as spousal abuse including spousal rape provides the grounds for freeing the *Tova'at* from her marriage without the giving of a *get*.

In light of the *umdana* that one cannot reside with a husband who is suffering from delusional jealousy disorder, a disorder which is accompanied by physical and emotional abuse as well as the engagement in spousal rape, Miriam is free to remarry without a *get* any Jew, even a *Kohen*.

---

45. *Teshuvot She'eilot Moshe EH* 2 (28).

46. *Teshuvot Avodat ha-Gershuni* 35, *Teshuvot Beit Yitzhak* 1:106; *Teshuvot Nishmat Hayyim* 129; *Teshuvot Maharsham* 2:110; *Teshuvot Heikhal Yitzhak EH* 2:25; File no. 861974/1, Tzfat Regional Beit Din, January 21,2013 (R. Y. Ariel's opinion)

In accordance with their view, invoking the *umdana* creates a situation of a *safek kiddushin*, a doubtful *kiddushin*, and for some *Poskim* such as *Teshuvot Maharbil* 1:17 one should refrain from being more lenient in *kiddushei safek* than a doubtful divorce. Nonetheless, *Teshuvot Maharik, shoresh* 171, *Pri Hadash, YD* 110 (end) dealing with *Sefek Sefeika, Teshuvot Maharsham*.8, *EH* 239, *Teshuvot Sha'arei Tzion* 3, *EH* 4, 22–24 and others follow the view of Ran in first chapter of Tractate Kiddushin that *safek kiddushin* creates a *hezkat penuyah*, a presumption of a single woman *me'deoraita*, on a Biblical level, and the rabbis ruled stringently due to the prohibition of *eishet ish* and therefore she requires a *get*.

47. See supra n. 13.

E.   A HUSBAND WHO ENGAGES IN SPOUSAL RAPE, REFRAINS FROM SUPPORTING HIS WIFE, EMOTIONALLY ABUSES HIS WIFE AND STEPCHILDREN AND REMARRIES WITHOUT GIVING A *GET* TO HIS WIFE

Facts of the Case

On August 7th and 11th, 2014, September 3rd, 2014, and August 10th, 2016, the aforementioned case was heard and submitted for resolution to this *beit din*.

Mrs. Bryna Stern (hereafter: *Tova'at*, the plaintiff) an *agunah* ("chained wife") for eight and a half years summoned Mr. Haim Stahl, her husband (hereafter: the *Nitva* – the defendant), before our *Beit Din* for the purpose of freeing her from her status of *igun* (chained to a marriage). During Chanukah of 2004, *Tova'at* requested a *get*, and in January of 2005, the *Tova'at* separated from *Nitva*. In the summer of 2007, the marriage was civilly annulled. To this very date *Nitva* will only grant her a *get* in exchange for monetary remuneration in the amount of $300,000.00. *Tova'at* refuses to comply with his condition and therefore *Nitva* refuses to give her a *get*. Subsequent to his demand for "a conditional divorce" *Nitva* has married another woman without giving a *get* to his second wife (*Tova'at*). On December 29, 2014, we obligated him to give a *get*. As we stated in our decision, according to most *Poskim* in a situation where a *beit din* obligates a *get*, the giving of the *get* by the husband cannot be contingent upon the wife fulfilling certain conditions. Given that he continued to refuse to give a *get*, on September 30, 2015, we directed the community to initiate religious, social and economic isolating measures in the form of "*harhakot* of Rabbeinu Tam"[1] against him in order to persuade him to give a *get*. To date, a *get* has not been forthcoming.

Now let's briefly summarize the facts of the case: Prior to the marriage which took place on July 4, 2000, the couple courted each other extensively. Both parties had been married previously and sired children from their respective marriages. There were over ten conversations between the parties during their courting and one-third to half of these conversations dealt with what each one expected of the other should they marry each other. Each one was very concerned to have this second

---

1. For a brief discussion of these isolating measures, see this writer's *Rabbinic Authority*, vol. 3, 291–293.

marriage be successful. Though the *Nitva* spoke to *Tova'at* about his expectations in the marriage, the majority of these conversations focused upon *Tova'at's* hopes. *Tova'at* alleges that she wanted to marry a person who would be kind and considerate to her and to her two sons, and as is the case with most prospective wives, was looking for someone who would be economically supportive in their marriage. Given that at the time, *Tova'at* was almost destitute; her concern to marry a breadwinner was a significant consideration in finding the proper mate. Already in 1987, *Tova'at* began working in order to supplement her first husband's income. As such, both her past marital history from the first marriage and her current economic situation propelled her to be concerned that *Nitva* would be economically supportive. And in fact, *Tova'at* alleges that *Nitva* treated her children nicely prior to their marriage. Regarding *Tova'at's* expectations that *Nitva* would be amiable, good-natured and caring with her children, this representation was corroborated by a woman who initially was a friend of *Tova'at* and subsequently during the marriage became a friend of the couple and had been told by *Tova'at* about this expectation during the marriage prior to *Tova'at's* decision to seek a divorce. The *Tova'at's* children corroborated to this panel that prior to the marriage their step father was kind and friendly towards them.

Immediately after the marriage commenced, *Nitva's* attitude and conduct towards his stepchildren radically changed. During family road trips when the children were between the ages of 6 and 13, *Nitva* would insist that they wear diapers and defecate in their diapers rather than stop on the road and allow them to go to the bathroom. As a controlling personality who dictated that *Tova'at* and her children accede to his many requests, *Nitva* instilled fear in the minds of *Tova'at's* two children and ejected one of her children who challenged his authority from the marital home for a few months. This ejection of one of *Tova'at's* children from the marital home for a period of a few months was corroborated by various individuals including the family rabbi. Whereas one of his stepsons tended to be attentive to his requests, the second son was a more independent personality as well as more aggressive and would not necessarily comply with all his wishes. At times, he would raise his hand against him, attempted once to hit him with a bat, and at other occasions throw things at him. As such, one can understand (not justify) the background of his ejection from the home. At one point, *Nitva* threatened to leave the marriage unless this stepson would permanently move out of the home. Testimony submitted to this panel indicated that this stepson was a fine individual. At times, he criticized his stepchildren for things that they didn't do and alleged that his children from his first marriage were better than his stepsons.

Throughout the duration of living together, on numerous occasions, *Tova'at* alleges that *Nitva* would engage, when she wasn't a *nidah*, in spousal rape in the context of both natural and unnatural intercourse. When he was angry, he would insist in engaging in intercourse despite *Tova'at's* protestations. On numerous occasions, despite *Tova'at's* protestations, he would say, "I want to rape you." And *Nitva* liked that *Tova'at* refused to engage in unnatural intercourse. In some of these incidents of spousal rape pain ensued either from the intercourse or from *Tova'at's* physical fights with the *Nitva* concerning the rape, pain which lasted for a few days. After their separation, *Nitva's* late father-in-law from his first marriage approached *Tova'at* and informed her that his daughter was a victim of spousal rape and wanted to know if she was also a victim of spousal rape. She replied "yes". After the third hearing, we contacted the *Nitva's* first wife in order to ascertain about matters relating to her marriage with the *Nitva*. She replied to us that certain matters in her marriage with the *Nitva* were fine except when asked "about the bedroom" she refused to respond to the *beit din*. Upon her suggestion, she advised us to contact her rabbi regarding this matter. Upon inquiry, the rabbi knew nothing about the nature of their intimate relations but surmised from her reluctance to talk about the matter that "things were bad".[2]

---

2. Though we summoned *Nitva* to appear at the hearing, he refused to attend. Generally speaking, regarding monetary matters both parties are required to be present at a hearing. However, assuming that the defendant was summoned to appear in a matter of *ishut* (personal status) such as a divorce matter, in the event he refuses to appear at the *beit din*, a hearing may be conducted in his absence. See *Teshuvot Noda be-Yehudah*, Mahadura Tinyana, *EH* 91; *Teshuvot Hatam Sofer, EH* 2:167; *Teshuvot Maharash Engel* 4:57; *Teshuvot Imrei Yosher ha-Hadash* 76; *Teshuvot Helkat Ya'akov* 1, *EH* 4; *Teshuvot Havatzelet ha-Sharon EH* 7; File 1/2/707, Supreme Beit Din for Appeals, Z. Warhaftig collection, pp. 140–141; *PDR* 6:265, 269–270; File 1-14-1393, Yerushalayim Regional Beit Din, March 5, 2003; File 924081/1, Yerushalayim Regional Beit Din, March 9, 2014; File no. 947820/5, Tel Aviv Regional Beit Din, April 6, 2016; File no. 865704/1, Tzfat Regional Beit Din, May 8,2017; Rabbi Y. Ariel, *Dinei Borerut*, page 302, Rabbi Dr. E. Shochetman, *Seder ha-Din be-Beit Din ha-Rabbani*, 2nd ed., pp. 521–522; Rabbi A. Dermbamdiker, *Seder ha-Din* 6:59.

Alternatively, a matter of *ishut* is governed by the same procedural rules as a monetary matter. Consequently, seemingly the absence of the husband to appear at a *beit din* hearing will proscribe the panel from commencing with a hearing. See *SA HM* 18:6; *Sma, SA HM* 18:3; *Shakh, SA HM* 13:8; *Tumim HM* 13:4; *Teshuvot Maharam Schick HM* 2; *Hazon Ish HM* 3:11. Yet, there are authorities who would validate proceeding with a hearing concerning a monetary matter in his absence in a situation of *sh'at ha-dehak*, in a time of emergency which is construed as a case of a *bedi'avad* (*post facto*). See *Bah, Tur HM* 13:8; *Ketzot ha-Hoshen* 13:1. Clearly, according to the *Poskim* when dealing with an *agunah*, as in our case we are dealing with a *sh'at ha-dehak*. See *Teshuvot Shevut Ya'akov*, 1:110; *Teshuvot Re'em* 37; B. Sternfield, *Teshuvot Sha'arei Tzion* 3:14; *Teshuvot Agudat Ezov Midbari EH* 9:2. Consequently, relying upon this minority opinion we have grounds to conduct a hearing in the husband's absence.

Cf. other *Poskim* who would mandate that all parties must be present at a *beit din* hearing in order to render a ruling concerning a matter of personal status. See *Teshuvot Divrei Malkiel* 3:145; *Teshuvot Divrei Hayyim* 1, *EH* 5; Rabbi Elyashiv, *Kovetz Teshuvot* 1:181, 3:202; File no. 865704/1, Tzfat Regional Beit Din, May 8, 2017(R. U. Lavi's opinion). The implications of their position is that in the wake of an *agunah's* claim to address the matter of the *get* and/or the possibility to void the marriage, such claims could not be heard and followed up with the issuance of a *psak din*, a decision without the husband's participation in the *beit din's* proceeding. In effect, in the Diaspora where *battei din* are not authorized to impose *get* coercion, an *agunah* may be left with no *halakhic* relief with the attendant results that she may abandon *Yiddishkeit*, Judaism, engage in promiscuous behavior and/or remarry without a *get* and sire children who are *mamzerim, halakhic* bastards. When dealing with an *agunah*, as the *Poskim* state one must find leniencies in order to free them from *havlei igun*, being chained to their husbands. See *Teshuvot Masat Binyamin* 44; *Teshuvot Maharashdam EH* 57; *Teshuvot Yabia Omer* 3, *EH* 20(34). The scope of the leniencies is not limited to the *beit din* seeking solutions to freeing her from her predicament. One of the leniencies is to procedurally be able to confront the plight of the *agunah* even if the husband refuses to appear in *beit din* by permitting the wife to air her claims in *beit din* during his absence.Given that we alluded to a *mesorah*, a tradition which permitted conducting a hearing in *ishut* matters with only one party, *battei din* ought to adopt such a posture.In fact, some *battei din* in the United States have adopted this approach.

Moreover, this couple has been separated for over eleven years. During this period of time, *Nitva* has refused to fulfill his marital duties such as engaging in conjugal relations in an appropriate fashion, furnishing spousal support and full child support and has remarried another woman(without a proper *heter nissuin, halakhic* permission to remarry) without giving a *get* to the *Tova'at*. We have summoned the *Nitva* to the *beit din* but he has refused to appear to address the matter of the *get*. Given that we are dealing with a case of *igun*, we are permitted to address the matter and render a decision even though the *Nitva* is absent from the proceeding. See *Teshuvot ha-Rashbash* 46; *Teshuvot ha-Mabit* 1:76; *Teshuvot Oneg Yom Tov* 168.

In sum, we may conduct a hearing in the absence of the husband for two reasons: Firstly, in a matter of personal status we may convene a hearing in the absence of a party. Secondly, since this case is clearly a situation of *igun*, we may conduct a *beit din* proceeding in the husband's absence.

Despite the fact that there is a basis for conducting a hearing in the absence of the *Nitva*, we are well aware that we must address the need to affirm the *hazakah*, presumption, "a wife does not dare to lie in her husband's presence" as well as accept testimony in his absence, yet we have a well-trodden *mesorah* which would address these concerns. In effect, the procedure adopted addresses the fact that the absence of a party from a hearing will not predispose the party who is attending the *beit din* proceeding from fabricating arguments which are deceptive and fallacious. See

Subsequent to the couple's marital separation, *Tova'at* alleges that *Nitva* had illicit affairs with an Asian woman and she told *Tova'at* that she was raped by him. For approximately a half year *Nitva* lived with her while she was in process of converting to Judaism and lived with her at her own expense. We attempted to contact her but were unable to reach her.

At the same time, *Tova'at* alleges that *Nitva* was emotionally abusive to her and a few times slapped her, threw a chair at her and pushed her once in the bedroom and once in the kitchen. When they moved from her parent's house to a second home, though *Nitva* failed to assist in the moving, he insisted that his pregnant wife of 39 years old who was considered "a high-risk pregnancy" move some of the heavy belongings from their attic from their old home to the new one which was located on the same block. And the reason *Nitva* made *Tova'at* responsible for the moving is because he did not want to move out of their first house. Though *Nitva* never screamed at his wife while interacting socially with their friends, however at home he would curse her using foul language and scream at her as well as raise his hand at her (as well as her children)

Rashi, Sanhedrin 7b; *Sma SA HM* 17:5.In fact, in the wake of a husband's absence from a *beit din* proceeding there are authorities will not trust a wife's trstimony that he husband is impotent. See *Teshuvot ha-Rivash* 127; *Beit Shmuel SA EH* 154:18. It is our understanding that their position would be applicable to the *Tova'at*'s allegation that the *Nitva* engaged in nonconsensual natural and unnatural *bi'ah*, intercourse with her.However, we choose to refrain from discussing the basis for the procedure we adopted which is recognized by numerous *Poskim*.

Moreover, her credibility has not only been corroborated by the procedure we implemented. Notwithstanding some authorities who will not recognize her trust-worthiness regarding an allegation of spousal rape (see *PDR* 4:342, 345), there are other *Poskim* who will trust her. See *Teshuvot Edut be-Ya'akov* 36; *Teshuvot Yaskil Avdi* 5, *EH* 69, 6, *EH* 25). Secondly, if a wife claims that her husband refuses to have conjugal relations with her and refrains from engaging in intimate relations in the conventional manner her words are to be trusted. See *Teshuvot ha-Rosh* 43:5; *Teshuvot ha-Rivash* 127. As Rema rules under such circumstances her words are trusted equivalent to a situation where we impart credibility to her plea that her husband is impotent. See *Rema SA EH* 154:7. In fact, the majority of authorities will accept a wife's claim that her husband is impotent. See *SA EH* 154:7; *Gevurat Anashim* 2, 50, 56, 67. Similarly, one may argue that alleging that one's spouse is engaging in spousal rape ought to be recognized.

Since *Nitva* was given the opportunity to appear and chose to abstain himself from the hearing, attempting to empower himself with the right to in effect prevent *Tova'at* to have " her day in *beit din*" we therefore have adopted the position of those *Poskim* who sanction having a hearing without *Nitva* as well as accepting testimony in his absence. For identical reasoning, see File no. 178–73, Beit Din Yerushalayim for Monetary Affairs and Inquiry into Yuhasin (M. Avraham's opinion).

and one time screamed at her in a retail store when they were purchasing a dining room table. At least three times, *Tova'at* warned him to cease his demeaning conduct. But the behavior persisted. At one point, *Nitva* threw a neighbor out of the house. Though none of the witnesses (children, relatives, friends and third parties) were able to corroborate the physical abuse allegations, nonetheless the family rabbi as well as a woman who was living with the couple from late 2003 until early 2004 stated that her allegations of emotional abuse were true and one witness said that he treated her "like a slave." *Tova'at* claims that he was sadistic and upon hearing that somebody passed away he reacted by laughing. Though there was no professional diagnosis of his conduct, after hearing about his behavior, one psychologist surmised that he was a sociopath.

Initially, in order to address their marital concerns, the couple attended various sessions with their family rabbi. Despite the prudent counsel which was provided by the rabbi, the marriage continued to disintegrate. However, already from 2001 through 2002, at *Tova'at's* request, the couple was attending marital therapy sessions. Though the couple saw three therapists during this period, *Nitva* allegedly felt that the problems in the marriage stemmed from *Tova'at's* behavior and therefore after attending one or two sessions with every therapist he failed to attend future sessions. After completing the sessions in 2002, *Tova'at* remained adamant in trying to continue the marriage for the sake of her children from her first marriage and her son sired from their marriage.

At the outset of the marriage, *Nitva* moved into *Tova'at's* home purchased by her parents and a while later the couple moved into another home purchased by her parents. Any funds expended for the purchase of the new home were covered by *Tova'at's* salary as well as money loaned to her by her parents. Though *Tova'at's* first husband was paying $3750 monthly child support and tuition for his two sons, after approximately three years into her second marriage, those monies ceased to be forthcoming for her children. Though he earned income, *Nitva* kept the overwhelming majority of those monies for himself. In fact, the couple filed their tax returns separately. In short, from the onset of the marriage, *Nitva* was living in his wife's house, she was providing the funding to maintain the domestic household including but not limited to repaying her parental loan, clothing, food and utility bills, and by the third year of the marriage his wife was supporting her family of her first marriage and in most instances paying their son's tuition and medical insurance. Furthermore, on alternate Shabbatot, *Nitva's* four children from his first marriage, ages 7, 9, 11 and 13 were guests in *Tova'at's* home.

Despite the fact that her husband's earned income was expended for the most part for his own personal needs rather than maintaining the domestic household and that *Nitva* allegedly reneged on his oral promise to *Tova'at* to pay her portion of the commission totaling $37,500 as well as $25,000 from the initial investment in a residential home that she sold (totaling $62,500), *Tova'at* remained in the marriage. Moreover, in certain years *Nitva* failed to pay tuition for his son and his wife's two children and to this very day, *Nitva* only pays basic child support for his child as mandated by the civil court and fails to pay for 36% of his tuition and the child's medical insurance as mandated by the civil court,[3] yet for the sake of her children she still wanted the marriage to succeed and therefore acceded to his every request. At the beginning of the marriage she was employed by an insurance agency where she worked 40 hours a week. Subsequently, in 2002 *Tova'at* became financially independent by starting an insurance agency which was open six days a week, supported herself, her two sons from the first marriage and their son, and paid a significant portion of the tuition. Yet, due to *Nitva's* unwillingness to defray expenses by transferring his salary to "the domestic purse," *Tova'at* had to borrow approximately $95,000.00 over a fourteen year period from her parents to defray her family expenses. (As of early 2015, she had repaid her parents a portion of her loan. As of that date, there still remains an outstanding loan balance. In other words, approximately eleven years later after marital separation, *Tova'at* still has not completely repaid the loan!)

As noted above by the woman who working in their home in early 2004, *Tova'at* still was unsure how to handle her marital situation, and she therefore again enlisted the services of a health care professional. From April 2004 until the time of marital separation, *Tova'at* attended marital counseling sessions given by a therapist for the express purpose of trying to determine who was responsible for the marital tensions. Again, *Nitva* participated in four sessions and then refused to continue to participate in any subsequent hearings. Having met *Nitva* a few times, one health care professional's impression (to be distinguished from a professional diagnosis) was that in his words "he was not a *mentsch* and

---

3. To corroborate these allegations, we received copies of the *Tova'at's* personal bank statements, copies of tuition statements and records of post-dated checks, a copy of the *Tova'at's* recent personal tax return, and a copy of the findings of fact, decision and order of the Family Court which in painstaking detail records the financial history of the couple. *Nitva* petitioned her in civil court in order to address the claims of child custody, child support, tuition and medical insurance. *Tova'at* received rabbinic permission to litigate in civil court.

a hateful individual" and that if you wronged him then in *Nitva's* eyes you are "sentenced to death." As such, the psychologist argues, one can understand how such a personality would be recalcitrant regarding the giving of a *get*. And we can understand why a pregnant *Tova'at* ended up having to shlep heavy items from the attic of her first home to her second home which was down the block. Even if the couple had consulted him three years earlier, the psychologist concludes he would have been unable to save the marriage.

Nonetheless, still desiring to keep the marriage and the family together, *Tova'at* attended dozens of sessions hoping to find "a light at the end of the tunnel." By the end of 2004, *Tova'at* realized there were no prospects for marital reconciliation and therefore requested of her husband to give her a *get*. Subsequent to the marital separation in January 2005, on August 9, 2007, the Family Court handed down an order of protection against the *Nitva* mandating that he "refrain from assault, . . . harassment . . . threats of any criminal offense against" *Tova'at* and her two children.

In reply to the question posed by the *beit din* panel to *Tova'at*, "If your husband would have acted properly to your children and supported you, would you have remained in the marriage?" *Tova'at's* reply was: "Given his conduct in the bedroom as well as his personality, I would have left him within two or three months into the marriage. Given his misrepresentation regarding how he would treat my children only showed his lack of trustworthiness, his unwillingness to support my family, his inappropriate behavior in the bedroom and his personality propelled me to get divorced" (*Tova'at's* approximate words). In fact, despite the fact that she already was pregnant with their child she told us that she would have left the marriage after two to three months. However, trying to save the marriage for her children who already had suffered from the behavior of their unfit natural father as well as hoping that there would be a possibility that *Nitva* would change were the reasons she stayed with the marriage for a few years. As a woman of forbearance, *Tova'at* attempted to keep her marriage together for the sake of her children, even with the attendant humiliating and abusive costs.

We asked one of the health care professionals the following question: "If this couple would have undergone marital therapy at the outset of the marriage, would there have been prospects to save the marriage?" Without any hesitation, his response was – "this marriage could never have been saved."

At the end of the day, the picture that was portrayed to us by family members, friends either of *Tova'at* and/or the couple and third parties, men and women (young and old) alike is that *Nitva*, though outwardly in the public eye was perceived either as charming, kind and considerate, "a harmless easygoing guy" and sometimes prone to "blowing up" if you disagreed with him, regretfully, in his marital and familial ties he was controlling, domineering, manipulative, emotionally abusive and subject to fits of anger.[4]

Discussion

A WIFE'S *UMDANA* (ASSESSMENT OF EXPECTATIONS) AFTER THE ONSET OF MARRIAGE

In contradistinction to *kiddushei ta'ut* which focuses upon an event prior to the marriage, namely the existence of preexisting grave flaw in the husband's physiology or behavior which if failed to be disclosed may under certain conditions be grounds to void a marriage (*bittul kiddushin*), *umdana* deals with an event (or events) which transpires after the inception of marriage.[5] For example, "had I known that my husband would have become a *mumar* (an apostate Jew), become a criminal or would have become mentally dysfunctional during our years of marriage I never would have married him" may serve as illustrations of a wife invoking an *umdana demukhah*, a major inference from assessed expec-

---

4. A friend of *Nitva* submitted testimony that he was a *mensch* and *Tova'at* was aggressive and could "eat him up for dinner," yet he pointed out that his testimony related to his interactions with them prior to the marriage. Though the friendship with *Nitva* continued after the marriage, he never observed them as a couple.

5. For our conceptual distinction between *kiddushei ta'ut* and *umdana*, see *Teshuvot Ohr Sameah* 2:29; *Teshuvot She'eilot Moshe EH* 2; *Teshuvot Zikhron Yehonatan* 1, *YD* 5. For decisors who invoke *umdana* as a tool to void a marriage, see *Poskim* cited infra n. 6.

It is important to stress that this *umdana* has been employed in the *teshuvot* both regarding *kiddushei ta'ut* as well as emerging *after* the onset of the *kiddushin*. In other words, concerning *kiddushei ta'ut*, once the major latent defect has been identified, some *Poskim* will employ the *umdana* by stating, "had she known prior to the marriage about this major defect she never would have married him." On the other hand, if the inappropriate behavior or *mum*, flaw, only began after the onset of the marriage and did not preexist prior to the marriage, there may be grounds to employ an *umdana* where she would (for example) exclaim, "had I known that he would become mentally dysfunctional during the marriage I never would have married him." For a discussion of these two types of *umdana*, see *Zikhron Yehonatan*, op. cit., subsection 17; infra case 8g.

tations (hereafter: *umdana*) which if proven may serve grounds to void a marriage without the giving of a *get*.[6]

Seemingly, the employment of an *umdana* here is open to challenge. As we know, for an *umdana* to be effective is dependent upon both parties. For example, a sales transaction involves the agreement of parties, the seller and the buyer: *"taluy be-da'at shenehem."*[7]

The voiding of the sale with the appearance of a defect subsequent to purchase would be predicated upon two conditions:[8]

1. The buyer would have not consummated the deal if he had realized that the item sold would be defective within a reasonable time. As Shulhan Arukh Hoshen Mishpat 232:3 states:

> If one sells another land, a slave, a domesticated animal, or other moveable property, and a defect, which the buyer did not know if, it is found in the purchase, the buyer may return it (to the seller and receive his money back – AYW) even if a number of years (have elapsed since the transaction – AYW), since this

---

6. For examples of various *umdanot* which served as a basis to void a marriage, see *Tosafot Ketuvot* 47b,s.v. *shelo*; *Teshuvot Maharam of Rothenburg*, Prague ed., 1022; *Teshuvot Noda be-Yehudah*, Mahadura Kama *EH* 88, Mahadura Tinyana *EH* 80(end), 135; *Teshuvot Beit ha-Levi* 3:3; *Teshuvot Hesed le-Avraham*, Mahadura Tinyana *EH* 55; *Teshuvot Shoeil u-Meishiv* 3, 1:61; *Teshuvot Torat Hesed, EH* 26; *Teshuvot Radakh, Bayit* 9; *Teshuvot She'eilot Moshe EH* 2(halitzah); *Zikhron Yehonatan*, supra n. 5; *Teshuvot Avnei Hefetz* 30; *Teshuvot Sha'arei Ezra* 4 *EH* 26; *Teshuvot Meishivat Nefesh EH* 73–77; D. Meisels, *Teshuvot Radad EH* 40; *Teshuvot Maharsham* 7:95 (a matter of a wife's mental dysfunction); *Iggerot Moshe, EH* 4:121; *Teshuvot Har Tzvi EH* 2:133. For a contemporary defense of employing this *umdana*, see M. Avraham "Voiding a marriage due to a major inference," (Hebrew) (manuscript on file with this author). Whether an *umdana* may serve as the sole avenue to void a marriage or as a *senif*, a supporting argument to void a marriage is subject to debate.

In our Chapter 8d, 8f and 8g we employ one *umdana* as the sole grounds to void a marriage. In our case here, we are utilizing a series of *umdanot* as the sole technique in voiding the marriage. In contrast to a case examined in this writer's *Rabbinic Authority*, vol. 3, pp. 306–327 where we invoke *umdana* as a *senif*, a supporting argument due to the fact there there are *Poskim* who reject the employment of *kiddushei ta'ut* as a vehicle to void a marriage, in the case found in Chapter 8c, we employ both *kiddushei ta'ut* as well as *umdana* to address two different issues emerging from the fact pattern of the case.

7. *Teshuvot Shoeil u-Meishiv*, Mahadura Kama 1:145, 197; *Teshuvot Noda be-Yehudah*, Mahadura Kama, *YD* 69, Mahadura Tinyana, *EH* 80; *Teshuvot Maharsham* 3:82, 5:5.

8. *Tosafot Ketuvot*, supra n. 6; *Netivot ha-Mishpat HM* 230:1.

transaction was based upon fundamental error, provided that the buyer did not continue to use the item after he became aware of the defect. If, however, the buyer continued to use the item after he saw (or became aware of – AYW) the flaw, he has (by his behavior – AYW) renounced (his right of rescission) and cannot return (the defective item and receive his money back – AYW).

2. The seller would negotiate the sale contingent upon the utility of the item being sold.

In other words, the voiding of the sales transaction is dependent upon the existence of both the seller's and buyer's implied conditions.

The requirement of "*taluy be-da'at shenehem*" as a precondition prior to the invoking of an *umdana* equally applies to marriage which is based upon the consent of both a man and a woman.[9]

For example, if a husband is engaged in criminal activity while married, the fact that a wife would exclaim, "had I known he would become a criminal, I never would have married him" would seem to offer no basis for voiding the marriage, since a similar statement must have either been articulated by the husband or be presumed on the husband's behalf. The husband's declaration would be – "If I become a criminal after the onset of the marriage, my marriage is invalid." In fact, the husband may not want to void the marriage in order to avoid his sexual intercourse being viewed as *be'ilat zenut,* an act of fornication. However, in contradistinction to the above view, adopting the views of Rabbis Mordekhai Hillel, Zvi Ashkenazi, Shmuel Landau, Hayyim Halberstam, Zvi Shapiro, Moshe Zweig, Moshe Feinstein, Ezra Batzri and others, in cases of a major *umdana* or what has been labeled as an *umdana demukhah* (hereafter: *umdana*) a major inference from assessed expectations expressed by one person suffices in order to void a commercial transaction and according to certain *Poskim* a marriage or a *halitzah* may be equally voided.[10]

---

9. *Tosafot Ketuvot,* supra n.6.

For a differing interpretation of *Tosafot,* op. cit. see Rosenzweig, "*Get zikui:* section on *bittul kiddushin*", (manuscript on file with this author); Avraham, supra n.6.

10. *Mordekhai, Yevamot* 4:29; *Teshuvot She'ailat Yitzhak,* 174, 186 (R. Stern's opinion); *Teshuvot Noda be-Yehudah,* Mahadura Kama, *YD* 69, Mahadura Tinyana *EH* 80,135; *Teshuvot Ohel Moshe* 1:62, Mahadura Tlitai 123; *Beit Meir, Tzal'ot ha-Bayit* 6; *Teshuvot She'eilot Moshe EH* 2 (4); D. Meisels, *Teshuvot Radad EH* 40; R.Y. Frankel, *Derekh Yesharah, be-Din Halitzah* in the name of R. Feinstein; *Iggerot Moshe,* supra n. 6; *Teshuvot Sha'arei Ezra* 4:26. For the basis of utilizing *halitzah*

This *umdana* which is known in Talmud Bava Kama 110b as "*ada'ata dehakhi lo kidshah nafshah*" (on this understanding she did not betroth[11] him") is to be understood as an implicit condition to the marriage.[12] In other words, in our case, as we will demonstrate given that the husband has failed to support his wife and in certain instances failed to maintain their son, engaged in spousal rape, physically and emotionally abused his wife, emotionally abused his stepchildren and remarried without giving his first wife a *get* is undermining *tenai'im*, conditions to the marriage and therefore we may invoke the *umdana* "*ada'ata dehakhi lo kidshah nafshah.*"

How does *Halakhah* view *Nitva's* acts of spousal rape as well as his engagement in unnatural intercourse which in certain instances resulted in pain to his wife? There is a duty upon a husband to have conjugal relations with his wife. Whereas according to some authorities the obligation is derived from the Biblical word in Shemot 21:10 "*she'erah* . . . he shall not diminish" or "*ve'onatah* he shall not diminish,"[13] others derive the duty by logical inference.[14] Elaborating upon this position, expounds Rabbi Naftali T. Berlin:[15]

> Reason informs us that (the husband) is so bound . . . as everyone knows, for this purpose that a bride enters into marriage. . . . Hence if he denies her sexual ties, she is deprived of her right.

In other words, *Halakhah* recognizes the wife's right to conjugal relations and therefore the husband has a duty to provide it to her.[16] In fact,

---

rulings to void a marriage, see this writer's *Rabbinic Authority*, vol. 3, 154, n. 44.

11. The word 'betrothal' is loosely translated as 'marry' in this context. As noted by *Teshuvot Seridei Eish* 1:90 and explicitly or implicitly by others the case in the Talmud deals with a husband's brother who became afflicted with skin boils *after* the onset of his brother's *kiddushin*.

12. *Teshuvot Binyamin Ze'ev* 71; *Teshuvot Terumat ha-Deshen* 223; Rabbi Shkop, *Sha'arei Yosher* 5:18. For understanding the *umdana* as "a *ta'ut*," an error, see *Sefer Ra'avyah, Teshuvot u-Be'urei Sugyot*, 1032; *Teshuvot Me'il Tzedakah* 2; *Teshuvot Shoeil u-Meishiv* 1, 197, 3, 1:61.

13. *Mekhilta de R. Yishmael Mishpatim* 3, ed. Horowitz-Rabin.

14. *Mekhilta de R. Yishmael*, supra n. 13; *Ketuvot* 48a.

15. *Birkat ha-Netziv, Mekhilta*, supra n. 13.

16. However, if the wife waives her right to engaging in intimate relations, the husband is exempt from his duty of "*onah*" provided that he has fulfilled the *mitzvah* of having children. See *Tosafot Ketuvot* in the name of R. Elchanan, *Ketuvot* 56a, s.v *harei zo; MT Ishut* 15:1; *Teshuvot Tashbetz* 1:94; *Hiddushei ha-Ramban, Bava Batra* 126b; *Teshuvot Maharik, shoresh* 10 in the name of Rabbeinu Tam, *Darkhei Moshe*,

for Rashba, a couple is mutually obligated one to another as result of the establishment of the marriage.[17]

Others such as Rabbi Avraham Min Hahar and Rabbi Berlin emphasize that the husband has a *kinyan* vis-à-vis his wife but only as regard to sexual relations.[18] However, although the husband's *kinyan* exists and she has a duty to engage in conjugal relations, her husband may not ravish her.

As Rabbi Yosef of Trani notes, "Certainly she is not subject to him incessantly when she does not desire it."[19] Almost two hundred years ago, there was a case reported to a *beit din* of R. Refael ibn Shimon in Egypt where the husband had relations with his wife incessantly during one night, leaving her tired and sleepless, and the holding of the *beit din* was that the wife was not deemed a *moredet* (a rebellious wife who refuses to engage in intercourse with her husband) and she was validated for her refusal to have intercourse in part based upon the earlier ruling of Rabbi Trani.[20] An improper performance of the duty of *onah* such as engaging in nonconsensual marital relations engenders emotional and psychological pain for the wife.[21]

A wife may cease and desist from having relations with a husband who advances excessive demands regarding conjugal relations and she will not be deemed a *moredet* who under certain conditions may be divorced by her husband.[22]

Moreover, implicitly relying upon the Talmudic dicta,[23] Rambam, Ra'avad, and Rabbi Yosef Karo rule that a husband may only have intercourse with the wife's consent.[24] In an earlier ruling in the Shulhan Arukh, Rabbi Karo states that if a husband is angry with her, intercourse

---

Tur EH 38:8; *Beit Shmuel, SA EH* 66:6.

17. *Hiddushei ha-Rashba, Nedarim* 15b.

18. A. Min Hahar, *Perush to Nedarim* 15b; *Birkat Netziv,* supra n. 15; *Ohr Sameah, Ishut* 4:2; S. Daichovsky, *Lev Shomeia le-Shlomo,* 226–227.Cf. *Ran, Nedarim* 20b; *Shitah Mekubezet, Nedarim,* ibid.; *Hiddushei ha-Rashba, Gittin* 69b. Others argue that his *shi'bud* (a duty) vis-à-vis his wife extends to supporting her. See *Mishneh Torah, Nedarim* 12:9; *Hiddushei Hatam Sofer, Bava Batra* 47b.

19. *Teshuvot Maharit* 1:5. See also, Mabit, *Kiryat Sefer, Ishut* 14.

20. *Bat Na'avat ha-Mardut* II, 2.

21. *Teshuvot ha-Radvaz* 4:118; *Teshuvot Yaskil Avdi* 6, *EH* 106(1).

22. See also *Teshuvot Yaskil Avdi* 5:69.

23. Rami bar Hama in *Eruvin* 100b and Rabbi Levi's statement in *Nedarim* 20b. Cf. *Nedarim* 15b.

24. *Eruvin,* supra n. 23; *MT, Issurei Bi'ah* 21:12; *Ishut* 15:17; Ra'avad, *Ba'alei ha-Nefesh, Sha'ar ha-Kedushah* 122; *SA EH* 25:2. See also *Beit Shmuel, SA EH* 77:4; *Maharit,* supra n.19; *Teshuvot Yakil Avdi* 6:25. Cf. *Atzei Arazim* 25:1.

is prohibited until she is persuaded.[25] In the words of Rambam, intercourse ought to be initiated "based upon conversation and joy".[26]

Unnatural intercourse (known in *halakhic* sources as "overturning the table") is permissible provided the husband has his wife's consent.[27]

Our presentation can be best summed up in the words found in Iggeret ha-Kodesh whose authorship is attributed to Ramban:[28]

> When a man has relations (with his spouse) he should not do so against her will and he should not rape her; the Divine Presence does not reside in such unions . . . he should persuade her with kind and enticing words and other proper and appeasing things. . . . Rather he should awaken her and arouse her with alluring words and desire as we said. In short: Before having intercourse, when a man is aroused he should make sure that his wife is enticed as well. In effect, your wife's mindset should correspond to yours.

Finally, the *halakhic* limitation of the freedom of contract – "contracting out of a *Halakhah* found in the Torah" underscores the centrality of *onah* for the matrimonial relationship. A husband is proscribed from preparing a prenuptial agreement which releases himself from his duty to perform conjugal relations[29] due to the fact that such abstention from relations engenders "*tza'ar,*" pain for his wife and/or is understood as entailing "the *ikar ha-nissuin*", the essence of marriage.[30] Notwithstanding the view of Talmud Yerushalmi and a few decisors,[31] adopting the

---

25. *SA OH* 240:3.

26. *Ishut*, supra n.24.

27. See *Ra'avad*, supra n. 24; *Yaskil Avdi*, supra n. 24.

28. *Iggeret ha-Kodesh*, chapter 6.

29. When dealing with monetary matters, generally speaking, *Halakhah* allows individuals including prospective spouses to determine their own monetary relationships, provided that the arrangement complies with a proper form, i.e., *kinyan*, and is not violative of any prohibitions such as theft or the interdict against taking *ribbit* (*halakhic* interest). See *Kiddushin* 19b; *SA, EH* 38:5; *SA, HM* 291:17; *Beit Yosef, Tur HM* 305:4; *SA, HM* 305:4; *Rema, SA HM* 344:1.

However "*onah*" is not a monetary matter. See *Rashi, Kiddushin* 19b; *MT, Ishut* 6:10, 12:7; *Hiddushei ha-Ramban, Bava Batra* 126b, s.v. *harei zu mekudeshet.*

Alternatively, it is viewed as *mehilah*, waiving her right to engaging in relations. See *Shitah Mekubetzet, Ketuvot* 56a in the name of Rashba.

30. *Rashi, Kiddushin* 19b; *Ramban, Hiddushei ha-Ramban, Bava Batra* 126b; *Ramban, Sefer ha-Zekhut, Ketuvot* 26 (on Rif).

31. *Talmud Yerushalmi, Ketuvot* 5:7 and *Bava Metzia* 7:7; *Hiddushei ha-Ritva,*

Talmud Bavli's position,[32] the majority of *Poskim* invalidate such a condition due to the fact that it is "*matneh al mah sha-katuv ba-Torah*," it is a stipulation in variance to the Torah.[33] As the Talmud notes "everyone knows why a bride enters the *hupah*, the bridal canopy" or as Tosafot observes, "matters which we marry for."[34]

In short, the performance of "*onah*" is one of the foundations of a *halakhic* marriage and consequently a husband cannot decide to unilaterally opt out of it.[35]

Given that today, at least in the *Golah*, the Diaspora, we legally and therefore *halakhically* aren't empowered to coerce a *get*, some *Poskim* argue that one must seek whether the conditions are ripe that enable a *Posek* to void a marriage based upon *umdana* in a situation where a *get* cannot be coerced.[36]

Consequently, the threshold question is whether engaging in spousal rape serves as grounds to coerce a *get*. This matter may be examined through the *halakhic* prism of a wife's plea of "*ma'is ali*" ("he is repulsive to me") and I therefore cannot have intimate relations with him.[37] Assuming a wife submits such a plea to a *beit din* accompanied by "*an amatla mevureret*", a clear pretext that in fact she is repulsed by her husband without having an interest in another man and waiving her right to the value of her *ketubah*, there are *Poskim* who will coerce the husband to give a *get*.[38] Based upon the facts presented to us, in effect *Tova'at* is

---

Kiddushin 19b, *Bava Metzia* 51a and *Bava Batra* 126b; *Mordekhai Ketuvot* 213 and *Bava Metzia* 369.

32. *Ketuvot* 56a, *Kiddushin* 19b, *Bava Metzia* 94a.

33. *Rashi, Ketuvot* 56a; *Ramban,* supra n. 30; *MT, Ishut* 12:7; *Tur EH* 38:12–13; *SA* and *Rema EH* 38:5.

34. *Shabbat* 33a; *Tosafot Ketuvot* 48a, s.v. *Rabbi Eliezer ben Ya'akov*; *Ritzva, Tosafot Yevamot* 65b, s.v. *ki*; *Teshuvot Rabbi Akiva Eiger ha-Hadashot* 51.

35. Though if a wife requests (or possibly sets a condition) before the marriage (or possibly during the marriage) that her husband refrain from performing *onah*, assuming the husband has fulfilled the *mitzvah* of having children, there are authorities who will validate this arrangement (see *MT, Ishut* 15:1, *SA EH* 76:6; *Mishneh le-Melekh, MT Ishut* 6:10; *Perishah, Tur EH* 76:17; *Hagahot Rabbi Akiva Eiger, SA EH* 76:1; *Teshuvot Shoeil u-Meishiv* 3:108). Clearly in our case no such arrangement was advanced by the *Tova'at*.

However, even a wife may only waive her right for a period of time rather than permanently because the essence of living together requires that intimate relations transpire. See *Bnei Ahuvah, Ishut* 17:2.

36. *Teshuvot Mahari Bruna* 211; Rabbi M. Posner, *Tzal'ot ha-Bayit* 6; *Teshuvot Shoeil u-Meishiv, Mahadura Kama* 198; *Teshuvot Divrei Malkiel* 4:100.

37. For the meaning and parameters of advancing this claim, see infra Chapter 8f.

38. *Teshuvot ha-Rashbash* 63; *Tosafot Rid, Ketuvot* 63b; *Hiddushei ha-Ritva,*

submitting a plea of *"ma'is ali"* with *"an amatla mevureret"* without having any interest in another man and waiving her right to the value of her *ketubah*. In pursuance to the aforesaid authorities *get* coercion would be permissible. [39] As such, given the inability to coerce a *get* where the couple resides, given *Nitva's* engagement in spousal rape we may invoke the *umdana*, namely *"ada'ata dehakhi lo kidshah nafshah"*.

As Rabbi Moshe Rozin, a twentieth century *posek* of Lithuania and subsequently of New York notes a husband's unwillingness to fulfil the *mitzvah* of *onah* is to be equated to an individual who conditions his marriage that it be devoid of engagement in conjugal relations in a proper fashion as mandated by *Halakhah*. Such a *tenai*, condition in Rabbi Rozin's mind is voided due to the deploying of the *umdana* of *"ada'ata dehakhi lo kidshah nafshah"* and therefore serves as as a rationale to void a marriage.[40]

Is there a basis for invoking *umdana* in a situation where *Nitva* fails to support *Tova'at* as well as their son, in various instances?[41]

Ketuvot 63b; *Teshuvot Tzitz Eliezer* 4:21; *Teshuvot Yabia Omer* 3, *EH* 18.

For additional grounds to coerce a *get* in our case of spousal rape see infra text accompanying notes 68–69.

Cf. other decisors who argue that the advancement of such a plea either obligates a *get* or may not obligate one at all. See *Teshuvot ha-Rashba* 1:573,5:95; H. Volozhin, *Teshuvot Hut ha-Meshullash* 1:2; *SA EH* 77:2; *Rema, SA EH* 77:3; *Beit Shmuel SA EH* 77:27; *Teshuvot Ezrat Kohen EH* 55–56; *Teshuvot Maharshal* 41; *Teshuvot Noda be-Yehudah* Mahadura Tinyana *EH* 90; *Teshuvot Mahari Bruna* 211; *Teshuvot Beit Ephraim EH* 129; Ra'ah ha-Levi, *Teshuvot Zekan Aharon* 149

39. It suffices that *Tova'at* argued at the hearing that she does not want to continue to remain married to him. There is no requirement that she state explicitly the words *"ma'is alai"*. See *Teshuvot Torat Emet* 186.

40. *Teshuvot She'eilot Moshe EH* 2(28,36,42).

41. The duty and scope of child support is based upon the laws of child support and the laws of *tzedakah*.

Whereas, *Nitva* is dutybound to support his wife (which includes food, clothing, lodging and medical needs) due to the fact that it is a husband's obligation, and he is obligated to support his son due to the fact that it is a father's duty to maintain his child (see *SA EH* 71:1; *Beit Shmuel, SA EH* 71:1; *Taz, SA EH* 1:2), there is no obligation to support his stepsons. Cf. *Iggerot Moshe EH* 1:106 who contends that a stepfather is obligated to maintain his stepchildren due to their being guests in his home.

However, given that the stepsons are not being supported by their natural father, in principle there is an obligation upon *Nitva* to pay for his stepsons' support based upon *hilkhot tzedakah*, the laws of righteousness (loosely translated: charity). In other words, he is obligated to pay support for four children from his first marriage and his son from his second marriage (see *SA EH* 71, *Beit Shmuel SA EH* 71: 3) as well as maintain *Tova'at* prior to supporting his stepsons. Nonetheless, since the

In fact, in a lengthy *teshuvah* we find Rabbi Moshe Rozin who invokes this *umdana* in the context of husband who was not prepared to support his wife. He focuses upon a *halitzah* situation employing the instrument of *umdana* to release the wife from her need to perform *halitzah*.[42] The case concerned a Jewish man and woman who married, and a few days after the marriage the husband committed suicide by poisoning himself.[43] Given the fact that the wife was childless and thus dutybound to marry her brother-in-law, *halitzah* was to be performed to enable her to remarry, but her brother-in-law's whereabouts were unknown and the wife became an *agunah* being either unable to marry him or being able to participate in *halitzah* which would allow her to be free to marry

---

Nitva does not have the financial means to support his stepsons, therefore, given his financial circumstances, he is exempt from paying for them. Since *hilkhot tzedakah* are only applicable if the person has the financial means (see *SA YD* 240:5, *Shakh, SA YD* 240:7), therefore given his financial means *Nitva* is exempt from paying support for them. Secondly, *hilkhot tzedakah* would mandate that *Nitva's* relatives who are in financial need would have priority over his stepchildren in receiving monies (see *SA YD* 251:3). As such, if *Nitva* had the financial means he would be paying his needy relatives prior to paying his stepchildren.

Absent an executed agreement between *Nitva* and *Tova'at* which was executed prior to the marriage whereby he would have obligated himself to pay for support of his stepchildren which would in effect preempt any third party support duty based upon *hilkhot tzedakah*, *Nitva* had no duty to support them.

Consequently, our question of the applicability of the *umdana* relates to the *Nitva's* nonsupport of *Tova'at* and their son only.

42. *Teshuvot She'eilot Moshe EH* 2 subsections 25–28.

Whether one can utilize the *halitzah* ruling to conclude that one can equally void the marriage of a husband who refuses to provide spousal support is open to much debate. Even though a *shomeret yavam* (a widow awaiting her deceased husband's brother to perform *halitzah*) is biblically prohibited to anyone else and her status is not as stringent as the status of a married woman who is biblically prohibited to anyone else, one may nonetheless apply *halitzah* rulings to marriage cases in matters of *kiddushei ta'ut*. See *Yevamot* 119a (Rava's dictum); *Teshuvot Terumat ha-Deshen* 250; *Teshuvot Noda be-Yehudah, Mahadura Tinyana EH* 66 (end) and compare with *Mahadura Kama Orah Hayyim* 21; *Hazon Yehezkel* on *Masekhet Zevahim, EH* 8; *Teshuvot Har Tzvi, EH* 1:95, 99. In fact, in addressing cases dealing with voiding marriages, contemporary *Poskim* (as well as earlier decisors) relied upon *halitzah* rulings as a precedent to void a marriage. See *Iggerot Moshe EH* 3:48; File no. 1-14-1393, Yerushalayim Regional Beit Din, March 5, 2003; File no. 870175/4, Haifa Regional Beit Din, December 29, 2014. We adopted this approach.

In light of the stringency of the status of a married woman, others such as *Teshuvot Torat Hesed Orah Hayyim* 29 and *Teshuvot Rabaz* 88 (3) would reject such an application of *halitzah* rulings to marriage situations.

43. As Rabbi Rozin notes we are not dealing here with a case of *"kiddushei ta'ut"* because it was not a foregone conclusion that he would poison himself.

somebody else. Given the fact that the circumstances indicate that this was a planned suicide, contends Rabbi Rozin that it is clear that the newly married husband never had intentions to comply with his marital duties, including but not limited to *mezonot*, providing food and clothing (as well as performing the *mitzvah* of *onah*, intercourse properly)to his newly married wife.

Rabbi Rozin claims that generally speaking a husband who conditions his marriage upon exempting himself from fulfilling his duty of providing spousal maintenance, clothing such a condition is null and void and the marriage is valid. Yet, in this scenario, given that his intent was to commit suicide he never intended to obligate himself with any marital duties, therefore the marriage is null and void.

Generally speaking, in all financial matters, two Jews, including a prospective marital Jewish couple and a Jewish husband and Jewish wife are permitted to determine their own business relationship or marital ties respectively.[44] In effect, in Rabbi Rozin's scenario the prospective husband is stipulating that the duty of support is inapplicable[45] or the above rule is to be understood that a prospective wife or a wife may choose to waive him of his obligation to spousal maintenance.[46] However, in our case at hand, prior to the marriage and during the marriage Bryna never agreed to waive her right to *mezonot* nor did he stipulate that the duty of support is inapplicable to him. Given that in Rabbi Rozin's scenario the husband planned his demise, it was similar to a prospective husband who conditions his marriage upon being exempt from complying with his marital duties. As Rabbi Moshe Sofer observes:

> Since he married her it was on the understanding that there would be support. And if there was no maintenance there is neither *ishut* (personal status) nor marriage.[47]

---

44. *Kiddushin* 19b; *Bava Metzia* 94a; *SA EH* 38:5; *Beit Yosef, Tur HM* 305:4; *SA HM* 291:17, 305:4; *Rema SA HM* 344:1.

45. *Hiddushei ha-Ramban, Bava Batra* 126b.

46. *Hiddushei ha-Rashba, Shitah Mekubetzet, Ketuvot* 56a; *Hiddushei ha-Ritva, Makkot* 3b.

47. *Teshuvot Hatam Sofer EH* 131.For additional authorities who contend that spousal support is intrinsically linked to *ishut*, personal status rather than reflecting a monetary debt which facilitates maintaining a life of matrimony, see *Tosafot, Ketuvot* 48a, s.v. *Rabbi Eliezer ben Ya'akov* in the name of Rashbam; *Minhat Hinnukh, Mitzvah* 66. Additionally, see this writer's "Contractual consequences of cohabitation in American law and Jewish law," 20 *Jewish Law Annual* 279, 306–308 (2013).

Just as we found earlier that Rabbi Rozin employs the *umdana* regarding a wife's unwillingness to be raped by her husband, similiarly he advances the same rationale for a wife's refusal to enter a marriage on the condition (notwithstanding an explicit stipulation) that she would be deprived of her *mezonot*, support.

Analogously, in our case, though *Nitva* promised during their courting days to be economically supportive of his new family, he never really intended to follow through on his commitment. Moreover, his track record regarding fulfilling this marital duty serves as testimony to his deception. As communicated to us by one of his friends, one of the reasons for his divorce from his first wife was because he was incapable of being a breadwinner for his family. More importantly, *Nitva* failed to fulfill his marital duties to support his second wife, the *Tova'at* as well at times their son. Therefore, based upon the *umdana, ada'ata dehakhi lo kidshah nafshah, Tova'at* never would have married him had she known that she would be supporting him, her family as well as their son! Furthermore, it was as if he conditioned his entry into marriage (without his wife's consent) to be exempt from his marital duty of support and proper conjugal relations which are a *tenaiim*, conditions to every marriage. Consequently, one can invoke *ada'ata dehakhi lo kidshah nafshah.*

On one hand, the marriage was civilly annulled in 2007 and therefore spousal support duty ceased.However, on the other hand, due to the fact that he has refused to give a *get*, he may remain *halakhically* dutybound to this very day to provide her with *mezonot*, spousal support even though they have separated. She has the status of "a *me'ukevet le-he'nasei*," namely she is incapable to remarry without the giving of a *get* and therefore she is entitled to *mezonot*.[48] Therefore, we invoke the *umdana,*

---

48. *Ketuvot* 97b; *Teshuvot Maharit* 1:113; *Piskei Din Rabbanayim* (hereafter: *PDR*) 1:74, 235; 3:44; 10:294. However, seemingly in pursuance to some authorities since she never filed a claim for *mezonot*, spousal support in a *beit din*, we view such reticence as a sign of *mehilah*, waiving her right to *mezonot*. See *Hiddushei ha-Ritva, Ketuvot* 96a; *Hiddushei ha-Ramban, Ketuvot* 96a; *PDR* 2: 289-291-292, 11:173.

However, as the aforesaid authorities explain that their conclusion is predicated upon the fact that the wife is "rolling with her husband". In other words, if *shalom* prevails in the marital home then and only then can one assume that she decided to be self-supporting and refraining from advancing a claim for *mezonot* means that she was waiving her entitlement to *mezonot*. Clearly the facts of our case demonstrate that this marriage was marked from the outset by strife therefore we cannot assume that Bryna waived her right to advance a claim of support against her husband, especially once she left him and he refused to give her a *get. See Rema SA EH* 70:5.

Given that *Nitva* had deposited a *get* and the value of the *ketubah* with a *beit din*, therefore in accordance with the view of Rabbi Eliyahu Mizrachi and Rabbi Shalom *ada'ata dehakhi lo kidshah nafshah* – *Tova'at* never would have married him had she known that she would be supporting herself, her family as well as their son even after their separation in January 2004 and after his decision to remarry without giving a *get! Tova'at* married him on the condition that he would provide spousal and family support.[49] In fact, argues Maharit that coercing a *get* is due to a husband's breach of a condition of marriage, namely to provide support.[50] And Maharit equates a husband who fails to support his wife to a husband who, after marriage, acquires *mumim*, defects which were not a condition to the marriage.

As we know, in a case of an impoverished husband who cannot provide material support, a husband of economic means who refuses to maintain his wife, and a husband who is imprisoned and cannot provide financial support, a *beit din* is authorized to coerce him to give a *get*.[51]

The *umdana* of *ada'ata dehakhi lo kidshah nafshah* "contemplates" that the wife expects that she will be able to exit the marriage if her

---

Schwadron he ought to be exempt from paying *mezonot* from that time onwards, however a review of this matter teaches us that this posture is a minority opinion. The majority of authorities contend that the duty of support continues until the wife receives her *get*. See *Teshuvot ha-Ran* 37; *Teshuvot ha-Rashbash* 411; *Helkat Mehokeik, SA EH* 77:3, *Beit Meir* 77; *Teshuvot Shevut Ya'akov* 2:140; *Teshuvot Besamim Rosh* 168; *Mishkenot Ya'akov* 67; *Sefer Hafla'ah*, Kuntres Aharon 77; *Pe'at Negev EH* 17. Consequently, *Nitva* would remain obligated in providing *mezonot* even after depositing the *get* and the value of the *ketubah* in the *beit din*.

However, should a *beit din* obligate a wife to receive a *get* and she refuses to receive it, then from that moment on a husband is exempt from providing *mezonot*, spousal support. See *Sefer Hafla'ah* 77:3,117:17.

49. *Kesef Mishneh, MT, Ishut* 12:11; *Maharit*, supra n. 48.

50. *Maharit*, supra n. 48. For others who endorse *get* coercion when a husband refuses to maintain his wife, see *Talmud Yerushalmi, Gittin* 9; *Ittur*, Ot Mem, Mered; *Teshuvot Yakhin u-Boaz* 1:30; *SA EH* 70:3; *Teshuvot Mohr ve-Oholot EH* 10; *Beit Meir* 70; *Teshuvot Hatam Sofer EH* 130.

51. *Piskei ha-Rosh, Ketuvot* 7:19; *MT, Ishut* 12:11; *Magid Mishneh, MT Ishut* 12:11; *Tur EH* 154; *SA EH* 70:3, 154:3; *Rema SA EH* 70:3, 154:3; *Beit Meir* 154:3; *Arukh ha-Shulhan EH* 154:20; *Teshuvot Oneg Yom Tov* 168. See also Rabbi Eliezer Ashkenazi, *Teshuvot ha-Rema* 36; *Teshuvot ha-Mabit* 1:76; *Teshuvot Ein Yitzhak* 2, *EH* 62, Anaf 12, 63; *Pithei Teshuvah, SA EH* 70:2 in name of Beit Meir and *Teshuvot Hatam Sofer* 154:6 in the name of Beit Meir; *Iggerot Moshe YD* 16 (2); *Teshuvot Shemesh u-Magen* 3: *EH* 27; *Teshuvot Shema Shlomo* 6, *EH* 16; *PDR* 4:169–173 (in the name of the majority of *Poskim*); File no. 1120087/1, Tzfat Regional Beit Din, August 7,2017. Clearly, there are authorities who reject *get* coercion where the husband is impoverished. However, in our case, *Nitva* was earning an income and refused to provide support to the *Tova'at*. As such, under these circumstances *get* coercion is equally appropriate.

spouse acts improperly by failing to provide for her as well as full support for their son.

The deployment of the *umdana, ada'ata dehakhi lo kidshah nafshah* in our case is not limited to *Nitva's* refusal to provide support and engaging in spousal rape which entail fundamental violations of the foundations of a *halakhic* marriage and extends itself to his lack of respect for the *Tova'at*, his wife. Our foregoing presentation of the facts conveys to this panel *Nitva's* lack of respect for his spouse. The *halakhic* imperatives of *kavod ha'beriyot* in general and *kavod ha'ishah* in particular are well known and well documented and do not require any further elaboration here. Suffice is to say that *Nitva's* cursing and screaming were inappropriate. Notwithstanding that Rabbi Babad argues that cursing without using one of Hashem's name does not entail an *issur*, a prohibition,[52] the students of Rabbeinu Yonah contend that there is a prohibition.[53] What we have here is a continuing violation of the rabbinic directive, "that a man ought to respect his wife more than himself and love her like himself . . . and he should not instill excessive fear and his speaking should be calm rather than be sad or angry."[54]

As the Talmud teaches us, a wife was given to a husband "for life and not for pain."[55] In our case, this marriage was marked by pain. Though the initiation of the marriage was consensual and thus affirmed the persona and integrity of both parties in establishing this matrimonial tie, regretfully, that affirmation of the self and respect of the individual began to dissipate immediately after the onset of the marriage. *Nitva* treated *Tova'at* in and out of the bedroom as an object rather than as a person. As one witness said – "*Tova'at* was a slave" and *Tova'at* was in fear of him. Despite the "toxic domestic atmosphere" in the marital home which encompassed being disrespectful to the *Tova'at*, every alternate *Shabbat*, *Tova'at* was considerate enough to have *Nitva's* four young children as guests in her own home, a domestic household which was being bankrolled by her rather than her husband!

Based upon the foregoing, there would be a basis to coerce a *get* due to the acts of disrespect that he exhibited towards *Tova'at*.[56] In short,

---

52. *Minhat Hinnukh, Mitzvah* 69. Cf, *Pithei Teshuvah, SA EH* 115:10 who is unsure regarding this matter.

53. *Shitah Mekubetzet, Ketuvot* 72b and *SA HM* 27:2.

54. *MT, Ishut* 16:19; *Be'air ha-Golah, SA EH* 154:10.

55. *Ketuvot* 61a.

56. *Rema, SA, EH* 154:1 (first opinion); *Bi'ur ha-Gra, SA EH* 154:11; *Pithei Teshuva, SA EH* 154:4 in the name of Maharam Alshakar who contends that this view reflects the consensus of the majority of authorities.

given that *Nitva* had been forewarned by *Tova'at* to cease from his cursing, he is *"oveir al dat Yehudit,"* transgressing the Jewish religion.[57] And if the spouse engages in cursing on a regular basis, some contend that there is no need for a warning.[58]

Since *get* coercion is a *halakhic* option, albeit unavailable today outside of *Eretz Yisrael*, given that Bryna lives in the United States there are grounds to invoke the *umdana, ada'ata dehakhi lo kidshah nafshah* due to his engagement in nonconsensual marital sex, acts of disrespect and failing to support his family.

Moreover, having to experience pain as a result of being a victim of spousal rape violates the Talmudic teaching that a wife was given to a husband "for life and not for pain." Such an experience is memorialized in *Halakhah*. Notwithstanding the view of Tosafot that payment of *tza'ar*, pain is only for the pain experienced by the injured party at the time of the commission of the act,[59] others contend that continuing pain is also compensated.[60] Consequently, should pain ensue from a coerced cohabitation, albeit more frequently the result of engaging in unnatural intercourse and last for a few days, a husband would be liable for *tza'ar*.

Being a victim of spousal rape in and of itself entails an infraction of *habalah*, battery. Having to undergo unnatural intercourse entails pain.[61] Having to be ravished by one's spouse and then undergo pain from that encounter is unconscionable. To rape one's wife who is supporting you and allowing him to live in her house *gratis* is beyond belief. To fail to cease and desist from such conduct after a wife entreats her husband to stop is unconscionable. Under such conditions, *Tova'at* is an object being exploited rather than a human being being respected.

As Rabbi Karo and Rabbi Shlomo Luria rule, a husband is liable for any injuries caused during consensual intercourse,[62] *a fortiori* should he force her to have relations against her will he has committed *"habalah"*, battery, and is liable for damages.[63] (Even in the absence of battery, as we

57. *Beit Yosef, Tur EH* 115:4; *Darkhei Moshe, Tur, EH* 115:5; *Teshuvot Rabbi Eliezer Gorden* 22 in the name of Ritva.

58. *Bi'ur ha-Gra, SA EH* 115:12; *Pithei Teshuvah SA EH* 115:10 in the name of Beit Meir.

59. *Tosafot, Ketuvot* 39a, s.v. *tza'ar*.

60. *Piskei ha-Rosh* in the name of R. Shimshon, *Bava Kama* 4:9; *Tur, HM* 420:17.

61. *Bereshit Rabbah* 80:4; *Rashi, Bereshit* 34:2.

62. *SA HM* 421:12; *Sma, SA HM* 421:10; *Yam shel Shlomo Bava Kama* 3:21. See further this writer's *Rabbinic Authority*, vol. 2, 81–102.

63. *Hazon Ish HM* 19:2; *Teshuvot Divrei Yatziv EH* 77:3. Whether an act of spousal rape without any attendant harm would constitute *habalah* is subject to

mentioned earlier in our *psak din* one is prohibited from raping one's wife.[64])

Consequently, whether one would coerce a *get* in our case of spousal rape which entailed battery may be derived from how *Poskim* ruled regarding coercing a *get* in the case of a battered wife. Notwithstanding that many *Poskim* reject *get* coercion in the situation of a battered wife,[65] there are others who under certain conditions will issue a compulsion order.[66]

---

controversy. See *Minhat Hinnukh*, Mitzvah 49.

64. See supra n. 24. See also *Sefer Ravan, Eruvin* 159; *Tosafot Nidah* 12a; *Ra'avyah* 3:994; *Ohr Zarua* 1, *Nedarim* 20b; *Piskei ha-Rosh Eruvin* 10:13. Cf. *Nedarim* 15b.

Whether a wife who is deemed a *moredet* (a rebellious woman who refuses to engage in intimate relations with her husband) can be forced to have relations against her will is a subject of controversy. See *Atzei Arazin*, supra n. 24; *Mordekhai Kiddushin* 530; *Hiddushei ha-Ra'ah Ketuvot* 63a; *Kiryat Sefer* 12:1.

65. *Beit Yosef, Tur EH* 154; *Darkhei Moshe, Tur EH* 154:17; *Teshuvot ha-Radvaz* 4:157; *Rabbi Kalfon Moshe, Teshuvot Shoeil u-Meishiv* 4 *EH* 14; *Teshuvot Mishpat Tzedek* 1:59; *Teshuvot Shoeil ve-Nishal* 2, *EH* 55:4, vol. 4, *EH* 14; *Teshuvot Tzitz Eliezer* 6:42, chapter 3; *Teshuvot Noseh ha-Ephod* 32 (15).

Many of the cited authorities arrived at this conclusion due to the fact that their understanding of Rosh's posture was that *get* coercion was improper regarding a husband who was a batterer. See *Teshuvot ha-Rosh* 43:3. Yet given the recent discovery of a manuscript it is clear that in fact Rosh, similar to other decisors endorses *get* coercion under certain conditions. See D. Birdugo, "*Get* coercion for a husband who is a batterer – An explanation of the responsum of Rosh," (Hebrew) 5776 *Kenas ha-Dayanim* 241.

For the role of manuscripts in *halakhic* decision-making, see Z. Lehrer, 16 *Tzefunot* 68 (1992); M. Bleich, "The role of manuscripts in halakhic decision-making: Hazon Ish, his Precursors & Contemporaries," 27 *Tradition* 22 (1993). In fact, some authorities have factored into consideration a newly discovered manuscript in their ruling. See *Avnei Nezer OH* 540, *YD* 312(71); *Teshuvot Ne'eman Shmuel* 106; *Teshuvot Hatam Sofer EH* 1:119.

66. For a similar scenario to the case before us, see *Tur EH* 154; *Beit Shmuel SA EH* 115:1; *Bi'ur ha-Gra SA EH* 154:11. In fact, some authorities view a batterer as an individual who is to be labeled as "an *oveir al dat Yehudit*" (lit. transgressing the Jewish religion) and assuming he is forewarned to cease and desist from such behavior and continues with his physically abusive behavior, there are grounds to coerce him to give a *get*. See *Bi'ur ha-Gra*, ibid. *Teshuvot Noda be-Yehudah, Mahadura Tinyana EH* 90–91; M. Yisrael, *Teshuvot Mas'at Moshe EH* 1:17; File no. 487862/1, Netanya Regional Beit Din, January 16,2011. Cf *Teshuvot Maharshal* 69.

As an aside, on the other hand, *get* coercion may be invoked in other situations of severe and/or continuous acts of husband's battery which may endanger a batterer's wife. See *Teshuvot Maharam of Rothenberg*, Cremona ed., 291–292; *Teshuvot Maharam of Rothenberg*, Prague ed. 927 in the name of Rabbeinu Simha; *Teshuvot ha-Rashba ha-Meyuhosot le-Ramban* 102; *Hiddushei ha-Ritva, Ketuvot* 77a; *Rabbeinu*

Furthermore, as we mentioned, *Nitva* was engaged in emotional abuse such as his treatment of his stepsons during their family trips, his cursing and screaming at them (as well as his wife), throwing one stepchild out of the home and forwarding an extremely inappropriate news release about his stepchildren to a national Jewish newspaper. In accordance with Mishnah, Talmudim and *Poskim* one may coerce a *get* when a husband emotionally abuses his wife.[67]

Noting the impropriety of emotional abuse of a spouse, Gaon of Vilna opines:[68]

> Even other matters that do not engender that much pain such as a husband who takes a *neder*, a vow that his wife should refrain from going to her father's home or to a house of mourning . . . *a fortiori* if he pains her physically.

In other words, implicitly following earlier authorities,[69] the Gaon is deriving the *Halakhah* of *get* coercion in the matter of spousal physical abuse from the *Halakhah* of *get* coercion in the case of spousal emotional abuse. Seemingly, Gaon's position is problematic due to the fact that Ramban's conclusion, regarding both types of abuse, is that one can only obligate a *get*. However, it is clear from Darkhei Moshe and Rema[70]

Simhah, *Ohr Zarua, Bava Kama* 161; *Teshuvot Tashbetz* 2:8; *Beit Yosef,* supra n.65 in the name of Agudah; *Bi'ur ha-Gra, SA EH* 154:17; *Rema, SA EH* 154:3 in the name of "*yesh omrim*"; *Teshuvot Maharshal* 69; *Beit Shmuel, SA EH* 154:9; *Teshuvot Perah Mateh Aharon* 1:60; *Teshuvot Hatam Sofer EH* 2:60; *Teshuvot Mateh Lehem EH* 1:8; *Teshuvot va-Yomer Yitzhak* 1, *EH* 135; *Teshuvot Shoshanim le-David* 2:20; *Teshuvot Noseh ha-Ephod* 32 (15); *Avnei ha-Ephod EH* 154:8; *Teshuvot Hayyim ve-Shalom* 2:112; *Teshuvot Maharsham* 5:38; *Hazon Ish Gittin* 108:14; *Teshuvot Tzitz Eliezer* 6:42(3); *Teshuvot Heikhal Yitzhak, EH* 1:3 (4); *Mishpatekha le-Ya'akov* 2:45; *PDR* 3:220; File no. 3426-21-3, Tel Aviv-Yaffo Regional Beit Din, January 29,2008; File no. 537502/4, Haifa Regional Beit Din, November 4, 2014; File no. 1056520/2, Tel Aviv Yaffo Regional Beit Din, April 10,2016; *Teshuvot Amudei Mishpat* 12; *Teshuvot Dibrot Eliyahu* 7:86.

67. *Ketuvot* 71b–72a; *Ketuvot* 77a; *Teshuvot Maharit* 1:113; *Teshuvot Tashbetz* 2:8; *Teshuvot Binyamin Ze'ev* 88. Notwithstanding Rabbeinu Hananeil who contends that the word "*yotzi*" in some of the above sources means "obligating a *get*," we are following Tosafot who argues that the word means "coercing a *get*". See *Tosafot, Ketuvot* 70a, s.v. *yotzi; Tosafot Yevamot* 64a, s.v. *yotzi; Piskei ha-Rosh Yevamot* 6:11; *Tur EH* 154(end) in the name of Rif and Rashi.

68. *Bi'ur ha-Gra, SA EH* 154:10.

69. *Teshuvot ha-Rashba*, supra n. 66; *Teshuvot Tashbetz* 2:8; *Teshuvot Yakhin u-Boaz* 2:43.

70. *Darkhei Moshe, Tur EH* 154:17; *Rema SA EH* 154:13.

as well as the Gaon that these matters require *get* coercion. In fact, others concur with their understanding of these *Poskim*.[71]

If *Tova'at* had been residing in *Eretz Yisrael* where *get* coercion is an option upon a husband withholding support, physically and emotionally abusing his spouse, engaging in spousal rape and marrying another woman without giving a *get*, albeit employed on a limited basis, her marriage may be dissolved by *get* coercion. And as we earlier mentioned in pursuance to certain *Poskim*, in light of the option of *get* coercion, *Tova'at* may have been unable to invoke the *umdana*. However, today outside of *Eretz Yisrael*, where *Tova'at* resides, there is no *beit din* which is legally and thus *halakhically* empowered to coerce a husband to give a *get*. Consequently, in the absence of the ability to coerce *Nitva* to give a *get*, based upon the submitted facts we may employ the *umdana* regarding *Nitva's* acts of spousal rape accompanied by acts of *habalah*. Here again, the *umdana*, *ada'ata dehakhi lo kidshah nafshah* is invoked due to a breach of a *tenai* in the marriage engaging in physical as well as verbal and emotional abuse.

The import and significance of applying the different types of *umdana* is underscored by the event that occurred after the marital separation and underscores a different type of *umdana*. At the beginning of 2014, *Nitva* received permission to remarry without giving a *get* to the *Tova'at* from a *beit din* which is located in Monsey, New York. In our files, we have letters as well as a letter authored by 20 *dayanim* and rabbis who reside in Yerushalayim, *Eretz Yisrael* as well as in Monsey, New York, who do not recognize the *gittin* in general and the *"heter nissuin,"* permission to remarry, in particular, of this *beit din*. In March 2014, one of the rabbis who was affiliated with this *beit din* officiated at the wedding of *Nitva* to another woman, even though he was still married to *Tova'at* due to the fact that he never gave her a *get*.

In light of *Nitva's* second marriage, he is violating the *Herem* (excommunication) of Rabbeinu Gershom of marrying a second woman while still remaining married to one's first wife. Nimmukei Yosef rules:[72]

> And Ritva in the name of his rabbi who said in the name of his rabbis that in a place where the practice is to refrain from marrying more than woman, then it is improper to marry another

---

71. *Teshuvot Binyamin Ze'ev* 88; File no. 9465-21-1, Netanya Regional Beit Din, February 14, 2007; File no. 966775/4, Netanya Regional Beit Din, February 8, 2016; File 990702/2, Netanya Regional Beit Din, June 23, 2016.

72. *Nimmukei Yosef on Rif Yevamot* 44a.

woman while still being married to one's wife. It is an *umdana de'mukhah* that she married him contingent on the fact that he would not marry anyone else. . . . As Tosafot wrote that Rabbeinu Gershom excommunicated a person who married more than one wife and we are obligated to coerce the two of them to divorce from each other.

To state it differently, as noted by other *Rishonim* and *Aharonim* there exists an *umdana* that no woman would marry a man knowing that the man would remarry without giving a *get* to his wife.[73] Unlike the other *umdanot* such as a woman would neither marry a man who would rape her or fail to support her which is an expectation which is specific to the case (i.e. the *umdana* emerges due to the husband's inappropriate behavior *during the marriage*) this *umdana* (i.e. no woman would marry a man knowing that the man would remarry without giving a *get* to his first wife) is an expectation of all women and is foundational to the creation of the marriage and emerges *after the couple has separated* and there exists no prospects for marital reconciliation.

Though there is no *mesorah* that permits the invoking of this *umdana* as an avenue to void a marriage, nonetheless, we do have a precedent for deploying a similar *umdana* as a means to void a marriage. Another example of such an *umdana* which emerges after marital separation and is foundational to the establishment of the marriage is the *umdana* that a woman would never marry a man who would refuse to give her a *get* should circumstances dictate that their marriage be dissolved. There are authorities who will void a marriage based upon the invoking of this *umdana*.[74] Both *umdanot* may serve as a *senif*, a supporting argument rather than as an independent ground to void a marriage.[75]

It is an implied condition to the marriage that no woman would marry a man who would decide to marry a second woman without giv-

---

73. *Hiddushei ha-Ritva*, *Yevamot* 44a; *Teshuvot ha-Rashba* 4:314; *Helkat Mehokeik*, *SA EH* 1:16; *Bi'ur ha-Gra SA EH* 1:25; *PDR* 3:257,262 (Rabbi Elyashiv's opinion).Though these authorities as well as *Nimmukei Yosef*, supra n. 72 invoke the implementation of an *umdana*, they refrain from addressing whether its employment is an avenue to be utilized in order to void a marriage.

74. Rabbi Eliezer Fried, *Teshuvot Hut ha-Meshullash* 3:5; Rabbi Petahiah Horenblass, *Pithei She'arim, Sheilot u-Teshuvot* 32. Whether Rabbi Tenenbaum would recognize such an *umdana*, we leave as an open question. See *Teshuvot Divrei Malkiel* 4:100. Cf. *Iggerot Moshe EH* 1:162(*halitzah*).

75. *Pithei She'arim*, supra n. 74.

ing a *get* to his wife.[76] Today, where the entire Jewish community as well as Western society view bigamy as prohibited conduct, common sense dictates that no woman would consent to marry a man on the condition that he is allowed to marry a second woman during the time that he remains married to his wife.[77] Furthermore, engaging in a bigamous relationship is *halakhically* deemed by Teshuvot Tumat Yesharim 84 as an act of emotional abuse. Finally, in a case where the husband married a second woman without giving a *get* to his wife, one must coerce them both to become divorced. The inference from his language is that the coercion is not based upon a wife's claim to become divorced but coercion is linked to the need to comply with *mitzvot*. Therefore, as Nimmukei Yosef writes, even if the husband and wife of the second marriage are prepared to live together (because the marriage after the fact is valid),[78] nevertheless a *beit din* has a mandate to dissolve either one of the marriages by coercing a *get* to comply with the performance of the *mitzvah* of giving a *get*.[79]

Even if it emerges that there were no grounds to issue a *heter nissuin* as there was in our situation, Rabbi Shlomo Luria and others already rule that a husband continues to transgress the *Herem* (the social sanction against bigamy) daily even if he is acting *be'shogeg* (unintentional sin) or due to *ones* (duress).[80]

---

76. *Teshuvot Maharshakh* 1:28; *PDR* 11:4.

77. As we know, during the eleventh century there emerged rabbinic legislation known as *takanot,* legislation of Rabbeinu Gershom. Among the pieces of legislation enacted at that time there was a prohibition upon a Jewish man to marry more than one Jewish woman. See *Teshuvot Maharam of Padua 14; Rema, SA EH* 1:10. Though numerous authorities argue that this legislation is inapplicable today for members in the Sephardic Jewish communities either because the legislation never was practiced in certain Sephardic communities or the legislation today is inapplicable in all Sephardic communities (see *Teshuvot ha-Ran* 38; *Teshuvot Mahari Bei Rav* 61 in the name of Radvaz; *Teshuvot Maharam Alshakar* 95; *Teshuvot Maharbil* 1:2; *Teshuvot Mishpat Tzedek* 2:1; *Teshuvot Hikrei Lev,* vol. 3, *YD* 87),nonetheless, there is a *min-hag,* a communal practice amongst Sephardic Jews to continue to forbid to this very day the engagement in a bigamous relationship. See *SA EH* 1:9; File no. 765725/1, Netanya Regional Beit Din, June 30, 2011; Israel's Chief Rabbi Yitzhak Yosef's letter to Dayan E. Shahar, 5 Kislev 5777 (letter on file with this author).

78. *Mordekhai Kiddushin* 522 in the name of Maharam; *Teshuvot Noda be-Yehudah,* Mahadura Tinyana *EH* 129.

79. *Ritva,* supra n. 73; *Teshuvot ha-Rashba* 4:304; *Beit Yosef Tur EH* 1; *Rema, SA EH* 1:10; *Arukh ha-Shulhan EH* 1:28; *Knesset ha-Gedolah, EH* 1, *Hagahot Beit Yosef,* 9. Cf. *Teshuvot Beit Yosef, Ketuvot* 14; *Pithei Teshuvah, SA EH* 1:20 in the name of *Teshuvot Noda be-Yehudah,* Mahadura Tinyana, *EH* 90.

80. *Teshuvot Maharshal* 14. See also, *Nimmukei Yosef,* supra n. 73 and *Ritva,*

Moreover, notwithstanding *Nitva's* daily transgression of the *Herem* of R. Gershom, the situation of *igun* which dates back over eleven years militates that a *get* be coerced for his wife.[81] As Rabbi Eliyahu ben Binyamin ha-Levi claims in the most unequivocal terms:[82]

> When the husband is not with the wife at all, one does not require the Mishnah of "*kofin*" (which enumerates the list of cases where we can coerce a husband to give a *get* – AYW). Our Torah scholars did not say that a woman should stand (live – AYW) without food, clothing and conjugal relations. . . .

To state it differently, there was no reason for our scholars of Mishnah and Talmud to specify that a husband can be coerced to give a *get* to an *agunah* who lives separate from her husband who neither furnishes proper intimate relations nor material support. *Sevara, halakhic* logic, dictates that under such circumstances *get* coercion is proper.[83] Addressing the case of husband who leaves his wife, refuses to comply with his marital duties, refuses to give a *get*, marries another woman and refuses to comply with his wife's plea for a *get*, such circumstances dictate that the creation of *igun*, a wife being anchored to a marriage mandates the coercing of a *get*! [84] In the absence of being able to employ

---

supra n. 73. Cf. *Teshuvot Maharshakh* 2:79 who contends that the *Herem* focuses solely upon the act of bigamy rather than the continuance of the second marriage without the husband giving a *get* to his first wife and therefore he rejects *get* coercion.

81. Obviously, given that the husband resides in the United States, one cannot legally and therefore *halakhically* coerce him to give a *get*. Yet, there is a basis to obligate a *get*. See File no. 641803/8, Yerushalayim Beit Din, September 5, 2010, *ha-Din ve-ha-Dayan*, no. 36. In fact, in a previous decision we obligated the *Nitva* to give a *get* unconditionally however he has continuously refused to give an unconditional one.

82. *Teshuvot Zekan Aharon* 149.

83. See also *Teshuvot Hakham Tzvi* 1.

84. On one hand, some authorities such as *Teshuvot ha-Rosh* 43:13, *Teshuvot Hakham Tzvi* 31, *Teshuvot ha-Mabit* 1:76 dictate *get* coercion due to the fact that the couple have been living separately for an extensive period of time with no prospects for marital reconciliation and effectively the husband fails to comply with his marital duties. See further, supra Introduction to chapter 8. On the other hand, the fact that the husband refuses to acede to his wife's request to give her a *get* and then proceeds to marry a second woman, for Rema mandates a *get* coercion. See *Rema*, supra n. 79. Others such as *Teshuvot Maharhash* 46, *Teshuvot Maharshakh* 2:79 and *Teshuvot Maharbil* 1, Kelal 2, Siman 16 disagree with his position.

get coercion, we are following a *mesorah* that we may invoke the *um-dana* under assuming certain conditions are obtained.[85]

And in fact, the above description conveyed by Rabbi Eliyahu reflects the plight of the *Tova'at*.

Seemingly, the lapse of time from the onset of the marriage until the *Tova'at's* decision to separate from the *Nitva* ought to undermine employing the *umdana* of "*ada'ata dehakhi lo kidshah nafshah.*" Based upon the cumulative evidence submitted to this panel, the marriage was consummated in the summer of 2000 and she requested a *get* during Chanukah 2004. Clearly, *Nitva's* acts of spousal rape, spousal disrespect, and his lack of spousal support occurred early on in the marriage and she should have requested a *get* by late 2000 or the beginning of 2001. However, our rendition of the facts of the case clearly indicates that given that she was a divorcee with three children, she desired to "make this marriage work." As she communicated to us in the final session, despite the fact that she was a victim of spousal rape, emotionally abused and in the eyes of one observer "she was fearful of him," she set aside her personal reservations and concerns in order to attempt to promote "*shalom bayit*" to the fullest extent of the words, peace and tranquility in her bedroom, for her entire family, newly born son and three children from her previous marriage. As such, she enlisted the guidance of her family rabbi on three different occasions, the counsel of four therapists which lasted until she requested her *get* and sought the advice of family members and friends. As we earlier mentioned, the reply to the boarder in *early 2004*, almost four years into the marriage says it all – The woman who worked a brief time in the marital home asked the *Tova'at*, "why are you staying in the marriage?" Her reply was "she was worried about the situation but she didn't know what to do" (her approximate words). In other words, despite the fact that "the writing was on the wall" dating back a few years regarding his treatment of the *Tova'at* and her children, *Tova'at* was a driven person who had already been divorced once due to an "unfit husband" and wanted to try every avenue to save this marriage for herself as well as for her kids. We asked one therapist the following question: "If the couple would have seen you earlier, could the marriage have been saved?" The informed and educated reply from a well-seasoned psychologist was – "It would not have made one iota of a difference. This marriage could never work." After reading the facts of this case, someone may say that that this marriage was doomed from its inception and therefore how could she have stayed with the marriage?

---

85. See infra n. 100.

Firstly, as Pirkei Avot states, "Do not judge your friend until you reach his place." Secondly, it is very possible that some women would have opted out of such a marriage much earlier and in fact two women who appeared in front of us submitted such a claim, but as a *beit din* we are dealing with the *Tova'at*, her personality and her expectations and aspirations, and it is crucial to rule in light of her situation. Her tolerance and drive "to see the good in every person" and hope to improve a bad situation drove her to remain in her first marriage for 16 years despite the highly inappropriate activity of her husband. The same attitude and disposition transpired in attempting to address her concerns regarding her second husband. As such, the facts of the case indicate that there are reasonable explanations why she remained in the marriage for an extended period of time hoping to salvage it. Once there was no hope in her mind to save it, she requested a *get*.

Seemingly, by Bryna's own admission that she became aware of her husband's conduct within three and half months from the time of the onset of the marriage and her decision to remain living with him under these circumstances for three and half years conveys to this panel that she was *mohail*, waived "the situation" and consequently there ought to be no grounds to void the marriage.

Drawing such a conclusion is open to *halakhic* challenge. As we noted earlier, this *umdana* of marriage of *"ada'ata dehakhi lo kidshah nafshah"* is to be understood as an implicit condition to the marriage.[86] In other words, in our case, given that the husband here failed to support his wife, engaged in spousal rape, abused his stepsons and was engaging in polygamy he is an undermining *tenaim*, conditions to the marriage and therefore we may invoke the *umdana "ada'ata dehakhi lo kidshah nafshah"*.

As elucidated by Rabbi Ariel Holland of our *beit din* panel, Shulhan Arukh states that if a man betroths his prospective wife on the condition that she has no defects and after the *kiddushin* (loosely translated: the marriage) defects appear, the couple is married provided that the defects have been cured.[87] In the event that the defects are incurable, the inference to be drawn is that the marriage is void. Relying upon this ruling, Tzvi Tiferet opines that the same conclusion ought to apply when a woman advances such a *tenai* regarding her prospective husband prior to the marriage.[88] This approach was subscribed to by Rabbi

---

86. See supra n. 12.
87. *SA EH* 39:7.
88. *Otzar ha-Poskim, SA EH* 39, 35 (1).

Dovid Friedman.[89] Moreover, as noted by Rabbi Holland, claims Rabbi Yehezkal Landau, in a line of argumentation endorsed subsequently by his son, that if one engages in a conditional marriage and then consummates the marriage via intercourse, the *tenai* is waived provided that the person does not incur a loss by waiving the *tenai*. However, if the result would be that the person incurred a loss then the *tenai is* operative and the marriage is voided.[90] In sum, once there was a *tenai*, and in our case it was an implied condition, there is no presumption of *mehilah* when a loss has been incurred by the act of marriage.

However, should we traverse from the world of *issurim* (prohibitions) to the world of *Hoshen Mishpat* (commercial matters) and apply the *halakhot* of sales to a defective item, in accordance with some authorities we would arrive at a different conclusion. If somebody purchases an item that has a defect and he used the item after discovering the defect, then we view the situation as a case of *mehilah* and he cannot rescind the transaction.[91]

Nonetheless, if a transaction materialized and there was a reason to void it, such as the presence of a defect and the buyer doesn't care that there is a defect, and the reason for his lack of concern is because he wants the sale to happen even under these conditions for another reason, the sale is rescinded. Similarly, Rabbi Navon and others contend that if a man marries a woman and he discovers a defect and he nevertheless is appeased by the monies that he received for becoming married to her, the marriage is not recognized due to the fact that his motivation for the marriage was for pecuniary satisfaction.[92]

It is understandable that the Talmud Bava Kama 110b which invokes the *umdana* as well as its subsequent application by various *Poskim* does not mandate that this *umdana* be employed immediately after the establishment of the act of marriage.[93] As we explained, a lapse of time does not mean necessarily that the wife waived her insistence to the continuing operation of an implied condition (or conditions) to her marriage.

Based upon the foregoing, there were various implied conditions in the couple's marriage. Given that the conditions were violated by the

---

89. *Yad Dovid* 2, *Piskei Halakhot, Ishut,* 149b (n. 110).

90. *Teshuvot Noda be-Yehudah,* Mahadura Kama, *EH* 54 (end); *Teshuvot Shivat Tzion* 90.

91. *MT, Mekhirah* 15:3; *Tur HM* 232:4; *SA HM* 232:3; *Arukh ha-Shulhan HM* 232:4.

92. *Mahaneh Ephraim, Ona'ah,* 5:12; *Hiddushei Rabbi Akiva Eiger, HM* 232:3; *Pithei Teshuvah SA HM* 232:3.

93. See supra n. 6.

husband's behavior, Bryna never waived these conditions. Rather, as the evidence has demonstrated, she tried to save her marriage. Once there was no hope in her mind to save it, she requested a *get*.

As such there are reasonable explanations why she did not separate from the *Nitva* immediately upon encountering his inappropriate behavior. Though in accordance with certain *Poskim*,[94] upon discovery of a major latent defect one must bolt the marriage immediately or refrain from remaining in the marriage for an extended period of time, nonetheless, in pursuance to Rabbi Moshe Feinstein and others who argue that she may continue to live with him provided she offers a reasonable explanation.[95]

Let's cite an excerpt from *Dayan* Tzion Boaron's ruling.[96] Dealing with a husband who was mentally dysfunctional, Rabbi Boaron describes the wife's mindset prior to discovering that her spouse had a mental disorder in the following manner:

> And one should not conclude that since she lived with him for seven years and gave birth to two children, she observed the defect and forgave him (*"mehilah"*). That is not the case. When dealing with such matters a person cannot understand the nature of the disease until much time has elapsed since sometimes due to her love for him she rationalizes his anger and temper and his agitated condition as being transient and she longs and hopes that the situation will improve. In particular, a person who takes medication regularly, there are times when he is content and silent. . . . One cannot say one observes and one is appeased as written in Maharsham . . . when he was asked about a couple who lived together for over 14 years. Since episodes of mental dysfunctionality occur from time to time and a man hopes to be cured and therefore . . . one cannot speak of seeing and being appeased.

---

94. *Tur* and *Beit Yosef EH* 154; *Teshuvot Maharik, shoresh* 24; *Teshuvot R. Akiva Eiger,* Mahadura Tinyana, 56.

95. *Iggerot Moshe EH* 3:45 (*"ta'am hagun"* or *"tirutzim nekhonim"*), 48, 4:113; *PDR* 1:5, 11–12. See this writer's *Rabbinic Authority,* vol. 3, 136–139. Though Rabbi Feinstein suggests the advancement of reasonable explanations for a delay in responding to the wife's awareness of a defect relates to invoking *"kiddushei ta'ut"* we are extending his position to a situation of employing *"umdana"* to void a marriage should there be a delay of time from the wife's initial awareness of the behavior which ensued after the marriage until she bolted the marriage.

96. *Teshuvot Sha'arei Tzion* 3, *EH* 4.

Consequently, in light of the aforesaid *mesorah* of Rabbis Feinstein and Boaron one may impart credence to the *Tova'at's* decision to remain in the marriage for three and a half years.

Based upon the cumulative evidence submitted to this *beit din*, notwithstanding contrary views which reject the deployment of an *umdana* as a means to void a marriage,[97] following a *mesorah* which we alluded to at the beginning of our discussion, we find that our analysis of the *umdana, ada'ata dehakhi lo kidshah nafshah* which may be invoked regarding spousal disrespect, spousal abuse, non-support and remarriage without giving his wife a *get* serve the grounds for freeing the *Tova'at* from her marriage without the giving of a *get*.

Finally, notwithstanding those authorities who reject *igun* as an *ilat gerushin* (a ground for divorce) for even obligating a *get* much less a basis for *get* coercion[98] there are other *Poskim* who endorse the view that *igun* may serve as grounds for sanctioning *get* coercion.[99]

---

97. *Tosafot Bava Kama* 110b, s.v. *de'adatei; Teshuvot Avodat ha-Gershuni* 35; *Teshuvot Beit Yitzhak* 1:106; *Teshuvot Heikhal Yitzhak EH* 2:25; File no. 861974/1, Tzfat Regional Beit Din, January 21, 2013 (Rabbi Y. Ariel's opinion).

In accordance with their view, invoking the *umdana* creates a situation of a *safek kiddushin*, a doubtful *kiddushin*, and for some *Poskim* such as *Teshuvot Maharbil* 1:17 one should refrain from being more lenient in *kiddushei safek* than a doubtful divorce. Nonetheless, *Teshuvot Maharik, shoresh* 171, *Pri Hadash, YD* 110 (end) dealing with *Sefek Sefeika, Teshuvot Maharsham* 8, *EH* 239, *Teshuvot Sha'arei Tzion* 3, *EH* 4, 22–24 and others follow the view of Ran in first chapter of Tractate Kiddushin that *safek kiddushin* creates a *hezkat penuyah*, a presumption of a single woman *me'deoraita*, on a Biblical level, and the rabbis ruled stringently due to the prohibition of *eishet ish* and therefore she requires a *get*. See also *Teshuvot Maharit* 1:138.

98. *Teshuvot Divrei Malkiel* 3:144–145; *Teshuvot Divrei Shmuel* 3:145; R. Y. Herzog, *Pesakim u-Ketavim* 7:133–134; PDR 1:162, 4:112, 7:108–109, 112–113, 9:211, 10:173, 11:362, 364; File no. 059133397-21-1, Beit Din ha-Rabbani ha-Gadol, *ha-Din ve-ha-Dayan* 18:12, December 25, 2007; File no. 764231/6, Haifa Regional Beit Din, May 25, 2014; File no. 698719/15, Yerushalayim Regional Beit Din, July 26, 2015.

99. *MT, Ishut* 14:8; *Shitah Mekubetzet, Ketuvot* 57a in the name of Ritva; *Shitah Mekubetzet, Ketuvot* 64a in the name of Ritva; *Teshuvot Hakham Tzvi* 1; R. Akiva Eiger, *Derush ve-Hiddush,* 91, Vilna ed.; File no. 910130/7, Netanya Regional Beit Din, June 3, 2015.For further acceptance of this position amongst the *Poskim* see sources cited by *PDR* 13:264, 269–271, H. S. Sha'anan, *Iyunim be-Mishpat* 1:28. For other *Poskim* who align themselves with this position, see supra, Introduction to Chapter 8, text accompanying notes 1–3.

Cf. with Rabbi Goldberg who argues in a *pilpulistic* fashion (loosely translated-engaging in casuistry) rather than *le-Halakhah* (in theory) and/or *le-ma'aseh* (in practice) that in the situation of an *agunah* we may coerce the husband to give a *get*. See Z. N. Goldberg, "In the matter of coercion due to *igun*," (Hebrew), in A. Tendler, *Treatise of sources & comments on get coercion* (Hebrew), 63–76, Jerusalem: 1998.

Given that his prolonged separation from Bryna, remarriage without giving Bryna a *get,* and his noncompliance with his marital duties of engaging in conjugal relations in a proper manner and furnishing spousal support creates an *igun* situation and therefore serve as grounds to coerce a *get* and in wake of the inability to coerce a *get* today in the United States, we may invoke the *umdana* of "*adaʾata dehakhi lo kidshah nafshah.*"[100]

Based upon the foregoing presentation, Bryna Stern is free to remarry without a *get* any Jew except a *Kohen.*

This *psak din* was approved by a renowned rabbinic authority.[101]

---

100. Rabbi Meir Posner, *Tzalʾot ha-Bayit* 6; *Teshuvot Shoeil u-Meishiv,* Mahadura Kama 198; *Zikhron Yehonatan* 1, *YD* 5.

101. Whether there is a *halakhic* requirement devolving upon a *beit din* to enlist the support of "a second opinion" or this rabbinic approval is reflective of "a *nohag*", a practice, see this writer's *Rabbinic Authority,* vol. 3, 256–262.

F.   A HUSBAND WHO ENGAGES IN PEDOPHILIA WITH HIS TWO STEPDAUGHTERS

Facts of the Case

On October 15th, 2009, Levi married Hindy in accordance with *Halakhah*. This marriage was a second marriage for both of them. During Hindy's first marriage she gave birth to five children. At the time of her second marriage, her children were the following ages: Miriam was fourteen years old, Yankel was 12 years old, Ahuvah was 11 years old, Ayalah was nine years old and Sarah was seven years old. Once married, Levi moved into Hindy's home. Throughout their marriage, despite the fact that he remained married to her, she paid the mortgage, utilities, paid most of the tuition and shared in financing family vacations. His contribution to the maintenance of the household was to pay for weekly groceries and provided her with attire for Yom Tov. In April 2012, Hindy separated from him. Subsequent to the separation, she requested Levi to give her a *get* and he refused. In the spring of 2013, Hindy opened up a file at a French *beit din* and the *beit din* summoned him to appear in front of them regarding the matter of the *get* but he was *mesarev le'din*, recalcitrant to appear for a *beit din* hearing and a few months ago, the Beit Din issued a *ktav seruv*, a writ of contempt against Levi and directed the members of the community to isolate themselves from him. A communication was sent by a French *beit din* to a rabbi in Germany and the synagogue where Levi was in attendance expelled him from praying at their *beit knesset*, synagogue.

To date, Levi has refused to give a *get* to Hindy and is only willing to execute a *get* on the condition that Ahuvah and Sarah, his stepdaughters, would admit to the police that their allegations of being sexually abused by their stepfather were fabricated. With the submission of these admissions, legal counsel has advised Levi that the two criminal convictions for abuse will be rescinded by the court. In a written communication to our *beit din*, Levi argues that his stepdaughters were brainwashed to submit their testimony by Hindy, their mother who herself was duped by his ex-wife to fabricate these stories. Upon the request of Hindy, we summoned Levi to appear for a hearing regarding the matter of the *get* but he declined to attend. On June 22, 2016, we conducted a hearing with Hindy Silver.

Hindy began her presentation by briefly discussing her three years of dating Levi and then communicated to us some of "the ups and downs" in her marital relationship with Levi. Thereafter, she told us about the incidents which eventually led to their marital separation and her eventual realization that Levi was a pedophile. In the summer of 2011, Hindy received a call from social services that they wanted to meet with Levi and her. At the meeting, the social worker informed them that there were allegations by Levi's natural daughter that she was abused by him but that the allegations were withdrawn by his daughter. In fact, Levi submitted to this *beit din* a copy of letter authored by Rabbi Y. M. Gruen in France wherein he states that in early April 2014, Levi's daughter appeared at his door without appointment and stated that her allegations of sexual misconduct against her father were false. And, in fact, during the same month a criminal court exonerated him of these submitted claims.

Approximately a half year later, one evening Sarah walked into one of her daughters' bedroom and found Levi sitting on her bed and the stepdaughter screamed at him. Asked by her mother what triggered such an outburst, Sarah's response was, "I hate him. I really hate him. He always comes to my bed and pinches me." Upon Hindy requesting of Levi to refrain from touching her children due to *halakhic* proscription and the petition of her children, Levi replied: "I'll listen to the *halachos* I want to listen to. You can't tell me what to do."

Subsequently, in March 2012, Social Services met with Hindy's children individually at their respective schools. Due to the conference with Sarah who communicated to Social Services that Levi touched her on her stomach, the police were notified and Hindy had a meeting with them. Though legal boundaries had not been crossed, the police didn't find anything of significant concern, nonetheless, police directed Hindy to speak to Social Services again in order to set up guidelines in terms of Levi's future interactions with his stepdaughters. By this time Hindy became vigilant and at least five times checked on Levi's movements around the house and couldn't sleep soundly due to the recent revelations of his behavior.

On April 21, 2012, Hindy's two sisters spoke to Hindy regarding Levi's behavior. Sara, Hindy's younger sister told Hindy that one of her children, who was a victim of the abuse, confided in her that her stepfather had gotten into bed with her as well as her sister and touched their breasts, events which were witnessed by Miriam, the oldest daughter. Additionally, Hindy's sisters told their sister that they recently convinced *Dayan* Cohen of the *beit din* that the children should be removed from the house immediately. After their conversations, Hindy and her sisters confronted Levi regarding his behavior. In their seven-minute conversation (which was recorded and submitted to the court as well as to our *beit din* as evidence), we overheard Chana, Hindy's sister, telling Levi that due to his acts of pedophilia either he immediately must leave the house or Hindy and her children would leave the house. His response was that he loves his children as well as his wife and sees no reason to leave the marital home. And then he adds, "if there is any error, I am more than happy to correct anything that went wrong." Chana's reply was, "it's too late – you have done it. The children are traumatized." The following day after Levi left Hindy's home, she changed the locks on the doors of her home. In retrospect, now Hindy understands why her husband used the small bathroom upstairs near the girls' bedroom instead of the main bathroom which was just a few steps away from their bedroom. By using this facility, his stepdaughters were able to view their stepfather showering and shaving and he was frequently caught by his stepdaughters peeking into their bedroom. And sometimes the children had happened to see Levi naked while walking into the bathroom which was ajar or when his towel slipped off him. Subsequent to their separation, one of Hindy's girlfriends told Hindy that Levi allegedly was only willing to remarry a woman who had daughters.

Subsequently, due to his stalking of Hindy, a restraining order was issued which prohibited him to be in close proximity to Hindy, and this order of protection will expire on September 3, 2017. Additionally, he breached a restraining order involving his son from his first marriage and consequently there is an arrest warrant out for him. Since that time, fearful of being imprisoned again, he left France and since 2015 has been leaving in another European country.

During the hearing, we spoke to one of the family's health care professionals who told us that it is clear that the victims of abuse who receive counseling have been traumatized rather than feigning that they were victims, and the therapist stated that the court's findings are correct. Secondly, both in oral testimony as well as in an affidavit, a rabbi in London told this panel that Levi admitted to him that he engaged in these acts of "inappropriate touching," including one where one of Hindy's sisters witnessed Levi touching one of his stepdaughters in the living room. Finally, though initially one member of a local *beit din* supported Levi's position, the Rabbi informed us that eventually the *dayan* had a change of heart and threw his support behind Hindy's claim for her *get*.

Given that Levi alleged that his stepdaughters were not traumatized due to being abused or witnessing the abuse and therefore his stepdaughters are attending sessions on a weekly basis "as a façade," we requested of Hindy to submit to us copies of various therapy bills (memorialized on the therapist's stationery) for her daughters' therapy sessions. Based upon our information regarding Hindy's financial situation as well as the health care professional's testimony and other reasons, we cannot impart credence to Levi's allegation that Hindy is willing to fund these sessions though they were allegedly only a façade.

Based upon the cumulative evidence submitted to this panel we affirm that in fact Levi acted inappropriately with Hindy's daughters. Hindy separated from him on the grounds that he was not a role model for her children. In short, she claims "*ma'is alai*" (lit. he is repulsive to me – I do not want this man) and therefore I want my *get*.

Until today, he has refused to give a *get*. Following in the footsteps of a communication dated December 22, 2013, a French *beit din* deemed Mr. Levi as "a *mesarev le-get*," as a husband who is *get* recalcitrant with all of its attendant consequences.

One of the consequences of being "a *mesarev le-get*" is to determine whether there are grounds to void their marriage, permitting Hindy to remarry without the giving of the *get*.

Discussion

1.   THE *MA'IS ALAI* (HE IS REPULSIVE TO ME) PLEA &
       KIDDUSHEI TA'UT (LOOSELY TRANSLATED:
       A MISTAKEN MARRIAGE)

The question is whether the wife's plea of "*ma'is alai*" (he is repulsive to me) is limited to circumstances where the wife cannot live sexually with her husband or encompasses a situation where she declares, "I do not want this man"? The panel asked her if Levi had not engaged in child abuse, would she have remained with him? Her reply was that she was unsure whether she would have stayed with the marriage. In fact, in the aforementioned recorded conversation which transpired the day before their separation during the hearing, Hindy affirmed that she was happy with Levi in terms of their marital relationship. Consequently, if the definition of *ma'is alai* is limited to sexual incompatibility, advancing such a plea, there would be no grounds to argue that Hindy was repulsed by Levi.

Notwithstanding some *Poskim* who contend that the two "*ma'is alai*" pleas are to be distinguished,[1] various authorities conclude that the

---

1. *Ra'ah, Ketuvot* 63b; *Beit ha-Behirah, Ketuvot* 63b.

claim includes a scenario where she doesn't want to be with her husband anymore.[2] To state it differently, her claim that "she doesn't want him anymore as a husband" suffices. Furthermore, there is no need for her to articulate the actual words *"mais alai".*[3] In contemporary times, various Israeli *battei din* have adopted this position.[4]

On one hand, as Rabbi Herzog observes:[5]

> *Ma'is alai* does not only entail plain hatred but an emotional fear of her husband and this is a secret from the secrets (inner dynamic – AYW) of the psyche . . . a person's soul recoils from touching the person. . . .

On the other hand, despite the emotional component of the *"ma'is alai"* plea, a victim has the ability to articulate the psychic and emotional feelings in rational terms by communicating to a third party (in our case, the *beit din* panel – AYW) the genesis for these feelings via an *"amatla mevureret,"* a clear pretext or explanation. In defining what an *"amatla mevureret"* entails, Rabbi Kook notes:[6]

---

2. *MT, Ishut* 23:16 compare with *MT Ishut* 14:8; *Teshuvot ha-Rashba ha-Meyuhusot la-Ramban* 138; *Teshuvot ha-Rashba* 1:573; *Teshuvot Maharik, shoresh* 102; *Teshuvot Maharit* 2, *EH* 40; *Teshuvot Maharitz ha-Hadashot* 172; *Teshuvot Maharashdam EH* 41; *Teshuvot Tzemah Tzedek EH* 262 (10); *Teshuvot Torat Emet* 186; *Teshuvot Tzel ha-Kesef* 2:10; *Beit Shmuel, SA EH* 77:11; Y. Hazan, *Teshuvot Yehaveh Da'at* 1, *EH* 13.

Moreover, it suffices that *Tova'at* argued at the hearing that she does not want to continue to remain married to him. There is no requirement that she state explicitly the words *"ma'is alai."* See *Teshuvot Torat Emet* 186.

For those authorities who define the *mais alai* plea as a wife's unwillingness to have conjugal relations with her husband, see *Hiddushei ha-Rashba Ketuvot* 64a; *Tosafot Rid Ketuvot* 64a; *SA EH* 77:2.

3. *Torat Emet,* supra n. 2; *Teshuvot Pnei Moshe* 1:55; *Ba'air Hetev, SA EH* 77:12; *Piskei Din Rabbanayim* (hereafter: *PDR*) 5:154, 157, 8:124, 126; File no. 316914761-21-1, Tzfat Regional Beit Din, October 29,2001 in 14 *ha-Din veha-Dayan* 10; File no. 980712/1, Haifa Regional Beit Din, October 27, 2014.

Additionally, she does not have to link her feelings of repulsiveness to any behavior exhibited by her husband but the *beit din* must be convinced by the merits of her claim and by the sincerity of her plea that the motivation is not due to her interest in another man. See *Tosafot Rid, Ketuvot,* supra n. 2; *Teshuvot ha-Rashba* 1:573; *Teshuvot Maharitz ha-Hadashot,* supra n. 2.

4. *PDR* 9:171, 181–184; File no. 32555/1, Ashdod Regional Beit Din, May 9, 2011; *Teshuvot Ateret Devorah* 1, *EH* 37.

5. *Teshuvot Heikhal Yitzhak* 1 *EH* 2.

6. *Teshuvot Ezrat Kohen* 56.

> It has to clear to the *beit din* that justice is with her and he de-
> serves, by his improper actions and practices, that she would be
> repulsed by him . . . that he caused everything.

However, the issue is whether the *"amatla mevureret"* must be verified
via the testimony of two eligible witnesses? As we noted in our earlier
decision, notwithstanding some authorities who mandate testimony in
order to assess the veracity of a wife's plea,[7] Tosafot Rid, Avnei Miluim
and Helkat Mehokeik do not require such verification.[8]

Even in the absence of a requirement to submit evidence, the advancing of an *"amatla mevureret"* does not suffice to impart validity to the
"ma'is alai" plea. As *Dayanim* Nissim, Elyashiv and Zolty opine, *"ein lo
la dayan ella amah she'einov ro'ot"* (a *halakhic* arbiter is mandated to
follow the discernment of his eyes) determines the veracity of the plea.[9]
Consequently, upon listening to the pretext of the plea and the awareness of the circumstances, a *beit din* panel must sincerely believe that
she is raising the plea for substantive reasons relating to her marriage
rather than as a ploy because she has an interest in another man.[10] Or
if it is clear that she is waiving her right to the value of her *ketubah*, we
can impart credence to a wife's plea of *"ma'is alai."*[11] In a recent *psak din*,
decision the Beit Din ha-Rabbani ha-Gadol rules that we endorse the
view of those *Poskim* who mandate that a *beit din* discern whether in
fact this plea is sincere and genuinely relates to the reason (or reasons)
for the dissolving of the marital ties.[12]

The question is whether a *beit din* may coerce a husband to give a *get*
based upon a wife's *"ma'is alai"* plea? Notwithstanding that there are
authorities who will mandate *get* coercion; [13]many *Poskim* will reject this

---

7. *Beit Shmuel, Kitzur Dinei Moredet*, 77 (end); *Teshuvot Maharit 2, EH* 40; *Hazon Ish EH* 79:16. See *Teshuvot Divrei Malkiel* 3:145 who requires corroboration via
witnesses or verification by 100 rabbis that she is telling the truth.

8. *Tosafot Rid, Ketuvot* 64; *Helkat Mehokeik, Kitzur Dinei Moredet* 77 (4). In
pursuance to *Avnei Miluim* 77:7 we trust her words.

9. *PDR* 3:201, 206–207; 20:193, 200. For earlier antecedents of this principle, see
Bava Batra 130b; *Sanhedrin* 6b; *Nidah* 20b; *Rema, Introduction to Darkhei Moshe*.

10. *Beit ha-Behirah, Ketuvot* 63a; *Teshuvot ha-Rosh* 43:6.

11. *Teshuvot Maharit 2, EH* 40; *Hazon Ish EH* 69:4; *Yehaveh Da'at*, supra n. 2 in
the name of Rema. Cf. *Teshuvot Yabia Omer 5, EH* 13:6; *Teshuvot Yehaveh Da'at 3,
EH* 33. For a recent summary of the position emerging from the rulings of Israeli
battei din, see File no. 1078402/6, Haifa Regional Beit Din, June 5, 2017.

12. File no. 992236/1. Beit Din ha-Rabbani ha-Gadol, May 17, 2015.

13. Rabbi Gershom, *Teshuvot Hut ha-Meshullash*, Tur 3, 35; *Piskei ha-Rosh,
Ketuvot* 5:34 in the name of Rashbam; *Tur EH* 77 in the name of Rashbam; *Teshuvot*

option and the husband may choose to divorce her. [14] Despite the fact

---

ha-Rema 96 in the name of Rashbam; *Tosafot Ketuvot* 63b, s.v. *aval* in the name of *"yesh meforshim"*; *MT, Ishut* 14:8; Ra'avad, *MT, Yibbum* 2:15, *Magid Mishneh*, ad. locum; *Orhot Hayyim* 2, *Ketuvot* 16; *Teshuvot Masat Binyamin* 44; *Teshuvot Re'em* 28; *Teshuvot Maharit* 2:40 in the name of Mahara Monson; *Teshuvot Betzalel Ashkenazi* 6:19; *Teshuvot Avnei ha-Ephod* 77. For additional *Poskim* who subscribe to this view see A. Horowitz, *Kuntres ha-Berurim*, 3–19.

The position of Rashi in accordance with certain opinions concurs with this view, see *Teshuvot Maharam of Rothenburg*, Berlin ed., 53, Prague d. 443; *Hiddushei ha-Ritva, Ketuvot* 63b; *Teshuvot Maharik, shoresh* 102. Cf. *Teshuvot Maharashdam EH* 41 in the name of Rashi; *Teshuvot Maharam Alshakar* 73 in the name of Rashi; *Teshuvot ha-Rema* 96 in the name of Rashi.

Whether Rambam, op. cit would require verification of the plea of *ma'is alai* prior to coercing a *get* is subject to controversy. See *Beit ha-Behirah, Ketuvot* 63a; *Beit Yosef, Tur EH* 77; *Teshuvot Maharashdam, YD* 140; *Teshuvot Maharit* 2, *EH* 40; E. Abergil, *Teshuvot Dibrot Eliyahu* 4:22.

In the event that a wife advances the plea of *"ma'is alai"* and it is clear that she has no interest in another man, some authorities will coerce a husband to give a *get*. See *Teshuvot ha-Rashbash* 93; *Teshuvot Yakhin u-Boaz* 2:21; *Hut ha-Meshullash*, op cit. However, others contend that we coerce a *get* only with regard to a husband's flaw which is enumerated in the Mishneh in Ketuvot. See *Sefer Meisharim, Netiv* 23, *Helek* 8; *Teshuvot ha-Rashba ha-Meyuhosot le-Ramban* 138; *Teshuvot Zekan Aharon* (Ra'ah ha-Levi) 149.

14. *Rabbeinu Tam, Sefer ha-Yashar, Teshuvot* 24 and 77 and *Hiddushin* 4; *Piskei ha-Rosh, Ketuvot* 4:34; *Teshuvot ha-Rosh* 43:6; *Ba'al ha-Maor, Ketuvot* 27a (according to pagination of Rif); *Teshuvot ha-Ran* 13 and 17; *Teshuvot ha-Rivash* 104 and 209; *Teshuvot ha-Rashba* 1:973, 1192, 5:95; *Tosafot Ketuvot*, supra n. 13 in the name of Rabbeinu Hananeil and Rashi; *Shitah Mekubezet, Ketuvot* 64a in the name of Rabbeinu Yonah and Rabbeinu Tam; *Hiddushei ha-Ritva, Ketuvot* 63b; *Tosafot Rid , Ketuvot* 63b; *Sefer ha-Behirah, Ketuvot*, Sofer ed., 268; *Teshuvot Tashbetz* 1:4, 2:69; *Teshuvot ha-Rivash* 104,209, and 361; *Teshuvot ha-Rashbash* 93 and 168 in the name of the majority of *aharonim* (later authorities); *SA EH* 77:2, Rema, *SA EH* 77:3; *Teshuvot ha-Rema* 36,96; *Beit Shmuel SA EH* 77:27; *Teshuvot Mahari Bruna* 24; *Teshuvot Masat Binyamin* 116; *Teshuvot Maharshal* 41; *Magid Mishneh, MT Ishut* 14:8; *Teshuvot Maharil ha-Hadashot* 189; *Teshuvot ha-Radvaz* 1:205, 2:430; *Teshuvot Maharashdam EH* 135; *Teshuvot Noda be-Yehudah*, Mahadura Tinyana, *EH* 90; *Teshuvot Tzemah Tzedek* (Schneersohn) 262:12; *Teshuvot Beit Yitzhak* 1:128; *Teshuvot Ein Yitzhak* 2:35(32); *Bah, Tur EH* 77:11; *Hazon Ish EH* 69:1; *PDR* 1:18, 3:224, 8:124, 15:145; *Iyunim be-Mishpat EH* 56.

Though in the wake of a *"ma'is alai"* plea in accordance with the above opinion we do not coerce the husband to give a *get*, under such conditions we refrain from coercing the wife to remain with her husband. See *Teshuvot ha-Rashba* 7:414; *Teshuvot ha-Rosh* 43:14; *Rashbash*, supra n. 13; *Teshuvot Mahari Weil* 20; *Teshuvot Re'em* 25; *Teshuvot Maharshal* 69; *Ba'air Hetev SA EH* 77:32; *Teshuvot Beit Ephraim*, Mahadura Tinyana, 1, *EH* 74.

Rabbi Avraham B. Gatinieu argues that the majority of *rishonim* (early authorities) subscribed to the position that *get* coercion may be applied in the wake of a

that outside of *Eretz Yisrael* one is not authorized to coerce the giving of a *get*, we are empowered to obligate the giving of a *get*. Though there are many *Poskim* who will equally refrain from obligating a *get* in a situation of "*ma'is alai*," even if the plea is accompanied by an "*amatla mevureret*

---

wife's "*ma'is alai*" plea. See *Teshuvot Tzel ha-Kesef* 13–14. A review of their rulings does not reflect his assessment that the majority view mandates *get* coercion in a situation that a wife advances such a plea.

In pursuance to this view, one neither coerces the husband to give a *get* ("*kofin legaresh*") nor obligates the giving of a *get* ("*hiyuv legaresh*"). However, under such circumstances a *beit din* may render a decision titled "*mitzvah legaresh*" (a duty to become divorced). See *Teshuvot Tashbetz* 1:1; *Teshuvot Terumat ha-Deshen, Peskaim u-Ketavim* 58; *Teshuvot Yabia Omer* 3, *EH* 17:13; *Iggerot Moshe YD* 4:15 (2). In other words, there is a debate whether a wife's plea of "*ma'is alai*" *may serve* as a basis to coerce or obligate a *get*. However, if one endorses the position that neither can a *beit din* coerce or obligate a *get*, then we are left with a situation of a potential *igun* situation where a husband may be recalcitrant concerning giving her a *get*. Consequently, under such conditions a *beit din* ought to render a judgment that there is a *mitzvah*, a *halakhic* duty for the husband to give a *get* lest the wife become an *agunah*. See File no. 810538/2, Beit Din ha-Rabbani ha-Gadol, April 28, 2011; File no. 880581-1, Beit Din ha-Rabbani ha-Gadol, July 31,2012; U. Lavi, "Is there an obligation to give a *get* when there is a plea of "*ma'is alai*" or only a *mitzvah* to give a *get*," (Hebrew) *Kenas ha-Dayanim*, 5776, 311, 316–317. Cf. other contemporary Israeli *battei din* that obligate a *get* in the situation of *igun*. See File no. 764231/6, Haifa Regional Beit Din, March 25, 2014; File no. 523426/2, Haifa Regional Beit Din, September 1, 2014; File no. 849440/19, Tel Aviv-Yaffo Regional Beit Din, July 14,2015; File no. 965579/2, Netanya Regional Beit Din, July 23, 2015; File no. 8293/5, Ashdod Regional Beit Din, February 2,2016; File no. 1009273/4, Haifa Regional Beit Din, September 6, 2016.

Our presentation of the issue whether a wife's submission of a "*ma'is alai* "plea is grounds for *get* coercion is limited to the context of understanding what the *din*, the *Halakhah* states as it emerges from the *Poskim's* rulings. However, there is an additional dimension which addresses the rabbinic legislation (*takanah*) regarding this matter, namely what has been labeled as "*takanat dina de'metivta*". In Gaonic times legislation was enacted that the submission of such a plea served as grounds to coerce a *get*. See *Hemdah Genuzah* 89; *Teshuvot Geonim*, Assaf ed. Vol. 2, 185; *Teshuvot Geonim, Sha'arei Tzedek* 4, Sha'ar 4, Siman 15; *Teshuvot Maharam ben Barukh*, Berlin ed., 494. There have been various challenges to the validity of this piece of rabbinic legislation. Some argue that this legislation never existed. Others challenged the authority of the Gaonim to enact such legislation which deals with matters of personal status. Some argue that the legislation was passed for a designated period of time and consequently it is inapplicable today. See *Piskei ha-Rosh, Ketuvot* 5:35; *Tur EH* 77; *Sefer ha-Yashar, Hiddushin* 24; *Hiddushei ha-Ritva, Ketuvot* 64a; *Ba'al ha-Maor, Hilkhot Alfasi*, 27a; *Teshuvot ha-Rashba* 1:1192, 1235; *Hiddushei ha-Ramban, Ketuvot* 63b. As such we have chosen to refrain from factoring this legislation into arriving at a conclusion whether the advancement of a wife's claim of "*ma'is alai*" may serve as grounds to coerce a husband to give a *get*.

"[15] yet there are authorities who recognize such a claim provided that the wife submits an *"amatla mevureret."*[16] Finally there are numerous *Poskim* who would permit *get* coercion on the condition that the wife submits an *"amatla mevureret".*[17]

Alternatively, in accordance with the *Poskim* who require evidence that in fact Hindy found Levi to be repulsive, at least in regard to his inappropriate relationship with her children, Hindy submitted evidence including: a criminal judgment, testimony by third parties that these events of pedophilia occurred and testimony by two Rabbis that Levi admitted to inappropriate touching of two of his stepdaughters. In March 2012, the daughter who was the victim of abuse communicated

---

15. *Teshuvot Maharam of Rothenburg*, Prague ed. 946; *Teshuvot ha-Rashba* 1:573, 1192; *Shitah Mekubezet*, supra n. 14; *Beit Shmuel*, supra n. 14; *Noda be-Ye-huda*, supra n. 14; *Teshuvot Beit Ephraim EH* 129; *Teshuvot Tzitz Eliezer*, 5:26 in the name of Rabbi Elyashiv; *Kovetz ha-Teshuvot* 1:174; *Teshuvot Ateret Shlomo* 1:32, 33 in the name of the majority of *rishonim*; *PDR* 7:3, 201, 204–206, 12:324, 339 in the name of Maharam, Rosh, Tur, Rema and Maharshal, 18:24; File no. 819158/3, Beit Din ha-Rabbani ha-Gadol, October 5, 2011. Cf. Izirer, 2 *Shurat ha-Din* 104 (5754).

Nonetheless, in a situation where the husband's behavior caused the wife to be repulsed by him and refuses to continue living with him, some of these authorities such as Rabbi Elyashiv would obligate the giving of a *get*. See *PDR* 3:77, 89, 9:94. As such, the facts of this case would propel a *beit din* to obligate the giving of a *get*.

16. *Sefer ha-Behirah* on *Ketuvot* 64a; *Hiddushei ha-Ritva Ketuvot* 63b; *Teshuvot Maharik, shoresh* 102 in the name of Rabbeinu Tam; *Rema, SA YD* 228:20; *Maharit*, supra n. 11; *Teshuvot Hut ha-Meshullash*, 2; *Ezrat Kohen*, supra n. 6; *Teshuvot Tzitz Eliezer* 4:21; 5:26; *Teshuvot Yabia Omer* 3, *EH* 18 (13); S. Werner, *Teshuvot Mishpetei Shmuel*, Mahadura Tinyana, 22:4; *Teshuvot Shema Shlomo* 3:19; Izirer, supra n. 15; *Dibrot Eliyahu*, supra n. 13; File no. 578173/1, Haifa Regional Beit Din, October 28,2013.

In fact, in accordance to Rabbi O. Yosef under such conditions there would be grounds to coerce a *get*. See other decisors who would concur that *get* coercion is permissible. See infra n. 17.

17. *Teshuvot ha-Rashbash*, supra n. 13; *Tosafot Rid Ketuvot* 63b; *Hiddushei ha-Ritva, Ketuvot* 63b; *Hut ha-Meshullash*, supra n. 13 (end of *teshuvah)* in the name of Maharam; *Teshuvot Yakhin u-Boaz* 2:21 in the name of Maharam; *Teshuvot ha-Ma-harit* 2:40 in the name of Rambam and Rabbi A.Munson; *Teshuvot Beit Ephraim* 126; *Erekh ha-Shulhan EH* 77:5; *Teshuvot Makor Barukh* 17; *Netivot Mishpat (Algazi)* 114a; *Teshuvot Zekan Aharon* 149; *Ezrat Kohen*, supra n. 6; *Teshuvot Devar Eliyahu* 13; *Teshuvot Tzitz Eliezer* 5:26(5),17:53; *Teshuvot Yabia Omer* 3, *EH* 18:4; File no. 917387/1, Yerushalayim Regional Beit Din, November 17,2013; *Kuntres ha-Berurin* 12 and 15 in the name of all the *Geonim* and *Rishonim* as well as *Aharonim*; PDR 15:18, 3:220,224. Cf. *Rema SA EH* 77:3; *Teshuvot Mahari Bruna* 211. Whether Ma-haram of Rothenberg would align himself with the opinion that there are grounds for *get* coercion under such conditions is an open question. See Y. Goldberg, *Eilu she'kofin le'hotzi*, 145, n. 3, 333–352.

her experience to a social worker. In short, the plea of *"ma'is alai"* is corroborated by evidence as well as by the *beit din's* positive assessment of Hindy's credence which is supported by character references, the absence of advancing a claim for monetary value of her *ketubah* either in this *beit din* or any other forum and no proof that she is interested in another man.

That being said, is child abuse an *ilat gerushin*, grounds for divorce that the wife may claim *"ma'is alai,"* I do not want to live with him? Addressing the case of a married man who was fondling young girls, incarcerated for four years and the wife desired to receive her *get*, Rabbi Shimon Hanover, *av beit din*, presiding *dayan* of the Wurtzberg Beth Din in Germany inquired of Rabbi Yehiel Weinberg who resided in Germany at the time whether there was a basis to obligate the husband to give a *get* utilizing the secular courts as an avenue to enforce the giving of the *get* based upon a wife's *"ma'is alai"* plea. Relying upon Rabbi Yair Bachrach's ruling that when dealing with matters of *ervah*, sexuality, one is required to forewarn the perpetrator and garner evidence regarding the matter prior to arriving at a decision.[18] In the wake of the absence of any forewarning, given that *Halakhah* does not mandate that the *get* be coerced under these circumstances, argues Rabbi Weinberg one cannot direct the secular courts to enforce *get* compliance lest we create a situation of a *"get me'useh,"* a coerced *get*. Nonetheless, Rabbi Weinberg admits that when dealing with a husband who is a pedophile, there is credence for a wife to claim *"ma'is alai,"* and implicit in his ruling, should there be evidentially proof which is *halakhically* valid there would be grounds to obligate a *get*.[19]

Seemingly, since *get* coercion fails to be a *halakhic* option, obligating a *get* equally cannot be implemented. However, in dealing with a husband who engaged in an illicit affair with his mother-in-law, following in the footsteps of *Hut ha-Meshullash*,[20] a Yerushalayim Beit Din contends that even those authorities who will object to obligating a *get* due to a *ma'is alai* claim would agree that such conduct is so repulsive that no wife would agree to live with a husband who commits such acts.[21] *Kal ve-homer, a fortiori*, in our case of a stepfather who engaged in illicit

---

18. *Teshuvot Hakham Tzvi* 133.

19. *Teshuvot Seridei Eish* 3:29. For grounds to advance a claim for terminating the employment of a pedophile who serves as an educator, see *Teshuvot Shoeil u-Meshiv*, Mahadura Kama, 1:185; *Teshuvot Hikrei Lev, YD* 47. See further, this writer's *Rabbinic Authority*, vol. 2, 101–109.

20. *Hut ha-Meshullash*, supra n. 13

21. File no. 1-21-2521, Yerushalayim Regional Beit Din, June 18, 2009.

touching of two stepdaughters and committed these acts in the presence of Hindy's oldest daughter who was traumatized by these incidents and is presently in therapy.

The argumentation advanced by *Dayan* H. Izirer in the above-cited *Beit Din* decision conveys quite clearly and eloquently the *ilat gerushin* here in our case. Obligating a *get* of a husband who committed "*ma'aseh ke'ur,*" repulsive acts with his mother-in-law, the *Beit Din* expounds:

> It is clear from the submitted evidence that the wife was unaware of the acts and from the perspective of the wife this is a major insult. Undoubtedly, the husband's conduct impacts negatively on the emotional world of the wife and it is worse than a husband who curses his wife . . . it is an attack on the personal honor of the wife, family values and family stability. It is attack like engaging in adultery but even more severe. . . .
>
> We must determine which *ilah* (ground – AYW) will allow us to obligate a *get*. If we view it from the vantage point of "an adulterer" then we are concerned with the dissipation of monetary assets but here there is no loss of assets. . . . When . . . he commits improper acts in his home and within the context of his private life one does not require the rationale of asset dissipation. This is an attack upon the essence of his life with his wife. In this case, he exploits his relationship with his wife in order to engage in affairs with his mother-in-law behind the hidden eyes of his wife. . . .
>
> Another ground: A husband who desires his mother-in-law that is older than him by tens of years, his behavior towards her entails sexual deviancy and mental dysfunction. . . . The fact that this matter repeated itself many times and during an extended period of time places him in the category of *oveir al dat Yehudit* (transgresses the Jewish religion) and there is no need for forewarning either because everyone knows and it is as if he forewarned or due to the fact that this is deviant conduct within the framework of a mental disorder and there is no ability to control the matter (his desires – AYW).

Upon reading the above, one can only conclude that the facts of our case are almost identical to the fact pattern presented by the Yerushalayim Beit Din. On one hand, we are dealing with a stepfather and stepchildren and the other *beit din* is focusing upon two consenting adults. However, on the other hand, in both scenarios the wife is unaware of what is transpiring and in each situation the husband is exploiting his ties with his wife. Whereas, in the other case, his ability to engage in an illicit affair with his mother-in-law is built upon his closeness to his wife, in our scenario Levi exploits the situation by utilizing his wife's home, including the bathroom near the girls' room to further his mission. Moreover, in terms of argumentation, the *Beit Din's* analogy to an adulterer is much more striking! Whereas, a husband's acts of adultery may entail asset dissipation and therefore a *get* ought to be obligated under such circumstances. However, here in our case, Levi is living in Hindy's home where she pays the mortgage, utilities, pays most of the tuition, and shares in financing family vacations. His contribution to the maintenance of the household was to pay for weekly groceries and provided his wife attire for the *Yamim Tovim*, the Jewish holidays. As such, there was no asset dissipation by Levi and yet *Halakhah* looks askance at his behavior. In the *Beit Din's* words:

> Undoubtedly, the husband's conduct impacts negatively on the emotional world of the wife and it is worse than a husband who curses his wife . . . it is an attack on the personal honor of the wife, family values and family stability.

Subsequently a few years later, citing the aforementioned ruling of the Yerushalayim Regional Beit Din, the Netanya Regional Beit Din reaffirmed a wife's repulsiveness vis-à-vis a father's abusiveness of his daughter.[22] A few months later, Yerushalayim Regional Beit Din again viewed the inappropriateness of such child abuse through the lens of a "*ma'is alai*" plea.[23]

Moreover, a wife's desire to be divorced from such an individual is not limited to the repulsiveness of the act of child abuse. In dealing with marital relations, as the Talmud states in various places, "one does not live with a snake in the same basket." Though the Talmudic context of this expression addresses a spouse who acts inappropriately in terms of his *halakhic* obligations, namely failing to comply with the *halakhot* of setting aside *hallah* (dough), a husband who refuse to support his wife and *halakhically* invalidating marriage to a *shoteh*, a person who is *halakhically* mentally dysfunctional,[24] in subsequent generations the statement has been utilized as a description of marital relations marked

---

22. File 860977/1, Netanya Regional Beit Din, May 20, 2013.
23. File no. 917387/1, Yerushalayim Regional Beit Din, November 17, 2013.
24. *Ketuvot* 72a, 77a, 86b.

by abuse as well as mental dysfunction.[25] The common denominator of all these examples conveys the notion that "one does not live with a snake in the same basket" means that a spouse cannot live with another spouse due to the other spouse's unwillingness to fulfill religious or marital duties or being psychologically impaired. However, in our situation we are invoking the expression that "one does not live with a snake in the same basket" in the sense that Hindy cannot live on the same premises ("in the same basket") with Levi due to his living in geographical proximity to her children, poses a threat which may potentially endanger her children's mental and potentially religious wellbeing.

2.   *UMDANA* – A WIFE'S ASSESSED EXPECTATIONS OF THE
       MARRIAGE

In contradistinction to *kiddushei ta'ut* which focuses upon an event prior to the marriage, namely the existence of a preexisting grave flaw in the husband's physiology or behavior which if failed to be disclosed may under certain conditions be grounds to void a marriage (*bittul kiddushin*), *umdana* (*ada'ata dehakhi lo kidshah nafshah* – with this in mind, she would not have entered into ther marriage) deals with an event (or events) which transpires after the inception of marriage.[26] For example, "had I known that my husband would have become a *mumar* (an apostate Jew), become a criminal or would have become mentally dysfunctional during our years of marriage I never would have married him" may serve as illustrations of a wife invoking an *umdana demukhah*, a major inference from assessed expectations (hereafter: *umdana*) which if proven may serve grounds to void a marriage without the giving of a *get*.[27]

---

25. *Teshuvot Harei Besamim* 4, *Mahadura* 4, 124; *Teshuvot Har Tzvi EH* 1:14–15; *Teshuvot Yaskil Avdi* 6, *EH* 61; File no. 969624/1, Haifa Regional Beit Din, May 26, 2016.

26. For our conceptual distinction between *kiddushei ta'ut* and *umdana*, see *Teshuvot Ohr Sameah* 2:29; *Teshuvot She'eilot Moshe EH* 2; *Teshuvot Zikhron Yehonatan* 1, *YD* 5. For authorities who invoke *umdana* as a technique to void a marriage, see *Poskim* cited infra n. 29.

27. For examples of various *umdanot* which served as a basis to void a marriage, see *Tosafot Ketuvot* 47b, s.v. *shelo*; *Teshuvot Maharam of Rothenburg* Prague ed., 1022; *Teshuvot Noda be-Yehudah*, Mahadura Tinyana *EH* 80 (end), 135; *Teshuvot Beit ha-Levi* 3:3; *Teshuvot Hesed le-Avraham*, Mahadura Tinyana *EH* 55; *Teshuvot Torat Hesed EH* 26; Bayit 9; *She'eilot Moshe*, supra n. 26; *Zikhron Yehonatan* 1, *YD* 5 (17); *Teshuvot Avnei Hefetz* 30; *Teshuvot Sha'arei Ezra* 4 *EH* 26; *Teshuvot Meishivat Nefesh EH* 73–77; D.Meisels, *Teshuvot Radad EH* 40; *Teshuvot Maharsham* 7:95 (a matter of a wife's mental dysfunction); *Iggerot Moshe, EH* 4:121; *Teshuvot Har Tzvi*

Firstly, based upon our discussion of the ongoing situation of "one does not live with a snake in the same basket," of ever-present and recurring pedophilia behavior with his steopdaughters in the marital home furnishes an example of the *umdana – ada'ata dehakhi lo kidshah nafshah*.

Furthermore, a second *umdana* in our case has been articulated by two *aharonim* (later authorities). Rabbi Eliezer Fried of Volozhin claims:[28]

> We have found a few times that we understand the nature of the wife and the nature of the matter that she absolutely does not accept the status quo . . . that she refuses [in retrospect – AYW] to be married to him and clearly then the *kiddushin* are invalid. And we encounter a few times in the Talmud that our Sages have authorized us to weigh demonstrable *umdanot*. And here if anybody would hear this particular *umdana* that it is unacceptable for her to be an *agunah* her entire life.

Subsequently, Rabbi Petahiah Horenblass, *Av Beit Din* (presiding *dayan)* of Warsaw concludes in a rabbinic matter:[29]

EH 2:133. Whether an *umdana* may serve as the sole avenue to void a marriage or as a *senif*, a supporting argument to void a marriage is subject to debate.

It is important to stress that this *umdana* has been employed in the *teshuvot* (responsa) both regarding *kiddushei ta'ut* as well as emerging *after* the onset of the *kiddushin*. In other words, concerning *kiddushei ta'ut*, once the major latent defect has been identified, some *Poskim* will employ the *umdana* by stating, "had she known prior to the marriage about this major defect she never would have married him." On the other hand, if the inappropriate behavior or *mum*, flaw, only began after the onset of the marriage and did not preexist prior to the marriage, there may be grounds to employ an *umdana* where she would (for example) exclaim, "had I known that he would become mentally dysfunctional during the marriage I never would have married him" For a discussion of these two types of *umdana*, see *Zikhron Yehonatan*, op. cit.

28. *Teshuvot Hut ha-Meshullash* 3:5. Whether Rabbi Tenenbaum would recognize such an *umdana*, we leave as an open question. See *Teshuvot Divrei Malkiel* 4:100. Cf. *Iggerot Moshe EH* 1:162(*halitzah*).

29. *Teshuvot Pithei She'arim, Sheilot u-Teshuvot* 32. Given that we employ the *umdana* "had I known he would be a criminal, I never would have married him," she has the status of "*a safek eishet ish*," a doubtful married woman on a rabbinic level (For the meaning of *safek kiddushin*, see *Ran*, on *Rif*, *Kiddushin* 5b; *Teshuvot Maharit* 1:38; see further Introduction, supra text accompanying n. 33.) Therefore we may invoke the *umdana* of *igun*. Rabbi Eliezer, supra n. 28 would concur with this position.

One can state, "with this in mind, I never would have married him," to remain an *agunah* forever.

In the wake of the directive of a French *beit din* that there are grounds to obligate a *get* and the couple has been separated for over four and half years, the invoking of the *umdana* that should she have known that she would become an *agunah* for the rest of her life she never would have married him resonates in our case.[30]

Upon her separation from Levi in what sense did she become an *agunah*? Firstly, Levi's decision to flee to another country to avoid criminal prosection *ipso facto* denied Hindy her entitlement to *onah*, conjugal relations.

Whereas according to some authorities the duty of engaging in marital relations is derived from the Biblical word in Shemot 21:10 "*she'erah* . . . he shall not diminish" or "*ve'onatah* he shall not diminish",[31] others derive the duty by logical inference.[32] Elaborating upon this position, Rabbi Naftali T. Berlin contends:[33]

> Reason informs us that (the husband) is so bound. . . . as everyone knows, for this purpose that a bride enters into marriage . . . Hence if he denies her sexual ties, she is deprived of her right.

In other words, *Halakhah* recognizes the wife's right to conjugal relations and therefore the husband has a duty to provide it to her. If a husband can in fact engage in conjugal relations and refuses to comply with his duty either out of hatred or anger vis-à-vis his wife or due to a marital quarrel or because "he cast his eyes on another woman," he is classified as "*a moreid*," a rebellious husband, and he can be coerced to give a *get*.[34]

Given the fact that Hindy separated from Levi due to child abuse and he has refused to give a *get*, in effect are we to view him as a *moreid* since it is due to the separation that he cannot live with her? As we mentioned, a *moreid* is a husband who is withholding intimate relations due to being angry or due to hatred of his wife. In our situation, the

---

30. In the wake of being an *agunah*, a husband may be coerced to give a *get*. See supra Introduction, text accompanying notes 1–3. Since *get* coercion is not an option today in the Diaspora, we may consider the employment of the technique of *umdana* to void a marriage. See supra text accompanying n. 42.

31. *Mekhilta de R. Yishmael Mishpatim* 3, ed. Horowitz-Rabin.

32. *Mekhilta de R. Yishmael*, ibid.; *Ketuvot* 48a.

33. *Birkat ha-Netziv,Mekhilta*, ibid.

34. *SA EH* 77:1; *Helkat Mehokeik SA EH* 77:1; *Hazon Ish EH* 108:13.

cessation of relations is due to the fact that he is *onus* (under duress) due to circumstances beyond his control, namely being separated from his wife, an action which was commenced by his wife. Thus, how can we consider him a *moreid*?

Seemingly, we may find support for such a position in the *Poskim* that a sick husband shall wait six months until he is cured before engaging in *onah*.[35] In other words, given his state of being an *onus*, since the husband's abstention from relations stems from his health rather than hatred for his wife, the husband is not viewed as a *moreid*. Analogously, the same should apply here where Levi's refraining from *onah* is due to Hindy's decision to separate from him rather than due to animosity towards his wife. In both cases, we should view the sick husband and the husband who is forced to move out of the marital home as a situation of *ones*. Consequently, should a husband be incarcerated due to criminal behavior, seemingly since his incarceration is due to his negligence, he should be viewed as a *moreid* given his inability to engage in intimate relations. However, some *Poskim* such as Rabbi Bezaleil Zolty construe the fact of imprisonment as creating a situation of being an *onus*, no different than a sick husband who is incapable of performing *onah* and therefore he isn't to be viewed as a *moreid*.[36]

Nonetheless, there are other authorities who disagree and argue that incarceration may occur either due to the husband's illegal behavior or due to circumstances beyond his control. On one hand, in a case where a husband was conscripted to the army for a specified time, akin to a husband who is sick for a prescribed time, a wife is *halakhically* required to remain in the marriage.[37] Given that the husband was coerced to serve in the army, we are dealing with a case of *ones* and therefore he isn't viewed as a *moreid* and thus there is no duty to dissolve the marital ties. On the other hand, serving in a prison is due to engaging in criminal behavior, consequently should a husband be incarcerated he is "*posheia*," responsible for being unable to have relations with his wife.[38]

---

35. *SA EH* 76:11; *Beit Shmuel, SA EH* 76:17.

36. *PDR* 5:329, 331.

37. *Hagahot Mordekhai, Ketuvot* 26a (on Rif) in the name of Riaz which is cited approvingly by *Darkhei Moshe, Tur EH* 76: *Beit Shmuel, SA EH* 76:18 and *Helkat Mehokeik, SA EH* 76:17; *Teshuvot Avnei Nezer, HM* 83. See *Teshuvot Imrei Mishpat* 10(2–3) application of Riaz's position to the case of a husband who is imprisoned and thus unable to comply with his duty of conjugal relations.

38. *Mordekhai, Ketuvot* 183; *Teshuvot Tashbetz* 2:68; *Teshuvot ha-Rashbash* 183; *Teshuvot Be'air Yitzhak EH* 10; *Teshuvot Beit Meir* 114; *Teshuvot Oneg Yom Tov,* 168 (end); *Teshuvot Hatam Sofer EH* 1:131; *Teshuvot Tzitz Eliezer* 6:42 (3).

Implicit in this view is that even if the imprisoned husband loves his wife and therefore unintentionally he cannot perform conjugal relations, by dint of his imprisonment he is transgressing the negative prohibition of refraining from having relations with his wife as well asfailing to comply with other marital duties[39] and as such he is to be viewed as a *moreid* and therefore *get* coercion is in place.

Secondly, his failure to support her for the last four and half years of separation engenders an additional reason why mandating *get* coercion is in place. Finally, the extended time of separation in and of itself mandates the issuance of a compulsory order to give a *get*. In short, Levi's failure to comply with his marital duties of engaging in conjugal relations and spousal maintenance coupled with his extended period of separation according to a well-trodden *mesorah* which recently has been memorialized in three Israeli *beit din* rulings requires that *get* coercion ought to be imposed due to the fact that Levi's behavior has transformed Hindy into an *agunah*. [40]

Finally, given that Levi fled France and moved from place to place in Europe there is a basis to coerce a *get*. [41]

In short, there are grounds to coerce a *get* based upon the wife's plea of "*ma'is alai*" as well Levi's unintentional withholding of conjugal relations and support coupled with his moving from place to place for four and half years since his separation from Hindy.

If Hindy had been residing in *Eretz Yisrael* where *get* coercion is an option, albeit employed on a limited basis in dealing with child abuse,[42] her marriage may be dissolved by *get* coercion. Additionally, if child abuse would be viewed through the prism of a *ma'is ali* plea accompanied by an "*amatla mevureret*," there is basis for *get* coercion.[43] Finally, given that Levi fled France (without his wife) fearful of being imprisoned in his native country due to the commission of a criminal act and refusing to

---

39. *Teshuvot Maharam Alsheikh* 50. See also, *Tosafot Ketuvot* 70a s.v. *yotzi*; *Piskei ha-Rosh Yevamot* 6:11; *Teshuvot ha-Ritva* 122. As Rabbi Refael Halperin aptly notes that a husband who is imprisoned and therefore cannot support his wife, even though he is *onus* is no different than a husband who is afflicted with skin boils and can be coerced to give a *get*. Similarily, the imprisoned husband ought to be coerced to give a *get*. See *Oneg Yom Tov*, infra n. 44.

40. See supra Introduction, text accompanying notes 1–3.

41. *Levush* 154:9 in the name of *Teshuvot ha-Rosh* 43:1–2.

42. *Pikei Din Rabbanayim* 8:124; File no. 9217-68-1, Tel Aviv-Yaffo Regional Beit Din, February 12, 2008.

43. See supra notes 13, 16–17.

comply with his marital duties such as conjugal relations and providing spousal maintenance creates an *igun* situation and therefore there is a basis to coerce a *get*.[44]

And in pursuance to certain *Poskim*, in light of the option of *get* coercion, Hindy may have been unable to invoke the *umdana*, "had I known that my husband would engage in pedophilia of my children during our years of marriage I never would have married him." However, today outside of *Eretz Yisrael*, where Hindy resides, there is no *beit din* which is legally and thus *halakhically* empowered to coerce a husband to give a *get*.

Consequently, in the absence of the ability to coerce Levi to give a *get* in contemporary times in the Diaspora we may employ *kiddushei ta'ut* and *umdana* as vehicles to void a marriage.[45]

Based upon our foregoing presentation and the cumulative evidence submitted to this *beit din*, notwithstanding contrary views recorded which reject the deployment of *umdana* as a means to void a marriage,[46] following a *mesorah* to which we alluded to earlier, we find that our analysis of the *umdana*, *ada'ata dehakhi lo kidshah nafshah* which may be invoked concerning an ongoing marital situation of "one does not live with a snake in the same basket," of ever-present and recurring pedophilia behavior with his stepdaughters as well as the *umdana* "one would have not married a man to remain an *agunah* forever" characterized by Levi's extended separation from Hindy with its attendant consequences of failing to comply with his marital duties provide two

---

44. *Teshuvot Oneg Yom Tov* 168; File no. 865704/1, Tzfat Regional Beit Din, May 8, 2017.

45. *Teshuvot Devar Eliyahu* 48; *Teshuvot Ein Yitzhak* 1, *EH* 24; R. Meir Posner, *Tzal'ot ha-Bayit* 6; *Teshuvot Zikhron Yehonatan* 1, *YD* 5; *Teshuvot Divrei Malkiel* 4:100; *Teshuvot Shoeil u-Meishiv*, Mahadura Kama 198.

46. *Teshuvot Avodat ha-Gershuni* 35; *Teshuvot Beit Yitzhak* 1:106; *Teshuvot Nishmat Hayyim* 129; *Teshuvot Maharsham* 2:110; *Teshuvot Heikhal Yitzhak EH* 2:25; File no. 861974/1, Tzfat Regional Beit Din, January 21,2013 (Rabbi Y. Ariel's opinion).

In accordance with their view, invoking the *umdana* creates a situation of a *safek kiddushin*, a doubtful *kiddushin*, and for some *Poskim* such as *Teshuvot Maharbil* 1:17 one should refrain from being more lenient in *kiddushei safek* than a doubtful divorce. Nonetheless, *Teshuvot Maharik*, *shoresh* 171, *Pri Hadash*, *YD* 110 (end) dealing with *Sefek Sefeika*, *Teshuvot Maharsham* 8, *EH* 239, *Teshuvot Sha'arei Tzion* 3, *EH* 4, 22–24 and others follow the view of Ran in first chapter of Tractate Kiddushin that *safek kiddushin* creates a *hezkat penuyah*, a presumption of a single woman *me'deoraita*, on a Biblical level, and the rabbis ruled stringently due to the prohibition of *eishet ish* and therefore she requires a *get*.

of the grounds for freeing Hindy from her marriage without the giving of a *get*.

Based upon the foregoing presentation of the existence of two *umdanot* ("she never would have married a pedophile" and "she never would have married someone who would be *me'again* her forever"). Hindy Silver is free to remarry without a *get* any Jew except a *Kohen*.[47]

---

47. In our actual decision, there is a "*senif*" (lit. – an appendage) which refers to a questionable *halakhic* view which buttresses the position in our case, namely the voiding of this marriage. We chose to refrain from elucidating the reason in our presentation here.

G. A HUSBAND WHO IS A BATTERER

1. A decision obligating a husband to give a *get*

THE FACTS OF THE CASE

In 1969, Ya'akov Markowitz married Rachel Markowitz in accordance with *Halakhah*. The couple had three children. One was born in 1971, the second child was born in 1973 and the last child was born in 1979. Prior to 1979, Ya'akov participated in a few incidents of violence at work and sometimes drove the car erratically. In 1979 Ya'akov became involved with people of ill-repute and Rachel alleges that this was the reason that Ya'akov began at that time to become physically being abusive towards her. Support for her claim was corroborated by copies of nine documents issued by doctors and hospitals which confirm that between 1983 and 1988, she was a battered wife. For example, in 1983, due to his assaults she experienced traumas to her arms, shoulders, brain bone and the neck. All these traumas required medical treatment. A year later, she was a victim of a severe head injury, an attempt of strangulation with marks on the throat and experienced psychological traumas which resulted in headaches, shivering, high blood pressure and depression. These acts of battery as documented by the doctors and hospitals continued for a few more years and during this period, in November 1985, she left the marital home because her life was threatened by him while brandishing a rifle. In late 1985 Rachel gave him a second chance after Great Rabbi Kling of Lyon, France, reproved Ya'akov for his assault as being in violation of the Jewish tradition but his involvement and words of admonishment were to no avail. In December 1985, she filed for civil divorce but she was still hoping that he would change and attempted for a third and final time to reconcile with him. Though Rachel attempted to reconcile with him and threatened him that if the battery didn't subside she would leave him, nonetheless in June 1986, he again attempted to strangle her and she finally separated from him permanently. Subsequently, on October 7, 1987, her husband entered her apartment, while she was in bed he stabbed her a few times, and their son saved her. Due to the stabbing, she was admitted to the intensive care unit of a local hospital with a life-threatening bleeding condition. For the attempted homicide, he was imprisoned for ten years by an Assize Court, a French criminal court due to his violation of Articles 2, 295, 296, 297, and 304 of the French penal code. In 1995, he was released from prison. In reply to our question whether her husband had a criminal record prior to their marriage, quickly and unhesitatingly she responded, "There was no criminal past."

Given that the acts of abuse began already in 1979, we asked her why she waited until 1986 to leave him. Her reply was that she feared for her life and he threatened her that should she leave him he would slaughter her siblings. On one occasion, she went to the police to report an act of domestic violence. Once she left the police the violence accelerated, and given that she continued to be fearful for her life she continued to stay in the marriage. Moreover, in the 1980's the police did not act on an order of protection. It was for these reasons that she never applied for an order of protection against him. Moreover, should her husband be incarcerated, it was her assessment that upon release he would threaten her life.

Being traumatized by her husband's conduct and feeling physically threatened, it was unsurprising that during the entire three and half hours of our hearing she focused upon her personal predicament of being a battered wife, with only a brief mention of her financial situation during her marriage and absolutely no mention of her children, except for her reply to our question, "do you have children?" It was only after the close of the hearing; she responded to our query and e-mailed the following communication to us:

> I have to add some important points concerning your question – "how was your life?" Every day my ex-husband came back home very late at night, sometimes at nine but most of the time at 2 AM or even later, and always with friends to drink alcohol and to make noise. He never told me where he was and what he did!
>
> When I came home with the children after work, around five o'clock, I was stressed to do so quickly the schoolwork with the children, their shower, to cook their dinner and to bring them to bed, before their father came home because I didn't want that they could see eventual scenes of violence.
>
> When he came home late at night, his meal was always ready on the stove but nevertheless he woke me up and I had to warm up his meal. That was my sad life.

After serving on divorce cases for close to two decades, it was the first time that during the entire proceeding a mother failed to even mention her children. This e-mail communication underscores for the *beit din* panel that the one time she speaks about her children it is done within the context of her life as a victim of spousal abuse.

In June 1988, a civil divorce was executed and the court concluded that the husband was responsible for the divorce due to acts of domestic violence. In 2005 and 2006, she demanded her *get*. However, to date, despite her request as well as the attempts of various rabbis to procure her a *get*, he has refused to give it to her.

DISCUSSION

According to *Halakhah*, raising your hand to strike a fellow-Jew, much less assaulting him, is a violation.[1] Moreover, one must respect the dignity of one's wife and one is prohibited from striking her.[2] Throughout Jewish history, rabbinical luminaries such as Rabbeinu Yonah and Rabbi Pelagi have railed against husbands who batter their wives and are unaware of the severity of the prohibition.[3] In fact, a batterer is liable to pay his wife for any injury incurred from the assault.[4] As an Israeli rabbinical court recently states:[5]

> A wife is not the acquisition of her husband, "for life she is given and not for pain." There is no place for distinguishing between a wife and a friend, and as the words of Rema state, "it is a sin like striking a friend". . . . On the contrary, in relation to one's wife, the husband is obligated to love her and respect her more than the duty concerning his friend.

That being said, the emerging issue is whether a wife is entitled to divorce herself from a batterer. Clearly, a wife who is a victim of battery is entitled to separate from her husband due to the Talmudic dictum, "one does not live with a snake in the same basket".[6] Under such conditions, can a *beit din* obligate a husband to give a *get*? Notwithstanding that there is a debate whether battery serves as grounds to coerce a *get*,[7] many *Poskim* in the past and in contemporary times will obligate a hus-

---

1. *Devarim* 25:3; *Sanhedrin* 58b; *Mishneh Torah* (hereafter: *MT*), *Hovel u-Mazik* 5:1.

2. *Bava Metzia* 59a; *Rema, Even ha-Ezer* (hereafter: *EH*) 154:3. See further this writer's *Rabbinic Authority*, vol. 2, 81–116.

3. *Sha'arei Teshuvah, Sha'ar* 3, 77; *Teshuvot Hayyim ve-Shalom* 2, *EH* 36.

4. *MT, Hovel u-Mazik* 4:16; *Ohr Zarua Bava Kama* 161.

5. File no. 4927-21-1, Petah Tikvah Regional Beit Din, 6 Tishrei 5765.

6. *Teshuvot Maharam of Rothenburg*, Prague ed., 946; *Teshuvot ha-Rashba ha-Meyuhosot le-Ramban* 102.

7. *Beit Yosef, Tur EH* 154:20; *Rema, SA EH* 154:3.

band to give a *get* under certain conditions.[8] Clearly, those *Poskim* who sanction *get* coercion for a batterer would concur that one can obligate a *get,* which in the hierarchy of *get* judgments entails a lower level of enforcement than a *get* compulsion order.[9]

Psak Din (Decision)

Based upon the cumulative evidence submitted to this panel, we obligate Ya'akov to immediately give a *get unconditionally* to Rachel.[10]

2.   A decision to void the marriage

DISCUSSION

In light of his *get* refusal, therefore we have to address the voiding of the marriage. Among the techniques that allow a *beit din* to void a marriage (*bittul kiddushin*) we encounter *kiddushei ta'ut*, loosely translated an erroneous marriage. Three conditions have to be obtained prior to invoking *kiddushei ta'ut* for the expressed purpose of voiding a marriage:

(1) The husband's defect must be a major one (a *mum gadol*), such as sexual impotency, refusing to have children, insanity, homosexuality, apostasy, a marital expectation communicated by the prospective husband prior to the marriage which turns out to be a misrepresentation, engaging in criminal behavior – such as business fraud and pandering prostitutes – or exposing one's mate to a contagious disease such as syphilis or HIV, but only if such a flaw was present prior to the onset of the marriage. All of the aforementioned examples of a husband's flaws have been characterized by one or more authorities as a *mum gadol*. Whether a particular defect serves as a major defect and therefore grounds for voiding a marriage is subject to the discretion of an arbiter

---

8. *Teshuvot ha-Rashba*, supra n. 6; *Teshuvot Maharam of Rothenburg*, Cremona ed., 291; *Tur EH* 154:20; *Beit Yosef, Tur EH* 74 (end); *Teshuvot Noseh ha-Ephod* 32:18; *Hazon Ish EH* 108:14; File no. 4927-21-1, Petah Tikvah Regional Beit Din, 6 Tammuz 5765; File no. 9465-21-1, Netanya Regional Beit Din, 26 Shevat 5767; File no. 3426-21-3, Tel Aviv-Yaffo Regional Beit Din, 21 Shevat 5768; File no. 537502/4, Haifa Regional Beit Din, 11 Mar Heshvan 5775.

9. *Teshuvot Binyamin Ze'ev* 88; *Piskei Din Rabbanayim* (hereafter: *PDR*) 11:328.

10. Once a *beit din* obligates the giving of a *get*, no preconditions can be advanced by the husband prior to executing the *get*. See *Teshuvot ha-Rashba* 4:256; *Bedek ha-Bayit on Beit Yosef – Tur Hoshen Mishpat* 143; *SA EH* 143:21. See further this writer's, *Rabbinic Authority,* vol. 3, 55–81.

or *beit din*. Consequently, there will be a difference of opinion concerning the severity and the magnitude of the defect that is required to void the marriage.

(2) The wife must be unaware of the defect prior to the inception of the marriage and must only discover it after the marriage. On the other hand, if, for example, a husband commits adultery or contracts Alzheimer's during the marriage, though both may be characterized as a *mum gadol* significantly impairing the matrimonial relationship, there would nevertheless be no grounds for a wife's claim that the marriage was consummated in error because the conduct or disease respectively occurred *after* the onset of the marriage.

(3) Finally, upon a wife's awareness of the major latent defect that her husband may have intentionally or unintentionally failed to disclose "the *mum gadol*," there is a debate whether she must immediately bolt the marriage or, if she has "a *ta'am ha'gun*," a reasonable explanation, in the words of Rabbi Moshe Feinstein,[11] she may remain in the marriage for a certain period of time.[12]

Given that we could not identify a preexisting flaw in the husband's persona, we were unable to void the marriage based upon "*kiddushei ta'ut*".

In bold contrast to the avenue of *kiddushei ta'ut* which focuses upon the presence of a major defect which existed **prior to the marriage**, as various *Poskim* note emerging from a Talmudic discussion, one finds another type of *bittul kiddushin* which talmudically is defined as "*ada'ata dehakhi lo kidshah nafshah*," loosely translated, with this understanding, if she had known at the time of the marriage that she would be married to a man with a certain defect, she would never have consented to the marriage.[13] In effect, the *Poskim* label this reasoning as an *umdana*, an assessed expectation of the wife which relates to future conduct which transpires **after the onset of the marriage**. For example, "with this understanding, had I known my husband would become a criminal during our marriage I never would have married him."[14]

Seemingly, the employment of an *umdana* here is open to challenge. As we know, for an *umdana* to be effective depends upon the consent of

---

11. *Iggerot Moshe Even ha-Ezer* 3:45.

12. See this writer's, *Rabbinic Authority*, vol. 3, 136–139.

13. *Bava Kama* 110b–111a.

14. For this difference between *umdana* and *kiddushei ta'ut*, see *Teshuvot Ohr Sameah* 29; *Teshuvot She'eilot Moshe, EH* 2 (1, 17); *Teshuvot Zikhron Yehonatan* 1, *Yoreh Deah* (hereafter: *YD*) 5; *Teshuvot Seridei Eish* 3:25 (21); *Teshuvot Har Tzvi EH* 1:99; *Iggerot Moshe EH* 4:121.

both parties. For example, a sales transaction involves the agreement of parties, the seller and the buyer – i.e. *"taluy be-da'at shneihem."*[15]

The voiding of the sale with the appearance of a defect subsequent to purchase would be predicated upon two conditions:

1. The buyer would have not consummated the deal if he had realized that the item sold would be defective within a reasonable time. As Shulhan Arukh Hoshen Mishpat 232:3 states,

If one sells another land, a slave, a domesticated animal, or other moveable property, and a defect, which the buyer did not know if, it is found in the purchase, the buyer may return it (to the seller and receive his money back – AYW) even if a number of years (have elapsed since the transaction – AYW), since this transaction was based upon fundamental error, provided that the buyer did not to continue to use the item after he became aware of the defect. If however, the buyer continued to use the item after he saw (or became aware of – AYW) the flaw, he has (by his behavior – AYW) renounced (his right of rescission) and cannot return (the defective item and receive his money back – AYW).

2. The seller would negotiate the sale contingent upon the utility of the item being sold. In other words, the voiding of the sales transaction is dependent upon the existence of both the seller's and buyer's implied conditions.

The requirement of *"taluy be-da'at shneihem"* as a precondition prior to the invoking of an *umdana* equally applies to marriage, which is based upon the consent of both a man and a woman.[16]

For example, if a husband is engaged in criminal activity while married, the fact that a wife would exclaim, "had I known he would be a criminal, I never would have married him" would seem to offer no basis for voiding the marriage, since a similar statement must have either been articulated by the husband or be presumed on the husband's behalf. In fact, the husband may not want to void the marriage in order to avoid his sexual intercourse being viewed as *be'ilat zenut* (an act of prohibited

---

15. *Teshuvot Shoeil u-Meishiv,* Mahadura Kama 1:145, 197; *Teshuvot Noda be-Yehudah,* Mahadura Kama, *YD* 69, Mahadura Tinyana, *EH* 80; *Teshuvot Maharsham* 3:82,5:5.

16. *Tosafot, Ketuvot* 47b, s.v. *she-lo; Netivot ha-Mishpat, Hoshen Mishpat* (hereafter: *HM*) 230:1. Cf. *Tosafot, Yevamot* 45b, s.v. *me.*

fornication). However, some *Poskim* argue in cases of a major *umdana* – or what has been labeled as an *umdana gedolah or demukhah* (a major inference expressed by one person) – that this suffices in order to void a marriage.

The emerging issue is whether *Halakhah* recognizes the *umdana*, "had I known he would be a criminal, I never would have married him," as a basis for voiding the marriage? Notwithstanding certain authorities who reject the possibility that a marriage may be voided on the basis of an *umdana*,[17] are there grounds to void a marriage in our case?

Take the following case: Prior to the marriage, a prospective husband fails to disclose to his prospective wife that he was arrested along with two other men on suspicion of counterfeiting coins. The woman was questioned and she knew nothing about the crime. Subsequently, the man and woman married and later she wanted to divorce from him. However, the husband was imprisoned (and the implicit assumption is that he was incapable to give a *get*) and given that she was *agunah*, the question posed to Rabbi Yosef Shaul Nathanson, a nineteenth century authority in Lemberg, Poland, was whether the marriage may be voided based upon *umdana*. Upon inquiry into the facts, the marriage was voided on two grounds: Firstly, he determines that the *seder kiddushin*, the betrothal ceremony, was invalid. However, he then states, "*hadashot*, innovative thinking, I am communicating to sanction this oppressed one" and suggests that we are dealing with a major latent defect due to the existence of an *umdana*. His analysis centers upon the Talmudic discussion of the childless widow who is obligated by the laws of *yibum* (levirate marriage) to marry her brother-in-law. Her brother-in-law is a *mukeh shehin*, afflicted with boils. Initially, Talmud Bava Kama 110b invokes the *umdana* that "had she known at the time of the marriage that she would have to marry a man with boils, she never would have married her husband." However, one of the reasons that the *umdana* is rejected by the Talmud is due to the doctrine that is better to be married rather than being single. Consequently, the fact that she is now bound to another man who is afflicted with boils would not serve as a reason for refraining from marrying his brother. In light of this discussion, argues Rabbi Nathanson,

> . . . I view this as a matter of *a fortiori* reasoning (from the situation of *mukeh shehin*). In that case (where she was clearly

---

17. *Teshuvot Beit Yitzhak* 1:106; *Teshuvot Nahalat Yoel Ze'ev*, 1, *EH* 58–59; *Teshuvot Heikhal Yitzhak EH* 2:25; Rabbi Uriel Lavi of Tzfat Regional Beit Din, File no. 861974/2, 20 Iyar 5774, 20.

married to her first husband who possessed no blemish), we say regarding the levirate husband who is a *mukeh shehin* that she would be able to be released to marry another without the performance of *halitzah* were it not for the doctrine that, "it is better for her to remain in this state of marriage." *A fortiori*, where the husband is sitting in jail, totally under the power of the government, and nobody knows his fate, she should be permitted to be free; for under these conditions, the doctrine, "it is better to be in such a state" plainly is inapplicable, because it is impossible for her to engage in marital ties with him. . . .

To state it differently, in light of the definitional guidance we may distill from the *umdana* regarding *halitzah*, Rabbi Yosef Shaul Nathanson arrives at the conclusion that a husband who is not living with his wife is precluded from engaging in conjugal relations and therefore the marriage may be voided.

Additionally, Rabbi Nathanson defines the *umdana* by stating:

> This is a major defect as it is written in Section 237(232 – AYW) in Hoshen Misphat clause ten that if he is subject to capture and execution by the government he has a defect and she can "return him". . . .

Following in the footsteps of Rabbi Eliezer ben Yoel ha-Levi and Rabbi Yonah Landsdorfer,[18] *umdana* is being defined by Rabbi Nathanson as "a mistaken transaction".[19] In other words, in pursuance to Rabbi Nathanson, the husband failed to disclose to his wife prior to the marriage that he would be serving time in prison. Consequently, the *umdana* here is being defined in terms of the *ta'ut*, the error that no woman would marry a man if she knew that he would be in prison.

In the same century, Rabbi Aharon Levine *av beit din* (presiding *dayan*) in Reesha in the Ukraine addresses the following question. Prior to the marriage, the prospective husband failed to disclose to his wife that he was a criminal dealing in a white slave business. After the marriage, he was imprisoned and was forced to civilly divorce her but refused to Jewishly divorce her, i.e. he was recalcitrant regarding the giving of a *get*. Relying primarily upon a *halakhic* impropriety in the wedding

---

18. *Sefer Ra'avyah, Teshuvot u-Be'urei Sugyot*, 1032; *Teshuvot Me'il Tzedakah*, 2.
19. *Teshuvot Shoeil u-Meishiv*, Mahadura Tlita'ah, *EH* 61.

ceremony, Rabbi Levine offers the following *senif*, supporting argument, to his ruling to free the woman without a *get*:[20]

> Since subsequently it was discovered that the groom was one of the criminals who engaged in a white slave trade business, it can be stated that even if there had been no defects in the ceremony, it is without validity, since there is no greater *umdana* than this, that the woman did not consent to marriage with this in mind.
>
> We have found in Bava Kama . . . that even though we may want to say that a childless widow who falls before a man with boils can be freed without *halitzah* due to the fact that "with this understanding she did not agree," we cannot do this because as Resh Lakish states, "it is better for a woman to be in such a state than be single . . ."

And though Rabbi Levine cites the ruling of Rabbi Nathanson as a precedent for his ruling which he readily admits is dealing with almost the identical fact pattern and relies upon the same Talmudic discussion of *halitzah* to serve as a ground to void the marriage, nevertheless, his understanding of the *umdana* is markedly different from Rabbi Nathanson's perception and he concludes:

> But this line of reasoning is inapplicable to our case because the groom was among those criminals whose lives are in continuous danger, and they dwell in perpetual fear, so it would be impossible for her to have a normal life with him. And, additionally, what woman would desire to live with a low-life and evil person such as this, and she did not agree to marry him with this understanding. And there is no *umdana* greater than this, that if she was aware of this she would have not married . . . if she had known of his criminality.

In contrast to Rabbi Nathanson who focuses upon the inability of engaging in conjugal relations with a husband who is incarcerated, Rabbi Levine focuses upon the negative aspects of being married to a criminal

---

20. *Teshuvot Avnei Hefetz* 30. Though we are relying upon Rabbi Levine's ruling which invokes the technique of *umdana* as a supporting argument to void this marriage, nevertheless there are other authorities who employ this mechanism as a sole argument to void a marriage. See *Teshuvot Noda be-Yehudah, Mahadura Tinyana EH* 135; *Teshuvot Har Tzvi EH* 2:133.

which stem from threats to the nuclear family in general and to the wife in particular, both from the outside world as well as from the husband himself. Whereas Rabbi Nathanson defines the ramifications of imprisonment in narrow terms, Rabbi Levine defines incarceration and the effects of criminality in more expansive terms. Finally, whereas, Rabbi Nathanson is arguing that one of the reasons that the marriage ought to be voided is due to *"kiddushei ta'ut"* which is defined in terms of an *umdana* contends Rabbi Levine that after the marriage, the husband became a criminal and in light of the *umdana* that no woman would marry a man who becomes a criminal, he voided the marriage. In other words, whereas Rabbi Levine utilizes the *umdana* to address the husband's criminality which emerges **after** the marriage, argues Rabbi Nathanson that the *umdana* can be employed to articulate the husband's conduct **before** the marriage. In effect, the *umdana*, in Rabbi Nathanson's mind defines the *ta'ut* which failed to be disclosed to his wife prior to the marriage. Despite the differences between Rabbi Nathanson and Rabbi Levine regarding the nature and scope of the *umdana*, in effect Rabbi Levine employs *medameh milta le-milta* (analogical reasoning) while explicitly stating that his ruling is based upon Rabbi Nathanson's *teshuvah*. The common denominator between the two *Poskim* is that they deploy an *umdana* dealing with the inability of a wife living with a criminal albeit an *umdana* leading to differences avenues to void the marriage!

Based upon the cumulative evidence submitted to this *beit din* panel, for seven years Rachel was living with a criminal who engaged in acts of domestic violence which culminated after their separation in his incarceration for attempted murder of his wife. Following in the footsteps of the aforementioned *mesorah*, tradition emerging from Rabbi Levine's ruling that recognizes that an *umdana* as it relates to a future event may serve as a vehicle to void a marriage, we invoke the *umdana*, "had I known he would be a batterer, I never would have married him," in accordance to the parameters established by Rabbi Levine in the context of an *umdana*, therefore we void the marriage and Rachel is free to remarry without a *get*.

In sum, we invoke an *umdana* which transpired after the onset of marriage in order to void the marriage. The *umdana* relates to the fact that the husband is a batterer.

Lest one challenge our conclusion in light of the fact that it took Rachel seven years to bolt the marriage due to his commission of criminal acts and therefore there is no basis to void the marriage, let us add the following. Given that already in 1979, his improper conduct commenced and she already realized that "this wasn't the person she expected to marry," she should have separated from him already at that time. And in fact, there are authorities who would contend that upon her awareness of his criminality she should have bolted the marriage.[21] Her decision to remain with the marriage until 1986 demonstrates *"savra ve'kiblah,"* she accepted the situation and therefore there ought to be no grounds to void the marriage.[22]

However, others may argue that in the event that there is a reasonable explanation for remaining in the marriage, one can still invoke the *umdana* and void the marriage.[23] As we explained, Rachel decided to remain in the marriage due to the threats upon her life as well as her siblings made by her husband should she leave him. Nonetheless, after a series of events spanning seven years, she realized that to continue to live with him was no longer an option and she separated from him in 1986. Given that sixteen months after their separation, he attempted to murder her and she only escaped from death due to the assistance of one of her sons corroborates and gives credence to her long-term concern for her own personal safety! As such, we can understand why she remained with him for such a long time.

In fact, the original source for the *umdana*, "had I known he would have a particular defect or act in a certain fashion, I never would have married him" is found in Talmud Bava Kama 110b and in that discussion there is no mention of any time limitation that is required before invoking the *umdana*. Secondly, there are *Poskim* who invoke the *umdana* years after the *kiddushin* was established. For example, addressing the case of a mentally dysfunctional husband who was hospitalized, Rabbi Tzvi P.Frank rules:[24]

---

21. See this writer's, *Rabbinic Authority*, vol. 3, 136.

22. *Tur and Beit Yosef EH* 154; *Rema, SA, EH* 154:1; *Teshuvot Rabbi Akiva Eiger, Mahadura Tinyana* 51, 106.

23. *Teshuvot Ein Yitzhak* 1, *EH* 24; *Teshuvot Maharsham* 3:16, 77, 6:160; *Iggerot Moshe EH* 1:79–80, 3:45, 48, 4:113.

The debate whether one must bolt the marriage upon the emergence of the improper behavior is raised in situations of *kiddushei ta'ut*. Here we are dealing with the presence of an *umdana*. Though there seems to be no discussion of whether the same controversy ought to be applicable when invoking the *umdana*, logically it should equally exist in this context as we found in *pesakim* and *teshuvot* dealing with *kiddushei ta'ut*.

24. *Teshuvot Har Tzvi EH* 2:133. Lest one challenge the authenticity of this *teshuvah* given that it was included in the collection of Rabbi Frank's *teshuvot* which were published after his demise, it clearly corresponds to his position as he authored in other rulings. See *Teshuvot Har Tzvi EH* 1:99 and *EH* 2:201. Cf. Rabbis Binyamin Be'eri and Eliyahu Bracha, *Mishnat Yosef*, Tevet 5776, 79–81, 415–417.

Additionally, I saw in Hesed Le-Avraham, Tinyana, at the end of siman (responsum – AYW) 55 that is applicable to our matter. Regarding a husband who became an apostate (a *mumar* – AYW), clearly had she known she would not have married him. And (his *psak* – AYW) should equally apply to our matter since he is insane and a person cannot live together with a snake in the same basket . . . and this is worse than a person afflicted with skin boils (*mukeh shehin* – AYW) and we may say had she known at the time of the marriage she would have not married him . . . and with an insane person one cannot live together and it is akin to an apostate. . . .

Clearly, Rabbi Frank's case which invokes an *umdana* does not indicate that the husband's succumbing to mental dysfunction transpired right after the act of *kiddushin*.[25]

What is the prerequisite for employing the *umdana*? As Rabbi Nathanson notes, in a situation where there are grounds to coerce a *get* and we are unable to employ coercion,[26] then we are permitted to invoke an *umdana*. In our case, due to his acts of physical abuse directed against his wife there are grounds for *get* coercion.[27] Given that we are

---

25. See also *Teshuvot Hesed le-Avraham*, Tinyana, 55 (end). For additional proof, see this chapter, case e, text accompanying notes 61–67. Finally, as Rabbis Fried and Horenblass note there is an *umdana* that a woman would never marry a man who would place her in an *igun* situation. Obviously, this *umdana* is being invoked years after the act of *kiddushin*. See infra text accompanying notes 34 and 35.

26. *Teshuvot Shoeil u-Meishiv*, Mahadura Kama 198.

27. Notwithstanding that many *Poskim* reject *get* coercion in the situation of a battered wife (see *Beit Yosef, Tur EH* 154; *Darkhei Moshe, Tur EH* 154:17; *Teshuvot ha-Radvaz* 4:157; *Rabbi Kalfon Moshe, Teshuvot Shoeil u-Meishiv*, 4 *EH* 14; *Teshuvot Mishpat Tzedek* 1:59; *Teshuvot Tzitz Eliezer* 6:42, perek 3), there are others decisors who will issue a compulsion order in situations of severe and/or continuous acts of husband's battery which may endanger a batterer's wife See *Teshuvot Maharam of Rothenberg*, Prague ed., 927 in the name of *Rabbeinu Simha; Teshuvot Maharam of Rothenberg*, Cremona ed., 291–292; *Hiddushei ha-Ritva, Ketuvot* 77a; *Teshuvot ha-Rashba* 1:793; *Teshuvot ha-Rashba ha-Meyuhosot le-Ramban*, supra n. 6; *Rabbeinu Simhah, Ohr Zarua, Bava Kama* 161; *Teshuvot Tashbetz* 2:8; *Teshuvot Yakhin u-Boaz* 2:44; *Beit Yosef* op. cit. in the name of Agudah; *Bi'ur ha-Gra, SA EH* 154:17; *Rema, SA EH* 154:3 in the name of "*yesh omrim*"; *Teshuvot Maharshal* 69, *Beit Shmuel SA EH* 154:9; *Teshuvot Binyamin Ze'ev* 88; *Teshuvot Perah Mateh Aharon* 1:60; *Teshuvot Hut ha-Meshullash* 4, Tur 3, 35; *Teshuvot Mateh Lehem EH* 1:8; *Teshuvot Hatam Sofer EH* 2:60; *Teshuvot Noseh ha-Ephod* 32 (15); *Avnei ha-Ephod EH* 154:8; *Teshuvot Hayyim ve-Shalom* 2:112; *Hazon Ish Gittin* 108:14; Y. Kobo, *Teshuvot Kokhav me-Ya'akov, EH* 9; *Mishpatekha le-Ya'akov* 2:45; *PDR* 3:220; File no. 537502/4, Haifa

bereft of the authority today to employ *get* coercion, even if years have lapsed since the act of *kiddushin*, in pursuance to Rabbi Levine's view we can invoke *umdana* and thus void the marriage.

In our case, the husband is not living with his wife for many years, he does not want to return to her and we have been told that he is living with a non-Jewish woman. This situation, as well as his past criminal acts, serves as a basis to coerce a *get*. In the wake of our inability to apply *get* coercion, one can invoke "*ada'ata dehakhi lo kidshah nafshah*" even years after the *kiddushin* and therefore void the marriage.

As some *Poskim* point out, prior to invoking the *umdana* one must be assured that there exists no basis to coerce the husband to give a *get*.[28] If *get* coercion is a distinct possibility, then her marriage could have been dissolved by *get* coercion due to *Nitva's get* intransigence In fact, there is a precedent for employing *get* coercion when dealing with a batterer who assaulted his wife as part of his habitual conduct, afterwards attempted to murder her and subsequently was imprisoned for his illegal conduct.[29] Relying upon the positions of Even Yisrael, Mateh Lehem and Avnei ha-Ephod, argues the *Beit Din* that the husband's imprisonment pre-cludes him from performing his marital duties such as providing spousal support and engaging in intimate relations, therefore we coerce him to give a *get*. Furthermore, even though many authorities such as Gaonim, Ramban and Rema will refrain from coercing a *get* regarding a batterer,[30] nevertheless, contends the *Beit Din* that such cases are dealing with assaults which are not life-threatening. However, should the battery be life-threatening, these *Poskim* would concur that a *get* coercion ruling should be rendered.[31] Given that in France, the Jewish community isn't

---

Regional Beit Din, November 4, 2014; File no. 1056520/2, Tel Aviv-Yaffo Regional Beit Din, April 10,2016. For additional *Poskim* who would coerce a batterer to give a *get* under certain conditions, see the recent *teshuvah*, responsum found in *Teshuvot Amudei Mishpat* 1:12.

In fact, some authorities view a batterer as an individual who is to be labeled as "an *oveir al dat Yehudi*" and assuming he is forewarned to cease and desist from such behavior and continues with his physical abusive behavior, there are grounds to coerce him to give a *get*. See *Bi'ur ha-Gra SA EH* 154:11; *Teshuvot Noda be-Yehudah*, Mahadura Tinyana *EH* 90–91. Cf. *Teshuvot Maharshal* 69.

28. Rabbi Meir Posner, *Tzal'ot ha-Bayit* 6; *Teshuvot Zikhron Yehonatan.* 1, *YD* 5; *Teshuvot Divrei Malkiel* 4:100; *Shoeil u-Meishiv,* supra n. 26.

29. *PDR* 3:220.

30. *Otzar ha-Geonim, Ketuvot,* p. 191; *Teshuvot ha-Rashba ha-Meyuhasot le-Ramban* 102; *Darkhei Moshe, Tur EH* 154:21

31. *PDR,* supra n. 29, 222. For earlier rulings, see supra n. 27. See also, *Teshuvot va-Yomer Yitzhak EH* 135 in the name of *Rosh, Rashba, Rivash, Tashbetz* and *Tur.*

legally empowered and therefore *halakhically* permitted to employ *get* coercion, in accordance to the above *mesorah*, tradition[32] we can invoke the *umdana*.

Finally, as Rabbi Eliezer Fried of Volozhin argues:[33]

> We have found a few times that we understand the nature of the wife and the nature of the matter that she absolutely does not accept the status quo . . . that she refuses [in retrospect – AYW] to be married to him and clearly then the *kiddushin* are invalid. And we encounter a few times in the Talmud that our Sages have authorized us to weigh demonstrable *umdanot*. And here if anybody would hear this particular *umdana* that it is unacceptable for her to be an *agunah* her entire life.

Subsequently, Rabbi Petahiah Horenblass, *Av Beit Din* of Warsaw contends in a rabbinic matter:[34]

> One can state, "with this in mind, I never would have married him" in order to remain an *agunah* forever.

Notwithstanding Rabbi Moshe Schacht's view that it is uncertain whether there is a basis for employing this *umdana*,[35] for both Rabbis Fried and Horenblass it was clear that there were grounds to invoking the *umdana* that should she have known that she would become an *agunah* for the rest of her life she never would have married him as a *senif*, as a supporting argument to void the marriage.[36]

Seemingly, creating an *igun* situation does not constitute an "*ilat gerushin*," grounds for divorce. As we know, a wife is entitled to advance

---

32. See supra text accompanying n. 28.

33. *Teshuvot Hut ha-Meshullash* 3:5. Whether Rabbi Tenenbaum would recognize such an *umdana*, we leave as an open question. See *Teshuvot Divrei Malkiel* 4:100. Cf. *Iggerot Moshe EH* 1:162(*halitzah*).

34. *Teshuvot Pithei She'arim* 32. Given that we employ the *umdana*, "had I known he would be a criminal, I never would have married him," she has the status of "*a safek eishet ish*," a doubtful married woman on a rabbinic level; therefore we may invoke the *umdana* of igun. Rabbi Eliezer, supra n. 33 would concur with this position. See case 8f supra notes 30–31.

35. *Teshuvot Ohel Moshe* 2.

36. In contemporary times, Rabbi Uriel Lavi, presently serving as an *av beit din*, presiding *dayan* of the Yerushalayim Regional Beit Din argues that the employment of any *umdana* may only serve as a *senif* to a decision to void a marriage. See File no. 861974/2, Tzfat Regional Beit Din, May 20, 2014.

a plea for divorce on the grounds of the existence of her husband's physical defects such as his contraction of an infectious disease or impotency and engaging in improper conduct towards her such as refusing to engage in conjugal relations[37] or being physically abusive towards her.[38] Under certain conditions and according to many authorities, a *beit din* will coerce the giving of a *get*. Though a husband who is *get* recalcitrant entails "withholding good from a friend" and is an infraction of "loving your neighbor like yourself,"[39] most *Poskim* would not consider freeing a woman from a situation of "*igun*" as an *ilat gerushin*.

However, Rabbeinu Yeruham introduces the notion that a husband's *get* recalcitrance may serve as grounds to coerce a *get*. He states the following:[40]

> My teacher Avraham ben Yishmael writes that it seems to him that a wife who says she does not find her husband pleasing and that he should give her a *get* and *ketubah*, and the husband says that he likewise does not find her pleasing, but does not want to give a *get* . . . we wait twelve months regarding the *get*, because possibly she will reconcile. After the year, we force him to divorce her. . . .

In short, in the wake of "a dead marriage" where there are no prospects for marital reconciliation, if the husband refuses to give his wife a *get*, but desires that his wife to remain an *agunah*, Rabbeinu Yeruham concludes that we compel him to give a *get*.[41]

Notwithstanding those authorities who reject *igun* as an *ilat gerushin* for even obligating a *get* much less a basis for *get* coercion[42] there are

---

37. *Ketuvot* 77a; *SA EH* 154:1; *Taz, SA EH* 154:1; *Beit Shmuel, SA EH* 154:1; *Yevamot* 65a–b; *SA EH* 154:6.

38. *SA EH* 76:11, 77:1; *Beit Shmuel, SA EH* 77:5; *Rema SA EH* 154:3; *Bi'ur ha-Gra, SA EH* 154:10. Cf. *Rema, SA EH* 154:21.

39. *Teshuvot Dibrot Eliyahu* 8:116.

40. *Sefer Meisharim, Netiv* 23, *helek* 8.

41. For differing interpretations of this ruling, see this writer's, *Rabbinic Authority*, vol. 2, 203–208.

42. *Teshuvot Divrei Malkiel* 3:144–145; *Teshuvot Divrei Shmuel* 3:145; R. Y. Herzog, *Pesakim u-Ketavim* 7:133–134; *PDR* 1:162, 4:112, 7:108–109, 112–113, 9:211, 10:173, 11:362, 364; File no. 059133397-21-1, Beit Din ha-Rabbani ha-Gadol, *ha-Din ve-ha-Dayan* 18:12, December 25, 2007; File no. 764231/6, Haifa Regional Beit Din, May 25, 2014; File no. 698719/15, Yerushalayim Regional Beit Din, July 26, 2015.

other *Poskim* who endorse Rabbeinu Yeruham's view that *igun* may serve as grounds for sanctioning *get* coercion.[43]

Based upon the foregoing, given that his prolonged separation from Rachel and his nocompliance with his marital duties of engaging in conjugal relations and furnishing spousal support creates an *igun* sitation and therefore serve as grounds to coerce a *get* [44]and in wake of the inability to coerce a *get* today in France, we may invoke the *umdana* of *"ada'ata dehakhi lo kidshah nafshah."*[45]

There exists an *umdana* that had she known that she would become an *agunah* for the rest of her life she never would have married him. In our case, the couple was already separated in 1986 and since that time Ya'akov has refrained from engaging in conjugal relations and providing support for Rachel. Being separated for over a quarter of a century from her spouse and being married to Ya'akov who refused to comply with his marital duties created an *igun* situation for Rachel.[46] On behalf of her, employing the *umdana*, the *beit din* states that had Rachel known that she would become an *agunah* she never would have married him.

In short, the inability today to employ *get* coercion regarding a husband who is a batterer as well as a husband who has created an *igun* situation serve as the bases of allowing us to invoke an *umdana* to void their marriage.

Moreover, utilizing this avenue of preventing *igun* to void a marriage indicates that the *umdana* may emerge years later after the consummation of the act of *kiddushin* and yet may serve as a vehicle to be *mevatel kiddushin*.

---

43. *MT, Ishut* 14:8; *Shitah Mekubetzet, Ketuvot* 57a in the name of Ritva; *Shitah Mekubetzet, Ketuvot* 64a in the name of Ritva; *Teshuvot Hakham Tzvi* 1; R. Akiva Eiger, *Derush ve-Hiddush*, 91, Vilna ed.; File no. 910130/7, Netanya Regional Beit Din, June 3, 2015. For further acceptance of this position amongst the *Poskim* see sources cited by *PDR* 13:264, 269–271 and H. S. Sha'anan, *Iyunim be-Mishpat* 1:28. For other *Poskim* who align themselves with this position, see supra Introduction to Chapter 8.

Cf. with Rabbi Goldberg who argues in a *pilpulistic* fashion (loosely translated – engaging in casuistry) rather than *le-Halakhah* (in theory) and *le-ma'aseh* (in practice) that in the situation of an *agunah* we may coerce the husband to give a *get*. See Z. N. Goldberg, "In the matter of coercion due to *igun*," (Hebrew), in A. Tendler, *Treatise of sources & comments on get coercion* (Hebrew), 63–76, Jerusalem: 1998.

44. See supra Introduction text accompanying notes 1–3.

45. See supra text accompanying n. 28.

46. Though Rachel only requested her *get* in 2005 and 2006, she already became an *agunah* years earlier due to the prolonged separation and his noncompliance with his marital obligations.

Psak Din

Notwithstanding contrary views which reject the deployment of *umdana* as a means to void a marriage,[47] we follow the *mesorah* of other *Poskim* who invoke the use of an *umdana* as a vehicle to void a marriage.[48] Based upon the *umdana* of expecting to receive her *get* rather than becoming an *agunah* for life, as well as the *umdana* of never expecting to be married to a criminal, we hereby rule that the marriage is voided and Rachel is free to remarry without receiving a *get*.

---

47. *Tosafot Bava Kama* 110b, s.v. *de'adatei; Teshuvot Avodat ha-Gershuni* 35; *Teshuvot Beit Yitzhak* 1:106; *Teshuvot Nishmat Hayyim* 129; *Teshuvot Maharsham* 2:110; *Teshuvot Heikhal Yitzhak EH* 2:25; File no. 861974/1, Tzfat Regional Beit Din, January 21,2013.

48. *Teshuvot Maharam of Rothenburg,* Prague ed., 1022; *Teshuvot Noda be-Yehudah,* Mahadura Tinyana *EH* 80 (end),135; *Teshuvot Beit ha-Levi* 3:3; *Hesed le-Avraham,* supra n. 25; *Teshuvot She'eilot Moshe EH* 2(*halitzah*); *Zikhron Yehonatan,* supra n. 14; *Avnei Hefetz,* supra n. 20; D. Meisels, *Teshuvot Radad EH* 40; *Teshuvot Sha'arei Ezra* 4 *EH* 26; *Teshuvot Meishivat Nefesh EH* 73–77; *Teshuvot Maharsham* 7:95 (a matter of a wife's mental dysfunction); *Iggerot Moshe, EH* 4:121; *Teshuvot Har Tzvi EH* 2:133.

H.   A HUSBAND WHO HAS A BIPOLAR PERSONALITY
DISORDER

The facts of the case

Prior to proceeding to our *beit din*, Sima had appeared in front of another *beit din* regarding the matter of a *get*. Prior to the marriage, the parties had signed a prenuptial agreement wherein it is stated that should Sima request her *get* and Shalom refuse to give a *get*, Shalom would pay $150 a day as a support obligation and that the matter of the *get* was to be re-solved by this *beit din*. After deliberation, the *beit din* obligated Shalom to give a *get* and awarded $75,000 to Sima due to Shalom's failure to give a *get*. The amount awarded was calculated based upon the number of days Shalom refused to give a *get*. Subsequent to that decision, in October 2014, the *beit din* addressed whether there were grounds to void the marriage. After extended deliberations, in September 2015, the *beit din* failed to void the marriage and permitted any other *beit din* to address the matter of *bittul kiddushin*, voiding the marriage. In March 2016, Sima opened up a case with this *beit din*.

Lest one challenge our right to revisit the merits of *bittul kiddushin* by invoking the Talmudic rule regarding *issurim*, prohibitions such as dealing with a case of a *hezkat eishet ish* (the presumption of Sima being a married woman), "if a scholar prohibited something, his colleague has no authority to permit it after it has already been forbidden,"[1] this rule may be inapplicable here. Firstly, the other *beit din* never actually issued a ruling. Secondly, even if the earlier panel of *dayanim* would have rendered a ruling which did not void the marriage, there is a basis to argue that this rule is inapplicable in contemporary times[2] or even if it is applicable today, when dealing with matters of *igun* one is permitted to revisit a request to void a marriage.[3]

After receiving no relief from the other *beit din*, Sima approached our *beit din* to address the matter. Despite being summoned by the other *beit din* as well as our *beit din*, Shalom failed to contact either panel and

---

1. *Berakhot* 63b; *Avodah Zarah* 7a. See further, this writer's *Rabbinic Authority*, vol. 1, 35 at n. 65.
2. *Arukh ha-Shulhan, Yoreh Deah* 242:63; *Teshuvot Maharsham* 9:79.
3. *Teshuvot Sha'arei De'ah* 100; *Teshuvot Miluei Even* 29 (end); *Teshuvot Heikhal Yitzhak EH* 2:45.

failed to appear for any of the proceedings. Both *battei din* conducted hearings regarding *bittul kiddushin* in the absence of Shalom.[4]

At our hearing, Sima submitted her presentation accompanied by evidence and testimonies regarding her marriage. In the summer of 2012, Sima, at the age of 21, married Shalom in accordance with *Halakhah*. On her wedding night, Shalom confessed to Sima that he failed his bar exam and he told her that he was depressed. He acknowledged at the time that he was depressed in the past and Sima understood the situation "as a happening in life" rather than a mental illness. During the next few months, Shalom spent the majority of time in bed. Sima was told that embarking upon marriage entailed "an adjustment period" and therefore Sima attempted to be supportive of him due to his feelings of embarrassment being unemployed. In retrospect, he was suffering from severe depression at the time but neither Sima nor her parents understood that his behavior at the time was symptomatic of a mental disorder. Sima's parents were impressed by his sincerity, ambition and intellect. In fact, their family rabbi who agreed to meet him prior to their engagement for the purpose of determining whether he was "a proper mate" for Sima had primarily a positive assessment of his personality. Yet, in January 2013, he began smoking marijuana on a daily basis.

After April 2013, his mental state began to improve. His mood improved and he was happier than previous months. Shalom became employed and subsequently quit his job hoping that he could be self-supporting with the assistance of inheritance money that he received which would be invested in the starting of a new company. By July 2013, he was energetic and working all the time. At the same time, he exhibited abnormal behavior such as refusing to board a plane before his name was called out by a steward and publicly yelling. After returning from his trip, wearing an expensive suit he gained entry to Henry Kissinger's apartment in the residential towers of the Waldorf Astoria by tricking the Secret Service. During that month, he communicated to Sima some of his crazy ideas including his plan to murder his business partner. By the end of the month, Shalom was impoverished and they couldn't afford the lease of their Fairlawn, NJ apartment and decided to move in temporarily with Sima's parents. Shalom took over a room in his in-laws' basement, called it "the war room," and he duct-taped the entrance and

---

4. Despite the fact that *Nitva* was absent from the various *beit din* proceedings there are *halakhic* grounds to conduct the *beit din* hearing in his absence. Moreover, we implemented certain *halakhic* procedures in order to corroborate the veracity of the wife's allegations. See supra chapter 8e, n. 2.

lined the windows with silver foil. Until this time, Sima's parents had never observed him exhibiting manic depression. By that time, Sima and her parents knew that he had completely lost it. At nights, he walked the streets, during the day he slept, and in his "waking hours" he was frequently ranting and raging about various matters and could not focus adequately upon his new business plan. While living with his in-laws, he told them that he was bipolar and he controlled his behavior by consuming marijuana rather than taking medication. One night during early August, after having an altercation with Sima while she was driving he jumped out of the car. Subsequently, he jumped on top of the car while it was in motion. He wasn't hurt and she left him there. Given his erratic behavior, both Sima and her parents told him that he would have to leave the house. Eleven months after their marriage, Sima had separated.

Subsequent to their separation, Sima learnt that he had attempted suicide twice in the past and that he spoke to his business partners about committing suicide and now again Shalom threatened her a few times that he may commit suicide. Allegedly, after the separation he was arrested for menacing in Woodstock and apprehended for running naked on a New York City highway and was tranquilized and hospitalized. By the time of marital separation, his inheritance money of $50,000 was depleted due to his failure in his business investments and according to the accounts of his business partners; Shalom was thrown out of the start-up company. Moreover, his bank account was overdrawn by $1700. Though Sima requested a *get* he has refused to give one. At one of the dinner conversations in his in-laws' home, he said that Sima is his property and since he is Sephardic he may marry more than one wife.

Discussion

I.   *Kiddushei Ta'ut* (lit. a mistaken betrothal, loosely translated as a mistaken marriage)

Prior to a wife invoking the tool of *kiddushei ta'ut* to void a marriage retroactively and claim that there was an error in the creation of the marriage, three preconditions must have been obtained:[5]

(1) The husband's defect must be a major one (a *mum gadol*) such as sexual impotency, refusal to have children, insanity, homosexuality,

---

5. The basis for a portion of our presentation may be found in our earlier discussion of *Rabbinic Authority*, vol. 3, chapter 8b.

apostasy, a marital expectation communicated by the prospective husband prior to the marriage that turns out to be a misrepresentation, if he
is engaging in criminal behavior such as business fraud or if he exposes
one's mate to a contagious disease such as syphilis or HIV; this flaw must
have been preexisting at the onset of the marriage. All of the aforementioned examples of a husband's flaws have been characterized by one
or more *Poskim* as a *mum gadol*. Whether a particular defect serves as
major defect and therefore grounds for voiding a marriage is subject to
the discretion of the *beit din*.

Based upon the cumulative evidence submitted, we find that *Shalom*
failed to disclose prior to the marriage that he was bipolar. Said conclusion is supported by testimony given by three of his friends as well as a
receipt from a psychotherapist who specializes in bipolar and mood disorders which attests that Shalom visited him ten months into the marriage. The receipt from this visit had a diagnosis code of 301:13 which
indicates a pre-existing mental condition of at least two years prior to
the visit. According to the DSM (Diagnosis and Statistical Manual of
Mental Disorders) the Code 301:13 identifies a bipolar disorder. Sima
submitted copies of check receipts of two psychiatrists who observed
him a year prior to the marriage.[6] Finally, there is documentation authored by Shalom where he admits having a mental condition prior to
the marriage, testimony from his friends that he suffered from PTSD
while serving as an Israeli soldier in the Gaza war, a copy of a Haifa
arrest in August 2010 for assaulting a former girlfriend and copy of a
September 2013 police report where he was arrested for assault with a
deadly weapon.

Based upon Sima's presentation and the testimony of her parents as
well as Shalom's friends, the symptoms of this mental disorder had been
observed and described in the form of severe depression, delusional and
manic behavior, assaults, drug abuse, suicide attempts and homicidal
threats. The question which emerges is whether this disorder is to be
labeled as "*a mum gadol*," a major defect.

The criteria for being classified a *shoteh*, mentally dysfunctional are
set down in Tosefta and subsequently cited in Talmud:[7]

> Our Rabbis taught: Who is a *shoteh*? One who goes out alone

---

6. Upon Shalom's departure from his in-laws' home, Sima found all these documents in his possessions that he had left behind.

7. *Tosefta Terumot* 1:3; *Hagigah* 3b.

at night, one who spends his night in a cemetery and one who tears his clothing.

Given that Shalom did go out alone during the night and appeared naked on a highway, there is Talmudic controversy whether one requires one type of erratic behavior to be deemed a *shoteh* or one requires all three types of abnormal conduct to establish mental incompetence. In fact, a subsequent passage in the Talmud adds a fourth form of aberrant behavior, namely one who destroys what is given to him.[8]

However, to argue that based upon these two specific manifestations of erratic behavior one ought to void a marriage seems to defy logic. In fact, a read of one of Rabbi Menashe Klein's *teshuvot* seems to lead one to the conclusion that signs of being a *shoteh* which may serve as grounds for *bittul kiddushin* are specifically the types of aberrant behavior noted above.[9] However, in our understanding the behavior deemed being irrational goes well beyond these forms of erratic conduct. As Talmud teaches us what we are really concerned with is whether there is a rational justification for acting this way. We need to understand what prompted such conduct. Is it symptomatic for an underlying psychological disorder or reflective of a thoughtful decision?[10] Moreover, notwithstanding some authorities,[11] as we learn from Rabbis Yosef Karo's and Moshe Issereles's rulings regarding the disqualification of witnesses, the list is not a closed list but encompasses any form of irrational conduct which may establish him as a *shoteh*, mentally incompetent.[12] In fact, numerous *Poskim* endorse their rulings and contend that the list is not exhaustive.[13] Furthermore, numerous *Poskim* argue that the psychotic behavior must have occurred at least three times in order to label him a *shoteh*.[14]

---

8. *Hagigah* 4a.

9. *Teshuvot Mishneh Halakhot* 14:146.

10. *Hagigah*, supra n. 7.

11. *Beit Yosef, Tur EH* 119 and 121 in the name of Rabbeinu Simhah of Speyers; *Teshuvot Maharik, shoresh* 19 in the name of Rabbi Avigdor; *Teshuvot Tzemah Tzedek EH* 153; *Teshuvot Hatam Sofer EH* 2: 4 in the name of Rashba.

12. *Beit Yosef, Tur EH* 121; *Darkhei Moshe, Tur, EH* 119:5; *SA HM* 35:8.

13. *Teshuvot Mahari Weil* 52; *Teshuvot Ateret Hakhamim EH* 18; *Teshuvot Divrei Hayyim EH* 53 (compare nos. 74–75); *Teshuvot Nefesh Hayah EH* 27; *Teshuvot Ohr Sameah* 13; *Teshuvot Oneg Yom Tov* 153; *Teshuvot Hatam Sofer, EH* 2:2; *Teshuvot Beit Ephraim EH* 89; *Teshuvot Sefer Yehoshua* 71; *Teshuvot Divrei Malkiel* 3:137; *Teshuvot Tzofnat Pa'aneah* 103–107; *Teshuvot Maharsham* 6:159; *Teshuvot Mishnat Rabbi Aharon* 56.

14. *Teshuvot Maharam ben Barukh* 455; *Pri Megadim YD* 1:23; *Sha'agat Aryeh,*

Addressing the case of a wife who had a few defects and refused to proceed with her spouse to a *din torah*, a rabbinical court proceeding relying upon a ruling of Rabbi Yosef Kolon, Rabbi Yoav Weingarten expounds:[15]

> . . . even if she is not insane, and simply does not know how to behave and conduct herself in the home due to her silliness and naïveté, this is considered a great, major defect and he is permitted to marry another . . . as discussed in Maharik. . . . The case was thus: the betrothed one lost her mind and could not help in any way in establishing a household. . . . And for this reason, Maharik voided the betrothal, even though the defect developed subsequently. Towards the end of his responsum he writes that even if she had properly married, the ban of Rabbeinu Gershom would be inapplicable. In that specific case, you must arrive at the conclusion that Maharik was dealing with someone who was not *halakhically* insane. For otherwise, why did he concern himself with the issue whether the prospective husband had to marry her, since an insane person is not marriageable? Therefore, one must conclude that the ban of Rabbeinu Gershom does not apply. . . .

Similarly, focusing upon a wife who is a hypochondriac and does not take care of the chores of the domestic household and cannot observe the *halakhot* of being a *nidah*, even though she does not meet the *shoteh* criteria set down in the Talmud, Rabbi Aryeh Lifshitz concludes that it is a major defect and the couple should divorce.[16] Such a line of argumentation was advanced by the Sanzer Rov that when dealing with whether a husband may remarry without his wife who shows *shoteh*-like conduct accepting a *get*, one need not demonstrate that the behavior is reflective of the Talmudic criteria of mental incompetence. One must only prove that a wife who cannot live with her husband like everyone else does is deemed a *shoteh*.[17] The same rationale for defining mental incompetence was endorsed by others.[18] Despite the fact that all of these

---

Ohr ha-Yashar 28–31; *Beit Ephraim*, supra n. 13; *Teshuvot Zikhron Yosef* 10.

   15. *Teshuvot Helkat Yo'av* 1:24.
   16. *Teshuvot Shem Aryeh EH* 2.
   17. *Teshuvot Divrei Hayyim* 1, *EH* 41.
   18. *Teshuvot Beit Shlomo EH* 95; *Teshuvot Shoeil u-Meishiv, Mahadura Kama* 3:108.

decisors were defining *shoteh* in the context of a wife's mental state and dealing with the permission of a husband to remarry without a wife's consent to receive her *get*, nonetheless their positions will equally apply to situation of a husband's irrational conduct.[19]

Notwithstanding Rabbi Klatzkin's view that it is too difficult to assess what conduct rises to the level of being a *shoteh*,[20] a review of the various *teshuvot* demonstrate that the *Poskim* entertain the possibility of voiding the marriage by labeling a husband as "a *shoteh*" or "a *meshuga*."[21] Furthermore, one is clearly left with the impression that if there is basis for voiding a marriage it is on the grounds that the husband's episodes of irrationality are overbearing to the degree that a wife cannot live with him. As Rabbi Feinstein writes:[22]

> Being a *shoteh* is a major defect as one is incapable of having intimate relations, as it is explicitly written in Yevamot 112 that our Sages did not enact legislation for a *shoteh* to marry, since we cannot sustain such a rabbinic enactment because a person does not live with a snake in the same cage. And therefore it is clear that a man who became a *shoteh* after the marriage if he can get divorced we coerce him to divorce . . . one must deem it as a mistaken transaction and void the marriage.

Based upon the presentation, submitted testimonies and supporting evidence, we are dealing with a husband who is incapable of having intimate relations lest he succumb to paranoia and mood swings with potential of meting out abuse, and his *shoteh*-like behavior occurred more than three times. Moreover, given his inability to focus, his failed start-up business and periodic sleeping during the daytime indicate a person who would be incapable of "holding a job" and therefore unable to be economically supportive of a wife, much less a family. As such, we are

---

19. For extrapolating the definition of a husband's defect from a wife's defect, see *Beit Shmuel, SA EH* 154:2 (compare with *Beit Shmuel, SA EH* 154:9); *Teshuvot Ein Yitzhak* 1 *EH* 24; *Teshuvot Beit ha-Levi* 3:3; *Teshuvot Havot Yair* 221; *Teshuvot Har Tzvi EH* 2:181. Cf. *Teshuvot Shevut Ya'akov EH* 110; *Beit Meir SA EH* 154:1.

20. *Miluei Even*, supra n. 3.

21. *Teshuvot Malbushei Yom Tov EH* 4; *Teshuvot Maharsham* 6, *EH* 159–160; vol. 8, *EH* 239; *Teshuvot Mishnat Avraham* 2:10; *Teshuvot Minhat Asher* 1:85; *PDR* 15:1,12; 20:239, 251; File no. 870175/4, Haifa Regional Beit Din, December 29, 2014.

Whether the husband must exhibit *shoteh*-like behavior as stated in Hagigah 3b–4a is subject to debate. See case 8d, supra text accompanying notes 14–17.

22. *Iggerot Moshe EH* 1:80.

dealing with a *mum gadol* which serves as grounds to invoke *kiddushei ta'ut*. Notwithstanding some *Poskim* who reject a wife's claim that the marriage ought to be voided based on a husband's failure to disclose his flaw (or flaws),[23] we are following the *mesorah*, tradition, which contends that failure to disclose a major defect prior to the onset of the marriage is construed as akin to a *mekah ta'ut*, a mistaken commercial transaction. If one sells a car without a motor and the buyer is unaware of this, we have a *mekah ta'ut*. Similarly, if a couple marries and the wife is unaware of a husband's major defect such as sexual impotence, a mental disorder or a criminal past, the marriage may under certain conditions be voided based upon the notion of *kiddushei ta'ut*, a mistaken marriage.[24]

What constitutes a mistaken transaction? As Shulhan Arukh rules:[25]

> Whatever the residents of a particular locale agree to term a defect in regard to an item sold, which defect shall be grounds for rescission shall in fact constitute grounds for rescission. Whatever the inhabitants of a particular locale agree is not a defect shall not be grounds for rescission unless (a right of rescission for such defect was) explicitly mentioned. For anyone who conducts business without specifying (any exceptions) he is relying upon commercial practice.

Given that commercial practice is determinative in defining what is a *mekah ta'ut*, should a defect be found in the transaction, the transaction is invalid based upon invoking the *umdana*, "on the understanding that the buyer is not purchasing the item" under such conditions.[26] Similarly, in the wake of discovering a preexisting *mum* after the onset of the marriage, we employ an *umdana* of *"ada'ata dehakhi lo kidshah nafshah"* (loosely translated: on this understanding she did not marry him). In our issue at bar, had Sima known prior to the marriage that Shalom was bipolar she never would have married him. Rabbi Yehonathan Abelman

---

23. *Beit Meir,*supra n. 19; *Hazon Ish EH* 69: 23; *Perushei Ibra*, 43. For additional authorities, see *Rabbinic Authority*, vol. 2, 140, n. 8.

24. *Havot Yair*, supra n. 19; *Teshuvot Ein Yitzhak, EH* 24 (6); *Beit ha-Levi*, supra n. 19; *Teshuvot Beit Av*, 7:28; *Iggerot Moshe, EH* 1:79 (1); *Teshuvot Seridei Eish* 1:168; *Har Tzvi*, supra n. 19; *Teshuvot Minhat Avraham* 2:10; *PDR* 10:249–260; *Teshuvot Sha'arei Tzion 2, EH* 20; File 1393-14-1, Yerushalayim Regional Beit Din, March 5, 2003; File no. 870175/4, supra n. 21.

25. *SA HM* 232:6.

26. *Rashi, Bava Metzia* 80a; *Tur HM* 226; *Taz SA HM* 306:5; *Misgeret ha-Shulhan* 224; *Mishpat Shalom* 232:11.

conceptualizes this understanding as "an *umdana* that emerges due to a *ta'ut*".[27] In fact, numerous *Poskim* have explained *kiddushei ta'ut* as a case of *Halakhah* invoking an *umdana*, "had she known about the error, she never would have married him".[28]

Alternatively, we are dealing in marriage with an implied condition. Generally, any mistaken commercial transaction is void due to the fact we presume that the purchaser expects to buy an item devoid of a defect. As such, it is as if he stipulated a *tenai*, a condition, in which case it be effective based on the *halakhot* of *tenai*. Similarly, we are dealing in marriage with a *tenai mutneh*, an implied condition. With the husband's failure to disclose the *mum*, the defect prior to the marriage, we construe this preexisting latent defect as a breach of her implied condition to the marriage.[29]

Seemingly our conclusion may be challenged as contradicting the Talmudic *hazakah* (presumption) that she is satisfied with *kol dehu* (the minimum) and therefore, "*tav le-meitav tan du mi-le-meitav armelu*" (better to live as two than live as one), and consequently a wife will tolerate a husband's physiological and/or character defects in order to remain in the marriage. Invoking this *hazakah* propels Rabbis Spektor, Posner,H. of Volozhin, Karelitz,Henkin and Waldenburg to reject the wife's right to advance the claim that her husband failed to disclose *mumim* that preexisted the marriage and therefore to argue that the marriage was consummated in error.[30] In accordance with their approach, Sima's claim has no basis.

However, numerous other *Poskim* argue that in the event that the

---

27. *Teshuvot Zikhron Yehonatan* 1, *YD* 5 (17).

On the other hand, as Rabbi Abelman notes, there is an *umdana* that emerges after a lapse of time. For example, a wife marries and after the marriage commences the husband begins to exhibit certain physiological or psychological disorders which did not exist prior to the marriage. For the use of such an *umdana* as a vehicle to void a marriage see in this chapter, sections C-G.

28. *Beit ha-Levi*, supra n. 19; *Havot Yair*, supra n. 19; *Teshuvot Birkat Retzeh* 107; *Teshuvot Shei'lat Moshe EH* 2; *Teshuvot Beit Av*, 7:14; *Teshuvot Sha'arei Tzion*, vol. 3, *EH* 4.

29. *Teshuvot Rabbi Akiva Eiger*, Mahadura Tinyana 51, 106. Cf. other authorities who reject this approach and advance a clear distinction between an error which relates to the past and a *tenai*, a condition which is breached *after* a transaction is voided. See *Beit ha-Levi*, supra n. 19; *Teshuvot Helkat Yoav EH* 25; *Hazon Ish, EH* 56 (9).

30. *Teshuvot Ein Yitzhak* 1 *EH* 23; *Beit Meir*, supra n. 19; *Teshuvot Hut ha-Meshullash* 3:4; *Hazon Ish EH* 69 (23); *Perushei Ibra*, supra n. 23; *Teshuvot Tzitz Eliezer* 1:42, Orhot ha-Mishpatim 1.

particular *mum* serves as a ground to coerce a *get*, then under certain conditions it may equally serve as a basis to void the marriage.[31] In other words, depending upon the circumstances of the case the *hazakah* may be rebuttable.[32] In fact , both Rabbis Feinstein and Yosef arrived at the conclusion that the *hazakah* is inapplicable when dealing with a husband who is a *shoteh*. [33]There may be instances when a wife finds the situation intolerable and will not want to remain in the marriage and should there be grounds for coercing a *get* there may be equally grounds to void the marriage. Given that there are grounds to coerce a husband who is a *shoteh* to give a *get*,[34] consequently we may entertain a wife's plea of *kiddushei ta'ut*.

Alternatively, Shalom's failure to disclose prior to the marriage that he suffered from a bi-polar disorder may be construed as inappropriate behavior (*"ma'aseh lo ha-goon"*) and is viewed as deceit. Consequently, relying upon the Rosh's ruling, Rema rules that if a man acted inappropriately and married her in such a deceitful fashion, we coerce to give a *get*.[35] Even if the defect is minor and its existence does not serve as a basis for *get* coercion should the failure of disclosure is viewed as an inappropriate act, we coerce the husband to give a *get*.[36] Clearly, in our case, this mental dysfunction is a major defect and therefore a *beit din* may coerce a husband who exhibits this defect to give a *get* due to the fact that he acted deceitfully.[37]

(2) The wife must be unaware of the defect prior to the inception of the marriage and only discover it after the marriage. On the other hand, if, for example, during the marriage a husband commits adultery or contracts Alzheimer's, though both may be characterized as a *mum*

---

31. *Teshuvot Ein Yitzhak*, 1, *EH* 24 (41); *Piskei Halakhot, Ishut* 1, *Yad Dovid*, 372; *Birkat Retzeh*, supra n. 28; *Teshuvot Ahiezer* 27; *Teshuvot Maharsham* 6:160; *Iggerot Moshe*, supra n. 22; *Teshuvot Har Tzvi* 2:180; *Minhat Avraham*, supra n. 24.

32. For a contemporary understanding of the rebuttability of the *hazakah*, see *Iggerot Moshe, EH* 4:83; File no. 870175/4, supra n. 21, at 59; A. Lichtenstein, *Shi'urei Harav Aharon Lichtenstein, Gittin*, 338. Cf. Rabbi Joseph Baer Soloveitchik, *"Talmud Torah and Kabalas Ol Malchus Shamayim,"* (Partial transcript of an address of Rabbi Joseph Baer Soloveitchik zt"l to the RCA Convention, 1975, on the topic of Gerut, Transcribed by Eitan Fiorino, INTERNET PARSHA SHEET ON VAESCHANAN, 5766, 11TH CYCLE, www.parsha.net/pdf/Devarim/Vaeschanan66.pdf).

33. *Teshuvot Iggerot Moshe* 1:80 (*halitzah*), 3:46; *Teshuvot Yabia Omer* 7, *EH* 7.

34. *Teshuvot ha-Rosh* 42:1 (note 2); *Teshuvot Maharhash* 2:33; *Teshuvot Ne'eman Shmuel* 66; *Iggerot Moshe*, supra n. 33; *Teshuvot Devar Yehoshua* 3, *EH* 30.

35. *Teshuvot ha-Rosh* 35:2; *Rema, SA EH* 77:3; *Teshuvot Divrei Malkiel* 3: 100.

36. *Beit Shmuel, SA EH* 117:11, 24.

37. *PDR* 1:10–11, 5:193, 203,10:241, 247.

gadol significantly impairing the matrimonial relationship, nevertheless since the conduct or disease respectively occurred after the onset of the marriage, there would be no grounds for a wife's claim that the marriage was consummated in error.

Based upon the cumulative evidence submitted, we find that Sima only became aware of Shalom's psychological disorder after the onset of the marriage. As Shalom's friends testified to the panel there was a consensus that Shalom knew how to "sweet-talk" people and manipulate them. In light of his personality, in their initial interactions with him they were unaware of his psychological problems. Eventually, they became aware of his character but chose for personal reasons to refrain from communicating to Sima, Shalom's prospective mate, his issues.

(3) Finally, upon a wife's awareness of the major latent defect, she must decide to leave the marriage. Regarding this condition, whether she must immediately leave the marriage or not is subject to debate. Though in accordance with certain *Poskim*, upon discovery of a major latent defect one must leave the marriage immediately or refrain from remaining in the marriage for an extended period of time, nonetheless, in pursuance to Rabbi Moshe Feinstein, *Dayanim* E. Goldschmidt, S. Karelitz, and Y. Bavliki, and others argue that she may continue to live with him provided she offers a reasonable explanation.[38]

Based upon the cumulative evidence submitted to this panel, during the first nine months of their living together, neither Sima nor her parents were aware of his psychological disorder. Having neither the background nor past experience with individuals who were mentally dysfunctional they were unable to assess the situation. In fact, even after a forty-five minute conversation with the family rabbi who had experience from interactions with many people, he was unable to discern the mental state of the personality who visited him.

As Rabbi Tzion Boaron, former *dayan* of the Beit Din ha-Rabbani ha-Gadol, insightfully observes:[39]

> With respect to the defect of insanity in a situation such as that before us it appears that this is certainly a case of mistaken

---

38. In pursuance to some *Poskim*, upon discovery of a major defect in her spouse, if a wife delays her decision to bolt the marriage for a reason (or reasons) which is acceptable to the *beit din*, the marriage may be voided. See *Iggerot Moshe, EH* 3:45 ("*ta'am hagun*" or "*tirutzim nekhonim*"), 48, 4:113; *PDR* 1:5, 11–12. See further this writer's, *Rabbinic Authority*, vol. 3, 136–139.

39. *Sha'arei Tzion*, supra n. 28.

transaction, for there is a strong presumption that no person will be reconciled to living his whole life, and to his children living their whole lives, in suffering and in fear, every day and every hour (as described above briefly).

And one cannot say that because she stayed with him for seven years and bore two children, that she saw the defect, and became reconciled to it. It is not so, for in such things a person does not clearly understand the nature of the illness until a substantial period of time has passed, for sometimes, out of love for him, she attributes his anger and his rage to tension and a passing state of nervousness, and she hopes and prays that the situation will improve. This is particularly so in relation to a person who is taking medication on a permanent basis, for then there are situations in which he is calm and quiet. And particularly, as the woman herself said, when he calmed down after each outburst, he would beg her to forgive him.

It transpires that in this case the *kiddushin* are precarious, both from the aspect of the presumption that a person does not become reconciled to such a defect, and that when the wife became aware of the true mental state of her husband she was not reconciled and the *kiddushin* are void, and also for the reason that even if she became reconciled when she became aware, according to all the above authorities, even though she was reconciled, the *kiddushin* are already void. Because the act was mistaken at the time of the *kiddushin* – for there is a clear *umdana* that if she had known about the illness prior to the marriage, she certainly would not have been content to marry him.

At the time of her marriage, Sima had no experience dealing with mentally dysfunctional individuals. Moreover, given his persona during the brief period of three months of courting, nothing triggered him to react psychotically and therefore no signs of mental dysfunction emerged which either Sima or her family observed. It was only in the last two months of their living together that it became crystal clear to Sima that he had a major mental illness and she observed him in a full manic state and therefore separated from him and requested her *get*.

Since *get* coercion is a *halakhic* option, albeit unavailable today outside of *Eretz Yisrael*, there are grounds to invoke *kiddushei ta'ut* based upon the severity of the *mum*, the defect as well as the deceitful conduct for failing to disclose the latent defect prior to the marriage.

Based upon the foregoing, we recognize that this case represents an example of *kiddushei ta'ut* and therefore we are voiding the marriage. Sima is permitted to remarry any Jew, even a *Kohen* without receiving a *get* from Shalom.

This *psak din* was approved by a renowned rabbinic authority.[40]

Final Thoughts

According to the Talmud and classical *Poskim*, a Jewish man may marry more than one Jewish woman provided he can provide support and engage in conjugal relations with each of them.[41] Over a thousand years ago, Rabbi Gershom Me'ohr ha-Golah passed rabbinic legislation that dramatically changed the landscape of *halakhic* family law for the Jewish community. Among his pieces of legislation was that a husband is proscribed from engaging in polygamy.[42] However, some authorities have argued that this legislation was operative only until the fifth millennium (i.e. 1240 C.E.).[43] Other authorities both Sephardic and Ashkenazic alike contend that the legislation that was passed is operative forever.[44]

The Ashkenazic community continues to accept this legislation to this very day. Consequently, if a Jewish husband married a second Jewish woman without giving a *get* to his first wife, we are mandated to coerce him to give her a *get*. And Pithei Teshuvah and Otzar ha-Poskim cite numerous *Poskim* who align themselves with this view.[45] Throughout the ages, a Sephardic *hatan*, groom under the *huppah* would execute an oath that he would not engage in polygamy.[46] Even for those Sephardic

---

40. Whether there is a *halakhic* requirement devolving upon a *beit din* to enlist the support of "a second opinion" or this rabbinic approval is reflective of "a *nohag*", a practice, see this writer's *Rabbinic Authority*, vol. 3, 256–262.

41. *Yevamot* 65a; *MT Ishut* 14:3; *SA EH* 1:9.

42. *Teshuvot Maharam of Rothenberg*, Prague ed., 153, 922; *Kol Bo* 116; *Teshuvot Maharam Mintz* 102. Whether the attribution of this legislation to Rabbeinu Gershom is correct we leave as an open question, See S. Eidelberg, 34 *Tarbiz* 278–288 (1965).

43. *Teshuvot Maharik*, shoresh 101; *Beit Yosef, Tur EH* 1; *SA EH* 1:10; *Darkhei Moshe, Tur EH* 1:10.

44. *Teshuvot Maharik*, shoresh 63; *Helkat Mehokeik, SA EH* 77:15; *Yam shel Shlomo Yevamot* 6:41; *Teshuvot Maharashdam YD* 140; *Teshuvot Maharam Alshakar* 95; *Teshuvot Hikrei Lev YD* 84; *Teshuvot Maharshakh* 2:36.

45. *Pithei Teshuvah, SA EH* 1:20; *Otzar ha-Poskim EH* 1:80.

46. *Teshuvot ha-Rosh* 33:1; *Teshuvot ha-Rashba* 1:812, 4:267; *Knesset ha-Gedolah, EH* 1:13.Whether failing to comply with one's oath serves as grounds to mandate *get* coercion is subject to debate. See *Teshuvot Maharashdam YD* 133.

Jews who were not bound by the legislation, ther were bound by oath as well as communal ordiance to support their wife until a *get* was given to her and may not engage in polygamy.[47]

Addressing members of the Sephardic Jewish community, Rabbi Yitzhak Yosef, Sephardic Chief Rabbi in *Eretz Yisrael* rules that once a Sephardic Jewish male is married he is prohibited from marrying a second Jewish woman without giving a *get* to his first wife unless he receives permission from a recognized *beit din* that addressed the issue in accordance with *Halakhah* and secular law.[48]

Based upon the foregoing, prior to having this matter addressed by a recognized *beit din*, there is no credence to *Nitva's* claim that as a Sephardic Jew he may remarry while remaining married to the *Tova'at*.

---

47. *Teshuvot ha-Ran* 38; PDR 3:176, 183.

48. Rabbi Y. Yosef, A letter to Rabbi E. Shahar, 5 Kislev 5777 (letter is on file with this author).

Index of Halakhic Sources

COMMENTARIES

RESTATEMENTS

ISRAELI RABBINICAL COURT DECISIONS
PISKEI DIN RABBANIYIM (PDR)

OTHER [ISRAELI] RABBINICAL COURT DECISIONS

JEWISH THOUGHT

About the Author

Since 1999, Rabbi A. Yehuda Warburg has served as a *dayan* on various *battei din* panels in the Hassidic, Modern Orthodox, Sephardic, and Yeshiva communities in the New York-New Jersey metropolitan area. He is a former research fellow at the Institute of Jewish Law at Boston University School of Law. He is a member of the editorial board of the journal *Tradition* and served on the editorial board of *The Jewish Law Annual*. For over two decades, Rabbi Warburg delivered classes in *Hoshen Mishpat* (business law) and *Even ha-Ezer* (family law) to rabbinical students at Rabbi Isaac Elchanan Theological Seminary, an affiliate of Yeshiva University. Rabbi Warburg received his rabbinic ordination from Rabbi Isaac Elchanan Theological Seminary and earned his doctorate of jurisprudence at the Hebrew University Faculty of Law. The author resides in Teaneck, New Jersey.